T0376209

في ذكرى

مارك لينز

Joseph Williams McPherson (1866–1946)

The Moulids of Egypt

(Egyptian Saint's Day Festivals)

by
J. W. McPherson MA (Oxon), BSc (Bris), Bimbâshî

Original Foreword by
E. E. Evans-Pritchard MA (Oxon), PhD (Lon), Bimbâshî

New Foreword by
Valerie J. Hoffman

Edited and Annotated by
Russell McGuirk

GINGKO

New Edition published in 2022 by
Gingko
4 Molasses Row
London SW11 3UX

ISBN 978-1-914983-10-8
e-ISBN 978-1-914983-11-5

Typeset in Times by MacGuru Ltd
Printed in the United Kingdom by Clays Ltd, Elcograf S.p.A.

www.gingko.org.uk
@GingkoLibrary

Front cover:
The formation of a procession on Cairo's Mu'izz lid-Dîn Street in celebration of Moulid el-Nebî. Photo by Zangaki brothers, late 19th century.

Rear cover:
Visit to the Moulid el-Nebî by the last Khedive, Abbâs Hilmî II, who was deposed in 1914.

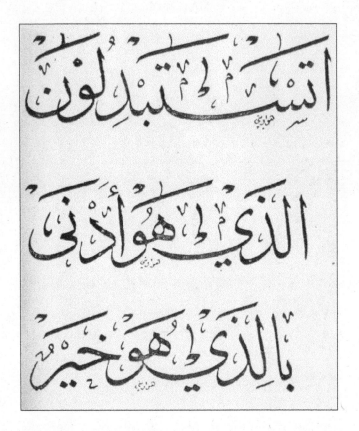

Would you exchange that which is better for that which is worse?
McPherson uses this quote from a Quranic Sûra (al-Baqarah, verse 61) to lend weight
to his plea to the Government and Islamic authorities to support the moulids.

Contents

Editor's Comments on the Text

In the original edition of *The Moulids of Egypt*, Arabic words were transliterated (i.e., rendered into English letters) in haphazard fashion, many appearing spelled in two or three different ways. In this new edition, I have standardised the spelling of these words using a simplified but consistent system which emphasises which vowels are long. This is virtually all that is required for non-Arabic readers to have a reasonable idea of how to pronounce Arabic words. The long vowels carry a circumflex: â, ê, î, ô, û. For the more ambitious of those readers, I have also indicated the difference between a "glottal stop", called *hamza*, and the guttural sound made by the letter *'ain*. The left-facing apostrophe is a glottal stop. For example, the word <gô'a> is two syllables with a "stop" in the middle: go-a. The letter *'ain* is indicated by a right-facing apostrophe. A simple way to approximate this sound is to say *ah*, and as you say it, try to swallow it – gently, as the sound does not need to be over-emphasised. <'aqaba> begins with a guttural "a"; <far'ônî> has a guttural "ô" in the middle; <shâri'> has a guttural "i" at the end.

In transliterating consonants, I (like McPherson) have ignored the emphatic versions of **d, s, t, z, l** and **r**; all are written as ordinary, non-emphatic letters.

Where McPherson puts an -ing or a plural -s on transliterated Arabic words, I have generally put the words in quotation marks; otherwise, most Arabic words which are not names of people or places are italicised, hence: *zikr*, but "zikrs" and "zikring".

The names of three members of the Egyptian royal family I have left as they would normally appear in English print: Fu'ad, Farouk, and Fawzia (rather than Fu'âd, Fârûq, and Fawzîya).

Unless otherwise stated, I have translated into English the various passages in Arabic, French and Italian which appear in the original edition of *The Moulids of Egypt*.

List of Illustrations

List of Maps

Editor's Note on Map Section

This book, as originally published, contains 21 maps of different parts of Cairo, plus one of Upper Egypt and another of the Delta and Fayûm. These were hand-drawn by McPherson himself. The Cairo maps purport to show where the city's moulids were held, each moulid being identified on its relevant map by a letter (generally the initial of the saint concerned) and a number to distinguish that saint from others with that same initial. McPherson was an inexpert cartographer, but his maps are a useful – and perhaps unique – record of precise moulid locations during the first half of the 20th century. To supplement the hand-drawn maps of Cairo and for greater clarity, each is next to a corresponding map of the same area cropped from a digital copy of The Survey of Egypt's "General Map of Cairo" (1920, scale 1:15,000).

The reader should note that there are very occasional inaccuracies on the hand-drawn map pages. For example, on Sectional Map XIII there is a A13 and H3 on the map to indicate the sites of Abû ʿAzâ'im's moulid and Hârûn's moulid respectively, but a A18 and H2 in the sub-title, and on the Sketch Map of Duqqî District there is a Z1 on the map to indicate the site of Zefeitî's moulid, but a Z2 in the sub-title. These are mere typos in the sub-titles and unlikely to cause confusion. We are leaving the maps uncorrected to show how they appeared in the original edition.

Foreword to the New Edition

Published in 1941, J. W. McPherson's *The Moulids of Egypt* is a rare gem of a book. A longtime resident of Egypt, McPherson became enamoured of Egypt's moulids (saint's day festivals), which are celebrated by both Muslims and Christians to honour holy men and women, especially those believed to be buried in Egypt, to seek their blessing and to enjoy the sociability of giving and receiving hospitality in the vicinity of their shrines. Although moulids take place in nearly every town and village in the country, this aspect of Egyptian life remains unknown to many, even some who live within a few streets of a major shrine. Fundamentalists attack the veneration of holy personages as blasphemy and modernists deem it superstition, but it is nonetheless an important part of the spiritual and social life of millions of people. As Biegman wrote, the moulids are in one sense "a world apart, which can easily be missed by those who find themselves in the top levels of society," but in reality "it is the upper-crust and the foreigners who are the world apart, for what is described here is nothing short of a mass phenomenon."[1]

McPherson wrote this book both as a plea for appreciation of the moulids and the secular festivities surrounding them, which were under frequent and sometimes violent attack by law enforcement at the time, and as a guidebook for those who would like to observe them. It is clear from his anecdotes that he enjoyed introducing members of the British expatriate community to these joyful celebrations. He writes of his personal experiences and observations in a lively, chatty style. In fact, one of the striking features of the book is its informality. For example, after speculating at some length on the likely similarity of the process of recognition of saints in Islam and Christianity, he notes that after writing those lines he was corrected on this point - but he does not remove the misleading

---

1 Nicolaas H. Biegman, *Egypt: Moulids, Saints, Sufis* (London: Kegan Paul; The Hague: SDU Publishers, 1990), p. 8.

paragraphs from the book; he merely adds this correction to the conversation. McPherson also includes letters to newspaper editors that support his opposition to government suppression of the moulids, especially the secular entertainments that surround them. McPherson argues that piety is strengthened by these secular activities, not diminished.

In his foreword to the first edition of this book, E. E. Evans-Pritchard argued that the moulids are not only religious festivals but have important secular dimensions. The truth of this observation needs no debate; rather, it has become necessary to insist that moulids serve religious purposes. When I gave a lecture on the moulids at the American Research Center in Egypt in 1988, an Egyptian history professor in the audience denied that the moulids have any religious significance at all. Therefore, I feel it is important to emphasize the centrality for Egyptian Sufism of devotion to the Prophet Muhammad, members of his family who are thought to be buried in Egypt, and other saintly figures. When I conducted fieldwork among the Sufis in Egypt in 1987–1989, I often asked them to define Sufism. Most often, they said it is the purification of the soul, genuine love for God, or the very essence of Islam. But one old man's response clarifies how many practitioners understand the method by which these are attained. We were conversing during the moulid of the Prophet's great-granddaughter, Fâtima -l-Nebawîya. The man was head of a group of Sufis that, like many others, had erected a pavilion in the vicinity of the shrine, offering hospitality to passersby. Sufis camp out in these pavilions for an entire week or more. He said:

> Sufism means love for the family of the Prophet. The Prophet is our
> intercessor and the one who brings us close to God, and it is through his
> family that we come close to him. [...] It is love for the family of the Prophet
> that causes us to be purified. This is why we come to the shrines of the family
> of the Prophet. [...] Why else would I leave my comfortable bed and come
> sleep on the pavement? I wouldn't be able to sleep on the pavement if it
> weren't for my love for the Prophet and his family. It is this love that purifies
> us and brings us close to God. That is why we do *dhikr*[2] here. That is why we
> come here to serve people.[3]

---

2 *Dhikr*, or *zikr* in its Egyptian pronunciation, is the "remembrance" of God through repetition of His "beautiful names" (el-asmâ' el-husnâ). McPherson explains its practice in Chapter 3.
3 Valerie J. Hoffman-Ladd, "Devotion to the Prophet and His Family in Egyptian Sufism," *International Journal of Middle East Studies* 24 (1992): 615–637 (quotation on pp. 617–618); Valerie J. Hoffman, *Sufism, Mystics, and Saints in Modern Egypt* (Columbia, South Carolina: University of South Carolina Press, 1995), pp. 50–88 (quotation on pp. 81–82).

This response makes clear that for him and many other Sufis, attendance at moulids is not only for blessing, entertainment, or sociability; it is a main focus of their spiritual development and service. For this reason, the lives of many devotees revolve around traveling the circuit of moulids. Moulids serve as occasions for members of different Sufi groups to meet and network and, because they are also popular festivals that attract large masses of people, they offer a venue for the orders to attract new members. Despite the wealth of information and detail contained in McPherson's book, these aspects of the function of moulids in Sufi life appear to have largely escaped the author's notice.

McPherson provides helpful hand-drawn maps to help visitors locate the shrines where the moulids are held. He also provides as much information as he can about when the moulids are held, although, as he points out, the dates are rarely exactly the same from one year to the next. The usefulness of McPherson's book as a guide to the moulids is limited by the fact that street names and the means of public transport, which he meticulously notes for each shrine, are subject to change, and the celebrations themselves are subject to change. Some of the moulids McPherson describes no longer take place. He even notes one moulid that he went to one year but was gone the next, the shrine destroyed and the body of the saint exhumed. On the other hand, some moulids, such as those of Ahmed el-Rifâ'î and Sayyida Nafîsa, which McPherson described as nearly extinct, are once again major celebrations. The impact on the moulid landscape of the Egyptian government's recent removal of thousands of tombs and historical monuments around the shrines of Sayyida 'Aysha and Sayyida Nafîsa remains to be seen, but it is likely to be considerable.[4] Those who are interested in seeing some of the activities McPherson describes but whose visit to Egypt does not coincide with a moulid may be interested in observing *zikr* at a shrine that has a weekly observance. *Zikr* after the afternoon and evening prayers may be observed at the following shrines: Sayyida Nafîsa on Sundays, Fâtima -l-Nebawîya on Mondays, Husein and Sayyida Zeinab on Fridays, and 'Alî Zein el-'Abdîn on Saturdays.

---

4 In January 2021, the Egyptian government announced that 2760 tombs, 360 families, and 23 shops in the area of the Sayyida 'Aysha shrine would be removed as part of its development of the area. The families would be moved to the Asmarât housing project in Muqaṭṭam (*Egypt Today*, 12 January 2021); the shops to the Tûnisî market; and the tombs would be removed to the 15th of May City in eastern Helwan (*Nawâfidh*, 30 January 2021). Likewise, in November 2021, the government removed some of the tombs in the area of the shrine of Sayyida Nafîsa in order to build a new bridge, arousing the ire of many people, including engineers, contractors, experts in the historical monuments of the area, and families whose members were buried in the targeted tombs (*Mubâshir Al Jazeera*, 18 November 2021).

McPherson describes a number of incidents of sometimes violent police suppression of moulids. These days, devotees face an even more pernicious threat.
In March 2011, following the resignation of former President Hosni Mubarak,
there were simultaneous, coordinated attacks on Sufi shrines in several cities,
allegedly perpetrated by Salafis,[5] though some cast doubt on Salafi culpability.[6]
Sufi responses included protest marches and calls for ordinary citizens to form
committees to guard the shrines.[7] The sheikh of the 'Azmîya order warned of a
civil war "beyond imagination, should the destruction of shrines persist."[8] Lest
we think that the government is antagonistic to Sufism, it is noteworthy that the
two leading representatives of the Islamic religious establishment in Egypt at the
time, the Sheikh of Al-Azhar and the Mufti of Egypt, were Sufis who roundly
denounced the attacks. McPherson notes the inconsistency of the government's
policy toward moulids, and that inconsistency remains today. Moulids can only
be held with government permission, which is sometimes withheld for various
reasons. In separate incidents, I and at least two other colleagues were prevented
by police from taking photographs or recording videos at saints' shrines, especially during moulids, although enforcement of such a ban (which is not official) is
inconsistent. A policeman told me that the government does not want such images
to be seen overseas. Long years of unjust Western criticism of Muslim societies as
lacking in rationality have prompted Muslim governments to promote an image
of Islam as a religion of reason, not of the sort of passion, ardent devotion and fun
that are seen at the moulids. But the vigilance of law enforcement at moulids is
now focused more on the potential for violent attacks on the celebrations than on
preventing the festivities.

Although there are academic works on the moulids[9] and Biegman's wonderful book of photographs, there is no book other than McPherson's that can serve

---

5 Mohammed Abdel Khaliq, "Salafi attacks on Sufi shrines violate Islam, declares Grand
Imam of Al Azhar Al Sharif," *Al-Ahram Daily*, 4 April 2011; Injy El-Kashef, "The Shrine
Affair," *Al-Ahram Weekly*, 7–13 April 2011; "Religious Endowments Ministry to Confront
Extremist Attacks," *Egypt Independent*, 7 April 2011. The term *salafi*, which means following
the ways of the early Muslims, was first used of modernist reformers in the early twentieth
century, but in the last few decades it has come to denote Muslim fundamentalists, who aim to
eradicate all practices that they regard as religiously illegitimate.
6 Jonathan Brown, "Salafis and Sufis in Egypt" (Washington, DC: Carnegie Endowment for
International Peace, December 2011), 8, 10.
7 "Egypt's Sufis to Form Popular Committees for Self-Defence," *Ahram Online*, 1 April 2013;
El-Kashef, "The Shrine Affair."
8 Ibid.
9 A fairly recent study is Samuli Schielke, *The Perils of Joy: Contesting Mulid Festivals in
Contemporary Egypt* (Syracuse, NY: Syracuse University Press, 2012).

as a guide for those who wish to observe a moulid. The book also serves as an artifact of a not-too-distant past. A contemporary reader of McPherson's book cannot help but be struck by the number of languages the author assumes the reader will understand, including Latin, Italian, French, and German. He also frequently invokes literary sources that might not be well known to contemporary readers. Today's readers will be grateful for Russell McGuirk's footnotes, which clarify these citations. No commentary is needed to appreciate McPherson's vivid descriptions, which take us into the world of traditional Egyptian piety, sociability, and joy.

Valerie J. Hoffman
University of Illinois Urbana-Champaign, USA
20 March 2022

Edward Evan Evans-Pritchard in Cairo
Evans-Pritchard (1902–1973) was Professor of Sociology at King Fuad I University
in Cairo from 1932 to 1934, during which period he and McPherson visited moulids
together. On a return visit to Egypt in 1938, he invited McPherson to join him on
a trip to Qenâ to see the Moulid of 'Abd el-Rahîm el-Qenâwî. Evans-Pritchard
suggested to McPherson that he should write a book about Egyptian moulids.

Foreword to the Original Edition

When my old friend Major McPherson asked me to write a foreword to his book on Egyptian moulids he broke a convention, for a pupil does not write a foreword to the writings of his teacher. What I know about the moulids of Egypt I have learnt from him. He has learnt nothing from me about them. I was introduced to them by him, and many are the enjoyable evenings I have spent with him in visiting the tombs of holy men in Cairo, and its neighbourhood, at the time of the annual fairs held in their honour. As I am an anthropologist, these visits were a profit to me as well as an enjoyment, for Major McPherson drew my attention to much that I would not have noticed had I been by myself and explained much that I could not have understood by reading books.

An anthropologist must at once be struck by many fundamental similarities between Egyptian moulids and the religious festivals of other peoples. It was for this reason, I fancy, that the author asked me to write a foreword to his book, and it was for this reason that I accepted the honour of doing so. I hoped to make in the foreword a short comparative analysis of religious feasts. This study must now wait for a more convenient season. When it is undertaken Major McPherson's book on Egyptian moulids will be one of its main sources. Such an enterprise needs, however, leisure and the use of a library, and I must write this foreword on a patrol on the Abyssinian frontier as far from the one as from the other.

I may, however, stress a fact of considerable importance which Major McPherson brings out in his book. To say that be brings it out in his book is, indeed, to do him an injustice, for it is its main theme. He says, and I agree with him, that a moulid is not, and cannot be, a purely religious ceremony. It has, and must have, a secular side to it. The sports, games, theatres, shadow-plays, coffee booths, beer booths, sweet stalls, eating houses, the meeting of friends, the singing, the dancing, and the laughter, are as much part of a moulid as the religious processions, the visits to the tombs of holy men, and the prayers in the mosques. The gay and secular side to religious ceremonies is an essential part of all popular religious festivals. No religion which lives in the hearts of a people can survive there without its feasts. If the feasting and the religious rites fall apart, it may well be that the feasting outlives the rites. An acute thinker, Pareto[1], has well said that in the history of peoples the reasons given for the holding of feasts may, and often do, change, while the feasts themselves show a remarkable uniformity from age to age.

I have frequently observed – and every student of the ways of primitive peoples has noticed the same fact – that in Central Africa a religious ceremony of any importance cannot be held without a banquet. There must be plenty to eat and drink, and the meats must be of a kind that are not daily eaten. Very few ceremonies are held without singing and dancing. So much is this so that Marett[2] defined one of the principal characters of primitive religions when he remarked that simple peoples dance their religion rather than formulate it as a theology. Religious ceremonies are always a holiday and a feast. I speak of primitive peoples because I have spent many years in the study of them, but what I have written of them in this respect might equally be written of the great religions of civilized peoples, of the religions of the peoples of Europe and of the East.

Religious ceremonies always tend to be associated with secular and festal activities. The secular festivities bring the people together and make the occasion a memorable one in their lives. A man remembers what he has enjoyed. The religious rites provide the festivities with a purpose and a centre round which they move. The festivities prevent the religious side from becoming a formal, lifeless, professional ritual performed by a few persons who have a local, or some other exclusive, interest in their maintenance. The religious rites prevent the festivities from becoming formless social gatherings, lacking the regularity and a special character of their own which alone enables them to endure. The religious and secular strands are interwoven together, and those who try to retain the one and discard the other, show little wisdom.

This is Major McPherson's main contention, but, though he tilts bravely at the puritanism and petty bureaucracy which seek to prohibit the secular side to moulids in Egypt, his book is in no way a polemic. It is a description of the moulids of Cairo, and of some of the principal moulids in the provinces and, as such, has great scientific value. It is a contribution to our knowledge of Egyptian life, a worthy supplement to the immortal writings of Lane[3]. Major McPherson

---

1 Vilfredo Pareto (1848–1923), Italian sociologist and economist.
2 Robert Ranulph Marett (1866–1943), British ethnologist.
3 Edward William Lane (1801–1876), British Orientalist and author of *The Manners and Customs of the Modern Egyptians* (1836).

has paid to the people of Egypt the debt which he freely acknowledges he owes them for the hospitality and kindness he has enjoyed at their hands for close on half a century.

E. E. Evans-Pritchard
Pocala, Sudan
1 November 1940

Qoseir
Qoseir is a port on the Red Sea, 170 km east of Luxor. McPherson
witnessed there "strange rites amongst the many tombs raised to
those who died here on the way back from Mecca…"

Introduction

The writer has spent more than half of a long life in Egypt, and thanks Allâh that such has been his privilege. From his early boyhood, it was his dream to live in Cairo, and from that as centre to see and know as much as possible of the places, peoples and languages all around the Mediterranean, but particularly in the Valley of the Nile.

He found Cairo an inexhaustible treasure house of interest and delight, and when alone wandered for hours exploring, till utterly lost, knowing that any '*arbagî*[1], donkey-boy or person, could take him or explain the way to some well-known spot such as the Ezbekîya Gardens or Qasr el-Nîl Bridge. He was fortunate, too, in falling into good hands during his first week and feels especially grateful for the hospitality of the family of the present Minister of Hygiene, Hâmed Bey Mahmûd, and that of Dr. Ibrâhîm Zakî Kâshif, at whose houses in country and in town, he had wonderfully interesting and enjoyable times; and to the family of the late Muftî, the Sheikh Muhammad Bikhît, with whom he wandered for months in Upper Egypt.

His work, too, civil and military, in later years gave him peculiar faculties for wandering almost anywhere and acquiring an otherwise impossible intimacy with strange places and people. This was particularly the case in 1919, the year of the most serious riots, and the few subsequent years, when his double military rank, British and Egyptian, and his post of "Mamur Zapt"[2] – a sort of Chief Inquisitor at the head of the secret police – necessitated frequent access to the interiors of palaces and huts; even at times the *penetralia* of harîms, for the masters of these and the occupants, when given the option, invariably preferred the officer to take on this delicate task, rather than one of the detectives of the other sex whose special work that is.

---

1 'arbágî = driver of an animal-drawn cart.
2 Ma'mûr Zapt = Director of the political Criminal Investigation Department (C.I.D.) for investigating political activists and secret societies.

As an extreme case, I may mention being instructed to find out and report what strange wild orgies were proceeding in a house suspected of harbouring seditious characters, on the edge of the *găbĕl*[3] east of Sidna Husein[4], and if necessary to arrest the lot. It proved to be a *zâr*[5], and I surprised a Priestess of the *djinn* engaged with her acolyte virgins in consummating a blood sacrifice at the "altar" with a view to casting out devils from a possessed woman. As I insisted on remaining till the last '*afrît*[6] had returned to Iblîs[7], or bringing in my small force and transferring all present to the Gamalia qism[8] (district police station) to explain the whole proceeding by a *mahdar*[9] (*procès verbal*), they ultimately elected to carry on, after the Medusa eyes of the '*âlima*[10], the exorcist, had done their best to turn me to stone like the enemies of Jason. (I know no other case of a man witnessing a *zâr*.)

On retiring, then, in 1924, I was left with more subjects of enquiry and observation, than I could deal with in my lifetime, and these never left me a dull hour.

Though more than contented with Egypt – except for the complacency with which modernism, Americanism, and many wretched forms of vandalism are suffered to ruin so many of the glorious old places and customs of the country – the writer, on finding himself absolutely free to live where he liked on retiring in 1924, set out to see if there were a better *pied-à-terre* in which to pass the rest of his days, and indeed found many a lovely spot in England, Italy, Spain, Greece, Tunisia and elsewhere, but none to equal Egypt for climate and general charm; none so cosmopolitan and so full of both Eastern and Western appeal.

It is not for him here to dwell on the glory of its mosques and monuments, the variety of its churches, surpassing any other town, nor on the *bonhomie* of its people, nor the facilities for pursuing any hobby and satisfying all tastes. Its old customs, and one of these – its moulids – is subject enough and more than enough for this essay.

A moulid is a popular religious feast in honour of some saint – in Egypt, usually of Islam – corresponding to the feasts and fairs of Europe (and its colonies) to honour some Christian saint; and although moulids hardly became a national institution in

---

3 găbĕl = hill; mountain.
4 The Sayyidna l-Husein Mosque near the Khân el-Khalîlî Bazaar.
5 zâr = ritual for appeasing or casting out evil spirits.
6 'afrît = demon, imp.
7 Iblîs = Satan.
8 Gamalia qism [more properly, qism el-gamâlîya] = the Gamâlîya district police station in Eastern Cairo.
9 mahdar = official police report or record of the facts of a case.
10 'âlima = literally, woman of learning.

Egypt till the 7th century of the *Hegira* (the 13th century A.D.), nor perhaps entirely recognised officially as such till two centuries later, they in many cases are a continuation of feasts held hundreds or even thousands of years before the Prophet, just as many Christian celebrations can be traced back centuries before Christ.

The first and greatest of moulids, excepting that of the Prophet, is the Feast of Sayyid Ahmad el-Bedawî at Tantâ, which is regarded by many Egyptologists as a revival of that of Shu,[11] the God of Sebennytus[12]; it owes some of its wonderful vogue to the mighty body and tremendous character of Ahmad el-Bedawî, suggesting subconsciously the "Egyptian Hercules,"[13] the hero of the ancient cult.

That cult vanished with the third branch of the Nile, the Sebbenytic, which flowed near Tantâ and the city of Shu, now known as Sammanud. Some ancient memories may have been kept just alive by the waters of the canal which borrowed the bed of that ancient river, and which I believe still exists.

One of the apostles of the Sayyid, Sheikh Ismâ'îl el-Imbâbî, died and was buried at his *zâwiya*[14] (cell) by the side of the Nile in the village known to Cairenes by his name[15], and is honoured by a moulid to this day; but that celebration does not follow the Islamic calendar, but is on or about the 10th of the Coptic month, Ba'ûna[16], 16 June, the date when ancient Egyptians watched for the mystic tear drop of Isis believed to fall at that time and that place into the river of Osiris. Long after the Night of Power, *Leilet el-Qadr*, the night when the archangel Gabriel brought down from heaven the revelation to Muhammad, had supplanted the Night of the Drop, *Leilet el-Nuqta*, crowds thronged the Nile bank watching for the mysterious "drop", and even now there are some who go for that reason in the middle of June as well, as for the blessing to be derived from a pilgrimage to the shrine of the sainted Imbâbî.

Wherefore all ye pilgrims to the *zâwiya* of Sîdî Ismâ'îl el-Imbâbî, come to the banks of the Nile opposite the Gezîra towards the end of "the second month of inundation", *aabet sen set*, the Alexandrian month of ⲠⲀⲰⲚⲒ still so written in the Coptic language and as Ba'ûna in English. That will be when we are nearing the time of the solstice, whilst the sun is yet in the zodiacal sign of Castor and Pollux.

---

11 The Greeks associated Shu with Atlas in their own mythology. Both were depicted as holding up the sky.

12 An ancient city of Lower Egypt, located on the Damietta branch of the Nile.

13 That is, the Egyptian god Shu.

14 zâwiya = small mosque, usually domed, over the tomb of a Muslim saint.

15 The village of Imbâba.

16 Ba'ûna = the tenth Coptic month running from 8 June to 7 July.

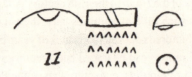

The Feast of Isis was a boat festival, for was she not the patroness of boatmen, and did she not teach them her invention of the sail? So, at the Moulid of el-Imbâbî the river swarms with feluccas and rowing boats, a lovely sight especially when Isis-Diana is bright in the heavens. You will do well to join them on the water, and above the laughter and the singing and "all kinds of musick"[17] you will doubtless hear the harsher rattle of the *sistrum,* associated with Cleopatra, the sacred instrument of Isis, used in her worship, as it still is in that of the Ethiopian Copts.

Quod semper, quod ubique quod ab omnibus![18]

The old leaders of Islam and of Catholicism were wise and reverent, and respected the traditions of their ancestors and those old celebrations which were the expression of the hearts of the people; and far from despising or destroying them, they adopted them into their own cult, purifying or modifying with as gentle a hand as possible. The great feast of Shamm el-Nesîm[19], observed by Christians and Moslems and all Egyptians alike, is in a way a moulid (though not included in those which follow), for it doubtless was held originally to celebrate the re-birth of the Phoenix and is a remnant of the cult of the Sun-God Ra by Egyptians of Pharaonic times. Those who doubt it should visit Matarîya, the old Heliopolis or "city of the Sun", before dawn on that day and see the crowds who have slept in the fields and the roads to see the sun rise near the obelisk which marks the site of the Temple of Ra. Few of these are more aware of the pull which draws them there, than are migratory birds of the urge which impels them to fly at the same time and to the same spot as their ancestors of ages ago. Yet those visitors are gay and happy and better for the holiday.

In describing the Moulids of 'Abd el-Rahîm at Qenâ and Yûsef el-Haggâg at Luxor, I have pointed out that the procession with boats dates back to the cult of Amun, as portrayed on the wall of the temple of Ramses III. This is of

---

17 Daniel 3:5 "That at what time ye hear the sound of the cornet, flute, harp, sackbut, psaltery, dulcimer, and all kinds of musick, ye fall down and worship the golden image that Nebuchadnezzar the king hath set up."

18 "…which is always, everywhere and by everyone [believed]".

19 Shamm el-Nasîm, meaning "smell the breeze", is a popular spring festival and holiday on the Monday after Coptic Easter.

Processional Boat once carried at the Moulid of 'Abd
el-Rahim el-Qenâwî, at Qenâ in upper Egypt

Funerary Boat of Tutankhamun, about 1500 B.C.
"But the great shock and disappointment was the absence in the procession of the
Boat, which has been a beautiful and distinctive feature of this moulid ... for centuries;
for thousands of years, in fact, seeing that Egyptologists hold that it was adapted by
Islam, as an integral part of this *zeffa* from the processions of Pharaonic times."

world-wide interest, and in 1357 (1938) pictures of these boats and fascinating bits of research on the subject appeared in *Nature*, in *Man*, and other magazines. Dr Evans-Pritchard, the anthropologist, invited me and one or two others to share rooms he had taken close to the Qenâ moulid to witness this unique sight. The moulid was indeed impressive though shorn of much of its original charm, but the local authorities had cut out the boats for no assignable reason. These boats are endeared to the people, not only by their antique traditions, but by more modern Islamic legends connecting them with the saint they are honouring, so why send half a million poor people, including ourselves, away disappointed and sacrifice one more of Egypt's real assets?

This, after all, is a small incident compared with what moulids all over the country have suffered of recent years and, therefore, what Egypt has lost in popular content, piety and happiness, and also of its native charm, and rich inheritance of beautiful customs.

This book of moulids, which should be a record of the popular expression of the exuberance of faith, goodwill and light-hearted merriment, is unhappily full of incidents like the above or far worse which perforce come into the picture of the moulid and can only depress and grieve the lover of the Egyptian people and their customs.

The joy of forty years delightful residence in Egypt has been marred for the writer, and who can say how many else, by seeing these ancient popular religious institutions, as indeed so much else that is picturesque and venerable, discouraged in many ways, and of recent years attacked by open vandalism and undermined by the sophisms of Pharisees and Puritans.

People of culture and taste who come to Egypt now for the first time and find much to charm and fascinate them, can hardly imagine how much more there was a few decades ago, and those who knew it then and return to it now, cannot, I think, fail to weep over the city. The loss of so many of its beauty spots, its modern streets ugly or at least banal like gashes across its oriental loveliness; the truncation of its picturesque customs, with the consequent damper on its native mirth and light-heartedness; so much that is unlovely and depressing; so much that Cairo might and should have escaped; so much indeed that is irretrievably lost. Happily, the vastness of the city has saved much of it, and of recent years the splendid efforts of a committee to protect venerable sites and buildings has checked much vandalism, but we still badly need some such group to defend its traditional customs.

Of course, the *Zeitgeist*, which blew mainly from the far west, to chill and blight Europe, has afflicted most of the world, Egypt included, with its false values, its substitution of mechanical cacophonies for human melodies, of amorphous sky-scrapers for shapely dwellings, of sordid materialism for the disinterested pursuit of beauty, of frenzied rush and blazing light and blatant noise for gentle living; in short, a new cult of savagery (not as they would claim, a new and special culture) for an old civilisation.

The Nebî Moses would ask us, as he asked the Benî Isrâ'îl[20], when they got their values all wrong:

"Would you barter blessed things for those which are base?"[21]

But if, as is indeed the case, Egypt has been more sinned against than sinning, she might have done more, and still might do, to check this outside contagion, this spiritual and artistic decadence. By a strange paradox the virtues of generosity and complaisance, so conspicuous in the Egyptians have tended to the loss of some of their priceless assets. Born and bred amongst such material and spiritual treasures, they do not realise their value, nor that a little *laissez-faire* may and does lead to irremediable loss.

And they get no return, no thanks for these sacrifices. All these up-to-date lures to tourists are the grossest mistake. Even the Westerners are repelled rather than attracted by the nasty cinema shows, nasty jazzy noises, nasty "bunny hugs" and "black bottoms", hideous buildings, and the rest of their own contributions to an anti-civilisation. They come here to escape the abominations they have brought on themselves and much of the world, and to bask for a while in the soft beauty of Eastern peace. They are not, thank God, votaries of these idols, not all of them; nor do they all appreciate the vulgar humour of Mark Twain who made his "hero" blow out the sacred lamp which pious hands had kept burning for centuries. I have in my mind at the moment a recent American visitor to Cairo, who although a millionaire had escaped the pettiness which millions are liable to bring. He, Mr C…, had known our city more than half a century ago and had visited it at intervals, and he mourned and deplored the ruthless changes.

But I am drifting into generalities, almost into personalities, a field which proved too vast for that great foreign friend of Egypt and the East, Pierre Loti, who wrote about "La Mort de Constantinople" and "La Mort du Caire". He was

---

20 Literally "the sons of Israel", i.e., the Jews.
21 Qurân, Sûrat el-Baqara [The Cow], verse 61.

also a Prophet, but of the Cassandra type – almost a *vox clamantis in deserto*[22]. Yet I think the East mourns now "*La mort de Loti.*"

This little book is simply and solely a plea for Egypt's moulids, which for the best part of a millennium have been an essential and valuable element in the religion, happiness and life of the people from the least to the greatest; but which in recent times, as I have said, for some deplorable reason, or lack of reason, seem to have been specially marked out for coercion, restriction, and what amounts to persecution, with chilling results on the hearts and souls of millions of dear people, who form the backbone of the nation. The *fallâhîn*[23] and the masses generally are poor enough as regards this world's goods, but they are rich in natural spirits, capacity for simple pleasures and innocent gaiety especially when they can fit these in with piety. It is a truism that religion and joy go hand in hand. Pharisees and Puritans who, with perhaps the best intentions, try to separate them, injure both, and unwittingly and unwillingly play into the hands of the enemy – the godless, the *bezbozhnik*,[24] the Bolshevik – who have warned us by the unhappiness of their people, as in Germany and Russia, that popular expression of religion cannot safely be suppressed.

Though any old stick, or rather new stick, seems good enough to beat the moulids, I have enquired diligently and have never elicited a valid reason for this attitude of antagonism or at least indifference, though there are plenty of reasons for sympathy and calls for support. The student class and the young "effendîs"[25] do not as a rule patronise them, but I have never known them actually hostile. They have their sports, their football, basketball, and innumerable games, and an excellent thing too, and they naturally go their own ways as the corresponding classes in other countries. But what have the poor got? Their spades, their *fu'ûs*[26] (hoes). But what games except a swing here and there, which they put up themselves usually, and a ride on their donkey, if it is not too tired for work. My windows look out on forty or more acres of playgrounds provided for the classes, and a splendid thing too, doubtless, for the physique of that section of the nation. The masses do not ask for that; they can amuse themselves if they are only allowed to do so. They can watch a conjurer or snake charmer or *Galli Galli*[27] man, a Punch and Judy or shadow play delightedly for hours, or a dancer

---

22 A voice crying in the wilderness.

23 fallâh (s.), fallâhîn (pl.) = native peasants, agricultural labourers.

24 Russian for "Godless".

25 Effendi = a Turkish title of respect. Here it refers to the educated class.

26 fa's or fâs (s.), fu'ûs (pl.).

27 A conjurer in the streets and ports of Egypt who says "galâ galâ" (hey presto!) Cf. Badawi & Hinds, *A Dictionary of Egyptian Arabic* (1986).

to some simple instrument, or an acrobat; but all these poor souls who made a modest living by amusing thousands up to a few years ago are chased from pillar to post, and seem to be looked on by the authorities as suspicious characters, and the little crowd of other poor souls, who like myself enjoy these antics, which are perfectly harmless, are scattered like a seditious mob. This is not only the case in the new and neurotic quarters but has spread like a blight over the native *manâshî* (squares)[28], and open spaces that of late were full of fun and life. Recently, on a Friday, I saw a clever conjurer ejected very roughly from amongst the tombs near Imâm el-Shâfe'î, where he and his little audience had taken sanctuary; and the last monkey I saw riding a goat was arrested and dragged off. "Manouli"[29] and the bow-wow had appeared as happy as the onlookers, but someone suggested that a SPCA fan had denounced "such cruelty" to dumb animals, and thought they were fit subjects for the boon of euthanasia. "Pity they were dumb!" I thought. "They might express other views." Others surmised that Manouli was only being taken to the *caracôl* (police station) to produce his *rukhsa* (licence), or his passport or birth certificate, or to fulfil one of those little formalities which have become so numerous and so important of late.

Of course, this is an age of repression and neurotics, not to mention narcotics, so much abused in Egypt these days. At the present rate of nerve destruction and decay, the great Plutocracies, Democracies, Aristocracies and the rest will have surrendered in a *War of Nerves* and merged before long into one grand Neurocracy. The trend of modern times, too, is a kill-joy trend, and the mania of modern people a kill-joy mania, and when they have killed joy and are bored to death, they kill one another and themselves. Thank God, this virus is so attenuated before it affects Egypt that we have escaped, so far, its most pernicious effects, even as the hurricane which wrecks ships in the Atlantic, and makes people very seasick in the Mediterranean, is reduced to slamming a few doors and raising a little dust in Cairo.

This rage for repression, though most evident at moulids, is by no means confined to such, as indeed I have indicated above. If a man may no longer laugh freely at a Punch and Judy show, nor smile at a dancing girl, he is reminded in many of the cafés that singing is prohibited by order of the Government. Women too may no longer indulge in lamentations for the dead, anyway in public.

---

28 More accurately, newly built villages or suburbs: manshîya (s.), manâshî (pl.).
29 Cf. This scene was recast in *Balthazar* (Alexandria Quartet, Vol. 2) by Lawrence Durrell as follows: "… Manouli the monkey in a paper hat brilliantly rode round and round his stall on the back of a goat."

The elders and notables of the land, like the students and *effendi* classes, are seldom seen at moulids and as a rule profess little interest therein, but I have never known one of them actually antagonistic. They too have their clubs and sports and their interests in art and literature and politics, which the poor have not, and they believe in the adage "live and let live". Many indeed go to the receptions (*tashrîfât*)[30] and the religious and historic ceremonies, which mark the opening and the close; and not a few actually support the popular sides also with money and influence. It is, for example, the lavish hand of the Minister of Hygiene, Hâmed Pâsha Mahmûd, which upholds the Tûkh[31] moulid, and that of Dr. Taha Husein which has saved that of his native town, Maghâgha. Many Christian and foreign notables help to defray decoration and other expenses and, as far as I have seen, they are all sympathetic. I have known them even supply a feast for the poor, and there is one who has restored the ancient tomb and Moulid of Sîdî Hârûn el-Huseinî on generous and beautiful lines.

It is a pity that, of recent years, rich and poor have drifted somewhat apart at festivals and functions common to both. Typical of this is the "Cutting of the *Khalîg*". This ceremony of the Bride of the Nile (*'Arûset el-Nîl*) has not changed materially, but a decade or so ago, the evening celebrations, *tashrîfa* (reception), fireworks, and the rest were all together at the *Fumm el-Khalîg*,[32] and there was a certain *Gemütlichkeit*[33] about it which was quite lost when the reception tents were erected in a special enclosure on Rôda Island, and the populace, not provided with special tickets, were prevented by mounted police from crossing the bridge to it and only able to hear the bands and see the fireworks from the other side of the water. In the same way, the intimate charm and atmosphere of friendly fellowship has gone from the *Mahmal*[34] and Holy Carpet festivals to a considerable extent. This will be found very marked in the accounts of the Moulids of Muhammadî, Imâm el-Shâfe'î and some others.

Moulids, as for many ages past, are still under the aegis of the Government. They are not held without a permission from the Ministry of Interior. Many of them are officially supported and attended – the greatest of all, that of the Prophet, by the King or his immediate representative. *'Ulamâ*,[35] ministers, the highest

---

30 tashrîfa (s.), tashrîfât (pl.).

31 A town in the Delta, near Benhâ.

32 Fumm el-Khalîg = "Mouth of the Canal", referring to the old Red Sea Canal, which reached the Nile by Rôda Island in Cairo. Now the name of that area of the city.

33 Friendly ambience (German).

34 mahmal = camel-borne litter sent by Egyptian rulers to Mecca at pilgrimage time.

35 'âlim (s.), 'ulamâ' (pl.) = trained in Islamic law and theology.

officials mingle at some of them. They are, in fact, a precious part of the religious and social life of the country. And yet many of them are being crushed out of existence, even that which centres round the head of the great Zein el-'Abdîn, son of Sidna Husein, and the once immense celebration of Sheikh "Tashtûshî".

Who then, or what, is behind this destructive movement? Not even the kill-joy and freeze-religion tendency of modern times with its almost universal blight can wholly account for it. Those who see a moulid spoiled by the stupid excesses of "'askarîs"[36] naturally blame the Police, but they are wrong in the main, ultimately, I believe, and the crowds seem to be realising that more and more. The writer was for a good many years a policeman of sorts and in a position most favourable to form an opinion, and he cannot remember any antagonism latent or expressed. And since he left that service, he has never pointed out a specific case of violence or interference through excess of zeal on the part of the rank and file to an officer, but the latter has checked this and mended matters.

Certainly, the police are not blameless. Some of the minor officers at the *aqsâm*[37] (police stations) carry their responsibilities heavily and seem to be unnecessarily nervous, lest a little moulid crowd or procession might disturb the peace or check the traffic. I wish they could see the crowds about Trafalgar Square or Buckingham Palace, or in the Piazza di Venezia at Rome, or any big towns and the absence of fluster or coercion on the part of the police. I am not speaking, of course, about strikers, political demonstrators or seditious mobs of any sort; the sooner they are broken up the better, and if such is not done, they get worse and things end badly. But the moulid crowd is the most harmless and best-disposed crowd in the world. Politics, tendentious speeches and such like have no part in them and are not tolerated by the people themselves if, as very rarely happens, a little extraneous party tries to introduce such. In the worst of the strikes and riots I have taken friends, including ladies, into the thick of a moulid crowd, and the peaceful contrast and air of safety has amazed and delighted them.

Of course, pickpockets and occasionally quarrelsome characters intrude as in any crowd, but such are easily dealt with on their own demerits, and the police have the sympathy and help of all the rest and no reason for spoiling the moulid and visiting their wrath on well-meaning decent people as, unhappily, I have had to relate in some of the accounts which follow.

This official nervousness passes down in exaggerated form to the "'askarîs", who often appear to think that they must interfere, even in things which they

---

36 'askarî (*s.*), 'asâkir (*pl.*) = a soldier or policeman.
37 qism (s.), aqsâm (pl.).

individually approve. The writer has often seen them enjoying the singing of a
sheikh or something amusing or edifying, and then suddenly become militant on
the advent of someone who looks official and break up the happy little show; and
sometimes the writer has been horrified to realise that his arrival is the innocent
cause of this, although he has come in as unofficial a manner as possible and
insisted that friends with him do the same.

It is regrettable, too, that moulids often suffer for events for which they are
entirely innocent and over which they can have had no control. As one example
of this, on 18 Sha'bân 1357 (12 October 1938), on returning from the great Qenâ
moulid in mid-Sha'bân, I went to that of Sultân Hanafî. This was the final night
and it had been working up before I went to Qenâ, but now I found practically
nothing but lots of "'askarîs" with long severe faces and a few rather frightened
and sad looking people. The mosque was most sparsely attended and from the
enclosure some distance away, where Punch and Judy, shadow shows, swings,
and the rest had amused a host of children, everything had been turned out and
darkness reigned. "Whatever has happened?" I asked. "Why, don't you know?",
someone said, "There was a row near the station a day or two ago and some
statesmen hurt." That was deplorable news, indeed, but I could not ascertain that
the smallest suspicion attached to anyone from that district, so why the votaries
of the holy Sultân had to suffer, or why *Qara Goz* (Punch) was arrested remains
a mystery. People go to moulids to obtain a blessing, and I am sure they ought
to receive an extra one for paying, as they sometimes do, for other peoples' sins.

The above was written before war broke out and was held over to see how
far this would affect us generally and the moulids in particular. As was hoped, in
general we remain unaffected in our lives, a most favoured and happy nation. God
has been indeed kind to us, but man has not been so kind to His moulid-going
poor. One calamity has been the non-observance of the great Tantâ Moulid of
Sayyid el-Bedawî, one of the greatest events of Islam, or at least its postponement *sine die*.[38] It has been a blessing to and the pride of Egypt for more than six
hundred years, bringing to it, it is said, more pilgrims than does Mecca to its own
holy places. Are we so overstocked with holy men that we freeze out the flower
of distant lands? And is it wise policy to anticipate the clouds of war, instead of
carrying on as long as there is nothing to prevent it, and so encourage the masses
to be of good cheer?

Cairo moulids suffered but not at first so badly. The 3 September 1939 on
which war was declared was 19 Rajab 1358. In the short period between then and

---

38 sine die [Latin] = indefinitely.

the start of Ramadân there are numerous moulids, and there was a rumour that they would be checked because of the alleged extra light, though up to the date on which I am now writing, 17 Shawwâl 1358 (28 November 1939), Cairo has remained *une ville lumière* except for rare and very brief blackouts, and I doubt if this has been officially applied even to moulids, but locally it seems to have been advanced in some cases as a reason (or a pretext) for their discontinuance. During the last few nights of Sha'bân the region below the citadel from the Bâb el-Wazîr to the tombs of the Mamelukes is usually a most pleasant sight: tiny moulids, dimly lighted shrines, little "zeffas" with their simple banners, torches and lanterns, the music of the tambourine (*târ*) and flute (*nay*), the rapt faces of sheikhs and happy enthusiasm of children; but in the year 1939 all was gloom each time I went. One of these nights, I saw a few disgruntled dervishes under that beautiful old archway near Sayyida 'Aysha with folded gonfalons[39] and one huge paper lantern burning dimly. I think they had been on their way to the tomb of el-Gîzî, which is amongst those of the Mamelukes. Proceeding to the place of the Moulid of Sheikh Sâleh Shâhîn el-Muhammadî, behind the Khalîfa police station, all was dark; but happily I found the important Moulid of Bahlûl, near the Bâb el-Wazîr, proceeding smoothly. It had been threatened, I was told, but had had a blessed escape. On the way there, I overtook a dervish whom I have known and respected for a long time. He was almost inarticulate with distress and emotion at the repressions, so I hope Bahlûl cheered him. Asking him why these little moulids had been dropped, he replied: "They say the Army objects to the light". Who "they" were I can't say, but it is impossible to believe such an absurdity, whether it emanated from the dervish himself or from "them", for at that very time, in addition to many lighted minarets, the citadel mosque was brilliantly flood-lit and high up blazed thousands of candlepower.

Of about twenty moulids I visited after war was declared, that is during the last days of Rajab and throughout Sha'bân, all were washouts, blackouts or doleful survivals, except four: el-'Azâ'im, Bahlûl, Matrâwî and last, but by no means least, Barsûm el-'Aryân. This last was a magnificent moulid worth a long journey to witness, perhaps surpassing that described of three years ago (which see), and indeed people had come from afar and settled there for a week or more. On the last night, thousands, tens of thousands, of Moslems mingled with the Coptic pilgrims at the shrine of this Christian saint. Such is the blessed spirit of tolerance amongst the people of Egypt. All was piety and joy, and there was not the smallest friction.

But that this brightest and happiest of moulids should be one of the few

---

39 Gonfalon, a banner, generally with streamers, hung from a crossbar.

surviving Coptic celebrations is very significant. It even suggests a clue to the quest which is the *leitmotif* of this preface – who is behind this repression of the moulids, this stifling of the people's natural expression of their piety and joy of life according to their hearts' dictates and the millennial custom of their country? Can it possibly be the very people from whom they might expect sympathy and support, an academic section of their leaders in religion, who, sacrificing the spirit for their own interpretation of the letter of the law with, doubtless, the best intentions tend to the same results as the modern *Zeitgeist* which we all deplore? Is it, indeed, the source to which we look for scholarly, constructive, guidance, that gives us instead scholastic prohibitions which are only destructive?

If this is the case, as I think is commonly supposed, though I am unwilling to believe it, it exonerates the police to a great extent, for it is the civil arm which has to execute punitive measures on those whom the Church deems "heretics", as in the days of the Inquisition.

I am sometimes told by theological pundits: "These moulids were not ordered by the Prophet, and therefore are not in our religion"; to which I reply: "Did he order your motor cars or half the things you have and do? If they are not in your religion why have your holiest men delighted in them for ages – your "Khalîfas"[40], your *Naqâ'ib el-Ashrâf*[41], your "Walîs"[42], your hosts of dervishes, and many whose tombs are now the objects of the very cult you discredit. Has modernism shed such a holy light that it reveals to you their errors and new truths unseen by them?"

There is a slogan specially applied to moulids: "Nothing against morals and religion!" This sounds excellent and certainly is in theory, but the application which is being given to it is working out very wrongly. No well-thinking person would do other than approve the elimination of anything specifically evil, but the amusements of the people which are being attacked now are, in the main, no more evil than eating or sleeping; indeed they are almost as necessary for the health, contentment and happiness of the people and the whole body politic. Is the graceful stick-play of the Egyptians against morals or religion, or their dancing and racing horses, or the "ringas" beloved of the Sudanese with their quaint music to which sometimes dancers fully clad do a *pas seul* suggestive of cockroach crushing; is singing wicked, or a little dancing for the matter of that? The Prophet

---

40 Caliphs; note that the Arabic singular is "khalîfa", never khalîf.
41 naqâ'ib el-ashrâf = heads of the descendants of the Prophet, the singular being naqîb el-ashrâf.
42 walî (s.), awliyâ' (pl.) = holy men, saints.

David (Nebî Dâ'ûd) danced in procession before the holy things[43], and to this day, at what is perhaps the most beautiful of all surviving religious pageants, the Palio of Siena, I have seen lads dancing the gonfalon dance[44] before the altar and in the house of St. Catherine there. Is it irreligious to be, or to watch, an acrobat, a snake charmer, a clever conjurer, a fat man or a dwarf, or even an amusing clown or a gifted strolling-player; or is it immoral to try your strength, or your skill at shooting at a micro-target or your resistance to electric shock? Those who try to make the world a more pleasant place will be damned if it is. Yet every one of these little joys which I have listed, I have seen ruthlessly checked or broken up again and again, and many more of the same type. The popular dwarf is now on the streets selling lottery tickets, the fat man is visibly slimming, and the rest – what has become of them, poor fellows? Again, poor *Qara Goz* (Punch) is no saint, but he has flourished for probably more than a thousand years in Egypt, Turkey, Persia, and the great Islamic states. Has he fallen into heresy? And have the marionettes of the equally ancient and popular shadow play (*khayâl el-zill*) come up against religion?

The great teacher, the Prophet Jesus, compared the Kingdom of Heaven to a field of corn in which an enemy has sown bad seed. When the tares (*zizania*) and cockle (*nagîl*)[45] sprang up the farm men wished to pull that up, but their Lord said," No, lest ye pull up the good wheat with it, leave it to the harvest."[46]

Though the field in the parable might well be the moulid ground, the similitude hardly stands as regards the tares, for that which the husbandmen decide to pull up and do so very thoroughly are not "tares", but the poppies and corn-flowers which add colour to the crop, or the fenugreek (*helba*) and hemp (*tîl*), which protect it as well as beautify it and increase its value. The holiday games which grow up about a holy day shrine become in a way part of it.

"…even as the trees
That whisper round a temple become soon
Dear as the temple's self…"[47]

The stark truth is that these well-meaning but misguided guides are tearing up religion itself. Anyone who saw a moulid

---

43 Cf. 2 Samuel 6:14.
44 A dance with banners.
45 Couch grass (*Elymus repens*).
46 [McPher.] Saint Matthew, Ch. XIII, 24
47 From Keats' *Endymion*.

"Before this sad disease of modern times," [48]

even a very few years ago, can check the truth of this by revisiting the same ceremony (if it still exists) and noting the dwindled number and enthusiasm of those
who visit the shrine, the broken "zeffas" and disgruntled sheikhs and dervishes.

It is curious, too, that of the few things which might have been regarded as
tares, gaming tables of all sorts still flourish, and I think more than they did before.
Perhaps from a Machiavellian point of view they may be deemed to do more
good than harm, for the odds against the youngsters who stake their *millièmes*
and *niklas*[49] are so great, that their inevitable loss should give them a distaste for
the gambling habit.

Those who read the accounts which follow of the Moulids of Sitna Fâtima
-l-Nebawîya bint Husein, of her great niece the other Fâtima -l-Nebawîya (bint
Ga'far el-Sâdiq), of Sîdî 'Ashmâwî, and alas of many others; or who have seen
them for themselves in the past and also in recent times, and are thus in a position
where comparisons are forced upon them, cannot fail to detect a subtle evil which
has crept in, undermining their whole-hearted sincerity; nor can they avoid the
conclusion that at least a contributory cause is the false interpretation and application of the catch-word about "morals and religion". Is it a triumph for religion
that in the first of the three cases here referred to, a very vulgar buffoon should
take the place, in an erstwhile solemn and dignified procession, of a descendant
and representative of the grand-daughter of the Prophet? Or in the second case,
that of the daughter of the Sixth Imam; is it a moral gain that the joyful precincts
of her beautiful little shrine should become as gloomy at her moulid as the prison
over the way; that the cave-like dwellings which re-echoed with "zikrs"[50] should
harbour a silent sulky party reduced to black tea and coffee, to smoking "shîshas"
and "gôzas"[51] in the semi-dark, and that the player on the *arghûl*[52], that fine old
reed instrument with its deep notes, should be ejected from the adjoining street as
though he had brought the plague?

And in the third case selected in this connection, that of Sîdî 'Ashmâwî, I think
a very obvious lesson is to be drawn from the little corner, formerly the scene of
innocent stick play, singing and such like, substituting these by a *zikr* in intended
conformity with the *mot d'ordre*, with results which were regrettable and profane.

---

48 This line, seemingly not from *Endymion*, remains unidentified.
49 "Penny and twopenny coins" (1000 millièmes = 1 Egyptian Pound; 1 nikla = 2 millièmes).
50 In Sufism, the repetition of words in praise of God, accompanied by music and dancing.
51 Types of waterpipe.
52 arghûl = a wind instrument roughly a metre long, consisting of two pipes.

The very virtue of the old moulid was the sincerity and openness of its piety and its joy. Anything, however well-meant, that induces secretiveness or hypocrisy tends, I hold, to unbelief and profanity, even to a spiritual retrogression, for which the people themselves can hardly be blamed.

Bliss, in his work on the religions of Syria and Palestine[53], attempts to sum up the position of the Dervishes in the scheme of the components of Islam, by saying: "The Dervishes seek God in the heart; the Ulama seek Him in the Book." The epigram suggests that if the former can be too emotional sometimes in their zeal, the latter are in danger of laying too much stress on formal religion and putting the letter before the spirit, of which indeed too many instances in the history of religion could be cited; but it is misleading in implying a sort of antithesis which ought not to exist – certainly not here in Egypt, where the *'ulamâ* include great leaders of the dervish orders, even the *Naqâ'ib el-Ashrâf* and the four sheikhs of the four orthodox sects, the Hanafîya, Shâfe'îya, Malakîya, and Hanbalîya.

In point of fact, I have never heard that the *'ulamâ* in general are inclined to coerce moulid-goers or that they are in favour of these irritating and sometimes violent repressions at present so harmful. That responsibility seems always to be laid at the doors of a certain potent authority of the great University of Al-Azhar. Chastisement is perhaps a tradition. Certainly, there are some classic cases on record, as that recorded by Lane of the Al-Azhar Professor el-Quweisinî[54], who celebrated his nomination as head of the 'Lodge of the Blind' (*Sheikh Zâwiyet el-'Umyân*), by having all his blind men (*'umyân*), about three hundred, mostly students, well flogged; not without reason, it is said, though they, failing to appreciate the reason, seized and bound the sheikh and flogged him. I can find no early records, however, of that use of the palm rod being extended to pilgrims and public at moulids.

Whilst penning the above lines it has been pointed out to me that Al-Azhar applies its castigatory rod to beast as well as man, the latest of God's creatures to give offence being none other than the Nebî's camel, which bears the *Mahmal* to the Holy Places, which one would have thought, indeed, the last to give offence.

There has, I am told, been considerable discussion of this *cause célèbre* in some of the papers, and it may not be out of place to append a copy of a letter to *The Egyptian Gazette*, which indicates that this august delinquent seems to have been handed over to the civil arm in the distinguished person of the political leader of the country.

---

53 F. J. Bliss, *The Religions of Modern Syria and Palestine* (Edinburgh, 1912).
54 El-Quweisinî was himself blind, a fact which clearly did not impress his fellow blind lodge members.

The Mahmal Procession

The *mahmal* was the decorated camel-borne litter sent by Egyptian rulers to Mecca at
pilgrimage time. It carried the *Kiswa*, the new covering for the Kaʻba. The tradition
began in the 13th century and ended in the mid-20th, about the time McPherson died.

25 April 1940

The Editor, Egyptian Gazette,
Dear Sir,
I had noticed recently polemics in the papers for and against the elimination of
the "Nebi's Camel", from the Mahmal celebrations,

ceu cetera nusquam bella forent[55]

and had wondered who could have so little useful to do as to open an attack
on a venerable and picturesque national custom. Surely Egypt's traditional
ceremonies have been sufficiently shorn of their beauty and significance in
these drab days without clipping the pilgrims' camel, the people's camel, the
Prophet's camel – *"ahsan min beni Adam"* (better than the sons of Adam) as I
have heard women ejaculate as they press forward to touch it.

A friend of mine and of Egypt, who regards the repeated uncalled for
little vandalistic moves which have already turned many of Cairo's brightest
moulids and pageants into little better than *mayātim*[56] (wakes), as nothing
short of a menace to the happiness and contentment of the people, has sent me
a cutting from the issue of 19 March 1940, which I find sad reading.

You commence an interesting and erudite article, entitled "Mahmal
Ceremony May Be Curtailed", with the information that Sheikh *Fulân* ["so
and so"] of Al-Azhar University "has suggested that the old tradition of
exhibiting the camel carrying the Mahmal should cease and that only the
Kiswa[57] should be exhibited. This proposal is now under consideration by the
Prime Minister."

Poor Hadgi Camel: Has he fallen into heresy?

Poor Prime Minister too, to be brought into the arena deuteragonist[58] in such
a gehâd![59] His Excellence, the pilot of our ship of state in these stormy seas!

Having sat at the feet of the late Mufti in Al-Azhar as he expounded
the Qurân, it is my proud boast that I can call myself a student of that most
venerable and noble source of learning and culture, and it is something

---

55 "You'd think no other battles could match its fury ..." Virgil, *Aeneid* 2:438–439.
56 meitam (s.), mayātim (pl.).
57 A brocaded covering for the Ka'ba, the *Kiswa* was made annually in Egypt and sent to
Mecca with the Pilgrimage caravan.
58 Second-rank actor.
59 jihad.

of a shock to find it tending to become also the source of petty pedagogic inhibitions.

I turn, Sir, with serene comfort to the accounts in your columns of the splendid appeal of the Congress of Social Reform and the note of calm constructive culture in the speech of its President, Dr Mansur Fahmi on "The Spirit of Conservation and National Characteristics". There is much these days which calls for such an antidote!

Yours very faithfully,
Abu Masaud.[60]

I think the dictum *mens sana in corpore sano* applies to moulids as to so many things. When the *corpus* (the popular side) is healthy and happy, the *mens* (the spiritual side) has every chance of being the same – not otherwise.

No plea for moulids can omit their political value; they make for happiness and content among the people, and therefore for loyalty and patriotism, invaluable assets to king and country. The Greek religious "moulids" with their popular games were most precious stabilisers of the State, and Rome would never have satisfied *Urbem et Orbem*[61] and kept her great empire together without lavish expenditure on festivals and games; *Panem et Circenses*[62] was not only the slogan of the masses, but also of a wise government.

An excellent article signed "R" appeared in *La Bourse Égyptienne*[63] of Thursday, 13 October 1932, headed "Nec Panem, Nec Circenses"[64] and pointed out that this was becoming the order in Egypt. He mentions Mazarin's remark when the French Revolution was brewing: "As long as the people laugh and sing and amuse themselves, there will be no rising." The article is too long to quote in full, but it ends:

"They're not given bread. They're not given games. Better yet, the few distractions they can find are disrupted. It's tantamount to allowing them yo-yos, but nothing else. A dangerous policy!"

---

60 [McPher.] Abu Masaud, I am told, was the name of the Prophet's camel. [The letter writer was McPherson.]
61 The City (Rome) and the World.
62 Bread and Circuses.
63 French newspaper published in Cairo.
64 Neither bread nor circuses.

The recent King's Speech[65] has happily spread a certain concern about "the bread of the people". *Inter alia*, I noticed in the *Balâgh*[66] near the end of November of the year 1939, an appreciation of this and some statistics showing how urgent the matter is. If the *Balâgh* is right, more than three quarters of the land of Egypt is in the possession of 6% of the people, which leaves not quite a *feddân*[67] per head for the rest to live on, or try to live on. What a field for the communist propaganda so rife amongst us! I was shocked in a Cairo restaurant at hearing a foreign politician remark: "The condition of the peasantry here is much like that of the French peasants was just before the revolution, and that of the notables will soon be like that of the French aristocrats shortly after the revolution began, if they do not soon do a good deal to ameliorate their lot." An impertinent and exaggerated remark, doubtless, but one which emphasises the value of the present movement in high places to "ameliorate their lot" with the best intentions and the most efficient organisation to give to all the *panem quotidianum*[68] and other material necessaries – but neither time nor expense to give them the equally desirable *circenses*.

Not by his exhortative words only, but by deeds has our King set a fine example; and of these *beaux gestes*, none, I think, is more appreciated by the people than their freedom to enjoy some of the royal spectacles and music in the Palace parade ground, and always the charming sight and sound of the "changing of the Guard". On the eve of the *subû'* [69] of the baby princess Fawzia (the octave of her birth), an immense happy crowd lined the great square enjoying the skirling of the *irba*[70] (bagpipes) and the music of many bands parading like polychromatic transparencies in the radiance of great searchlights. These, too, in searching for a *tayyâra* (aeroplane) on which was inscribed the name "FAWZIA", bracketed the moon and *el-zuhra* (the planet Venus) and many a glorious heavenly body, till one half-expected them to find the royal name amongst the constellations, as Conon of Samos found the shorn tress of the Empress Berenice, which had been snatched up by the Gods.

A few weeks later, on the occasion of the sixth anniversary of his accession, at the end of a perfect day of music and pageants, *finis coronavit opus*[71] in the form

---

65 The Egyptian king, i.e., Farouk.
66 "el-Balâgh" was an Arabic language newspaper of the period.
67 1 feddân = 1.04 acres.
68 "Daily bread".
69 subû' = ceremony marking the seventh day after the birth of a child.
70 (q)irba = bagpipe or waterskin.
71 The end [result] crowns the work.

of a very amusing cinema in the same royal square, with thousands of seats to accommodate first the children of the public and then their elders.

All were supremely happy at these royal entertainments because they were left in peace! No sticks or canes! No bullying! No pedagogic or official fussing or interference! A rumour that the King had come out and was somewhere there incognito added a delicious thrill. Even if this were not so, I hope at least His Majesty saw how much his humble subjects appreciated these memorable evenings and may himself come to realise how his country's moulids are threatened.

Would that the royal eyes could have been turned for a moment from that pleasant scene on the night of his accession, to the seemingly wanton desolation that was being wrought about the shrine of the granddaughter of the Prophet and throughout a wide district on this which was also the night of her once honoured moulid. I will not spoil the picture of the royal entertainment in the 'Abdîn Square by painting here such a dismal contrast. A note thereon will be found in the account of the Moulid of Sitna Fâtima -l-Nebawîya which follows later.

As the war only overlapped the moulid season of 1358 (1939) during forty days and forty nights (from 19 Rajab to 29 Sha'bân, i.e., 3 September to 13 October), it was not conclusive how far its pretext would be used to further abase them, though things looked pretty bad when on the last night moulids were blacked out even in the tombs, whilst the Citadel mosque was flood-lit, as mentioned above. Perhaps, however, it was deemed preferable to risk the city's stronghold being bombed than the dead being disturbed. A pious thought indeed!

A cheering incident was the observance, after all, of the Tantâ moulid, though on a considerably reduced scale on 19 Shawwâl (30 November), albeit six weeks after the normal date; but, unfortunately, few outside of Tantâ knew of this till too late. Its non-observance in October was probably not entirely due to the war, but also to Ramadân beginning in the middle of October, which would have necessitated the date being put forward about a week if held in that month. As the Scottish people say:

"We maun be thankfu' for sma' mercies!"

Or as we express it more elegantly here:

el-hamdu l-illâh alâ kull hâl[72]

---

[72] Praise be to Allâh, in any case.

Alas! Alas! the resuscitation of Ahmad Sayyid el-Bedawî and a fairly good opening of the season by the Bayûmî procession in the month of Safar only raised false hopes for 1359 (1940), for whilst the war has caused rather a boom in Cairo, and sports, cinemas, fashionable cafés, bars and such like have carried on with marked *éclat*, the repression and suppression of the immemorial prerogatives of the people in the way of moulids and other public events have gone so far that the people are most undesirably scared and upset.

That this is asking for political trouble, especially at this time, seems to me, and I should think to all who have studied history and feel the pulse of the people, obvious and serious.

Rather than dwell on this phase, I will add *in extenso* a letter which appeared in September 1940 (Sha'bân 1359) in one of the papers published in Egypt.

Egypt's Real Danger

The Editor,
Egyptian Gazette.
Dear Sir,
It is surely of prime importance to any country, at any time, that its peasantry and masses should he contented and happy; and vitally necessary when it is threatened as ours is now; and any forces, however plausibly insinuated, which tend to lower the morale and spirit of the people, naturally so high and sanguine, and to scare and disgruntle them, should be combatted with all the power of those which have it.

There are such forces, and one of the worst in its effects, but happily the easiest to remedy, is the repression of the people's moulids and public fêtes – their only joys, the only outlets for their natural high spirits and piety. Poor dear souls, they have not much of this world's goods – an average of about an acre apiece to live or starve on according to an article in "El-Balâgh"; no basket-ball, or sports of any sort like the better-off – perhaps a swing or two which they put up at their own expense and by their own enterprise, to be torn down ruthlessly as often as not these days, as happened at the erstwhile immense Duqqi Moulid of Zefeti. At the moulid of the granddaughter of the Prophet, 16 Rajab (20 August), I noticed two swings, a "goose nest" for infants, many little gambling tables and an expanse of sand, as the recreation section for the half million pilgrims and visitors expected on this great celebration. I am told the number of swings was reduced the last night. These crowds could hardly share the holy shrine from noon till midnight, nor confine themselves to zikrs, so being disappointed at finding no innocent amusements

as of yore, no music, no singing, they were driven to the Esbekia quarter[73]
or to a doubtful film or perchance to listen to the poisonous enemy wireless,
another deadly demoralising force.

What a lesson we might draw from [the Greek island of] Tinos! When
the *Helle* was sunk under the eyes of the pilgrims and visitors to the Moulid
el-Athra [of the Virgin Mary], the first care of the king and prime minister
was to telegraph to the leaders of the moulid to see that that suffered as little
as possible, and that nothing must prevent or spoil the procession, and that all
possible help and protection be given to the people.[74] And it was so, for there
were no narrow or timorous-minded persons to thwart the royal solicitude
for his people. Our own King, God bless him, would show equal solicitude
for his people as he has proved on many occasions by delighting thousands
of them in the royal square, with cinemas and bands of music and other
entertainments, as at the [*subû*] celebration of the baby Fawzia.

This spirit of repression, which is now a political danger, is to a great
extent of course the modern kill-joy mania, but I find the people largely
attribute it to a specious slogan enunciated by some doubtless well-meaning
pundit – "Nothing against morals and religion". This sounds all right, but
by the way it is being applied it is having a more and more pernicious effect
on the *bien-être* of the people and on their religion. Are swings, shadow
shows, acrobatics, laughter, music, singing, happy faces and the rest against
morals and religion, that on that pretext or that of the war, the people should
be deprived of the festivals that gave colour and brightness to their lives?
The joyous ceremony of the Bride of the Nile was always enjoyed by tens of
thousands until this year, when it was shared, according to the pictures, by
two sheikhs, a high civic official and, I think, an onbashi[75]. The next Mahmal
procession, or at least the prophet's camel, is threatened with emasculation.
The moulids are crushed even in the country, including that of Ismail Imbabi,
which blended so beautifully on land and on the Nile with that millennial
Egyptian fête of "Leilat el-Nukta". Last Friday, "Leilat el-Maarâg [Mi'rag]"[76],

---

73 Generally considered to be an insalubrious part of the city in McPherson's time.
74 On 15 August 1940, i.e., on Assumption Day, the Greek cruiser *Helle* was sunk by an
Italian submarine just off the main port of Tinos. This was witnessed by the crowds gathering
to celebrate the feast. McPherson has Arabized the feast by referring to it as Moulid el-'Athrâ.
The King and Prime Minister referred to are those of Greece. "Our own King", two sentences
later, refers to Farouk.
75 onbâshî = corporal.
76 The night of the Prophet's ride on the horse Burâq to Jerusalem and Paradise.

a few people had a pleasant reminder of the Prophet's ride to Jerusalem and Paradise, by seeing the cars of the great going to and returning from the Mosque of Muhammad Ali, with its brilliantly lit minarets, and some the great joy of a glimpse of their much-loved king; but the great populace of Cairo and the thousands who came from afar, as also the Ulama and leaders of the people, no longer flock to the shrine of the great Cairene miracle worker Tastoushi to do him and the Prophet honour and hear of the shaking of the Lote tree[77] of Paradise.

One is taught that the Walis [saints] are living entities. What do they think of the declining honours paid to them and their moulids being turned into "meitums" [wakes]? How unfair it seems that the cinemas, the dancing halls, the cabarets and the like should be benefited by the war, and only the moulids and time-honoured festivals of the poor *blacked out*!

As a matter of the country's welfare, how much better to encourage them in the face of crises than to fill them with apprehension; and why flatter the enemy in this way, whose lying wireless has already accused us of shivering with fear in our shelters? It is they and our fifth column who score by these repressions and their effects on the people; they who are rejoicing over this gift of a priceless asset.

And now, Sir, for the love of the Lord and the people, I implore you to air these simple truths in your enlightened columns.

Yours very faithfully,
(El-Hag) Abu Masaud

If this book not only arouses the interest and sympathy of the general reader in the subject of moulids and the claims of the people to be amused or at least to amuse themselves, but also induces those in power to reflect on the subject and to relax the present restrictions, to grant liberal *circenses* and, particularly, to give full scope to the piety and gaiety of the humble classes at their Moulids, the writer will feel that he has not written in vain and has repaid to a small extent the debt of gratitude he owes to the dear people amongst whom he has made his home, and

Sublimi feriam sidera vertice.[78]

---

77 A variety of Christ's thorn (*Zizyphus spina Christi*).
78 Horace: "With head lifted, I shall strike the stars."

Photograph of the Moulid el-Nebî by Zangaki brothers, late 19th century.

I

Moulids: Their Origin and Objects

A moulid may be defined as a religious and popular local feast in honour of a reputed saint.

The Egyptian moulids described below form what may be regarded as a pioneer list, as it comprises only those which the writer has repeatedly seen, or those about which he has direct and reliable information. It has not seemed to him necessary, nor even desirable, to list Moslem and Christian moulids separately, their nature, origin and objects being broadly the same. The word *moulid* (birthday or birth-place) is rather more applicable to the Moslem celebrations than the Christian, because the former are held by preference on the believed birthday of the sheikh, whilst the latter are approximately on the supposed day of death (the day of his birth into eternal life). *Hic dies postremus, aeterni natalis est.*[1]

We must seek the origins of moulids in the ancient roots of society and religion, in an instinct of wholesome veneration of those who have left examples of holiness or merit, too high perhaps for common attainment but not too high to be striven after; and in the impulse which brings men together to find free scope for their divine aspirations and their animal spirits. They crop up in the records or folk lore of most countries and were great assets in the lives of the Greeks and Romans, who doubtless spread their observance in other lands, in willing soil, already not entirely strange to them.

The "Moulid of Anchises"[2] at the foot of Mount Eryx in Sicily, where Trapani (the ancient Drepanum) now is, was typical, embracing all the criteria of our definition. Virgil in the Vth book of the *Aeneid* describes vividly the religious observances at the tomb, and the sports which were so popular with his Trojans

---

1 "This [his] last day is [his] birth into eternity."
2 The father of Aeneas.

and the natives, and doubtless the veneration in which Anchises was held was mainly due to his having been the favourite of a goddess, just as Moslem and Christian Saints are with us the favourites of God. Naturally in ancient times the moulid was about the shrine of a god. This was the case in Egypt, or of a deified king, in many instances, instead of that of a human saint, but in those days the anthropomorphic conception of the Deity was very pronounced and the distinction between the divine and the human not so clearly drawn.

Some of the Egyptian moulids of today retain practices which have come down from Pharaonic times, notably those in the Theban district. Those old customs, and then the observances at the tombs of Coptic saints, centuries before Islam, led up to the Egyptian moulid as we now know it, though its great vogue and, to a great extent, its form seem to date from the death of Ahmad Sayyid el-Bedawî in the 7th century of the *Hegira* (the 13th of the Christian era).

Ahmad's transcendent personality, and his reputation for valour, piety and miracle, not only made a unique appeal to the masses, but constrained the greatest sheikhs of those days of faith to acknowledge him their superior, and that not in Egypt alone but almost throughout the Moslem world even before he was sent as a gift from heaven to Egypt. He had crossed North Africa, had lived twenty years at Mecca meeting and impressing the world's pilgrims, and had been received as a Prophet in Iraq; and so, as the news of his death spread, his tomb became surrounded, not only by Egyptians, but by pilgrims from the Indies and all the Moslem world. Naturally, such a throng over a considerable time in Tantâ gave an impetus to the markets and the general life and prosperity of the little place, and the re-meeting of old friends who had perhaps first met at the Ka'ba, the making of new acquaintances and the hospitality of the people of the town soon lent a social and then a festive side to the occasion, which, blending with the air of sanctity about the very body of such a favourite of Allâh, created the perfect moulid atmosphere. It was natural to arrange a similar meeting for future years, and the same time of the year was chosen, the Coptic month Bâba (October), which date has been retained, without reference to the Arabic date, with two minor celebrations also following the solar calendar.

The prestige and prosperity of Tantâ had so soared that Desûq, which is not far away, decided to honour the bones of their great Walî Ibrâhîm in the same way, and Damanhûr and other towns followed the example. Moulids thus spread, and the more readily in districts (like the west of Cairo) where Sayyid el-Bedawî had posted the apostles he sent out, notable amongst which is Sîdî Ismâ'îl Imbâbî, whose moulid is still one of the most typical and attractive.

Cairo is fortunate, unique in fact, in that a number of its moulids centre about the relics or actual bodies of members of the immediate family of the Prophet.

The following list could not be equalled by any city in the world, I am convinced, not even by Mecca, certainly not now that vandal Wahhâbîs have shamefully destroyed the tomb of 'Aysha and many others.

Sidna Husein boasts the head of that "martyred" grandson of the founder of Islam.

Sidna Zein el-'Abdîn ('Alî -l-Asghar) is also represented by his head.

Fâtima his sister by her body, and

Sakîna his other sister, by relics.

These last three were all the children of Husein.

Sayyida Zeinab their aunt, sister of Husein, has her celebrated mosque and moulid and a tomb whose authenticity is doubted.

Fâtima -l-Nebawîya daughter of the Sixth Imâm, Ga'far Sâdiq, and 'Aysha her sister, are similarly honoured, Fâtima's body being believed to be enshrined in the street of her name near Bâb el-Khalq. These two are descended in a straight line from Muhammad through 'Alî, Husein, Zein el-'Abdîn and Ga'far Sâdiq.

Sitna Nafîsa who shares the Moulid of Sakîna is similarly Nebawîya in descent, being the great grand-daughter of the Imâm Hasan, younger brother of Husein. She lived in Cairo for seven years, died and was buried here.

Hârûn whose tomb is on the premises of Major Gayer-Anderson,[3] by the Ibn Tûlûn Mosque, and whose moulid has been revived might be added, as he is certainly "Huseinî".

Sitna Rugaiya whose tomb is near the Mosques of Nafîsa and Sakîna is, I am told locally, closely related to these and therefore also "Huseinî". (I have not been able to obtain particulars or confirm her moulid.)

---

3 Robert Grenville Gayer-Anderson (1881–1945), whose long sojourn in Egypt nearly coincided with that of his friend McPherson. The premises referred to is now the Gayer-Anderson Museum.

Sîdî 'Abdullah el-Hagr whose *tâbût*[4] (sarcophagus) outside of his mosque near Sitna 'Aysha is the centre of a tiny moulid, is testified to be of the Prophet's family, by the inscription: "This is the place of Sîdî -l-Sheikh 'Abdullah of the family of the Husein."

Of the remaining moulids, a very large proportion of the Saints honoured thereby are Ashrâf, descendants of the Prophet.

The term "Huseinî" is applied to such of the Ashrâf as are descended from the Husein branch of the Prophet's family. It will be clear from the attached very abbreviated genealogical tree that Sakîna, Zein el-'Abdîn, 'Aysha, and the two Fâtima -l-Nebawîya are Huseinî, but that term cannot be applied to Nafîsa, who is *sharîfa* (high-born) through Hasan. The Âghâ Khân is of course both *sharîf* and Huseinî, as well as Ismâ'îlî.

The tree (below) will also show at a glance the exact relationship of the eight great saints heading the above list, to each other and to the Prophet.

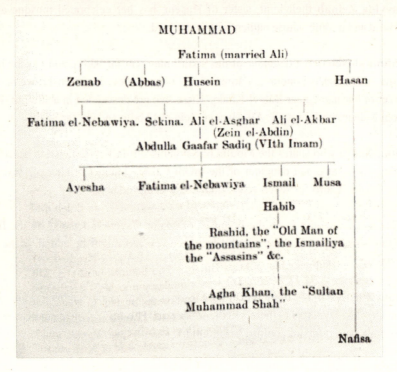

---

4 tâbût, also a casket or coffin.

The influence of the Fatimites, who ruled Egypt from the 4th to the 6th century A.H. (the 10th to the 12th century A.D.), greatly favoured the status of moulids, paving the way to their full governmental and royal recognition. Their making el-Qâhira (Cairo) their seat of government, coupled with their cult of the relics of the Prophet's family, and the introduction of many of these, did much to bring about Cairo's high position as guardian of the holy things of Islam.

Cairo, too, is easily the leader (*facile princeps*) in the number and eminence of the sheikhs and "walîs" (holy men) it honours, not necessarily in the number of the noble and high-born (Ashrâf), who are strictly local. Egyptian monarchs like Salâh al-Dîn and Hasan have their mosques, but King Sâleh has his mosque, his tomb, and his moulid to this day in the Nahhâsîn district[5], where he sat in a ragged woollen cloak (*dilq*) mending baskets and exhorting to piety, and through which he passed in triumph after he had captured Jerusalem, Damascus, and Ascalon. Afterwards, it was "written" (*maktûb*) of him that he should also be recognised as a saint. Sâleh was doubly Sultân, as King of Egypt, and in the religious sense in which the title is applied to "Sultân" Hanafî, "Sultân" Maghrûrî, and others, as sovereign amongst saints.

Sultân Sâleh's tomb at once came into repute and was visited by Sultân Beybars, amongst many pilgrims, and quite probably became quickly honoured with a moulid, as Sâleh died about 647 A.H. (1249 A.D.) ten years after Ahmad Sayyid el-Bedawî's death at Tantâ had given such an impulse to these observances.

Then in 890 A.H. (1485 A.D.) the great Abû -l-'Elâ died and was buried near the Nile at Bûlâq. The beginning of the 10th century A.H. (16th century A.D.) was singularly notable. In the one year 930 A.H. (1523 A.D.) died and were buried in their own "zawiyas", the miracle-worker Dashtûtî (Tashtûshî), and the two anchorites, Marsafa, who after fighting in Persia under Qâitbâi lived 30 years in a Muqattam cave, and el-Muhammadî -l-Demardâshî; and almost at the same time the other Muhammadî (Shâhîn), who was also an anchorite of the Cairene "Thebaid"[6], the Muqattam Hills (*vide* their moulids).

The objects of these moulids are evident from the above, and from their very origin, that is "to glorify God by venerating one of his favourites," as I heard an old dervish express it; contingently to acquire a blessing and a friend and intercessor in the heavenly court; and thirdly to recreate and refresh soul and body, with

---

5 The Nahhâsîn district, where the "coppersmiths" are located.
6 The Thebaid was an administrative district in Upper Egypt for several hundred years from the Ptolemaic period. The area became famous for its Christian hermits during the 4th and 5th centuries A.D., the best-known being St. Anthony. McPherson is using "Thebaid" metaphorically to indicate that Muqattam, too, had its hermits, though much later.

thankful joy, and with freedom for everybody to visit the local shrine and take part in the amusements.

A ceremony such as the commemoration of the great Muhammad 'Alî does not constitute a moulid, nor can the "Fête of the Bride of the Nile" be considered such. Nor are the ordinary religious services of church or mosque, such as Sunday Mass or the Friday Prayer, though perfect in their way; nor the Persian threnody of the 'Âshûrâ; nor the solemnities of the *Mi'râg* (ride and ascension of the Prophet), and of the Night of Power, *Leilet el-Qadr*. Many of the Saint's Day feasts in Europe are true moulids, and many of the country fairs are so. Unhappily, we must exclude the fairs of "Merry England", since the Reformation and Puritanism crushed and chilled the soul of them, leaving them mere markets, more or less merry.

Not that a moulid need exclude buying and selling from its liberal scheme. Some of the most typical of Egyptian moulids are also fairs, for example, that of Sîdî Huneidiq, in the desert by Lake Timsâh. Its great enclosure is almost made up of booths where fruit, toys, sweets, &c., can be bought; but all the multitude visit the local tomb and enjoy the horse and camel races and sports.

Even the greatest Cairene (and Islamic) moulid, that of the Prophet Muhammed (Moulid el-Nebî) is not so typical, *qua moulid,* as those of Sidna Husein, Barsûm el-'Aryân, Sîdî Bayûmî and most of the others listed below, because it does not centre round any spot specially hallowed by the Prophet. Even in my time it has been held in at least three different places. It is a general rather than local feast.

For the same reason, I have excluded the supreme Christian moulid, Christmas, because it is so general, and its component parts divided between church and home and not localised popularly at any one spot.

Likewise, we have in Egypt, as far as I am aware, no Catholic moulids, in the sense of being religious, recreative, local, and free to all; though there are many in a more restricted way. I read, for example in the *Giornale del Oriente* of 2 February 1940:

> On next Sunday, the 4th of February, the Salesian Institute of Rôd el-Farag
> will celebrate the feast day of its founder, Signor Giovanni Bosco, with a
> religious service in the morning and a party in the afternoon.

Then follow details of the Mass and its officiants, and the music, plays, singing &c., the features of a moulid, except that it is more for a community than the general populace – inevitable in such a case. Perhaps the nearest approach is the

Feast of St. Teresa[7] at Shubrâ in October, when all the populace that can find room on the premises is there, a crowd much more Egyptian than European (*ifrângî*)[8], with Moslems, Jews, Greek Orthodox, and members of every religion and caste taking part or bringing votive offerings to the shrine of the "Little Flower".

Naturally it is only the Egyptian Moslems or Copts, those attached to the soil (*adscripti glebae*[9]), who can arrange a typical Egyptian moulid according to its traditions; and it is one of the many instances of their blessed tolerance and friendliness that all dwellers in Egypt and visitors of whatever creed or nationality are made perfectly free and welcome.

---

7 St. Thérèse of Lisieux (1873–1897).
8 ifrângî = literally, a Frank or Frankish, meaning West European.
9 "Adscripts of the soil", a term referring, in feudal times, to farm labourers who could be sold and transferred with the land.

The Feast of St. Thérèse of Lisieux (1873–1897) was in the Cairo quarter of Shubrâ, "with Moslems, Jews, Greek Orthodox, and members of every religion and caste taking part…"

II

Moulids: Their Place, Times and Seasons

As the paramount object of this little work is to interest people in the moulids of Egypt, a necessary auxiliary object is to explain where and when they can best be seen, since it is astonishingly easy to miss them. For that reason, each moulid described has been treated somewhat in guide-book fashion, the easiest way of approach being given, and notes as to its most probable date.

As with almost the sole exception of the Moulid el-Nebî, they centre about shrines which are fixed objects, and their location is simple enough. Yet even so, the recent tendency to keep the religious and secular sides apart makes it sometimes difficult for a stranger to find the latter. For example, the amusement booths of Sidna Husein[1] have fringed the *gabel*[2] at the extreme end of the continuation of the Mûskî[3], but the last two or three years, what remains of them have been crowded into a bit of waste land considerably nearer. Those of Sayyida Zeinab, which were originally near the mosque in the Baghâla district, were moved to Darb el-Gamâmîz[4], and then to a place not far from Ibn Tûlûn[5]. Those of Muhammadî have retired from the main approaches to the mosque, to a quasi-concealed fold in the contour of the village of Demardâsh. At the Moulid of Sîdî Hillî the mosque is on one side of the main road to Rôd el-Farag (via Bûlâq) and the amusement park away on the other.

When at a moulid, the manifold lights, sounds and decorations are assertive enough, yet one can pass very near and not notice them. This is even the case in

---

1 By the Mosque of Sayyidna l-Husein.
2 The hill referred to here is that part of the Muqattam Hills east of Old Cairo.
3 That is, at the eastern end of Shâri' el-Mûskî in the Khân el-Khalîlî.
4 Darb el-Gamâmîz ("Road of the Sycamores") is the name of a crowded district in east Cairo.
5 The Mosque of Ibn Tûlûn.

so central a moulid as that of 'Ashmâwî. Indeed, so inconspicuous are they that the writer wandered about Cairo for a quarter of a century without knowing of the existence of more than a dozen or so.

If the locality is simple, the date is often most elusive, especially to those not familiar with the lunar calendar, naturally used for Moslem feasts, which advances on the Gregorian 11 days every year, making a complete round of the solar year three times in a century. Even so, I can only recall about half a dozen important moulids where the same date is rigidly adhered to every time. These are, giving the eve of the feast in each case:

On 10 Rabî' I	'Ashmâwî
On 11 Rabî' I	el-Nebî
On 26 Rajab	Dashtûtî ("Tashtûshî"), and some small ones.
On 14 Sha'bân	Matrâwî and several minor moulids
" " "	'Abd el-Rahîm el-Qenâwî
" " "	Yûsef el-Haggâg
On 29 Sha'bân	Bahlûl, and a number of quite little ones

It is to be noted that of these dates, 26 Rajab, is a very special night, the eve of the Prophet's Ascension, *Leilet el-Mi'râg*.

In Lane's time, a century ago, the Tashtûshî moulid was the actual great Cairo celebration of *el-Mi'râg*. Now the latter takes place at the Citadel mosque of Muhammad 'Alî, which doubtless partly accounts for the "pumpkinification"[6] (αποχολοχυντωσις) of Sheikh Tashtûshî.

Some moulids are announced in the Arabic papers, and a few of the most important in the European Journals. But there is a pitfall in the form of these announcements into which the writer has fallen more than once, and which is the cause of scores of persons, particularly visitors, missing each year the greatest spectacle of all, the Moulid el-Nebî. For instance, in the year 1939, the papers stated that on the occasion of the solemnity of the Moulid el-Nebî, Tuesday, 2 May would be observed as a public holiday, all government offices would be closed, and so on, that being 12 Rabî' I, the birthday of the Prophet. Those who

---

6 apocolocyntosis, literally "gourdification". This refers to a Roman political satire, *The Gourdification of the Divine Claudius*, said to have been written by Seneca the Younger in the 1st century A.D. McPherson presumably uses the word to imply the trivialisation or down-grading of Sheikh Tashtûshî.

ignored the fact that in Islam, as in Genesis, the evening and the morning constitute the day, and were unaware that a thoughtful government fixes the holiday for "the morning after the night before," naturally went to see the great function and the fireworks on Tuesday and discovered that all had been consummated the afternoon and evening of the Monday. It is for that reason I have given the date of the Moulid el-Nebî as 11 Rabî' I and have followed this system for all the others. It may be taken that the great night is always the eve of the actual day, i.e., the evening before it, as we should reckon on Gregorian lines; though in some instances it continues into that day, which may be reserved for the grand procession (zeffa). This is the case with Sayyid el-Bedawî, 'Abd el-Rahîm, el-Haggâg and a few others, but with the rest there is then only the very mild observance of the khâtima[7], the closing of the whole moulid.

As for the great majority of moulids, their date is subject to fluctuation from so many causes, and often without apparent reason, that it is only by careful watching and enquiry on the spot that one can be at all sure. Even the man on the spot, the very sheikh at the mosque door, often misleads one, probably through having no certain knowledge himself or through the date being altered after he has given his information. At one time, I fancied that they looked on me as a suspicious character and purposely diverted me from their moulid, but on sending my Moslem helpers (murâslât)[8] I still got wrong answers, sometimes as many as the number of emissaries sent. By repeatedly going, however, in successive years and noting the day of the week and of the Arabic month, it has been possible to arrive at something like a formula in many, but not in all cases. The days and dates of the moulids which follow and any conclusion which can be drawn from them are therefore given as some guide.

There are many reasons for this uncertainty, among them that the exact birthday of the saint is seldom known, and a date has arbitrarily to be chosen, which itself may be subject to local or seasonal changes, such as the death of a benefactor – a cause which once greatly delayed the Moulid of Zefeitî – or delay in collecting the cost of decorations, etc., or the date (which, if by the Arabic calendar, passes through all the seasons) falling at a time when the piece of land required is under cultivation. That is the case frequently with country celebrations. I have known it happen to those of Mazlûm and Farag.

Imbâbî indeed has had such baffling modifications, including a postponement because of cattle plague in the district, that ranging from Safar to Rabî' II in seven

---

7 khâtima or (in Egyptian dialect) khatma = "end" or "conclusion".
8 murâsla (s.), murâslât (pl.) = a military term meaning "orderly" or "batman".

years, and seemingly enjoying summer without reference to the lunar calendar, I was completely baffled till I discovered that its date followed that of an ancient Feast of Isis, which fell shortly before midsummer.[9]

There are certain other Moslem moulids which follow the solar calendar instead of the lunar, notably that of Sayyid el-Bedawî, held always in the Coptic Bâba (that is, October), and, therefore, also those of Desûq and Damanhûr which closely follow it; also, that of Bayûmî which Murray[10], writing in 1888, said was always celebrated in that same month, presumably because the Bayûmîya dervishes are a branch of the Ahmadîya, the *tarîqa* (Sufi Order) of Sayyid el-Bedawî; but now seemingly in the month of Baramhât (March). It results from this that these and all such moulids must clash every thirty years with Ramadân, which is *mensis non* from this point of view[11] and then struggle through the pilgrimage months, very lean times for local feasts. Such a coincidence, as long as it lasts, involves the putting back or forward of the date and the conducting of the moulid on reduced lines; and what is much more unfortunate, it gives that selfish element which grudges the people any open expression of their piety or joy, a pretext for checking the renewal of the moulid on its old lines when it emerges from this sort of eclipse. The great Sayyid el-Bedawî has now[12] entered into the *umbra* of this perilous period, more gloomy perhaps than the *penumbra* of the war.

Within the general communion of Islamic saints there appears a certain symbiosis between individual "citizens in that holy City of Saints" *sodales sanetorum civium*,[13] which is reflected in a *rapprochement* of their moulids. As a first example, I will mention Sîdî Marzûq, about whom I know nothing but that he has a moulid with a wonderful *zeffa*, and a most puzzling and elusive date, varying from the month of Zû -l-Qa'da to that of Safar between 1352 (1933) and 1356 (1937), and that the conduct of his moulid and *zeffa* are suggestive of Sîdî Bayûmî, particularly in the prominence of red banners. Now on comparing the dates of Bayûmî and Marzûq on the three occasions I have noted both, I find that twice Marzûq has been celebrated exactly a week after Bayûmî and on the third exactly a fortnight, and that both their moulids fall in Baramhât or Barmûda (March or April). These rather empirical premises, though not justifying a conclusion, suggest that Marzûq

---

9 [McPher.] *Vide* Introduction and detailed account of the Moulid of Ismâ'îl Imbâbî.
10 *Murray's Handbook for Egypt.* John Murray is the publisher.
11 That is to say, no moulids are held during Ramadân.
12 i.e., the late 1930s, early 1940s.
13 From last two verses of *Ecce! Panis Angelorum* (Behold the Bread of Angels) by St. Thomas Aquinas.

depends on Bayûmî, and like the latter ignores the Arabic lunar calendar in favour of the Coptic and solar system.

Bayûmî had another important satellite, the great 'Afîfî,[14] whose moulid amongst the tombs always followed immediately after that of Bayûmî. I fear that it is now quite extinct. It is clear that this also must have followed the solar not the lunar calendar.

Sutuhîya at the Bâb el-Futûh, at or near the end of Sha'bân, has her satellites in el-Qâsid, Gamel, 'Abd el-Kerîm and 'Abd el-Bâsit; and, in Bûlâq, Galâdîn, Wâstî, Kurdî, Khasûsî and Awlâd Badr seem to group in time as in place about Sîdî Nasr.

The most definite case is that of Imâm el-Shâfe'î which, normally falling on the first Wednesday of Sha'bân, pins down el- Leithî to the following Friday week and Samân to the Thursday week, and controls also Abû Deif, Abû Zeid, 'Alî -l-Gîzî, 'Adwîya, Gamîla and sundry small fry.

There are also imponderable influences, hardly dreamt of in our philosophy or theology, which sometimes determine the date or ensure the observance of the moulid. In 1357 (1938), I found on or just before the final night that the Moulid of Mazlûm had been stopped for no real reason, the suggestion that it was on account of the fairly recent death of King Fu'ad being rather a stigma on the memory of that kind-hearted monarch, who would have been the last to accept such an equivocal honour. But the disgusted ghost of Sheikh Mazlûm appeared to the local authority responsible, and so alarmed him that the moulid started afresh and proceeded to the final night with all honour and *éclat*.

An instance of historical note is the appearance of the Prophet himself to the pious Sheikh el-Bahâ'î at the shrine of his grandson Husein, to assure him that the noble head was really there, thus establishing the prestige of the mosque, the tomb and the moulid. Similar supernatural occurrences are associated with the tomb and Moulid of Sultân Sâleh, and many others. The last case with which I am acquainted dates back only a few months. In Sha'bân 1358 (1939), the Moulid of Sîdî Hârûn "el-Huseinî", which was revived a few years ago by Major Gayer-Anderson, on whose ground the little tomb stands, failed to eventuate when due at the beginning of the month, owing to the Major's return being delayed by the outbreak of war. When he arrived, Ramadân (in which month no moulids are held) was so near that he reluctantly abandoned it for a year, the more unwillingly as I think he deemed the war no reason for such an omission, but rather a calamity calling for an extra effort to encourage the people in the simple and pious customs and pursuits, which tend to their contentment and happiness and the very stability

---

14 [McPher.] *Vide* Bayûmî.

Sheikh Suleimân el-Kreitlî, "Custos et Genius Loci & Adscriptus
Glebae" – custodian, spirit of place, attached to the soil

of the realm in a crisis. But alas, it did not seem humanly possible to arrange all the details of a moulid in a few hours! That, however, was reckoning without the ghost of Sîdî Hârûn. That blessed spirit lost no time in appearing in the night watches to Sheikh Suleimân el-Kreitlî, the guardian of Hârûn's last resting place, explaining that no excuses would be accepted for the omission of the ritual due to him. Suleimân is as ancient, venerable and picturesque as Eli or Simeon (and as myope as Father Jacob[15]). He is a sort of reincarnation of a long line of Kreitlîya, who occupied the Beit el-Kreitlîya (in which Gayer-Anderson Bey now dwells) through the centuries, and is definitely *adscriptus glebae* [bound to the soil]. He claims that his *silsila,* or pedigree, goes back beyond these to the sons of the Prophet and friends of Hârûn. Thanks to this humble representative and devoted adherent of the saint, and with the Major as Fairy Godmother, the moulid blossomed as by magic, and Sîdî Hârûn had every cause to shower blessings on them both – and so another legend is added to the many which cluster about the Beit el-Kreitlîya.[16]

It has been mentioned elsewhere that the date of Sayyid el-Bedawî follows the solar calendar, and for that reason it will clash somewhat from now (1358 / 1939) on with Ramadân and the practically non-moulid months, till it emerges again into Muharram. Abû Hareira of Gîza, though Islamic, adheres to the Coptic order of movable feasts, being always celebrated on Easter Monday with the great pan-Egyptian holiday of Shamm el-Nesîm. It, however, retains elements far older than Islam or Christianity and may reasonably be believed to be derived from sun worship and the Phoenix cult. Desûqî, Bayûmî and Imbâbî take their cue from Sayyid el-Bedawî, and follow the seasons, not the moon. (Also, I think, Marzûq, and possibly Shuhadâ'.)

As for the few Coptic moulids, they coincide with the feast of their patron saint, or culminate within a few days of it. Of these I have listed the following:

---

15 Jacob was a patriarch of the Israelites, and in old age his sight began to fail. "Now the eyes of [Jacob] were dim for age, so that he could not see." (Genesis 48:10) His son Joseph thought, wrongly, that this was why Jacob, approaching death, blessed his younger grandson, Ephraim, with his right hand; and his older grandson Manasseh, with his left hand – thus acknowledging that Ephraim would be the greater of the two.

16 [McPher.] Many of my readers are already familiar with the weirdly attractive character of Sheikh Suleiman, from Major Gayer-Anderson's "Twelve Legends of the Bayt el-Kredlea [sic]" which began to appear in *The Sphinx* on 23 December 1939. This " mysterious old man" is indeed egregious, but still illustrative of a type which continues to wield strange spiritual influences. [These legends were republished as a book, *Legends of the House of the Cretan Woman,* by R. G. 'John' Gayer-Anderson Pasha, (AUC press, Cairo, 2001).]

Mâr Girgis (St. George)	in Barmûda	April	Coptic Catholic
Mâr Girgis (St. George	in Bashans	May	Coptic Orthodox
Sitna Damiâna	in Bashans	May	
Sitna Mariam	in Misrâ	August	
Sîdî Marsûm el-'Aryân	in Tût	September	

It is to be hoped that there are many others in the provinces, and certainly the Feast of the Assumption in Misrâ (15 August) takes the form of a moulid in a number of places, as it does in very numerous countries. The Palio at Siena is in honour of the *Assunzione,* and I was fortunate in witnessing the same under the name of Ἡ Κοιμησις της Θεοτοχου[17] at Cremasto on the Island of Rhodes. Ample religious observances, including the visit to ikons of Our Lady, were followed by Rhodian lads and lassies singing the songs and dancing the dances of ancient Greece most beautifully.

Butler in his book on the Coptic churches[18] mentions three moulids which I have not been able to confirm:

St. Mercurius (Abû Seifein)	15 Hâtûr (in November)
St. Cyrus and St. John of Damanhûr	4 Abîb (in July)
St. Sergius (Abû Serga)	18 Amshîr (in February/March)

In fact, in the case of the first of these, I went to the *deir*[19] of Abû Seifein on 15 Hâtûr 1650 (24 November 1933), and not only was there no sign of a moulid, but people living in the *skêtê* assured me that it was long since extinct.[20]

---

17 "The Dormition of the God-Bearing [One]."

18 *The Ancient Coptic Churches of Egypt,* by Alfred J. Butler (1884).

19 Monastery.

20 [McPher.] Though the Arabic word *deir*, and the Greek σκητη *skêtê*, both mean monastery, they *may* refer to a group of such with their churches and dependencies, including the dwellings of lay folk connected in various ways with the foundation, the whole being enclosed by a protecting wall. The Deir of Abû Seifein may be used therefore (as Wallace Budge in *The Nile* uses it) in the latter sense to include not only the church and monastic buildings of St. Mercurius (Abû Seifein) with the enclosed chapels of Barsûm el-Aryân, Girgis, Michael, Buktor, etc., but the distinct churches of El-Athrâ (the Virgin), and Anba Shenûda, the "Convent of the Maidens" and all the little streets and houses within the ancient

The Copts, of course, keep many other feasts which, not being moulids, are out of the province of this book, of which are the Christian movable feasts of Palm Sunday, Easter, Whitsuntide, etc., and many fixed Holy Days. Of these

'Eid el-Ghatâs   Epiphany, in Kîhak (19 January)
'Eid el-Salîb   Festival of the Cross, in Tût (27 or 28 September)
'Eid el-Rusûl   Feast of the Apostles, in Abîb (12 July)

Also, Christmas ('Eid el-Mîlâd), which, though a moulid in a supreme sense, is not included here for reasons given in Chapter I.

Certain Feasts of Our Lady are kept publicly with most of the characteristics of a moulid, of which I have included 'Eid el-Iddi'â[21], The Assumption, in Misrâ in an account of Moulid Sitna Mariam at Mustarod (and at Duqdûs), with a reference to 'Eid el-Bishâra, The Annunciation, in Baramhât.

Similarly, there are of course many Moslem celebrations which cannot be included in a book of moulids, as for example:

The two "Bairams"
The two *Mahmal* (and *Kiswa*) ceremonies, on the departure and return of the Pilgrims
Cutting the *Khalîg*, or *'Eid Arûset el-Nîl*
Leilet el-Mir'âg and *Leilet el-Qadr* (and *Leilet el-Nuqta*)
Commemoration of Muhammad 'Alî
and the *'Âshûrâ*

It will save many disappointments if it is remembered that with the exception of the very few moulids assigned to a particular day of the month (*vide supra*)[22], they usually have a preference for a definite weekday, often adhering strictly to such, e. g.,

---

boundary wall: the Greek word in its colloquial form σκητη (skêtê), I have always found to have this general sense.
21 'Eid el-Iddi'â' appears to be a mistranslation of Assumption, which in Arabic is normally 'Eid Su'ûd el-'Athrâ'; iddi'â' means assumption as in "It is our assumption that this word is mistranslated".
22 vide supra [Latin] = see above

Sunday	El-Kurdî	Rajab or Sha'bân
	Galâl	Muharram or Safar
	Mazlûm	Muharram to Rabî' II
Monday	Fâtima -l-Nebawîya	the last in Rabî' I usually
	Abû Hareira	Shamm el-Nesîm
Tuesday	Fâtima -l-Nebawîya bint Ga'far Sâdiq	early Sha'ban
	Hasan Anwar	Rabî' II to Sha'bân (on 6 out of 7 visits)
	Sâleh el-Haddâd	first after mid-Sha'bân
	Sidna Husein	last of Rabî' II usually
	Sayyida Zeinab	that nearest the middle of Rajab
Wednesday	Imâm el-Shâfe'î	the first of Sha'bân usually
	Sultân Hanafî	first after mid-Sha'bân
Thursday	Abû Atâta	from Rabî' I to Gamâd I
	Abû -l-'Elâ	early in Rabî' II
	Abû -l-Sebâ'	from Rabî' I to Gamâd II
	Bayûmî	Baramhât (March)
	Ismâ'îl Imbâbî	Ba'ûna (June)
	Marzûq	Baramhât (March) or Barmûda (April)
	Muhammad el-Bahrî	from Muharram to Safar
	Muhammadî (Demardâshî)	in latter half of Sha'bân
	Sayyid el-Malek	Safar to Gamâd I
	Selîm	Gamâd II to Rajab
	Farag	Rabî' II to Rajab
Friday	'Abdullah	Rajab to Sha'bân
	'Abd el-Dâ'im	Muharram to Rajab
	'Amrî	Sha'bân
	Hamza	Gamâd II (once on Sunday in Sha'bân)
	Imâm el-Leithî	near the middle of Sha'bân
	Ma'rûf	Rajab to Sha'bân
	Sa'ûd	early in Sha'bân

| Saturday | Marsafa | late in Sha'bân |
| | Zein el-'Abdîn | Gamâd II (but has ranged from Safar to Sha'bân) |

I am sure this list could be greatly extended, especially for Thursday, the eve of Friday, and for Friday itself, but I have only ventured to put down moulids which I have attended again and again and always found adhering to one day of the week.

Zefeitî seems to oscillate between Sunday and Thursday, and a few have no apparent preference. El-Hillî, for example, I have known on Tuesday, Thursday and Saturday, and ranging over several months.

It would be easy to draw up a consecutive list of Christian Saint's Day Feasts (Catholic, Orthodox or Coptic) simply following the calendar in each case, the sequence being preserved; but the above list will show how impossible that is with the Moslem moulids. I have, however, preceded the detailed accounts which come later in this book by an approximate Calendar of the Feasts described. This, at least, will indicate which moulids may be expected about any given date. Where the range in time varies so that it may occur in one of several months, the first of these is given.

It is important to remember that a few Moslem moulids follow the Coptic, solar calendar, and not their own lunar reckoning:

Abû Hareira	The Coptic Easter Monday (Shamm el-Nesîm)
Bayûmî	Baramhât (March)
Ismâ'îl Imbâbî	Ba'ûna (June)
Sayyid el-Bedawî	Bâba (October)
Ibrâhîm el-Desûqî	Bâba (October)
Marzûq	Barmûda

and probably this is the case with some others, notably Shuhadâ' in Barmûda (*vide* Shuhadâ').

Apart from supernatural intervention, the dominating influence most potent in determining the ultimate date of a moulid is that of the Ministry of Interior. Its permission must be obtained, and any limitations or postponements it may impose must be complied with. Occasionally it withholds permission altogether.

The indications regarding place and date given in this chapter and in lists, etc., which follow, are not based in any way on anything official, but simply on personal observation and deduction over a series of years, up to this year of the *Hegira* 1359 (1940), and of course liable to modifications in the future.

Also, as I have emphasised elsewhere, the 126 moulids which follow are far from being a complete list. They comprise only those I have assisted at, or about which I have the most direct first-hand information. I know there are many others (of which some are big and important), but how many I have little idea.

For example, I believe that there is a moulid of some importance at Damanhûr, but not having had an opportunity of seeing it, and enquiries having elicited only vague and contradictory reports, it is left out altogether.

Again, Major Gayer-Anderson, who visited the tomb of Sheikh Salîm el-'Aryân, on the eastern bank of the Nile about a mile from Nag' Hammâdî kindly sent me a long account from the lips of Sheikh Salîm's nephews, who cultivate the eight "feddâns"[23] about the tomb presented by the Khedive Ismâ'îl in recognition of a notable miracle witnessed by His Highness. This famous hâgg[24] who never wore clothes, to whom all animals were tame, and who lived in austere sanctity must surely have a moulid, but the Major not being able to ascertain the date or even to confirm this, I must not group it with the rest.

Lane's statement written a hundred years ago, that "where there is a sheikh's tomb, there is almost always a moulid", confirmed me in my determination to include only twentieth century celebrations of which I have direct knowledge.

It is strange that the great detailed, voluminous, and conscientious writers on Egypt – Lane, Budge, and Murray, and the rest, as far as I know – should cull only the most flamboyant and conspicuous flowers from the garden of moulids, for in over two thousand pages of the three named, now before me, I can only find the description of about fifteen, of which some are little more than references, and two at least, Sîdî 'Afîfî and Sultân Rifâ'î, are, I fear, quite extinct. But "kind hearts love the little flowers", and I am sure the kind hearts of my readers will be interested in and sympathise with these little moulids, struggling, many of them, to keep their place in the sun. (Of the two moulids 'Afîfî and Rifâ'î which had a great vogue in 1888, when Murray wrote about them, the first is referred to in my account of the Moulid of Bayûmî. The other, Murray says, was "one of the most remarkable festivals that occur during the year". At it, the Rifâ'î dervishes, encamped in the necropolis between the tombs of the Mamelukes and Imâm el-Shâfe'î, were in great force and exhibited their most wonderful feats. The mid-day procession through the city also was unique. The account in *Murray's Handbook of Egypt*, 1888 issue, is a revelation of what a moulid could be in those days.)

---

23 1 feddân = 1.04 acres (4200 m²).
24 hâgg = pilgrim; more especially, one who has been on pilgrimage to Mecca.

There have been great changes in the past, and doubtless will be in the future, but let us hope and pray that they will be favourable to Egypt's moulids.

A Saint's Tomb at el-Marg (northeast edge of Cairo).

III

Moulids: Their Devotional Side

A moulid, being the celebration of some saint, centres naturally about the spot where his body, or at least a relic, has been laid. This may be under his *tâbût*[1] in a mosque or in one of the picturesque shrines, surmounted by a dome (*qubba*) called *maqâm*, his "place", or *dareih*, his grave, or *zâwiya*, his corner. The last term was applied by an anchorite to the cell in which he elected to live and in which he preferred to be laid for his eternal rest, as in the cases of Marsafa and Muhammadî, but it naturally extended to the "comb" of cells grouped sooner or later round about it, forming the rudiments of a monastery.[2] Marsafa's *zâwiya*, though still underground, ranks as a *masgid* (mosque) with the inscription over the door, "The Mosque of Sîdî 'Alî -l-Marsafa" (*vide* his moulid).

The *tâbût* is sometimes in a private house, as in the cases of el-Ansârî and of el-'Azâ'im, whose moulids are described below, and I once witnessed a tiny moulid and saw the *tâbût* in the house of one of the Romali family, but do not remember the name.

Even before the Ministry of Interior has approved and fixed a period (which is usually a week, but may be two and even three, or as little as a single day), the number of worshippers at the hours of prayer greatly increases at these places, not only because of augmented zeal on the part of the local people, but on account of

---

1 tâbût normally means "wooden coffin", but in the present context it refers to the wooden cover over the vault in which the body is laid. This cover is usually draped with silk or linen on which are verses from the Qurân. Cf. Lane, *Manners and Customs*, Ch. 10, "Saints".
2 [McPher.] Mîrâlâi [Colonel] Gayer-Anderson tells me that the Senousi regularly make use of this natural system of cell division for the propagation of their tenets. One-cell *zawâyâ* (the plural of *zâwiya*) are established with the view to each one producing a group, still called a *zâwiya*, each new occupant receiving instruction from the original anchorite, until he is qualified to go forth and found another nuclear cell, and so on.

the afflux of visiting pilgrims; and more *zikrs*, often preceded by little processions, may be remarked. At the same time decorations begin to appear in the district, little flags, coloured lamps and globes, and so on. Big framed pictures representing circumcision doctors at their work are put up over the barbers' shops, often with a notice that this operation will be performed gratis; and gay stalls appear for the sale of '*arûsas*, little sugar figurines brilliant with tinsel; and swings and many other things, to be treated more fully in the next chapter on the popular amusement side of a moulid.

The opening day being fixed, there is an inaugural ceremony of a religious nature, often official, with readings from the Qurân, a panegyric of the Saint, *zikrs* and other devotional exercises. This may be presided over by a local sheikh, usually of one of the dervish orders (*tŭrŭq*), frequently a spiritual or blood descendant (or both) of the founder whose feast is being honoured. Or the government may nominate some high ecclesiastical dignitary, such as one of the '*ulamâ*. The greatest of these, the Sheikh el-Bakrî, lineal descendant of the first *khalîfa*, Abû-Bakr, used always to lead the moulid of Tashtûshî, which was also the celebration of "el-Mi'râg", taking up temporary residence on the spot.

He is the head of all the numerous orders of dervishes, with the title of *Naqîb el-Ashrâf*, prince of the *ashrâf*, ("sharifs" or members of the family of the Prophet), and as descendant of Abû-Bakr el-Siddîq "occupies" the supreme "carpet" (*sigâda*)[3] of that great founder, with the further title of *Sâhib Sigâda*, the *sigâda* being the spiritual throne. The direct descendants of 'Alî and 'Omar have each his "carpet", but these rank after that of the Sheikh el-Bakrî.

These dervishes become more and more *en évidence* as the days of the moulid go on, as the *zikrs*, the visits to the tomb, and all the essential characteristics work up in a rapid crescendo to the great *apodosis*[4] of the feast. This usually is at the octave of the opening ceremony, and then they are the heart and soul of the culminating *zeffa* (procession), of which indeed they are the essence and nucleus, though multitudes of the laity accompany them, vying with them in zeal and enthusiasm.

Many non-Moslems have a singularly vague and cramped idea of what the term "dervish" implies. Quite recently a "person of culture", after asking me, "What is a moulid?", and my explanation involving a mention of dervishes, added, "Oh, I

---

3 [McPher.] This word *sigâda*, though also used in our ordinary sense of carpet, has the original meaning of something spread for prayer. The verb to pray is "*Săgădă*". This sacred mystic meaning may account for the strange legends of "flying carpets" which transported their possessors whither they willed.

4 In the Eastern Orthodox Church, the final day of a period of feasting.

know all about the dervishes: they are or were the 'howling' and the 'whirling', *n'est-ce pas,* but I thought they were done away with!"

Apart from cases like this of simple ignorance, the fact that there is not the same clear line of distinction between clergy and laity as exists in Christendom, makes it difficult to assess the number and importance of those who may be regarded as in "holy orders", major or minor. The initiation of the simplest member into the brotherhood of any of the Sufi orders (*tŭrŭq*) is a form of consecration, but need afford no outward and visible sign to the outsider, except on such rare occasions as that of a *zeffa*. I met my own *syce*[5] at a moulid in the white and green of the Order of the Shâzlîya[6], sash and other insignia, and carrying a gonfalon, and have recognised since in the *zeffa* many others whom I never dreamt possessed the *sanad* and *silsila*[7] of a dervish.

In point of fact, they are both the heart and framework of Islam, and have been since the time of the great founders, Abû Bakr, father in-law of the Prophet and 'Alî, his son-in-law.

The idea (which particularly underlies Sufism) of spiritualising Muhammadism by means of "orders" has resulted in perhaps about a hundred *tŭrŭq* (plural of *tariqa*, a "way") all acknowledging and enjoying the *bărăkă* which, though ordinarily meaning a "blessing", has in this case the further implication of something resembling "Apostolic succession". For every dervish has been a *tâlib*, a postulant, and passed to *murîd* under catechumenical instruction by a *murshid*, a guide, to full initiation by *ward* and *zikr*, receiving a sort of laying on of hands and complying with numerous canons, and acquiring his *sanad bi-silsila* (diploma and chain), the *sanad* certifying to the inviolability of the *silsila* (chain) of spiritual ancestry which unites him with the founder of his order, and through him to the Prophet himself. Many of these genealogies are rather awe-inspiring, even some of those in the hands of quite simple souls, who make no boast of their ancestry, or hardly value it, seemingly, except in this sacred connection. They remind one of St. Joseph's family tree and similar biblical records. (They also bring home to one the ghastly irony of Nazi "racism" – that one without blood or breed should have the infinite impudence to stand as arbiter in such matters and assign to a lower plane than himself anybody is revolting enough, but to do so with a race of millennial descent and immemorial civilisation is beyond comment! This digressional

---

5 Stable groom.
6 Shâzlîya = a Sufi order of Sunni Islam.
7 Both words refer to the lineage or spiritual chain of a Sufi, sanad being the diploma of initiation and silsila the pedigree. (Cf. Glossary).

lapse has nothing to do with the war; it is the citation of a shocking freak case in natural history.)

The *ward* corresponds pretty closely to the Church's use of the Rosary: it involves a telling of beads; and it is significant that though in its verbal sense it means "to arrive", as a substantive it is the Arabic name of a rose.

The *zikr* is essentially the repeated utterance of the name God, "Allâh, Allâh, Allâh," the word *zikr* meaning "to mention", but extends to the Witness of the Unity of God, and the Apostolate of Muhammad, "There is no God but God, and Muhammad is His Prophet". This is known as the *Kalima* (the Word), and is of such significance that its utterance by a non-Moslem in some countries is liable to entail forcible circumcision.

It is, I think, invariably preceded by the *fâtiha*, the little opening chapter of the Qurân, a beautiful little prayer not unlike the Pater Noster, and may be accompanied by many a sacred strophe, *zarb*[8], such as *Allâh sâmi'! Allâh bâsir! Allâh 'âlim!* – "God heareth! God seeeth! God knoweth!"[9]

In the case of the initiatory *zikr*, there is much else which varies with the order, of which certain parts are not supposed to be divulged. The ceremony, too, contains the elements of a "Sacrament of Penance" – the *wudû'* (ablution); and a general confession by the *murîd* to his *murshid, (pîr)*[10], with vows of amendment, and subscription to a covenant *'ahd* of heart-service to his God, and faithful allegiance to his spiritual father, whose hand he is clasping, from whom he receives an implied absolution.

This handclasp, which I have compared to the episcopal "laying on of hands", with the thumbs raised and pressed together, and the hands veiled by the sleeve of the dervish, is similar to that of a couple at their betrothal and has its counterparts in Coptic and other Christian functions, particularly in the East. I have noticed marked cases in Greek villages which were long under Turkish domination, and recall a dramatic incident in the history of the Moors in Spain, when the Lady of Lara adopted Mudarra, the illegitimate son of her dead husband by a Moslem girl, by enveloping him in her very capacious sleeve.[11]

Though the dervishes date back to the very early days of Islam, their

---

8 More correctly, zarb [darb] is a musical term meaning rhythm.
9 McPherson's Arabic here is grammatically correct, but it is possible that these three words would normally be samî', basîr and 'alîm as that is how they appear in the list of God's 99 attributes, el-asmâ' l-husnâ.
10 Pîr = "old man" in Persian. The word refers here to a superior in a Sufi order of dervishes.
11 See Lope de Vega's *El Bastardo Mudarra*, based on a legend of family feuding in the much earlier epic Spanish poem Cantar de los Siete Infantes de Lara.

reorganisation on lines which have changed little to this day, was the work of 'Abd el-Qâdir el-Gîlânî in the 6th century of the *Hegira* (12th century A.D.), so that his followers, the Qâdirîya, constitute the parent order, *el-tarîqa -l-aslîya* of which the main branches are the Rifâ'îya and the Sa'dîya. All three of these are very prominent in Egypt, but the Sa'dîya has lost the great prestige it enjoyed at the time of the *dôsah*, when only its ruling sheikh was deemed qualified to ride on horseback over the backs of a host of prostrate dervishes. That ceremony which was the crowning feature of the moulids of el-Nebî, Sidna Husein and Tashtûshî never resulted in any recorded injury, but was abandoned before the present century. The founder was Sa'd el-Dîn el-Gebawî.

The Rifâ'îya are remarkable for the wonderful way in which their spiritual exaltation triumphs over pain and physical limitations. Their walking in fire and eating the white-hot embers, also glass and poisonous creatures – things which normally cause death or the most grievous bodily disturbances – have never been explained on material grounds. Exhibitions of this sort are frequently referred to in the notes on specific moulids, particularly those of Zefeitî and el-Ansârî. The case described of the human chandelier whose flesh was perforated and burnt in many places, but who showed no trace of blood or injury after the Sheikh el-Rifâ'î had moistened his finger with his own tongue and touched the wounds, is paralleled by that of a dervish whom I saw at an obscure *zikr* in Bûlâq. He held a bundle of thorns in the fire of a *mesh'al*, a sort of brazier[12] till it blazed, then lifting his one flowing garment for a moment, crushed it against his ribs so that the thorns might have a firm grip, and then spun round and round like an ever brighter and fuller fire balloon, till just as suddenly he withdrew the fiery mass and gave a friendly face-slap with it to some of the sheikhs who were "zikring" around him.

Naturally the order of the great Sayyid el-Bedawî of Tantâ called the Ahmadîya is popular and important, as also its branches, which include the Bayûmîya, named after 'Alî -l-Bayûmî (*vide* his moulid), the Sha'râwîya, the Shinawîya, and the Awlâd Nûh. These last attract attention by their youth, the conical *tartûr* on their heads, their wooden swords, beads, and little cord whips (*farqilla*). They are much *en évidence* at the Tantâ procession.

There are also the Burhânîya of Sheikh Ibrâhîm el-Desûqî, the Bakrîya, the Demardâshîya, each with local and general repute, and a small new order, the 'Azâ'imîya, and others.

---

12 The mísh'al is perhaps more torch than brazier. Lane describes it as "...a staff with a cylindrical frame of iron at the top filled with flaming wood..." and provides an illustration. *Manners and Customs*, Vol. 1, Ch. 6, on "Marriage".

"Tombs of the Mamelukes" and Ancient City Gate
"One of these nights, I saw a few disgruntled dervishes under that beautiful old archway
near Sayyida 'Aysha with folded gonfalons and one huge paper lantern burning dimly."

Of the rest, the "way" of the Shâzlîya, founded by the Meccan, Abû Hasan el-Shâzlî in the 7th century of the *Hegira*, must by no means be omitted, for it is singularly strong and wide spread in the Cairo district, and has, I am sure, a very beneficent influence amongst the *fallâhîn*, artisans, and the youths of the villages, being *par excellence* the Order of the Laity, if that is not a contradiction in terms.

Bliss, the author of *The Religions of Syria and Palestine* deems the Shâzlîya the most spiritual of all the *tŭrŭq*. Its initiates are neither mendicants nor thaumaturgists[13], nor of the whirling, "howling", or fire-eating types; are singularly unassuming and free from camouflage and show, and judging by many I know personally, have been drawn into the Shâzlîyan fold by an earnest desire for a higher spiritual life. People who are careful that those they employ or have dealings with be in possession of *rŭkhăs*[14] (licenses), or *shehâdât* (testimonials), and such like recommendations, might perhaps be still better advised to attach importance to the guarantee of the *sanad* of a Shâzlî. One can only speak as one finds, but I can testify that Shâzlî lads whom I have had as *syces* [grooms] have never let me or my horse down, and I cannot recall having ever known a real "bad hat" amongst them. They are just simple honest souls who never quite forget the *"Allâh sâmi', Allâh bâsir, Allâh 'âlim!"* (God hears, God sees, God knows!)

Though the founder was buried near the Ka'ba, he has had worthy representatives in Egypt. The name of Muhammad el-Shâzlî appears on many of the banners, and in front of the Mosque of Sultân Hanafî is, or was, a shrine superscribed, "The cell of the order of the Shâzlîya" (*zâwiat el-sâda -l-shâzlîya*).

The divers *tŭrŭq* can be distinguished frequently by a prevailing colour appearing in the banners, turbans or caps, the sash and the *brassard*[15]. That of the Rifâ'îya is black; of the Qâdirîya white; of the Sa'dîya, Burhânîya and Shâzlîya green; and of the Ahmadîya red, as also its branches, the Bayûmîya, etc.

Before leaving the special consideration of the dervish orders, it may be useful to tabulate the dates of the founders of those with which we are most concerned:

	Founder	*Buried A.D.*	*A.H.*
Qâdirîya	'Abd el-Qâdir el-Gîlânî	Baghdad, 1165	561

---

13 Miracle-workers.
14 rŭkhsa (s.), rŭkhăs (pl.).
15 Arm-band [Fr.].

	Founder	Buried A.D.	A.H.
Rifâ'îya	Ahmad el-Rifâ'î	Basra, 1182	578
Shâzlîya	Abû Hasan el-Shâzlî	Mecca, 1258	657
(Sufi)			
Maulâwî	Galâl el-Dîn el-Rûmî	Konya, 1273	672
Ahmadîya	Ahmad Sayyid el-Bedawî	Tantâ, 1276	675
Burhânîya	Ibrâhîm el-Desûqî	Desûq, 1278	677
Sa'dîya	Sa'd el-Dîn Gêba	Jêba, 1335	736
(Bektâshî)	el-Hâgg Bektâsh[16]	(Anatolia), 1357	759
Senûsî	Muhammad ibn el-Senûsî	Jarabub, 1859	1276
'Azâ'imîya	Muhammad Mâdî Abû -l-'Azâ'im	Cairo, 1938	1357

The name of Galâl el-Dîn (Rûmî) comes naturally in this list, not only because his Sufi principles made love and beauty and renunciation into self-ladders up to God and prime factors in the ultimate apotheosis of man (thus softening the austerities and asperities of the Islam of those hard days, with the humanities of the Alexandrian school and the poetical conceptions of Iran), but also because his Order of the Maulâwîs is strongly represented in Egypt. That was very apparent up to a few years ago, before the great and touching Persian ceremony of the 'Âshûrâ was crushed and the misunderstood and unappreciated ecstasies of the whirling dervishes banned. Still we meet occasionally with their characteristic dress, their garb of Indian mourning, and see at moulids the mystic dance of the samâ' which Galâl el-Dîn introduced at Konya.

The Bektashîs, closely allied to the Maulâwîs in origin, history and cult, and like them happily absorbed into Islam, are little seen at moulids or in the streets of Cairo, but a visit to their monastery and beautiful garden at the mosque cave of Sultân Maghrûrî in the Muqattam Hills, and a talk to the monks and their urbane Bâba is a fascinating and illuminating experience.

The Senusis have little place in this book of moulids, but appear in the list as

---

16 McPherson has not provided place of burial, and has given 1357 as year of burial. The Bektâshîs say that the founder was buried somewhere in Anatolia and estimated year of death as 1341 A.D. [cf. "Haji Bektash Veli and the Bektash Path in Albania and Macedonia" by Arben Sulejmani, *Occasional Papers on Religion in Eastern Europe*, Vol. 34, Issue 1, George Fox University.]

evidence of the persistence through the centuries of the dervish idea, whose mysticism and faith in God cannot be killed by modernism, materialism and atheism.[17]

A startlingly pleasant local proof of this is the birth and development within the past few years of the *tarîqa* of the ʾAzâʾimîya (*vide* Moulid of ʿAzâʾim), whose reigning head is the son of the enshrined founder himself. A pity that one cannot reckon on a series of metempsychoses enabling one to note the progress or decay of such an infant order! Will it pass into oblivion as many, many others must have done, or will honoured descendants of the founder point back to him through a long *silsila* as a star in the galaxy of "walîs"?

The *zikr* already referred to in connection with initiation is the all-prevailing religious observance at every moulid, and is so named from *zăkără*, "to mention", as its essential is the reiterated calling on the name of God, Allâh![18] It is performed inside or outside the mosque or *zâwiya*, in the streets, in private houses, everywhere. Some orders such as the Bayûmîya may introduce words or gestures peculiar to themselves, but these are hardly noticeable to the ordinary observer, as after the opening prayer, the *fâtiha* and another exalting the Prophet and the favourites of God, there is great scope in what may accompany or be associated with the actual utterance of Allâh! Allâh! Allâh! Certain strophes have been already quoted and these may be greatly extended, names or attributes of God being generally chosen, as *yâ dâʾim*, O Everlasting One, and the whole "ninety-nine names of God" may be introduced. One of the most venerable of the company usually leads, frequently with a *nay*, a sort of flute, or other simple instrument, and the tempo and rhythm are impeccable. The musical element may take a lofty and complex form, as in a *zikr* I have described below – that of Sîdî -l-Ansârî. The beauty of the sounds produced by skilled hands in ecstasy was a memorable treat, enhanced by the graceful shape and colour of the instruments put to such good purpose – the *nay* and the "sĭbs" and other flutes, the drums and kettle-drums, *naqrazân*[19], *tabl baladî*[20] and *tabl shâmî*[21] and the *bâz*[22], the cymbals, and strange and powerful

---

17 [McPher.] If it is true, as I have read and heard, that the Senusis destroyed Moslem tombs with the fanaticism of the Wahhâbis and then raised a monument to their own founder, they cannot be held in much esteem, and in any case their iconoclastic efforts discredit them.
18 [McPher.] As Major Gayer-Anderson has reminded me "Allâh" may be substituted by some other divine appellation, such as "huwa" (He), "El-Wâhid" (the One), "Allâhu hayy" (God lives), "Yâ hayy" (O living One), etc.
19 naqrazân like a kettledrum but smaller.
20 tabl baladî = bass drum.
21 tabl shâmî = shallow metal kettledrum with a laced head.
22 Also called tabl bâz, another variety of small metal kettledrum, but this is one beaten with a strap.

tambourines, and the rest, which I will not further describe, as that will be found in some detail in the account of the moulid referred to.

Apart from the rhythmic utterance of "*Allâh!*", and the chanting of strophes and prayers, singing is not excluded, "mǔnshĭds"[23] being specially called upon to render "qasîdas", or elegies, often of the eroto-spiritual type that joys the heart of a Sufi, and remarkably resembling the lovely and graceful "Songs of Solomon".

It is beyond the scope of this work and the competence of its compiler to transcribe in detail what is said and sung at a *zikr*. In any case, Lane in that wonderful achievement of his, *The Manners and Customs of the Modern Egyptians*, has done so, and I strongly recommend to those not already familiar with it the perusal of his account of the combined moulids of the Prophet and Sîdî 'Ashmâwî, in which many "qasîdas" and other matter are given, and also the musical score of the *kalima*, the *lâ ilâha illa Allâh*, etc., of which the place in a *zikr* should be stressed as much as that of the *fâtiha*.

Another feature of a moulid (closely associated with the *zikr*) to be stressed is the recitation of the Qurân. Sometimes a *khatma* is performed, the reading of the entire book. The Hadîth, the sayings of the Prophet, is also much read.

Lane in the same chapter gives a vivid account of the now obsolete *dôsah*, and of the reactions of some of those who assisted at the *zikr*. He mentions, *inter alia*, the ejaculation by the "mǔnshĭds" of the word *meded*[24] as an invocation for divine aid (or strength). I have heard the same and am struck by the parallelism of this with the word "dynamis" (δυναμις) which is ejaculated in parts of the Greek Orthodox mass, and is quite liturgical, and occurs in St. Chrysostom.

Lane's black eunuch who became *melbûs*[25], and ultimately epileptic, and foamed at the mouth, and his soldier who shook and groaned horribly, are by no means uncommon sights to this day. I have seen many on the very spot Lane wrote about, and they enter into my account of the Moulid of 'Ashmâwî and others. It is extremely rare for any suspicion to be roused that the subject is "putting on" his symptoms or that they are due to other than the extreme zeal of his devotions.

The command to make mention of the name of God, and the belief that it

---

23 mǔnshĭd = singer, reciter.
24 [McPher.] This word mĕdĕd had indeed a profound mystical significance with the Sufi poets and others. Nicholson, in his *Divani Shamsi Tabriz* commenting on an ode of Galâl el-Dîn [Rûmî] says: "this term is employed by Jalal'uddin to denote the perpetual replenishment of the phenomenal world by a succession of emanations from the Absolute." One wonders if selah, so often interpolated in the Psalms of David, had any such significance [selah being a Hebrew word of unknown meaning, possibly a musical direction].
25 In a state of frenzy or religious ecstasy.

cannot be too often repeated has led through the ages to this extraordinary development. Through the cult of the Sufis and other mystics, the goal of the *zikr* is the *Gazb*, the ecstatic trance when the soul sheds all earthly dross and is absorbed for a time in the "All-Soul." *Magzûb* from *găzăbă* meaning "drawn (by God)" is a better word than *melbûs* for this condition in which things terrestrial have lost all hold and realities are apprehended in another sphere.

If the uninitiated onlooker finds the raucous ejaculations of those involved in the *zikr*, and their contortions, and the outward form of a *zikr* almost grotesque, and the ultimate symptoms of the *gazb* rather dreadful, his wonder and admiration must be called forth at the ecstasy and utter aloofness from the world arrived at, and also at the amount of physical endurance shown.

He must remember, too, that the East is freer than the West from self-conscious restraint and *pudor malus*[26], and means strange to the conventional eye are taken to throw off the trammels of earth in cults other than that of Islam – for example, flagellation, and "omphaloscopy"[27] in Christendom.

In Lane's time, seemingly, the whirling dance of the *samâ'*[28] was frequently employed in a *zikr*, and I am glad to say I have seen it more often again in moulid "zikrs" of very recent years, and marvelled at the entire absence of fatigue and giddiness after a vertiginous top-like spin of ten or more minutes.

The *zikr* is by no means confined to dervishes or even sheikhs; the ordinary laity may and do take part freely – old men and youths and even young boys, and occasionally women. Sometimes groups of tiny children organise a "zikrlet" of their own behaving exactly as their elders, who do not interfere as long as their intentions are obviously good.

It is usual to lead up to those *zikrs* by processions, which may be of the simplest character, just a few sheikhs and others with a big paper lantern (*fânûs*) at the opening of a moulid. As its *apodosis* approaches, however, they assume a more and more imposing *envergure*[29], till on the eve of the feast, or in a few instances on the day itself, they present, when at their best, one of the finest spectacles of a religious nature that the East affords and even at small moulids may be extremely well worth seeing.

The paper lanterns give place or are added to by cressets or braziers of open iron work on poles. Each *mesh'al* as these are called, is constantly fed by quick

---

26 False shame.
27 Examination of the back part of the eye. Here, presumably, "looking at the beam in your own eye".
28 samâ', literally "listening".
29 Scale, significance [Fr.]

kindling wood for the double purpose of illumining the way if the procession is at night and of stiffening the skins of the tambourines, called "târs" and similar instruments. The execution of the dervishes on these, especially on the great tambourines known as the *bandîr qadrî* and *bandîr 'arûsî* is startlingly effective, sometimes resembling a volley of musketry, the more so as they manipulate them most gracefully, above their heads, performing at the same time a kind of dance, sometimes as the *zeffa* proceeds and sometimes circling at a halt.

Then there are the *bawâriq*[30] of the various orders bearing Islamic mottos, and the names of Muhammad and his "khalîfas" ('Alî, 'Omar, 'Uthmân, Abû Bakr, etc.,) or the style of the *tarîqa,* and the name of its section. The *beiraq* is a sort of gonfalon, swung on a pole, topped by a crescent or the word "ALLAH" in brass, or some other sacred symbol. The number of these banners at a big moulid is immense. Even at that of Abû -l-'Elâ in the year 1357 (1938), where the *zeffa* was a sort of compromise held at 10 in the evening. I noticed about thirty of the *Shâzlîya* alone, with the title *el-tarîqa -l-hâmidîya -l-shâzlîya* and the local name of the division, including the name of my own village, Bein el- Sarâyât, and neighbouring "'ezbas"[31], such as Duqqî and Mît 'Uqba (*vide* Abû -l-'Elâ).

The dervishes on these great occasions of course appear with their insignia and colours, and may to a great extent be recognised by these and by the inscriptions on the gonfalons; but there is some confusion about the green as it is not only a favourite colour for the *tŭrŭq* but is, or should be, the distinctive colour of a *sharîf.* The green of these descendants of the Prophet is however of a more or less distinctive shade and their turbans are usually particularly ample. The kaleidoscopic effect is increased by the patchwork of ragged "dilqs", home- and hand-spun garments, and traditional robes of many colours; also by the varied and striking staves, wooden swords and the like, and the headgear, turbans and caps of innumerable shapes and colours, and the *tartûr* which is by no means confined to the Awlâd Nûh[32] but is much affected by children, and which also takes strange devotional forms, by exhibiting sacred symbols and invocations to numerous saints.

Lane, at the celebration of the 'Âshûrâ (tenth Muharram) deciphered on a *tartûr* of sorts in the mosque of Sidna Husein:

---

30 (Turkish) banner, standard (of a Sufi Order). beiraq (s.), bawâriq or (more correctly) bayâriq (pl.).
31 Rural settlements. Needless to say, Bein el-Sarâyât, Duqqî and Mît 'Uqba are no longer rural, nor villages, having been absorbed into the extremely over-crowded city of Cairo.
32 The descendants of Noah.

The Dilq
"The kaleidoscopic effect is increased by the patchwork of ragged
'dilqs', home- and hand-spun … robes of many colours…"

Yâ Abû Bakr

Yâ 'Omar

Yâ 'Uthmân

Yâ 'Alî

Yâ Hasan

Yâ Husein

Yâ Sîdî Ahmad Rifâ'î

Yâ Sîdî 'Abd el-Qâdir

Yâ Sîdî -l-Gîlânî

Yâ Sîdî Ahmad el-Bedawî

Yâ Sîdî Ibrâhîm Desûqî

The central figure in the *zeffa* is the *khalîfa*, chosen as the nearest available representative of the *walî* or *sheikh* who is being honoured, often a direct descendant.

It is well to be present at the very beginning when the different units assemble with all their panoply and this dignitary is solemnly mounted on his brilliantly caparisoned steed, frequently with a little lad of his tribe prettily dressed in Bedouin attire. This takes place often far from the destination, a favourite place being the precincts of the mosque of Sidna Husein. This is the case with Sîdî Bayûmî (which see), at about 3 in the afternoon, and the groups are most picturesque; and the whole course to the mosque (which takes about two hours) is through a most glorious bit of the old city. The Marzûq *zeffa* assembles at about the same time in the historic tract outside the Bâb el-Nasr, the 'Adlîya district, and affords a brave sight. It then proceeds to the mosque by a round-about way, cutting into the Mûskî, and circling Sidna Husein (*vide* Marzûq).

In the old days, the *zeffa* – or as it seems to have been then called, the *ishâra* – was in the case of Tashtûshî a national and Islamic event (*vide* Dashtûtî) and that of Abû Hareira at Gîza on the Coptic Easter Monday morning was until recently vast, most ancient and important (*vide* Abû Hareira) and still has some vogue and interest. That of Sheikh Hamza assembled till recently, and I trust will again, in the afternoon at the mosque of 'Ashmâwî. Sîdî Salîm in Bûlâq still has a fine afternoon procession, where the distinctive insignia of the Rifâ'îya, Qâdirîya and Shâzlîya can be well studied.

Of the evening *zeffas*, Ansârî's circulates from and back to the tomb itself, always pausing on its course at the underground mosque of Marsafa, whose moulid is on or near the same date. That of Abû -l-'Elâ assembles at about 9 at Saptia[33],

---

33 el-Sabtîya, a district of Cairo to the south of Shubra.

where the Shâzlîya has a sort of depot for their banners, etc.

Although the tambourines already referred to are the most striking instruments to be seen and heard on these occasions, they are by no means the only ones. Amongst others are the cymbals, *kâs*, various reeds from the small *zummâra*, to the immensely long and deep-voiced *arghûl*, and many kinds of *naqqâra* which latter are of earthenware, open at the smaller end and closed by a stretched skin at the other. Then in some moulid processions drums in great variety vie with the "tars", for instance in the day *zeffa* of Sîdî 'Abd el-Rahîm, where the immense camel drums and others of the kettle type are a sight to see as well as an experience to hear.

Sometimes wandering minstrels or professional strolling musicians cut in, as other extraneous elements, of which some through long custom enjoy a sort of symbiotic acceptance; of these the Alexandrian acrobats who act as forerunners to most big "zeffas" are a picturesque and harmless instance. Also, private celebrations, particularly circumcision processions frequently join up with a *zeffa* to the general advantage, as a rule, of both.

Naturally there are pauses at intervals *en route*, and these may be punctuated by special exhibitions of ritual dancing including occasionally the whirling *samâ'*, with music usually, and at night with "mesh'als" (cressets), "sirâgs", *fawânîs*[34] (two types of lantern) and many illuminating devices. The 'Azâ'im paraded in 1358 (1939) with enormous chandeliers connected with proportionately large cylinders fitted with a pumping apparatus as in the case of the Primus stove – a highly luminous but not very picturesque innovation. They paused at the Bâb el-Mitwallî and elsewhere for Quranic recitations and the *fâtiha* and other prayers, by no means an unusual proceeding at a *zeffa*.

The Rifâ'îya too, or allied orders, sometimes amaze all present by fire-eating or other feats of wonder, though that is not so common as of yore; and, indeed, one who frequently accompanies a *zeffa* has many startling experiences and surprises. I cannot better end these remarks on the processional part of a moulid than by referring readers to my subsequent account of the Moulid of Zefeitî.

The salient feature was a revival of the *dôsah* with the differences that the representatives of Zefeitî were not on horseback when they walked upon and over the recumbent dervishes, and that these were only in contact with the ground by their fingers and toes, and perhaps some by their heads. Their bodies and throats

---

34 [McPher.] sirâg, etc. – sirâg, sûrûg though used in Arabic, Turkish and Persian as a general term for lamp, seems here to be applied mainly to a little oil lamp with floating wick, like an altar lamp, which when found in a zeffa is carried, probably in a mesh'al (cresset) to be deposited in the tomb. Fânûs, fawânîs, though also lantern in general, is in Persian the special term for Chinese lantern.

were supported on the points of long, rigid, and sharp daggers of the dervish type, known as *dabbûs*[35], which also are described in detail in that account. The date was 1357 (1938).

Before coming to the ceremonies which conclude a moulid, there are certain religious and quasi-religious customs to refer to. Of these are "free" circumcision, street preaching and the distribution of protective charms – "hegâbs".

I have already referred to the circumcision booths and the barbers' shops, temporarily converted into such, to be seen at all big moulids near the mosque or tomb. They can be recognised at once by the large picture sign. Ritual mutilation is performed on both sexes, certainly with wonderful skill and speed and success for a few piastres, or quite gratis with the very poor. The general atmosphere of a "Figaro's" establishment – anyone being welcome to sit and watch or gossip – is maintained. Those who desire a fuller and more private ceremony can have the operation performed at home, but even then the patients, wonderfully attired, are paraded with their harîm friends in open carriages in the streets, in preference at the time of a moulid, when they may augment the *zeffa* by a brass band as well as their own colourful *cortège*. The doyen of the faculty, Dr. Mahmûd 'Enâyet-Allâh, whose headquarters are at Imâm el-Shâfe'î, has a gorgeous booth there with innumerable coloured lamps and decorations and entertains his friends, clients and visitors freely, and displays the same sumptuousness at some other moulids, notably at Tantâ where black lads in their war paint so amuse the little victims by their antics and "tartûrs" and other lures, that these become of the *mutahharîn*, i.e., the purified before they fully realise why they have been so brought into the lime-light; or in stubborn cases their cries are so drowned, that there is little risk of their panic spreading amongst waiting candidates for circumcision. For further notes on this subject, I refer the reader to the Moulid of Fâtima -l-Nebawîya.

As regards preaching, there are of course in addition to the authorised and orthodox discourses and panegyrics from the *minbar,* or pulpit and otherwise, sermons of a less formal nature introduced into "zikrs", sometimes very powerful, of which an example is cited under "el-Ansârî", but in using the term "street preachers", I am referring more to zealous revivalists who take up a position where they can attract a crowd and thrill their listeners sometimes with their fiery eloquence. Such an extreme case as that described under "Zein el-'Abdîn", where the orator literally hypnotised some and terrified others, is unique in my experience. An extreme in the other direction is the gentle and reasonable blind Hâgg Husein, to whom reference is made under "Sitna 'Aysha", who always rounded

---

35 dabbûs (s.), dabâbîs (pl.). The normal meaning is "pin".

off his homily by the ninety-nine sacred names and the distribution of Quranic texts. I have missed him the past year or more, but hope he is still "in the bond of life" as I have heard him express it. I last saw him at a Moulid of Sultân Hanafî, quite unmoved by a storm of torrential rain which soaked him and his listeners.

The distribution of "hegabs", religious charms or talismans, frequently follows the open-air sermon, and indeed often appears to be the end and object of it. The Hâgg Husein always wrote the name of the recipient on his *hegâb*, and made no regular charge, though a small coin was usually given him. This seems to be the usual proceeding, and though there are exceptions, most dervishes whom I have seen engaged in this way seemed more bent on pious works than on money-making. I knew a nice old fellow who stood near the door of the mosque of Sidna Husein at moulid time, who would by no means part with a *hegâb* till after he had made the applicant long exhortations accompanied with a panegyric of the Hasa-nein[36] and citations from the Qurân, and he refused to part with more than one at a time. There were so many applicants that whilst he accumulated a few piastres he might have taken as many francs had he been worldly-minded.

Naturally the central religious act at a moulid is the visit to the shrine in honour of the sheikh who, if a *walî*, that is, a sheikh of peculiar holiness – one of God's favourites – is deemed to be still living and to obtain a blessing.[37] A simple ritual is followed and a few prayers uttered (mainly to the sheikh for intercession), and offerings are made for or directly to the poor. Though there are plenty of willing recipients, I have very rarely been solicited by religious mendicants, whom Lane found ubiquitous and persistent a hundred years ago. I only remember being pestered once, and that at an early night of the Tantâ moulid, but I suppose I brought it on myself by the injudicious way in which I distributed a sum of money delivered to me by a Cairene friend, who could not come himself, and who had specially asked me not to put it in the chest for that purpose in the mosque, but to give it to deserving cases. These cropped up like the heads of Briareus[38], and when the sum was exhausted, I beat a retreat, trying to cover that by surrendering my own small money. Then it seemed to me that a miracle occurred! The blind eyed me from afar; the lame and legless coursed after me like stags; palsied and paralysed hands

---

36 The Hasanein = Hasan and Husein, the martyred grandsons of the Prophet Muhammad.
37 [McPher.] This simple ritual usually includes the placing of the hands first on the tomb and then on the face, and of circulating round it with ejaculations eulogistic of the sheikh. The prayers always include the *fâtiha* (opening chapter) of the Qurân.
38 In Greek mythology, one of three monsters called *Hecatoncheires*, i.e., the 100-handed. Each had 100 arms and 50 heads and were sons of the Uranus (Heaven) and Gaea (Earth). Cf. *Iliad*, Book 1, lines 401–404.

gripped me like jiu-jitsu champions; the bedridden left their litters and joined in the pursuit; and it appeared to me that the dead were rising from the number of ghastly faces, hollow orbits and fleshless outstretched arms. I ran and only felt safe when I reached the clocktower in the square. The form of charity I sometimes adopt since then, is to bestow on the thirsty ones a *sebîl ullâh*, a fountain of God. This sounds a lot but it simply means buying up a *qirba*, skin of water, or a *dôraq*[39] of *tamar hindi*[40], *'erq sûs*[41], or some such iced and sugared drink, and leaving the onus of distribution on the vendor, whilst I evaporate. Once I bought up an ice-cream seller's stock of *dandurma*[42], but he hunted me up after to complain of severe manhandling (sic) by the mothers of little boys who came too late, and he wanted compensation for his torn clothes and damaged "machina".

Of the larger forms of charity are government grants and private gifts and bequests for the upkeep of the shrine, the expenses of the moulid and for the poor; also, one very popular form, dinners for the needy. Those may be remarked at the moulids of the Prophet, of Sidna Husein, Muhammadî, Sayyida Zeinab, and others, and on a small private scale at nearly all. They may be on any or every night during the run of the moulid, but, of course, mainly on the last. Perhaps the most conspicuous feasts at the time of the *'ashâ* (i.e., dinnertime) are on the east side of the Mosque of Sidna Husein. A very curious incident I witnessed at a dinner given to the poor of the 'Ashmâwî district is described under that moulid.

Moulids which are deemed important end, or virtually so, by a ceremony similar in the main to that with which they were opened. This takes the form of a *tashrîfa*, a reception, amongst the chief of which in Cairo are those of the Prophet, Imâm el-Shâfe'î, and Muhammadî, all described or referred to under those names and, of which the first is quite a national as well as Islamic event, under the *aegides*[43] of the king, the *Naqîb el-Ashrâf*, the *'ulamâ* and the ministers.

The usual elements are a visit to the shrine, readings of the Qurân with a panegyric of the Saint and a sort of *polychronion*[44] of his living representatives, some speeches and a word with the personality who presides, who may be a member of the Muhammadan hierarchy or the local *khalîfa*, or the doyen of the particular

---

39 Pitcher.

40 Tamarind – in Arabic, literally "Indian dates."

41 Licorice root.

42 Egyptians now seldom use this word for ice cream, preferring instead the Italian *gelati* (always in the plural).

43 That is, aegis – McPherson gives the Greek plural form in the text above.

44 Polychronion [Gr., Πολυχρόνιον] = a solemn hymn of praise chanted in the liturgy of the Eastern Orthodox.

mosque or order, or sometimes a lay notable. The last was the case in 1357 (1938) at Qenâ, when the *mudîr*[45] occupied the chair of honour. (He may be, however, quite likely, and for all I know, in dervish orders.)

Sometimes ceremonies of special solemnity are added, as one referred to under Muhammadî where white robes and lighted tapers were brought into requisition. The *'ulamâ'*, ministers and notables attend these "tashrîfas", and many of the general public. Coffee, sweets and cigarettes have been in evidence and welcome at all "tashrîfas" I have seen, and sometimes music has been added. Not infrequently, the performers are the lads of the band of the Reformatory at Bein el-Sarâyât, who until recently were to be heard also at the moulids of Tashtûshî and some others during the whole of the final evening.

The ultimate "seal" is the *khâtima* – from *khătămă*, i.e., to seal – some time on the theoretical day of the saint, following the great "eve". At Sidna Husein it involves the circling of the mosque at noon by some of the orders with their banners, etc., but usually (exception being made for the few cases in which the great procession is merged into the *khâtima* on this last day) these last rites are so mixed up with the pulling down of decorations, the departure of visiting pilgrims and a certain natural reaction, that there is something of the air of a *katabasis*[46] about it, after the *anabasis*[47] of the early days and the climax of the great night.

I am afraid that it will savour almost of eschatology to call up anything after this last day of the *khâtima*, but I cannot refrain from noting a little rite I observed seven days after the conclusion of the moulid of Fâtima -l-Nebawîya bint Ga'far Sâdiq, renewing some of the moulid observances at the tomb on a reduced scale. I had never seen or heard of this, and on my expressing surprise to a sheikh at the *tâbût,* he exclaimed: "Seven days after the birth of a child, we celebrate his *subū'* so why not that of a great saint seven days after her birthday?" I could only repeat, "Why not?"

---

45 mudîr = head, director or administrator.
46 Greek for "descent". Here the writer probably means "anticlimax".
47 Greek for "ascent".

The Dôsah

"… a considerable number of darweeshes and others… laid themselves down upon the ground, side by side, as close as possible to each other, having their backs upwards, their legs extended, and their arms placed together beneath their foreheads. They incessantly muttered the word Alláh! About twelve or more darweeshes, most without their shoes, then ran over the backs of their prostrate companions; some, beating 'bázes,' or little drums, of a hemispherical form, held in the left hand; and exclaiming Alláh! and then the sheykh approached: his horse hesitated, for several minutes, to tread upon the back of the first of the prostrate men; but being pulled, and urged on behind, he at length stepped upon him; and then, without apparent fear, ambled, with a high pace, over them all, led by two persons, who ran over the prostrate men; one sometimes treading on the feet; and the other on the heads. The spectators immediately raised a long cry of 'Alláh lá lá lá lá láh!' Not one of the men thus trampled upon seemed to be hurt; but each, the moment that the animal had passed over him, jumped up, and followed the sheykh."

(E.W. Lane, *Manners and Customs of the Modern Egyptians*)

IV

Moulids: Their Secular Side

The word '*secular*' is used here in its original proper sense of '*saecular*', as in the *Carmen Saeculare*, the "Secular Hymn" composed for the Roman sports[1], and in the expression "secular bird" as applied to the Egyptian Phoenix; as something venerable which has stood the test of the ages. I would prefer the word "profane", but a perverse generation has similarly perverted its significance, which as *pro-fanum,* meaning "before the temple," exactly describes a moulid crowd before the shrine of their sheikh, honouring God and him by worship in an atmosphere of light-hearted joy. Indeed, it is with unwilling obedience to a convention that I separate the "devotional" from the "secular" sides, for surely a thankful appreciation of the good things created largely for our enjoyment is an acceptable form of devotion.

And is it not clear from the ancient and classical writers of East and West, that games owe their development, if not their very origin, to religious observances? Who in the long pages of Homer can recall a single one of the many accounts of games in which they are not the accompaniment of devotional ceremonies, an essential indeed when these were of a popular nature?

I have referred in Chapter I to Virgil's account of a typical moulid of the olden times – that of Sîdî Anchises at his *dareih* (tomb), in Sicily – worship, games and a sacrifice for the people.

Those who are divorcing games from the worship of our modern moulids are leaving the sacrifice, but a sacrifice which is not for the people, but a sacrifice of the people, of their inherited rights, of their joys and, with these, of their religion.

---

1 Commissioned by the Emperor Augustus and written by Horace, this was sung on the occasion of the *Ludi Saeculares* (Secular Games), celebrating the end of one century (*saeculum*) and the beginning of another.

This point of view does not touch the fact that there is place and more need than ever now for the austere and meditative dervish soul to whom *res severa est verum gaudium*[2], of which the East has produced so many. These get the intuitions and revelations out of the scope of human science and reason, from which those from whom such are withheld, by temperament or by the whirl of life's incidents, are wise to draw what benefit they can.

Trasumanar significar *per verba*
non si poria; però l'essempio basti
a cui esperïenza grazia serba.

[The passing beyond humanity may not be set forth
in words: therefore, let the example suffice any
for whom grace reserves that experience.][3]

The monks and anchorites of Islam (especially the Sufis) have preached love and joy in earthly matters as leading up to rapture in heavenly things; and the Christian Church is superlatively hedonistic in the right way. The Church which has bred an army of martyrs, and a host of eremites, ascetics and contemplatives, uses a liturgy which is full of calls to joy and song; the Introits to its Masses begin frequently with such exhortations as *Gaudete! Laetate!* and the serious-minded St. Paul places charity and joy at the head of all the *Fruits of the Spirit.* Solomon, wisest of men, Prophet of Islam, and author of the lovely "Canticles" and other canonical books of the Church, limns in the "Book of Wisdom" the attitude of the ΑΓΙΑ ΣΟΦΙΑ [Holy Wisdom] when God was creating the world:

Cum eo eram, says the Holy and Eternal Wisdom, *cuncta componens, et delectabor in singulos dies, ludens coram eo omni tempore, ludens per orbe terrarum:*

[Then I was the craftsman at his side. I was filled with delight day after day, rejoicing in his presence, rejoicing in his whole world...][4]

The Holy Wisdom, though essential in "composing all things", was playing

---

2 "True joy is a serious thing" – said by Seneca.
3 Dante, *Divine Comedy, Paradise*, Canto 1, lines 70–72. (Charles Singleton translation.)
4 Proverbs 8:30–31.

about, literally skylarking, and greatly enjoying Herself, "playing every day, playing before Him all the time, playing throughout the world," whilst the Almighty was toiling in creating a beautiful place for us unworthy and unappreciative creatures. Yet She was not indifferent to our race, for Wisdom Herself adds:

et deliciae meae cum filiis hominum.

[and delighting in mankind.][5]

Surely no Pope, Khalîfa, Monarch, Prince, Potentate, Ruler or Teacher, no Man who ruthlessly or unnecessarily wipes the smile instead of the tear from the face of the people, can hope for God to smile on him or to wipe away his tears.

Forgive me, dear reader, for thus excursing, and let us away to a moulid through the gaily beflagged and brightly lighted streets, the decorated cafés and shops, guided by the ever-augmenting glare and blare, and the recurring report like a pistol shot, which indicates that some lusty youth has propelled the *babûr*[6] up the inclined track with such force as to fire the *cap* at the top; past the glittering rows of "'Arûsas" on the sugar stalls, and the swings and goose-nests and roundabouts, and innumerable little stalls and hand-barrows, and through the crowd till we reach the shrine, and perhaps witness a *zeffa*, or at least see a *zikr*. Then, having paid our "visit" to the sheikh, on to see *Qara Goz*, our old friend Punch, and the accompanying shadow show and conjuring display, augmented perhaps by fire-eaters, snake charmers and the like. Then a rest in one of the more ambitious variety theatres, or a tent of performing dogs, or some surprise attraction; or in the open air, join the ring of people watching graceful stick play and dances, or the tricks of a *hâwî*, or listening to a raconteur. If you are a horseman, you can admire the beautiful creatures, dancing or prancing, or pawing the ground in search of hidden treasure, or at a country moulid, racing with stalwart and picturesque Bedouins up. If you are a crack shot, you can fire with minute rifles at a tiny target at minimum range, and if you are a dunce at the game, you will probably be just as successful. If you are great at throwing-in a cricket ball, your skill will stand you in good stead at the nine-pins, or other cock-shy; or if your *forte* is Samsonian

---

5 Proverbs 8: completion of verse 31.
6 This can refer to a stove or a variety of smoke- or steam-producing machines, including motor-driven vessels and locomotives. Here it loosely means "engine". Presumably from the Turkish equivalent, vâpûr (itself from the English word "vapour").

deeds, you can bring down the house by firing the percussion cap with a record weight on the *babûr*, or by ringing the bell at the top of a pole by a hefty smite with a mallet on an anvil, or by actual *jeu de poids et haltères*[7], or by driving nails into a log.

If you are a gambler and have brought no *millièmes* with you, you can change your piastre at one of the "bankers" and squander the coins so obtained on pin-tables of divers kinds; or a game of dice whose coloured sides correspond to squares on which you put your stake; or a kind of "shove-millième" in which you throw your stake onto a *table quadrillée*, gaining if it falls into one of the many squares without impinging on the lines; or you can gamble on the station – Cairo, Tantâ, Benhâ or Alexandria – at which a revolving hand stops; or back your fancy from a team of homing pigeons or rats; or with a *nikla* buy a biscuit which may or may not contain a coin up to a *barîza*[8]; or acquire a bottle of *sharbât*, or a doll or some other treasure at the very amusing *ma-lum*[9] table, by purchasing a lucky envelope. You may even exceed the usual money limits and lose a big piastre at the three-card trick, if no police are in sight.

Skill is brought in, in many variants of ring-throwing, the objective in one of these being a swimming duck, which disappears from the pool if her neck be encircled, to reappear in the fullness of time, I suppose, on the thrower's table. Luckily for the duck's feelings, she is now generally represented on the water by a wooden bird, which is swapped for the real thing if won.

Fleeing from the snares of the Monte Carlo department, we hurry through the freaks – Zubeida, of sixty years and less than half that number of inches; the calf with five legs, on which she has been going strong for quite fifteen years and does not look a day older (therein the greater marvel); the giant,

...and many more too long,
Gorgons and hydras chimaeras dire.[10]

Near the circumcision booths we see a minor but equally permanent act of mutilation going on – tattooing. This is done with great expertise and is interesting, and perhaps still more so the framed pictures of designs painted on glass from which to

---

7 Weights and dumbbells [Fr.].
8 10 piastres.
9 Word uncertain, but likely to be *el-ma'lūm*, which can mean payment, though usually to a beggar or such workers as dustmen, sweepers, etc.
10 Two snippets from Milton's *Paradise Lost*: "...and many more too long," is part of line 473, Book 3; "Gorgons, and Hydras, [and] Chimaeras dire", line 628, Book 2.

choose – purely geometrical for the strict Moslem, or Quranic texts in *sŭlŭs* characters[11], or a name and address, or the record of a vow (*nadr*); for the rest, snakes, lions, birds, trees, their sweethearts, etc., and sometimes very strange selections. (I once saw an effeminate long-haired youth, whom Lane would have certainly classified as a "gink"[12], being tattooed with the names of his patrons, as far as appropriate surface space would allow. That was near an arch of Muhammad 'Alî's aqueduct, fairly remote from the moulid then proceeding of Hasan el-Anwar.)

From the *Bûza* booths[13] we hear a persistent note of metal struck on metal in perfect rhythm, with other strange music. This is in accompaniment to equally weird Sudanese dancing. But that calls for rather a more special notice, as do several of the "attractions" catalogued above.

We are assailed but not tempted by piquant odours from stalls and from sizzling trays on little fires – sausages, *ta'mîya*, *fûl* (beans), *kebâb*, *kufta*, *ruz* (rice), and many other delicacies,[14] and offered iced water, *lîmonâta*, *tamar hindî*, *'erg sûs*[15], *sharbât*, and sundry other drinks. Cigarettes, too, including Wills's Flag, usually bought one at a time for a *nikla* (two *millièmes*); the seller rather looks askance at you if you demand a whole packet. *Sabâris*[16] (cigarette and cigar ends) was popular till a year or so ago, when legislation forbade the collecting of *mégots*[17] in the street or dealing in the same, giving rise, I fear, to a good deal of illicit trade therein, and the manufacture by an enterprising little clique of local Havana cigars, for which Spanish labels were locally printed.

One thing I miss, and indeed have not seen since the moulid of Sidna Husein in 1357 (1938), is the *Piste à la Mort* of the intrepid Canadian, Billy Williams, which for years was a unique attraction. A sort of bear-pit round whose tall vertical walls Billy circulated at vertiginous speed on his motor-bike.

---

11 thŭlŭth = an ornate style of Arabic calligraphy.

12 "gink" is a Turkish word referring to cross-dressing male dancers, usually, according to Lane, "Jews, Armenians, Greeks and Turks" (Cf. *Manners and Customs*, Vol. 2, p. 113).

13 Lane (*Manners and Customs*, Vol. 1, Ch. 3) defines *booza* as "an intoxicating liquor made with barley-bread, crumbled, mixed with water, strained, and left to ferment, … commonly drunk by the boatmen of the Nile, and by others of the lower orders." He further notes that a similar beverage was made by the ancient Egyptians. For an interesting account of the apparently Turkic origins of the word, see "On the Possible Oriental Origin of our Word Booze," by Berthold Laufer, *Journal of the American Oriental Society*, Vol. 49 (1929), pp. 56–58.

14 [McPher.] *vide* Glossary.

15 'erg sûs = a licorice drink.

16 sabâris = despite the mentioned legislation, this word is still used to mean cigarette butts gathered from the street for re-use.

17 Cigarette butts [Fr.].

Having lost a near relation or two at the game, he has carried on alone and it is much to be hoped that he has not shared their fate. Billy's feat of blindfolding himself whilst dashing up and down to a few inches from the top and bottom of the pit, thus riding without hands or eyes must have been unique, and seeing that he did that at intervals of less than half an hour throughout a moulid, one cannot help fearing the worst.

In addition to these characteristic and usual items there are plenty of sporadic happenings and surprises, sometimes disappointing or even shocking, and sometimes very much the reverse, reminders of Pharaoh's day or of Greek and other bygone influence or startling up-to-date innovations, and what is always interesting – the by-play and the reactions of the onlookers who know not boredom.

Of the items which perhaps call for rather less summary mention than that made above is the first named, the Sugar Booths. The seller is perched up amongst his shelves of sugar figurines, to which the general name of 'arûsa is applied, a word which means bride, and which may also indicate a doll, because the prevailing type is that of a gorgeously dressed maiden. I have seen them pouring the hot sugar, red or white into wooden moulds, at a place close to the Bâb el-Futûh, but how that is done and the result marvellously arrayed in paper garments, with tinsel of gold, spangles, and the rest and then sold at prices ranging from a small piastre (five millièmes) to about half a franc (twenty millièmes) is a mystery.

In addition to the 'arûsa proper, there are horsemen, ducks, rabbits, dogs, goats, &c., sole or grouped, sometimes in a manner coarsely conceived and rudely executed, though recently some of the naughtiest seem to have been suppressed in Cairo (though still on show in certain provincial centres). En revanche for this expurgation, a very up to date model has appeared, representing a bridal chamber with mirrors and couch and the young couple, the 'arîs and 'arûsa. I am told this is a revival of an old classic known as 'Azîza wa-Yûnis. Other popular examples are the heroes Abû Zeid and 'Antar, armed and mounted, and sundry brigands such as Abû 'Alî Saraq el-Ma'za (i.e., Abû 'Alî-stole-the-goat).

These and other names suggest folklore and present scope for anthropological research, as the resemblance of these ancient puppets to the Tanagra figures[18] and to much that was turned up at Pompeii make them interesting to the archaeologist. In point of fact, I have found professors of these branches who have accompanied me to moulids rather fascinated by the 'arûsa stall, but their fragile selections have usually crumbled up or been devoured by ants before they have photographed them or left any permanent record to science.

18 Mould-cast Greek figurines of terracotta from 4th century BC.

"… gay stalls appear for the sale of 'arûsas, little sugar figurines brilliant with tinsel".

I am glad to be now told by Prof. Evans-Pritchard, who read the above, that his '*arûsa* figurines did not perish in the usual way, but that after photographing them he gave the collection to the Pitt Rivers Museum at Oxford.

The late Prof. Hocart[19] of the Egyptian University was prevented by his much-deplored death from leaving (as far as I am aware) a permanent record of the collection I helped him to build up.

Mîrâlâi Gayer-Anderson Bey kindly took me to a place in the Gamâlîya district where these are made by pouring melted sugar into wooden moulds. He has since had made permanent plaster models of some of the more striking.

Apart from the Tanagra figures and such like, they remind one of the *Santons*[20] *de Provence, les bonhommes de pain d'épices*[21] of French fairs, and the old gilded gingerbread men and animals, from which the gilt is now off, if they are not actually an extinct species.

As a sop to religion, the '*arûsa* stall sometimes presents representations of the *Haram* or the Ka'ba; and as an extra temptation to children, a variety of minor sweets – *simsimîya, hummusîya, gôz el-hind*, &c. (*vide* Glossary).

Qara Gôz merits, I think, a high place in the list of attractions, for I find my personal predilections from earliest youth for a Punch and Judy show, are shared by all the "walads" (boys) of Egypt and *chojokler*[22] of Turkey, and I think also by the *petits gosses*[23] of Europe, who get either the classic Punch himself or at least the Guignol or other of his bastard offspring who inherit his quaint *bonhomie* and petulant audacity. I am told, too, that by peaceful penetration he has taken up strong positions in the hearts of the *chechees*[24] of the Far East.

Orthodox Christianity identifies Punch with Pontius Pilate; and Judy with Judas Iscariot, who presumably betrayed his sex as he did his Master; Toby being no other than that very attractive boy, Tobias, in whose reflected light the Archangel Raphael so shines in the liturgies and 'old masters', the puppy his inseparable companion, taking his place in the little drama. But I suspect Punch of much greater antiquity and that he apostatised from some pagan cult, as later he seems to have gone over to Islam under the style of *Qara Gôz*, "Black-Eye" (suggestive of the number of black eyes he collected on his knuckles in his attacks on policemen

---

19 Arthur Maurice Hocart (1883–1939), an anthropologist in the Department of Philosophy at Cairo University from 1934 till his death on the eve of World War II.
20 Terracotta figurines, particularly for Nativity scenes, made in Provence.
21 Gingerbread men.
22 çocuklar = "children" in Turkish.
23 French slang = "little children".
24 Possibly refers to "cēcci" in Malay, though it means "sister".

and others). I have seen this title otherwise rendered, as *Qara Qôja*, "Black (bad) Husband," in reference to his unmarital conduct towards his wife Bakhîta, who, one must admit in his defence, is a bit of a Xanthippe[25]; also here in Egypt by a somewhat different spelling: *Qara Qûs*.

The show is too crudely mediaeval to be exactly edifying and is not to be recommended to a nun-conducted "crocodile," but Mr. Punch is intensely amusing, and his voice and gestures are sustained in the local shows with extraordinary skill. His *savoir faire* and versatility too are such that he is a rapid expurgator on the arrival of visitors whom he diagnoses as highbrow, to whom he alludes in his patter with great *bonhomie,* with pretty compliments and blessings, not forgetting hints concerning cigarettes and *niklas*, which are usually fruitful.

Khayâl el-Zill, a shadow show, is generally seen in the same booth under the aegis of Mr. Punch, alternating with his exhibition and conjuring tricks, fire eating and minor attractions, for all of which the entrance fee is a *nikla* (two *millièmes*), drums and other music included. Visitors, who are always well received, are accommodated with chairs, if there are any procurable and, if not, armfuls of children are thrown into corners without their showing the smallest resentment, to make room on the benches. Unfortunately, there is no provision for conditioning the atmosphere. Beyond veiled hints, such as those of Punch's spokesman, or of the clever manipulators of the marionettes behind the sheet (whose manual acts are worth watching also from behind the screen), there is no touting for baksheesh, and the gift of a *piastre* or so to the music or the performers is taken with smiles of gratitude and showers of blessings.

Here, too, the jests and gestures are not of a very refined type, and the visitor must be prepared for shocks, and to take a lady to *Khayâl el-Zill* is as risky as a visit to the monkey house at the Zoo; but there is nothing so essentially immoral, nor so vulgar, as many of the nasty films we get from the other side of the Atlantic, which so damage the prestige of the western races in the eyes of the East and are said in India particularly to be doing more harm than all the other propaganda. Incidentally, too, there is nothing in Punch's funny squeak or in any of the voices to disintegrate one's marrow like the awful "twang" – or twyank – the "talkies" have added to the nastiness of the "movies".

The conjuring tricks which I have noted as often thrown in with Punch and *Khayâl el-Zill* are often childishly simple, like the magic ball on a vertical cord, which stops in its descent at any point at the word of command; but others are extremely clever and baffling, and almost always highly amusing, though often at

---

25 The shrewish wife of Socrates.

the expense of some good-tempered person in the audience. The Egyptian conjurers are experts at card tricks and other feats of *légerdemain,* as witness the *galli-
galli* men in the streets, but the Indians have still greater prestige in these matters.
Of these a certain Hâgg Ahmad el-Hindî runs an independent show in his own
booth and at moulids is the *doyen* of the thaumaturgists[26].

At these performances, even if *we* are not amused all the others present are and
provide us with a fine tonic by their laughter and merry appreciation, occasionally
tumultuous, and their friendly attitude towards us leaves a pleasant impression.

The Variety Theatres are run on the whole on a much more ambitious scale
than the little places just described; yet they range from a platform outside a café,
shop or house; or a screen of canvas or tent-work in the corner of a court, or in
a passage between the buildings, where a few comic turns and a little singing or
dancing may be witnessed, to a vast tent with rising tiers of benches about an
arena big enough for a circus, with a varied entertainment of the circus style. In a
big country or *gabel* moulid[27] there may be quite a number of these.

The characteristic of the bigger tent-theatres is a lofty wooden platform on each
side of the entrance, one of these for a brass band, the other to accommodate at
frequent intervals some or all of the performers – singers, dancers of both sexes,
clowns, dwarfs, giants, muscle-dancers, who give samples of their art until the
enthusiasm of the crowd is excited to the point of buying tickets, and then the
big performance commences inside. The last named, clad in little but loincloths,
always men, stand immovable, but for their muscles – pectoral, abdominal, bra-
chial – which dance in a marvellous way, aided by unbelievable movements of
the diaphragm. The *danseuses*, if allowed to show themselves at all, must emulate
in sobriety the steps and undulations of the *Thesmophoriazousae*[28] invoking the
chaste Demeter. It is true that a few years ago they were adopting less laudable
classic steps and becoming somewhat too Greek, but they always danced fully
dressed and never with men, and never attracted the gilded youth or the jazz fan,
who knew that for a half-naked bunny-hug they must seek the richer bowers of the
most respectable cabarets and hotels. When a few years ago, the city fathers (or
grandmothers) or whoever it is who arbitrates somewhat arbitrarily on the matters
of Terpsichore[29], vetoed the ancient *danse de ventre*[30], and the public so clamoured

---

26 Workers of magic (or, in the case of saints, of miracles).

27 i.e., a moulid on a hill.

28 Greek women celebrating the 3-day religious festival in honour of Demeter, goddess of
harvests; "Thesmophoriazousae" is also the name of a play by Aristophanes.

29 Greek Muse and goddess of dance.

30 Dance de ventre = belly dance.

for it, monotonous though it be, that the *artistes*, who moreover knew nothing else, lapsed into it, strange evasions were resorted to. On one occasion, this dance was interrupted by a lad (set to watch) announcing that police were approaching the entrance. The *première danseuse* with great presence of mind, and imitated at once by the others, turned the other side towards the door and danced with the muscles of that. There being no legislation against *la danse de lune*[31], that was not deemed a contravention.

A very well-known character, a star unique in his way, has not been *en évidence* very recently. He danced always in the dress, ornaments, hair, lipstick, and manners of a woman, and people who watched for the umpteenth time could hardly be made to believe that he was not what he appeared. He generally made a simpering round of the audience, and with a smirk presented his photo under which was printed "The celebrated Egyptian dancer, Husein Fu'âd", and his address for private appointments to weddings, &c.

Whether of his own free will, he "walked sober off," or whether he attracted the attention of the "city fathers" and was shoved off, I cannot say.

The last time I think that I saw Husein Fu'âd was at a big New Year party at an English house near Zeitûn, under the caste-leader, Mahmûd Lalû, who himself manages one of the moulid tents. He brought good and amusing performers, and a highly conventional party were as delighted as they were surprised at an atmosphere of fun entirely new to nearly all of them. (The writer added an almost too successful thrill, by raiding the house, after secretly dressing up his own servants, one as a police officer, the others as "ghafîrs"[32]. The sweet blarney and faces of our ladies, who took it entirely *au sérieux*, obviated the execution of the "police" threat to rope us all together and take us to the *caracôl*[33] – I think rather to the disappointment of some of the men.)

To a great extent, the amusement side of a moulid is served by a special professional class which follows them from place to place, even throughout the provinces, so that wherever one goes, he is likely to see familiar faces and to be himself recognised by their owners, and a subtle ear may recognise Punch's voice to be the same in Cairo, Tantâ or Asyût. The same applies to the circumcision doctors, but most of all, to the managers and artists of the theatrical shows.

The most popular of these shows is run by "Professor" Shawwâl, a great character and a mighty man of muscle and strength. He might be Castor or Pollux for

---

31 An interesting parallel to the somewhat vulgar English expression "to moon".
32 ghafîr, *pl.* ghufarâ' = guard, watchman.
33 caracôl = gaol.

his prowess, and from his ovate form preserving the contour of Leda's egg. He introduces each of his caste and invites to the marvels of his theatre by a funny speech in which he punctiliously observes the grammatical forms, *waqf* and *wasl* and *tanwîn*[34] – for well he knows that if you do not talk over the heads of an Egyptian audience, they will metaphorically trample you under their feet. This rhetorical effort is always applauded and is always the same, and at its peroration he generally perches the whole of his male staff on his head or his shoulders or abdominal prominence, and lightly revolves with "all up" – this as an earnest of what you may expect when he begins to show his strength. He is exceedingly zealous for the reputation and orderliness of his house and its precincts, and never asks for, nor allows, occasion to bring in the invidious collaboration of the police. I have seen a host of would-be gate-crashers attempting to gain free admittance or accumulating so about his gates as to form a rather rowdy mob, but quickly with his little *farqilla*[35] of many cords, he scatters the crowd "in the imagination of their hearts". Once I saw him go to the assistance of the police trying to separate and subdue two hefty belligerents (for occasionally a fight starts in the best regulated moulid) and picking up a delinquent under each arm, he gave each a tender bear-hug, then threw him limp and gasping at the feet of the law.

Shawwâl's *contre-partie* in the *gô'a* (troop) is a dwarf, most unprepossessing in appearance, but his sense of time and rhythm is so subtle that his movements when he dances are positively graceful in spite of bandy little legs. He has a hundred funny ways, but he is not funny when his irascible temper gets the better of him. I have seen him hurl a wrestling opponent three times his size into the midst of the spectators.

I mentioned rats and pigeons being made accessories to the gambling indulged in on a tiny scale. As I have never seen them put to this use elsewhere, I will describe the procedure in the case of the rats. (The pigeon play is similar.) The rat-table is a wooden disk of about a metre in diameter, with minute "houses" round its periphery, whose doorways are big enough for a rat to enter. Each house bears a number corresponding to those on a board for the stakes. When these are laid, a big white rat is placed in the centre of the table and the number of the house into which he ultimately decides to enter indicates the winner. It is difficult for Abû Fîrân, the "father of rats," to prevent undue influence being brought to bear on

---

34 Terms of classical or literary Arabic grammar, which subject many speakers of the colloquial language find daunting.
35 farqilla = leather-thong whip generally used to drive animals.

his rodent's choice. I have seen, for instance, a little lad surreptitiously projecting fragments of cheese into the house of his chosen number.

The Sudanese *ringo* (or *ringa*), which is always associated with the consumption of their national drink *bûza,* has (I have found) always had a special interest for savants, especially those who have travelled in the districts south of Egypt. There are recondite features connected with the origin and analogies of this weird institution that attract these gentlemen, but no one can fail to be struck by the unique nature of his surroundings in one of these *bûza* booths. (The Sudanese at home call this form of beer, *marîsa*, a term hardly ever used here in Egypt.)

The treadmill-like step of the dance, and the weird instruments, which include a bit of a railway line, are not quite like anything else, and the rather sour and cloudy Sudanese beer (*bûza*) served in bowls or gourds by ebony hands is equally strange; luckily tea, coffee or *qirfa* (cinnamon tea) can be indulged in instead. The crescendo of the vogue of the *ringo* in Egypt within the last decade is, I suppose, the result of its novel features. From being a rarity, it is now found at almost every big moulid, sometimes duplicated or triplicated, and it is established in a few places in Cairo on a more permanent basis apart from the moulids.

As it is referred to in the description of the Moulids of Fâtima -l-Nebawîya, Muwaffaq, and some others, instead of extending remarks on it here, I will conclude them by quoting a letter written on the subject to an anthropologist friend, which deals specially with one of the instruments employed, the *sistrum*, and the theories of an ex-professor of the Egyptian University concerning it.

26 November 1935
(30 Sha'bân 1354)

The Sistrum – Shakhshaakha

Dear Evans-Pritchard,
The quest of the Sistrum has proved a pleasant, if rather long and not very fruitful one. Though, I suppose, originally Egyptian, and introduced into Greece with the cult of Isis, its home now, anyway as a musical instrument, seems to be south of Egypt, for though common enough here in Cairo, it is always in the hands of Sudanese or Berberines, or at least in their "Ringas" or Booza booths, or ceremonies at which they predominate. Strangely enough it seems hardly known intermediately. Mousa, my Theban valet, and others from Upper Egypt, assure me that they never saw nor heard of it till they came to Cairo. (I should be interested to know if you found it prominent in Abyssinia).

With the Sudanese it seems to play the role of the Egyptian *Zumara*.
As that seems hardly to exist without the Tar, the Shakshaakha sistrum is
symbiotic with the Ringu, and the Kuria. You will remember the Ringu, which
either gives its name to the whole show or takes it from it, the Ringa, that kind
of harmonium with vertical wooden keys, and pipes or painted gourds, which
wobbles eternally; and the Kuria which is or exactly resembles a section of
a railway line, from which perfectly rhythmic notes are elicited by two iron
rods.

In reference to a point raised by Prof. N[ewberry], I cannot find that
the sistrum is specially used in ceremonies connected with puberty, but in
conjunction with the Ringu and Kuria, at practically all ceremonies such as
Circumcision and Marriages, Moulids and the Zarr, as well as at simple social
gatherings for frolic and the consumption of *Booza*.

I have never known the use of this form of Sistrum divorced from the
dance – a dance that is usually suggestive of the treadmill or beetle crushing
but, notwithstanding, graceful and rhythmically perfect; but occasionally a
dancer with two sistra in each band leaps from the circle into the air with great
élan. The usual *motif* of the dance is the circling of some half dozen amorous
swains about a *Nigra-sed-formosa*[36], displaying their charms and "sistral"
talents and, one by one, taking her in his arms, till at last one is accepted.
Their singing, if indulged in at all, is ejaculatory and croony, and St. Jerome's
criticism – "Gemitum pro cantu habent"[37] – would be better justified than as
he applied it to his doves. Occasionally in Arabic, they go a little further, the
limit I have heard being:

> "Aiwa, Aiwa, min es-Sudan,
> Sirig es-sanduq Muhammad,
> Lakin 'muftah maai'.
> [Oh yes, oh yes, from the Sudan
> Muhammad stole the box
> But the key's with me.]

The "Ringa" we witnessed on 18 Tût (29 September 1935) at the Coptic
Moulid of Mar Barsum el-Aryan, at Maasara (near Helwan), was quite typical
of its form in Egypt, whether accompanying Moslem or Coptic celebrations,

---

36 A girl; the Latin meaning "I am black but beautiful" comes from the *Song of Songs*.
37 "By way of song, they can only moan."

and probably only differs from the purely Sudanese article, in that bowls of *booza* are supplemented by cups of coffee or qirfa. Occasionally one sees young and very handsome girls dancing, but more often (as Mrs. Hocart, who accompanied me to the moulid of Sidi Muafaq with the Professor some nights ago, remarked) they suggest Epstein creations. On the other hand, some of the youths have features as delicate as one could find in statuary.

The sistrum is a cylinder of hard white metal, rather more than a foot long with handle and conical cap, and containing pebbles. From one to four are held high and in front of the dancer when shaken. The form rarely differs from the two I posted to you yesterday, but very occasionally, there is a handle deluxe of ornamented yellow metal. One such, suggesting both fish and phallus, I tried to purchase at a recent moulid, but the super-Epsteinienne held to it, she explained, in memoriam of her fisher lover, who perished in the Nile. (She too was a fisher of sorts, by assumption of the Petrine mandate[38].)

I first observed the sistrum in 1919 at a Zarr; the *Aalima* (or Godeya[39]) circling with it a kind of altar, after a blood sacrifice in a rite suggesting a mourning for Adonis (*et ecce ibi mulieres plangentes Adonidem[40]*).

In this case, neither she nor the family of the possessed woman were Sudanese, but the djin to be exorcised were, and I think some of the assistants.

Here too the handle of the sistrum was suggestive of the ithyphallic[41] cult of (the god) Min in ancient Egypt before the vogue of Isis, but, I imagine, by pure coincidence.

I do not recall seeing it again until the moulid of Fatima el-Nebawiya, at which there were several Ringas, 27 Rabî I 1353 (9 July 1934), and though probably I had missed it when visiting moulids, I am sure its vogue and that of the Ringa, have enormously increased recently. You may have noticed, when with me, Ringas at the Moulid el-Nebi, and the Moulids of Bayumi, Matrawi, Muhammadi, and Mazlum (the last being the moulid in the fields where the brigand was unveiled and lynched). This month (Sha'bân, which ends today, and is a carnival of feasts before the fast of Ramadân), I have visited Ringas not only at Muafaq, referred to above, but at the moulids of Imam el-Shafei, Matrawi, Mansi, Saleh Haddad, Sultan Hanafi, and Awlad Badr. There were

---

38 The right to assume possession. Historically, this was the right, accorded by the Vatican, to dominion over lands discovered by Christian nations.

39 kôdya = the leading woman at a zâr.

40 "And behold women sat there mourning for Adonis", from Ezekiel 8:14. The correct phrase is: *et ecce ibi mulieres sedebant plangentes Adonidem* .

41 Ithyphallic = with erect penis.

two at Sultan Hanafi, one of which I visited with Mrs. Wyman Bury[42], and the other with Prof. Hocart, and at the very small moulid of Awlad Badr two days ago there were two flourishing Ringas. They are prominent also at the feast of Sayed el Badawi.

It is important to note that although an attribute of religious feasts, it is always in the "amusement park", and never in Egypt brought into mosque or church, or employed at a Zikr.

So far, I have only dealt with one form of the Sistrum, but I am sending you three of an entirely different type, made of coloured basketwork, in the shape of an orb of 3 or 4 inches diameter, with a handle. Since your letter on the subject, I visited a Sunday afternoon ceremony, which takes place every week in the court of the great mosque of Sitna Nefisa and purchased those I am sending at the door of the mosque. I had seen this type in the hands of some children at Bein el-Sariat a year or more ago. I have now, with the help of Gad el-Moula traced the children and find that their parents bought these *sistra* at or in Sitna Nefisa when visiting that saint ceremonially; and I have not been able to ascertain that they can be obtained elsewhere. Gad assures me they are in pious memory of Sitna Nefisa, who was very fond of them. (This reminds me of Siena, where the little horses and other toys of St. Catherine are preserved and reproduced as her souvenirs for the faithful. I fear Nefisa's originals have been lost.)

It may interest Prof. Newberry, as a great Egyptologist and *sistrum* specialist, that some of the children about the mosque had lengthened their *sistrum* into a sceptre-like object by means of a cane.

There is yet a form of *sistrum,* still more sceptre-like, borne on a pole, in the *zeffa* (procession) of many moulids, and I think on some other occasions. Though much more ornate than the ordinary *shakhshaakha,* it is called by the same name. You must have seen it, surrounded and followed by men and sometimes dervishes, gorgeously attired and given to whirling and divers contortions. This I have known for about thirty years, and its use seems on the decline, though I was glad to see it in all its glory last Wednesday afternoon, though the full *zeffa* with banners and the mounted "Khalîfa" was not allowed (on account, they said, of the riots).

---

42 Florence Ann Marshall, a nurse and the wife of George Wyman Bury (3 January 1874–23 September 1920). He was a naturalist, explorer, Arabist and political officer in the British army, who died in Egypt of tuberculosis after the First World War. They met when he was a tubercular patient at Westminster Hospital, London, in 1911.

Now do make any use of this you like (if it has any), mentioning my name or not as you wish. Ibrahim, the black Ringa-dancer and others, have helped me, but Mousa, keen on the quest as he knows it is for you, has been by far my most intelligent and reliable informant; he obtained the metal *sistra.*

The moon of Ramadân has been seen, so Ramadân karîm, yâ azîzî[43].

Yours,

J. W. McPherson

In replying to the above letter, Prof. Evans-Pritchard told me *inter alia* that the *sistra* sent him from Egypt were now in the Oxford Pitt Rivers Museum. He mentioned that amongst the many associations of the *sistrum* with Egypt, was the use to which Cleopatra put it at the battle of Actium, where it acquired the name of "Cleopatra's trumpet".[44]

He, and still more Prof. Newberry, would be interested in the *dabbûs*[45] I examined some years later at the Moulid of Zefeitî and whose description will be found under that head, as, apart from its mystical use by the dervishes, it combined all the requisites of the ideal primitive royal sceptre – the typical spherical shape with long handle, the loaded *sistral* head with the addition of resonant bits of metal for calling to order, and potential death at each end to enforce such. I was unable at the time to obtain and send one to Oxford, but have acquired one recently, by the kindness of Major Gayer-Anderson, which, however, owes its rattle qualities wholly to the bell-like bits of metal on chains, and has no loose particles for that purpose within the hollow head.

I think in this and the preceding chapter, I have enumerated enough of the characteristic things which one sees or hears at a moulid, that edify, amuse or interest, without more than the most passing mention of the quacks who tempt you with *dawâ'* (medicine) to cure all ills, the doctors who charm out aching teeth, or the fortune teller and his writing on sand, *darb el-raml*, or even the rarer exhibitions

---

43 Said during the month of fasting to downplay its severity, ramadân karîm means "Ramadân is generous"; and yâ 'azîzî means "O my dear [friend]".

44 Virgil, *Aeneid* 8:685 ff., translated by David West, adapted by the editor: "On the other side, with the wealth of the barbarian world and warriors in all kinds of different armour, came Antony in triumph from the shores of the Red Sea and the peoples of the Dawn. With him sailed Egypt and the power of the East from as far as distant Bactria, and there bringing up the rear was the greatest outrage of all, his Egyptian wife! ... In the midst, [Cleopatra] cheers on her troops with the sistrum ..." (...Regina in mediis patrio vocat agmina sistro... line 696).

45 Literally "pin", here *dabbûs* is a ceremonial dagger.

of television by looking into ink in the medium's hand, known as *mandel*,[46] and such like occult matters. There are often surprises that may constitute the particular interest of the evening on both the devotional and secular sides. Much of what I have described or omitted to mention is, of course, highly banal or extremely primitive, and so far removed from the conventional and fashionable evening's programme that there must be many to whom it will have little appeal, but no one can be indifferent to the simple piety and light-hearted enjoyment which pervade the atmosphere of a moulid.

There is the freedom to move about when and where you will, *semel huc, atque illuc*[47], and to leave at once any item which displeases for something better – none of the prison atmosphere, so specially irksome to a claustrophobe, which discounts even good theatrical performances, concerts, picture shows and the like, and becomes a martyrdom when one goes for a supposed treat and instead sits through hours of complete boredom, looking in vain for the happy, enthusiastic, unsophisticated, unsatiated moulid faces to cheer one through it.

The writer appreciated and frequented the simple unsophisticated and human attractions of moulids, more and more, *pari passu* with the regression of those qualities in conventional entertainments, due to the ousting of music by its spurious substitute jazz, with its nasty concomitants, and the ghastly error that the Muses can be mechanised. It was too sad a role to assist at the victory of blatant cacophonies and nauseous croonings over the inspired harmonies and lovely melodies which the genius and the souls of the great masters had bequeathed us through the centuries. Sad, too, to witness the surrender of the artistic public to this soulless invasion; and sad to know that the professional musicians who had delighted us, real and good musicians many of them, had to choose between murdering their own art or starving.

But the great tragedy, or so it seems to me, is that the young generations born into this can have no vivid idea of all that was sacrificed, and, therefore, no more or little more urge to combat this bondage which has enthralled music and the arts, than a young Fijian, "to the manner born", to renounce the cannibalism which from his cradle he has regarded as natural.

Hasan Pâsha Anîs, who is a keen musician as well as a supreme master of aeronautics, once told me that in jazz he has frequently recognised primitive African music, of the *ringa* and allied types. That is interesting but does not console us for

46 This type of "magic" has the fortune-teller prophesying while looking at a mirror-like surface, in this case evidently provided by a still pool of ink.
47 "To and fro", from 2 Kings 4:35.

what was better than *ringa* or jazz, especially as it has lost its soul and simplicity in its migration to American negro bawdy house, and its exploitation by enterprising purveyors to dubious taste first in the New World and then in the Old, till it has come to roost again in Africa.

"Who will roll away the stone from the mouth of the sepulchre" of the Muses, and deliver us from this cult of the grotesque, ugly, discordant and indecent, with its objective representation on the Hollywood screen and its raucous support by the radio, to the extent that people of culture and refinement with revolt, it is to be hoped, in their hearts, are mesmerised by the fashion of the cult into distorting their haunches with arms akimbo, slapping their own buttocks and poking their thumbs out, like stable lads and fishwives, in a way that would have earned them, not so long ago, the stocks or the spinning house at home or the bow string out here. Surely, we are a race of sheep, caring little whether we be black, white or ringstraked[48], and following any false shepherd who has such abnormal bluff and impudence as to impose his fashion.

Taking up this evening's *La Bourse Égyptienne*, I am glad to see that my views are not held by an isolated few. I read :

> To wriggle about, move their buttocks from one side to the other, slap hands and feet, toss their heads in excruciating fashion like a hanged man, scream as if they're in the jungle – such is the savage symphony which our dance halls offer at the moment.

Some readers may retort that I have hurled no Jeremiads at the *ringa* dancers and their grotesque music, have indeed written rather sympathetically on the subject. To which I reply that though I have never seen anything actually vicious or repellent in a *bûza* booth and would hesitate to put the *ringa* on as low a plane as our jazz, I do not cite it as an edifying item of a moulid, but rather as a curiosity to be seen, heard or studied once or twice, and should resent and resist its being dragged into our salons, "best" hotels, and all places of entertainment, to dominate everything and everybody and oust the music of culture and the masters. It, like jazz, is too primitive and coarse. Happily, unlike jazz, it has no propagandists nor protagonists to bring about this preposterous result. The evil is in the excess; a spot of jazz might lend piquancy to an entertainment, like a few freckles on a comely countenance, but when freckles become a confluent pigmentation on the face of society, if looks like an ugly contagion.

---

48 "Marked with circular stripes" (archaic).

If an acid test of real natural gaiety, as opposed to forced hilarity, is the absence of all tendency to the morbid and the macabre, then the fun of the moulid fair shows up well. Morbidity and intentional irreverence are unknown, and the *macabre* has no place even if the moulid is held in a *maqbara*[49]. Nor do any of its shows suggest the *Cabaret du Néant*, or *Le Ciel*, or *L'Enfer*[50] of *La Ville Lumière*[51], much less a "Black Mass" in the Catacombs. Happily, the atmosphere of this blessed country is all against that sort of entertainment, though an article in *La Bourse Égyptienne* of 26 March 1940 indicates that the macabre trend is progressing even in Egypt. The article, entitled *Le mystère des voix d'outre-tombe*[52], describes the invasion of Chatby Cemetery by five hundred cars and five thousand people who left their cabarets, their fox-trotting and the rest, to hunt down an alleged ghost.

But any of my readers who were in Berlin some twenty years ago (or since, for all I know), will have realised to what macabre depths jazz can fall, and it is significant that it was more eagerly welcomed and cultivated there than elsewhere in Europe. The changes were rung on "Dances of Death" – *Waltz Macabre, Der Tanzende Tod (Valse Boston), Shimmylieder* – and Foxtrots of the same; and the *Programm,* of a popular *Tanzsaal,* or a fashionable *Tanzfest* for *das vornehme Leben*[53] was hardly complete without the sung-dance, "Fox Macabre Totentanz", of which the refrain ran:

'Berlin, dein Tänzer ist der Tod !
Berlin, du wühlst mit Lust im Kot!
Halt ein! lass sein! und denk ein bischen nach:
Du tanzt dir doch vom Leibe nicht die Schmach,
denn du boxt, und du jazzt, und du foxt auf dem Pulver-fass."

[Berlin, your dance is the dance of Death!
Berlin, with joy you whirl about in filth!
Halt! Stop! and think about it a bit:
You won't dance the shame out of your belly,
for you box and you jazz and you fox-trot on a powder-magazine.]

---

49 maqbara = "Tomb" or "graveyard". To associate "macabre" with the Arabic "*maqâbir*" (pl.) is a clever play on words, and indeed the latter word is the likely etymology of the former.
50 Names of three cabarets (of the void, of heaven, and of hell) at the foot of Montmartre in the 18th arrondissement. They were demolished mid-20th century.
51 By which he means Paris.
52 "The mystery of the voices from the beyond".
53 Posh society, distinguished Germans.

This was advertised by a huge nightmare of a picture – of gay company dancing on a bridge which spanned the bottomless pit at the moment the bridge was collapsing and letting them down. This was all so near the superlative of ghastly decadence that it is difficult to conceive what the *Mutterleib*[54] can have produced further for this war, for seemingly the only next step would be:

Berlin, dein Tänzer ist die Hölle![55]

But, to these polemics and *cauchemars*[56] a truce, and let those who love the macabre go to the heart of Germany, and the jazz fan to the οικηματα [oikêmata][57] of the far West where the Conga, the Bunny Hug and the Black Bottom may be seen and heard in their pristine *purity,*

...Juvat integras accedere fontes,
Atque haurire.[58]

or since

Non cuivis contingit adire Corinthum.[59]

"Hell's Kitchen" or the *bas-fonds*[60] of Frisco or Chicago might serve, not to mention places nearer home, but those who prefer an atmosphere of simple natural devotion and joy, and the fresh air of heaven without the umbra or penumbra of the macabre, might do worse than come with me to a moulid, for preference, a country one.

You may even say or think, with Byron:

...sweet are our escapes
from civic revelry to rural mirth.[61]

---

54 Mother's body.
55 Berlin, your dancers are [the epitome of] Hell!
56 "Nightmares" [Fr.].
57 Οικηματα = literally "houses", but can also mean, as here, "brothels" [Gr.].
58 "May He help [me] to reach and drink my full from clear fountains" (Lucretius).
59 "It is not everyman's lot to reach Corinth" (Horace).
60 Literally "the shallows" (Fr.). Here, presumably "slums".
61 *Don Juan*, cxxiv.

Beit el-Kreitlîya and Ibn Tûlûn Mosque
Aerial shot of Beit el-Kreitlîya showing its proximity to the Ibn Tûlûn Mosque.

V

Moulids: Their Individual Features

The preceding pages have envisaged moulids in general, though drawing illustration from specific cases. This chapter is of the nature of a guide, portraying their individual features or idiosyncrasies as far as the writer has observed on repeated visits to nearly all of them and, in the few remaining instances, from first-hand current information. He has never seen, nor applied for, official lists or particulars, which would doubtless have made this a much more valuable document technically and statistically, but which he leaves to others; for this compilation is intended to be of the nature of very mild research in a neglected but highly deserving field. Being such pioneer work, there are very numerous *lacunae* which want filling up, notably in the non-inclusion of important provincial moulids, for want of personal contact and direct reliable information.

Though all moulids must essentially have their devotional side, this varies from being their sole aspect in some of the small ones, especially those of a quasi-private nature, such as el-'Azâ'im, to others such as el-Hillî, which tend the other way. Others, like el-Nebî, have a sort of official character; some borrow a charm from ancient or beautiful surroundings; desert and country meetings have their own picturesque items; immemorial customs are shadowed in a few; dervishes or musicians may have surprises for us so that as a result few moulids are devoid of some points of individuality.

As explained in Chapter II, the date on which a moulid is actually celebrated fluctuates so greatly, sometimes over several months, that for the Islamic feasts which are in a very large majority, it is not possible to construct a calendar which is anything more than roughly approximate. An attempt at such is appended, which at any rate will give an idea of when to begin looking out for a particular moulid, but reference to the moulid as described later in this chapter will bring one much nearer.

It will be noted that in the Calendar I have only ventured to put in the actual day of the month in eight cases, and one of these Bahlûl, on 29 Sha'bân, is not rigorously exact, as it is, I believe, intended for the eve of Ramadân, and there may be 30 days in Sha'bân, though usually 29. The same probably applies also to several of the small moulids about the "Bâbs" of Futûh and Nasr[1], and elsewhere. In Chapter II also are given the approximate dates of the relatively few Coptic moulids, according to that Calendar. It has been mentioned that the Moslem Moulid of Abû Hareira at Gîza ignores the Moslem calendar in favour of the Coptic Easter Monday, and that Sayyid el-Bedawî follows the solar, not the lunar months, falling in October, the Coptic Bâba. Also, Bayûmî is in March (Baram-hât), and Imbâbî in June (Ba'ûna).

As importance is often attached to the day of the week, rather than that of the month, the Table near the end of Chapter II should be useful.

The 126 moulids which follow are arranged alphabetically.

Readers not familiar with Arabic are reminded that there is a Glossary of the Egyptian words used, arranged alphabetically according to the English transliteration.

Approximate dates of Moulids which follow the Islamic Calendar

(Where the date may vary more than a month, the first probable month is given.)

Muharram	'Abd el-Dâ'im	Cairo
	Abû Tarâbîsh	Helwân
	Galâl	Cairo
	Khalîl	Shubrâ
	Muhammad el-Bahrî	Cairo
	Mazlûm	Sharâbîya (Cairo)
	'Omar	Cairo
	Qărănî	Wâsta District
	Shatbî	Cairo District
	Tûnsî	Cairo District
Safar	Sayyid el-Malak	Cairo (Saptia)

---

1 Bâb el-Futûh and Bâb el-Nasr are two of the three remaining gates in the walls of the Old City of Cairo. The third is Bâb Zuweila.

10 Rabî' I	'Ashmâwî	Cairo
	Fâtima -l-Nebawîya	Cairo
11 Rabî' I	el-Nebî	Cairo ('Abbâsîya)
	Sâleh, Sultân	Cairo
Rabî' II	Abû -l-'Elâ	Cairo
	Farag	Cairo District
	Farghâl	Abû Tîg
	Husein	Cairo
	Nasr	Cairo
	Shibl	Shuhadâ', Manûf
	Tartûrî Hasan	Cairo District
Gamâd I	Abû Atâta	Gîza District
	Abû -l-Leil	Benî Mazâr
	Abû -l-Sebâ'	Cairo (Bûlâq)
	Ahmadein	Cairo
	Badrân	Cairo
	Benhâwî	Cairo
	(Desûqî)	Gezîret el-Dahab)
	Galâl el-Dîn	Asyût
	Gûda	Minyâ -l-Qamh
	Hamza	Cairo
	Hilâl	Cairo
	Huneidiq	Ismâ'îlîya
	Qureishî	Zinein
	Sakîna	Cairo
	Salâma	Cairo
Gamâd II	'Ârif	Tîla, Menûfîya
	Abû 'Umeira	Kerdâsa
	Gamâl el-Dîn	Kafr Turmus, Saft
	Gharîb (el-Gharîb)	Mît 'Uqba
	Hasan Anwar	Old Cairo
	'Uthmân	Pyramids
	Lâshîn	Mît 'Uqba
	'Uqbî	Mît 'Uqba
	Salîm	Cairo (Bûlâq)
	Tartûrî	el-Hatîya (Mît 'Uqba)
	Zefeitî	Duqqî
	Zein el-'Abdîn	Cairo

Rajab	'Abdullah	Cairo
	Abû Qafas	Helmîya, Zeitûn
	'Agamî	Alexandria District
	'Azâ'im	Cairo
26 Rajab	Dashtûtî (Tashtûshî)	Cairo
	Ibrâhîm	Matarîya
	Kurdî	Cairo (Bûlâq)
	Ma'rûf	Cairo
	Muwaffaq	Cairo
	Qâsid	Cairo
	Shâmî (el-Shâmî)	Gezîret el-Dahab
	Wâstî	Cairo (Bûlâq)
	Zeinab	Cairo
Sha'bân	'Abdullah el-Hagr	Cairo (Khalîfa)
	'Abdullah Kafr el-Darb	Cairo (Khalîfa)
	'Abd el-Bâsit	Çairo (Bâb el-Nasr)
	'Abd el-Karîm	Cairo (Bâb el-Nasr)
	'Abd el-Qâsid	Cairo (Bâb el-Nasr)
14 Sha'bân	'Abd el-Rahîm el-Qenâwî	Qenâ
	'Abd el-Wâhid	Cairo (Bûlâq)
	Abû Badîr	Cairo
	Abû Deif	Cairo (Imâm)
	Abû Zeid	Cairo (Imâm)
	'Alî -l-Gîzî	Cairo (Mameluks)
	Ansârî (el-Ansârî)	Cairo
	Arba'în	Cairo
	Awlâd Badr	Cairo (Bûlâq)
	Awlâd Shu'eib	Cairo
	'Aysha	Cairo (Khalîfa)
	'Aysha -l-Tûnsî	Cairo (Khalîfa)
29 Sha'bân	Bahlûl	Cairo
	'Amrî	Cairo (Muhammad 'Alî)
	'Amrî	Cairo (Tûlûn)
	Fâtima -l-Nebawîya bint Ga'far	Cairo (Bâb el-Khalq)
	Galâdîn	Cairo (Bûlâq)

Gânib	Cairo (Sarûgîa)
Hanafî, Sultân	Cairo
Hârûn	Cairo (Tûlûn)
Kharûsî	Cairo (Bûlâq)
Leithî	Cairo (Imâm)
Mansî	Cairo
Marsafa	Cairo
Matrâwî	Matarîya
Muhammadî, Demardâshî	Demardâsh
Muhammadî, Shâhîn	Cairo (Khalîfa)
Qâzâzî	Cairo (Gamâlîya)
Sâleh Haddâd	Cairo
Samân	Cairo (Imâm)
Shâfe'î, Imâm el-	Cairo
Sutuhîya	Cairo (Bâb el-Futûh)
Yûsef el-Haggâg	Luxor

(Fuller particulars as regards dates, etc., will be found in the detailed account of each *sheikh*, which follows.)

The Arabic months	The Coptic months
Muharram	Tût
Safar	Bâba
Rabî' I	Hâtôr
Rabî' II	Kîhâk
Gamâd I	Tûba
Gamâd II	Amshîr
Rajab	Baramhât
Sha'bân	Barmûda
Ramadân	Bashans
Shawwâl	Ba'ûna
Zû-l-Qa'da	Abîb
Zû-l-Higga	Misrâ
	Nasi

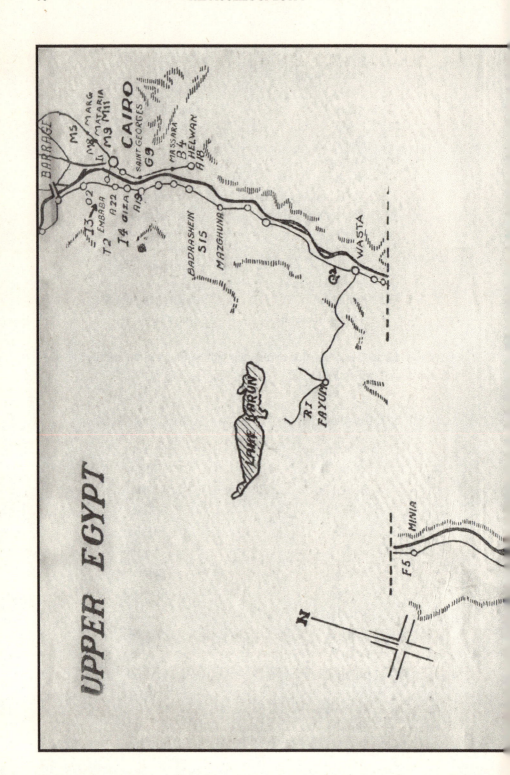

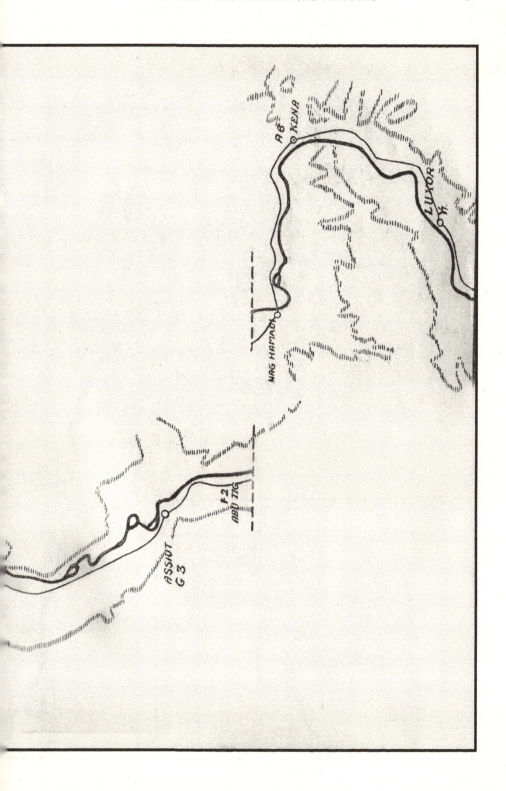

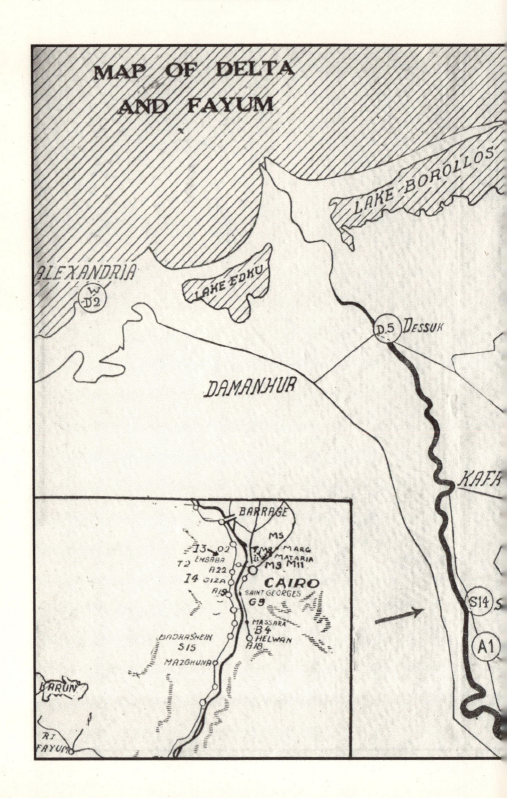

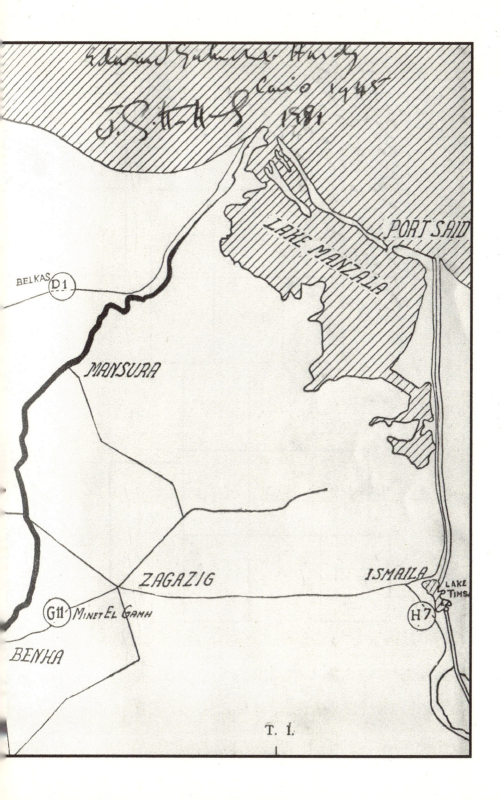

Index to Sectional Maps of Cairo

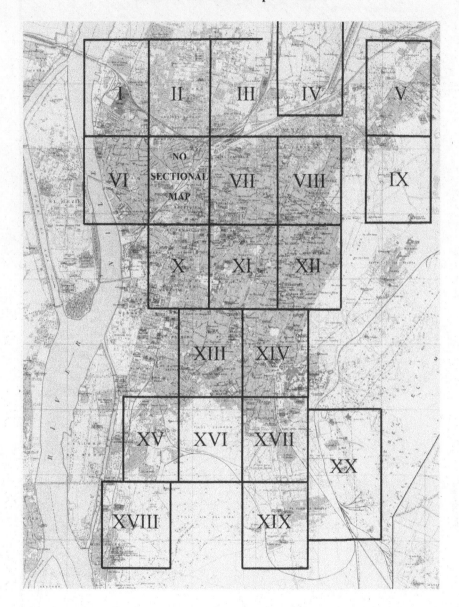

Table of Sectional Maps of Cairo

	Moulid	Section			Moulid	Section
A	2 'Abd el- Bâsit	VIII	H		3 Hârûn	XIII
	3 'Abd el-Dâ'im	X			4 Hasan Anwar	XV
	4 'Abd el-Kerîm	VIII			5 Hilâl	VI
	7 'Abd el-Wâhid	VI			6 Hillî	I
	8 'Abdullah	X			8 Husein	XII
	9 'Abdullah el-Hagr	XVII	I		2 Ibrâhîm (Sûq el-Silâh)	XIV
	10 'Abdullah Khafîr el-Darb	XVII	K		2 Khasûsî	VI
	13 Abû -l-'Azâ'im	XIII			3 Khudeirî	XIII
	16 Abû -l-'Elâ	VI			4 Kurdî	I
	23 Abû -l-Sebâ'	VI	L		1 Leithî	XIX
	27 Ahmadein	VI	M		1 Ma'rûf	X
	28 Ansârî	XI			3 Maghrabî	X
	29 Arba'în	XI			4 Mansî	VIII
	30 'Ashmâwi	XI			6 Marsafa	XI
	31 Awlâd Badr	VI			7 Marzûq	XII
	33 'Aysha	XVII			9 Mazlûm	IV
	34 'Aysha -l-Tûnisî	XVII			10 Muwaffaq	VI
B	1 Badrân	II			11 Muhammadî (Demardâsh)	V
	2 Bahlûl	XIV	N		1 Nafîsa	XVII
	3 Bahrî	VII			2 Nasr	VI
	5 Bayûmî	VIII			3 Nebî	IX
	6 Benhâwî	VIII	Q		1 Qazâzî	XII
D	3 Darghâm	XI	S		1 Sakîna	XVII
	4 Dashtûtî	VIII			2 Salâma	XI
E	1 Emery I = 'Amrî I	XI			3 Sâleh Ayyûb	XII
	2 Emery II = 'Amrî II (Tûlûn)	XVI			4 Sâleh el-Haddâd	XIII
F	1 Farag	I			5 Samân	XVII
	3 Fâtima -l-Nebawîya	XIV			6 Sa'ûdî	XIV
	4 Fâtima -l-Nebawîya bint Ga'far Sâdiq	XI			8 Sayyid el-Mâlik	VI
G	1 Galâdîn	I			9 Salîm	I
	2 Galâl	III			11 Shâfe'î	XIX
	6 Gamâl	VIII			13 Shatbî	XX
	7 Gânib	XIV			16 Sutuhîya	VIII
	9 Girgis	XVIII	W		2 Wâstî	VI
	10 Gîzî	XVII	Z		2 Zein el-'Âbdîn	XV
H	1 Hamza	X			3 Zeinab	XIII
	2 Hanafî	XIII				

Sectional Map I

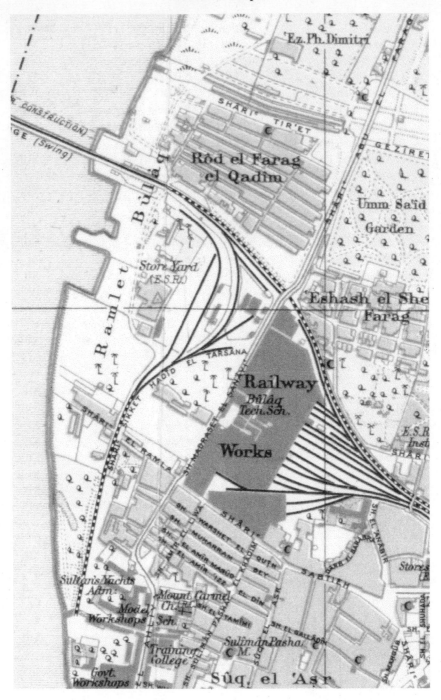

Sectional Map

I

Bulaq (and Rod el-Farag direction)

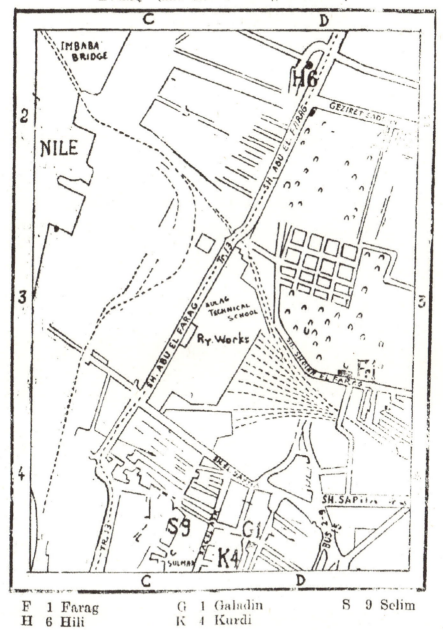

F 1 Farag   G 1 Galadin   S 9 Selim
H 6 Hili   K 4 Kurdi

Sectional Map II

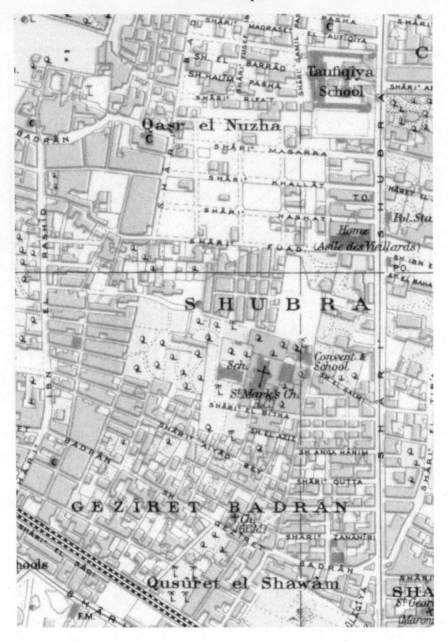

SECTIONAL MAP
II
GEZIRAT BADRAN.

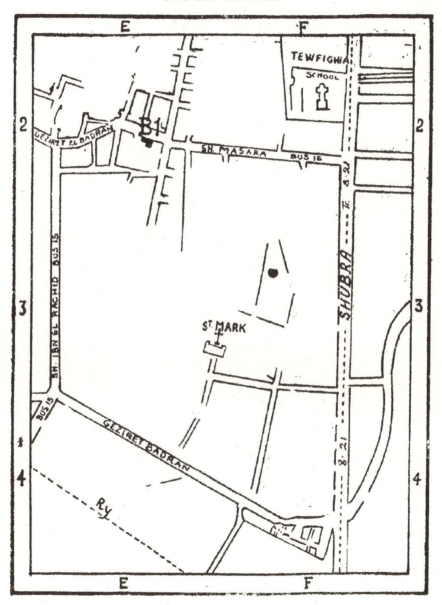

B 1 Badran

Sectional Map III

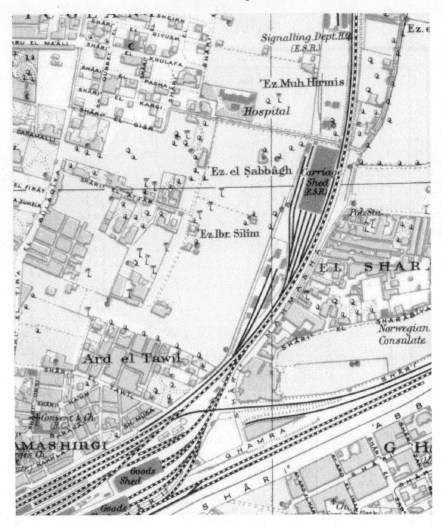

SECTIONAL MAP
III
SHARABIA

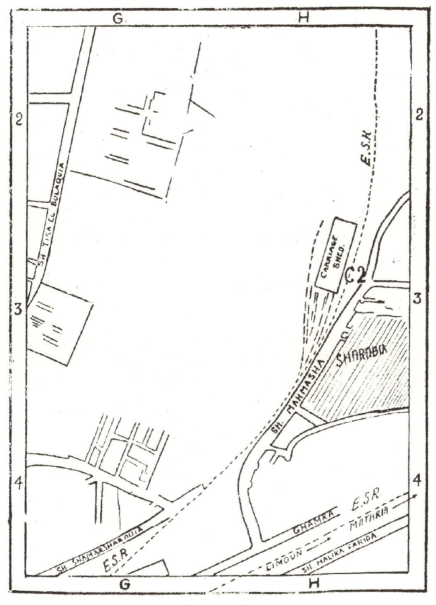

G 2 Galal.

Sectional Map IV

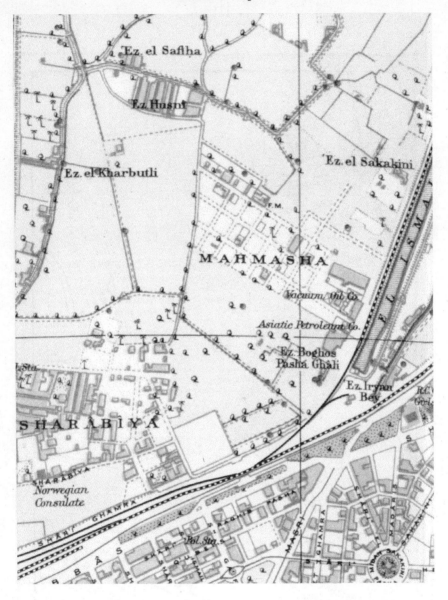

SECTIONAL MAP

IV

EZB. SAFIHA, (N. of Sharabia).

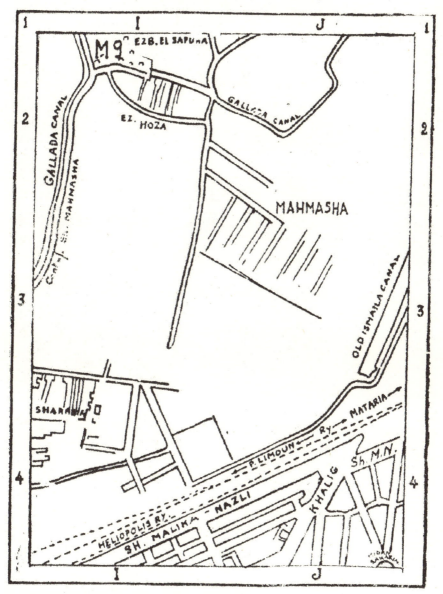

M 9 Mazlum.

Sectional Map V

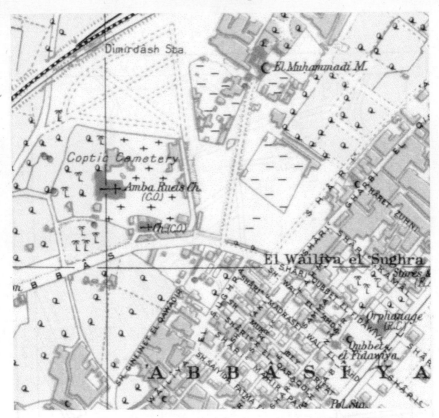

Sectional Map
V
N·E Cairo : (nr. Demardash).

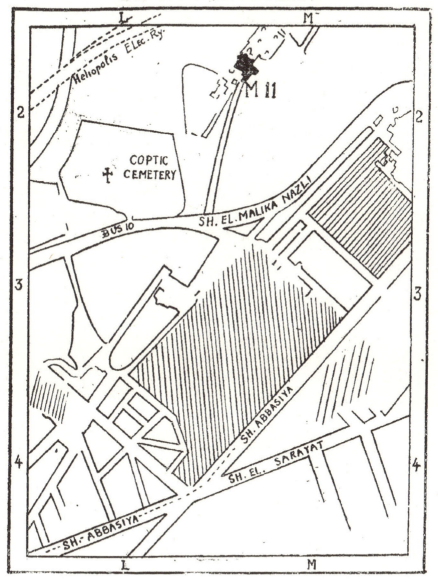

M 11 Muhammadi.

Sectional Map VI

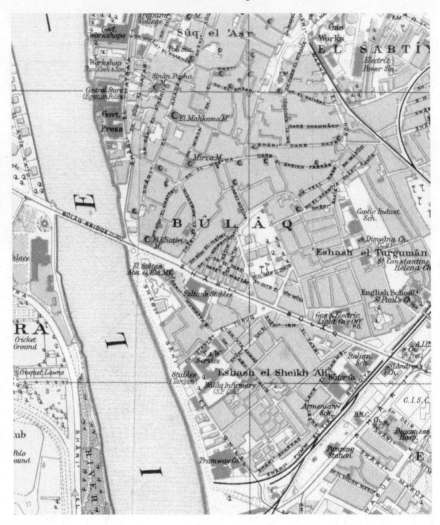

SECTIONAL MAP
VI
BULAQ.

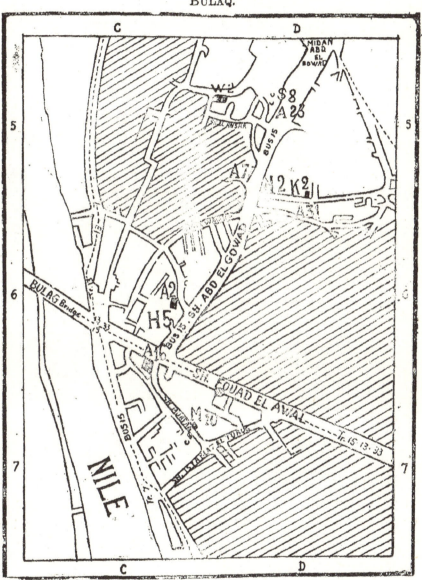

A	7	Abd el-Wahid	A	31	Awlad Badr	N	2	Nasr
A	16	Abu el-Ela	H	5	Hilal	S	8	Sayed el-Malak
A	23	Abu Sabaa	K	2	Khasousi	W	2	Wasti
A	2(27)	Ahmadein	M	10	Muafaq			

Sectional Map VII

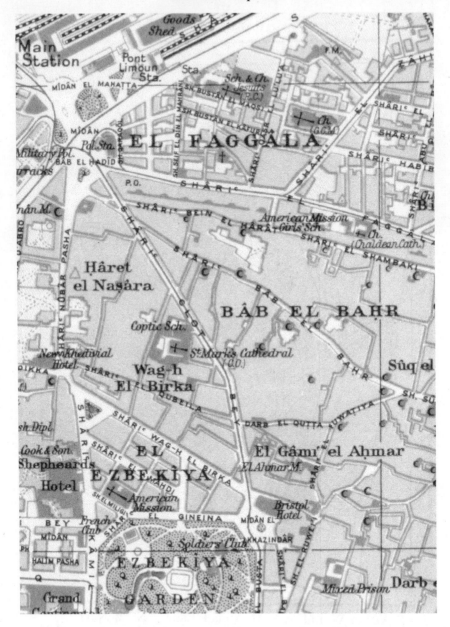

SECTIONAL MAP
VII
CLOT BEY DISTRICT.

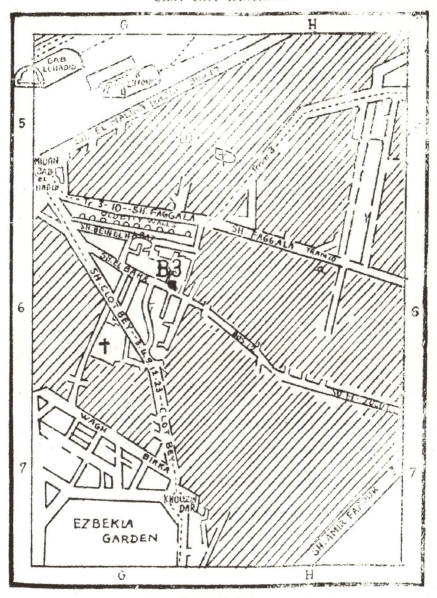

B 8 Bahri

Sectional Map VIII

SECTIONAL MAP
VIII
BABS EL-NASR & FUTUH: and vicinity of Sh. Farouk.

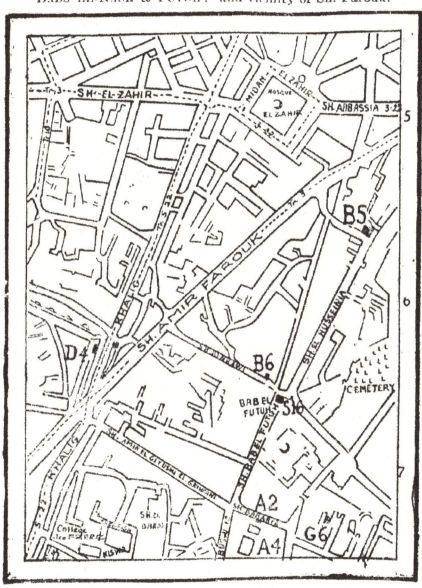

A	2 Abd el-Basat	B	5 Bayumi	D	4 Dashtouti
A	4 Abd el-Kerim	B	6 Benhawi	G	6 Gamal
	M 4 Mansi			S 16 Sutuhia	

Sectional Map IX

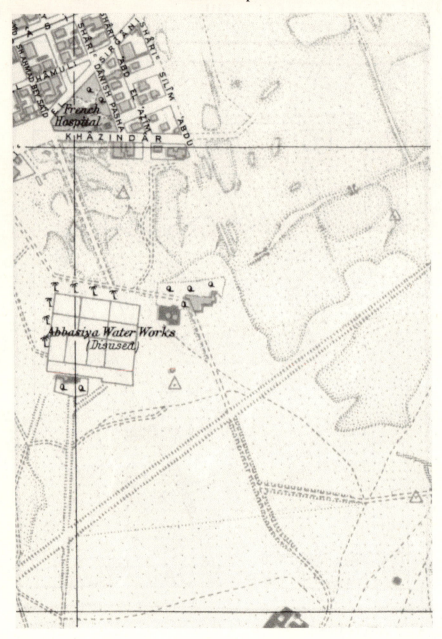

SECTIONAL MAP
IX
ABBASSIA.

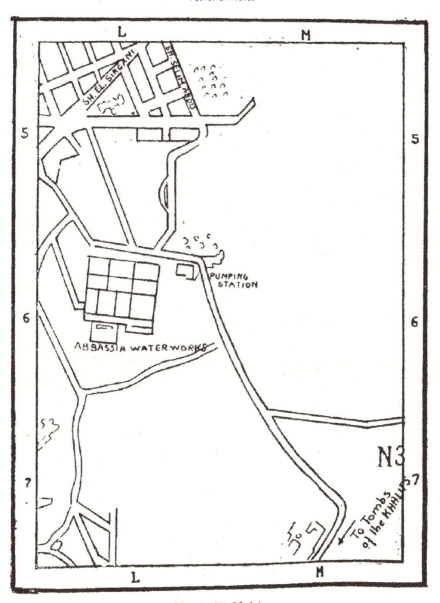

N 3 El-Nebi.

Sectional Map X

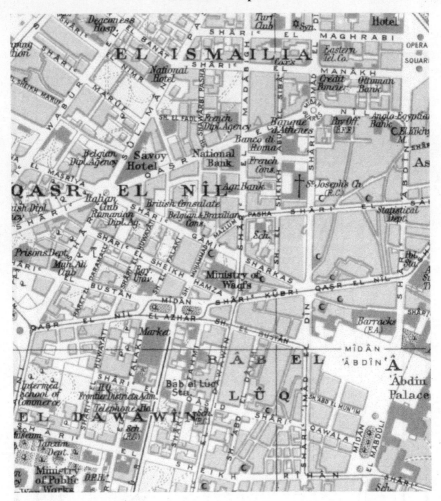

SECTIONAL MAP

X

ABDIN &c.

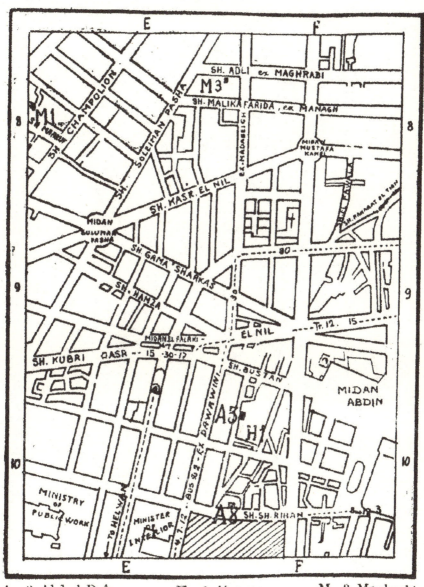

| A | 3 | Abd el-Daim | H | 1 | Hamza | M | 3 | Maghrabi |
| A | 3 | Abdulla | M | 1 | Maaruf | | | |

Sectional Map XI

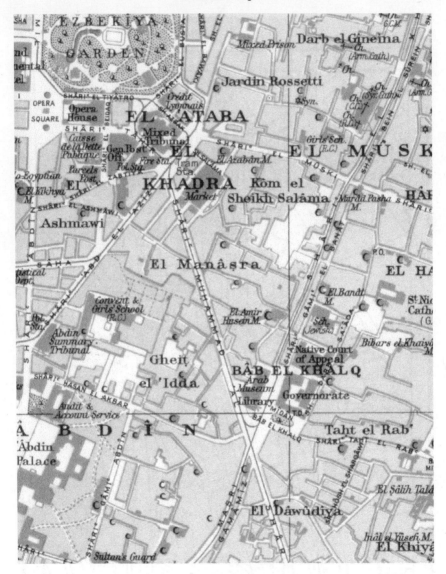

SECTIONAL MAP
XI
ABOUT SH. MUHAMMAD ALI.

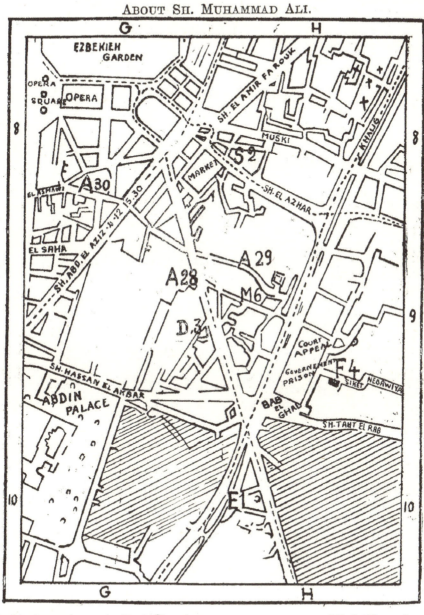

A 28 Ansari	D 3 Dargham	M 6 Marsafa
A 29 Arbein	F 4 Fatima el-Nebawiya, bint Gaafar	S 2 Salama
A 30 Ashmawi	E 1 Emery	

Sectional Map XII

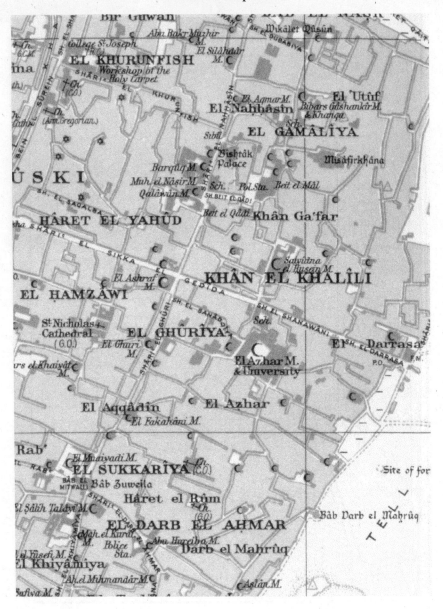

SECTIONAL MAP
XII
MUSKI DISTRICT.

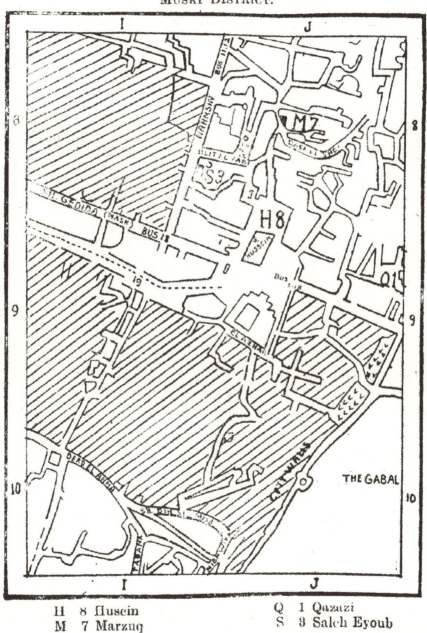

H 8 Husein   Q 1 Qazazi
M 7 Marzuq   S 3 Saleh Eyoub

Sectional Map XIII

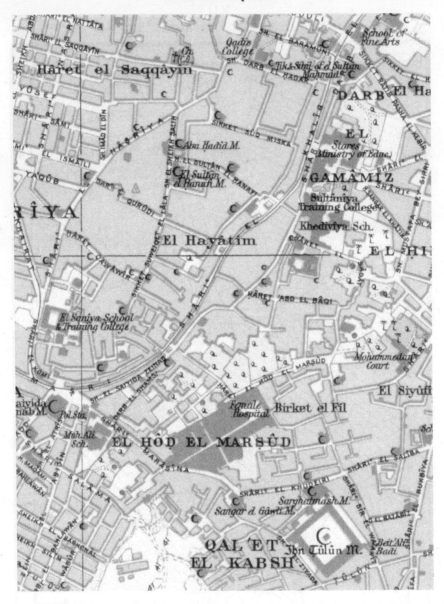

SECTIONAL MAP
XIII
SAIDA ZENAB & IBN TOULOUN
DISTRICTS.

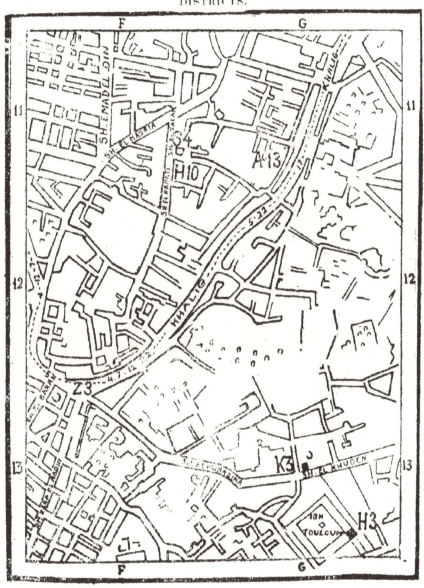

A 18 Azaim	S 4 Saleh el- Haddad	H 2 Haroun
H 2 Hanafi	Z 3 Zenab	K 3 Khuderi

Sectional Map XIV

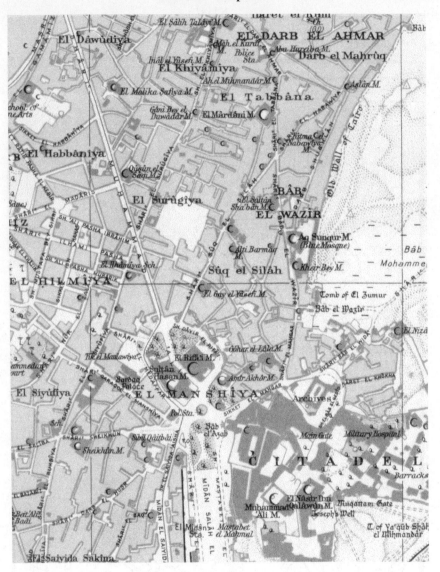

SECTIONAL MAP
XIIII

SOUTH-EAST-CAIRO :—
          neighbourhoods of Bab el-Wazir and Suq el-Silah.

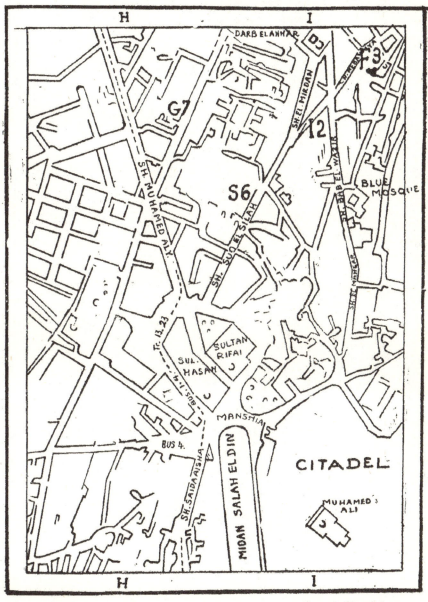

B   2   Bahlul
F   3   Fatima el-Nebawiya
G   7   Ganib

I   2   Ibrahim
S   6   Saudi

Sectional Map XV

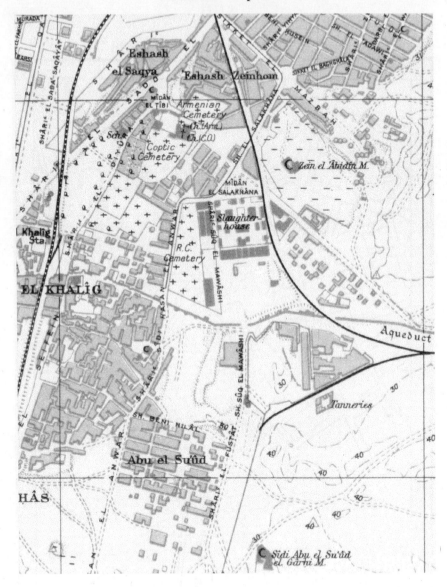

SECTIONAL MAP

XV

"ABATTOIR DISTRICT."

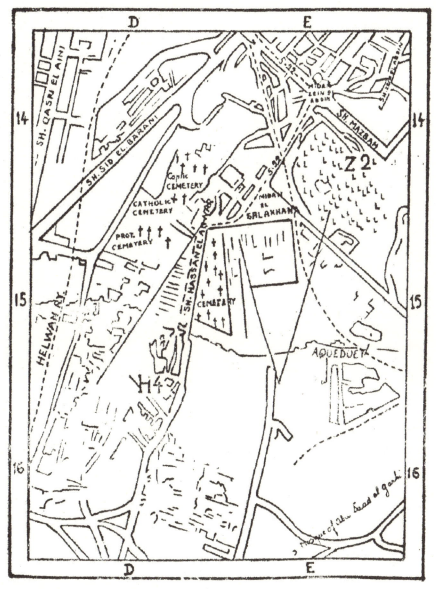

H 4 Hasan Anwar   Z 2 Zein el-Abdin

Sectional Map XVI

SECTIONAL MAP
XVI
IBN TOULOUN DISTRICT.

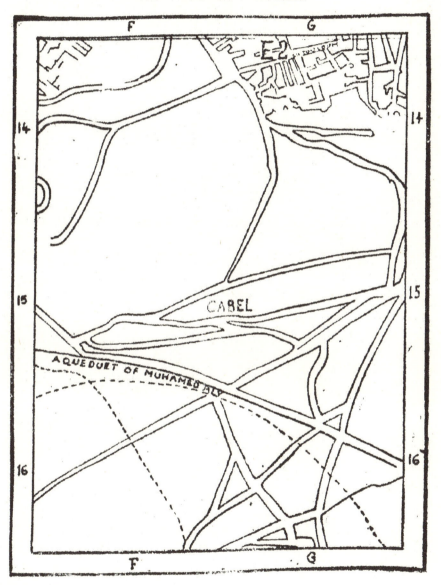

E 2 Emery.

Sectional Map XVII

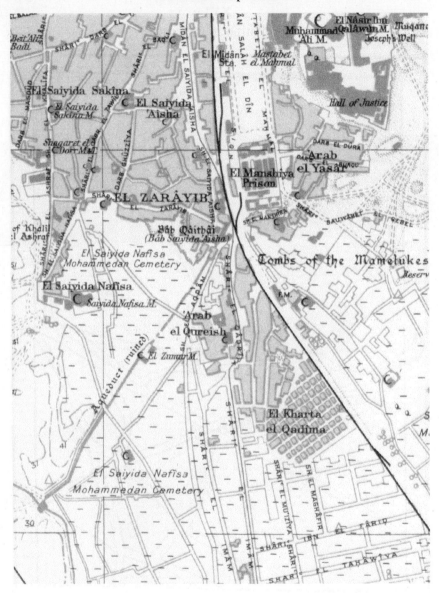

SECTIONAL MAP
XVII
ABOUT TOMBS OF THE MAMELUKES AND ABBASIDE KHALIFS.

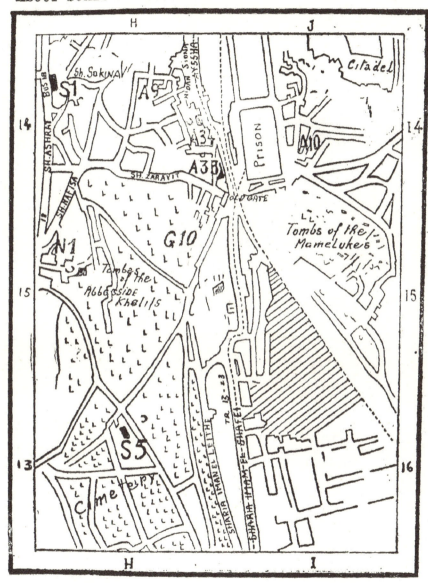

A 9 Abdulla el-Hagr	G 10 Gizi
A 10 Abdulla Khafr el-Darb	N 1 Nafisa
A 33 Ayesha	S 1 Sakina
A 34 Ayesha el-Tunisi	S 5 Saman

Sectional Map XVIII

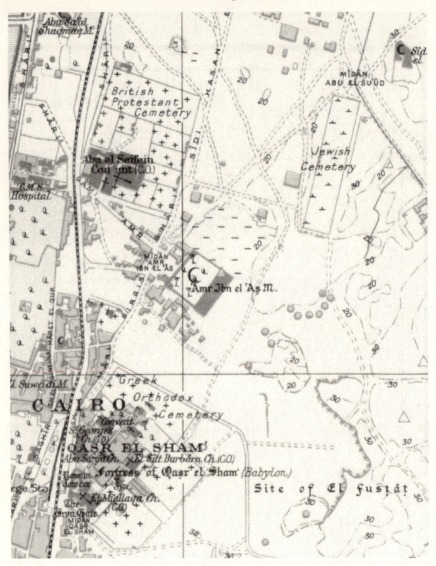

SECTIONAL MAP
XVIII
FORTRESS OF BABYLON.

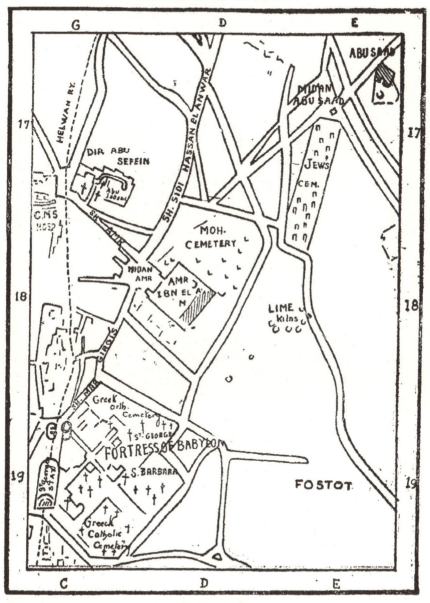

G   9 Girgis

Sectional Map XIX

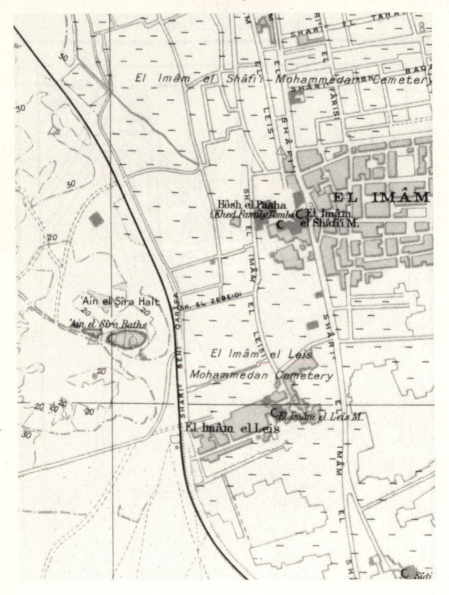

SECTIONAL MAP
XIX
NECROPOLIS OF IMAM EL-SHAFEI

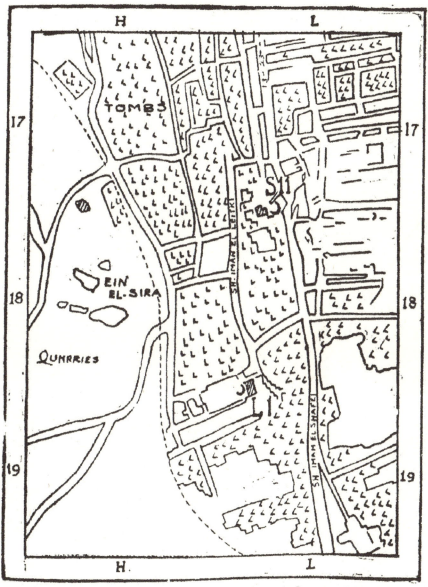

L   1 Imam el-Leithi   S   11 Imam el-Shafei

Sectional Map XX

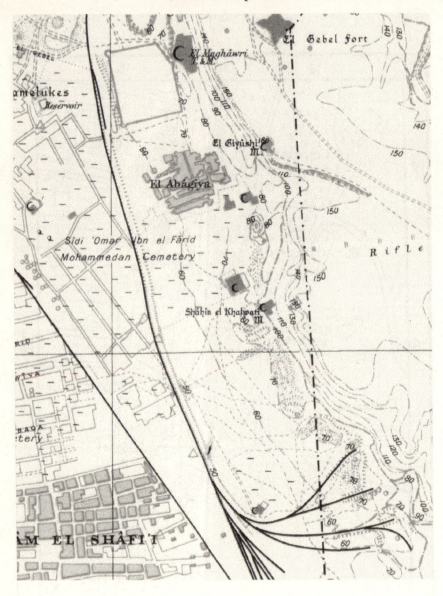

SECTIONAL MAP

XX

UNDER THE MOQATTAM HILLS.

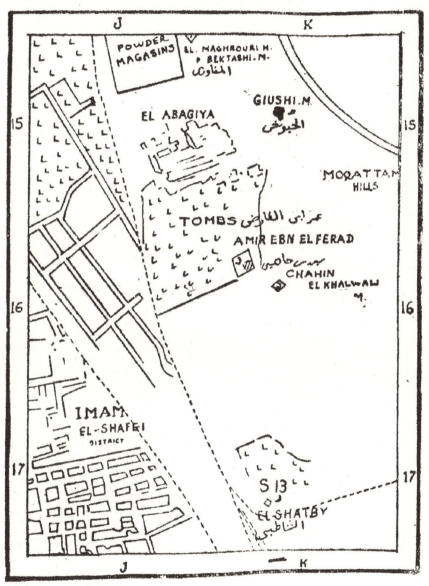

S 13 Shatbi

Duqqi District

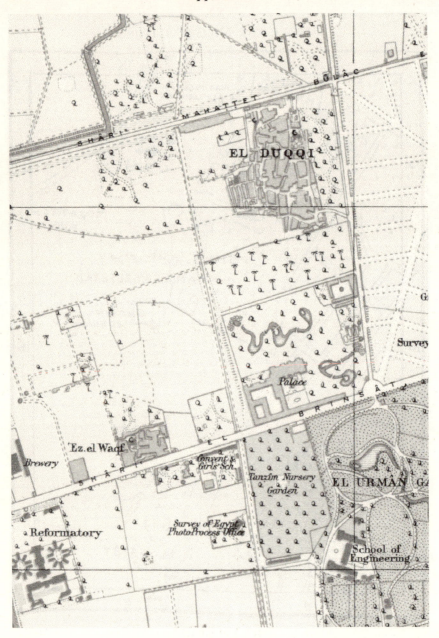

SKETCH MAP
OF
DUQQI DISTRICT.

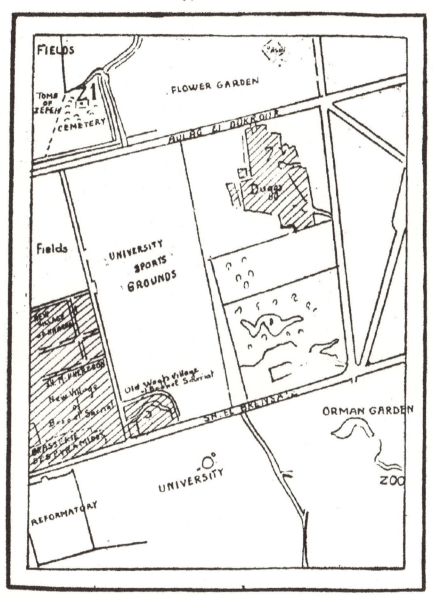

Z 2 Zefeti.

Railway Guide to Upper Egypt

	Moulid	Railway Station
A	6 'Abd el-Rahîm el-Qenâwî	Qenâ
*	18 Abû -l-Tarâbîsh	Helwân
*	19 Abû Hareira	Gîza
	22 Abû Qureish	Zenîn
*B	4 Barsûm el-'Aryân	Ma'sara, Helwân
F	2 Farghâl	Abû Tîg
	5 Fûlî	Minia
G	3 Galâl el-Dîn el-Asyûtî	Asyût
*	9 Girgis	Old Cairo – St. George
*I	1 Ibrâhîm	Matarîya
*	3 Imbâbî	Imbâba
	4 Itmân = 'Uthmân	Pyramids
*M	5 Mariam	Mustarod, Matarîya
*	8 Matrâwî	Matarîya
*	9 Mazlûm	Sharâbîya
*	11 Muhammadî	Demardâsh
*O	2 Oqbi = 'Uqbî	Mît 'Uqba
Q	2 Qărănî (Uweis el-Qărănî)	Wâsta district
*R	1 Rûbî	Medînet el-Fayûm
S	15 Shuhadâ'	Mazghûna
*T	2 Tartûrî	Hatîya, Mît 'Uqba

Note: Those starred appear also in the Delta and Fayûm Railway Guide.

Railway Guide to Delta and Fayûm

	Moulid	Railway Station
A	1 'Ârif	Tîla, Menûf
	18 Abû Tarâbîsh	Helwân
	19 Abû Hareira	Gîza
	21 Abû Qafas	Helmîya
B	1 Barsûm el-'Aryân	Ma'sara, Helwân
D	1 Damiâna	Belqâs
	2 Danyâl	Alexandria
	3 Desûqî	Desûq
G	11 Gûda	Minyet el-Qamh
H	7 Huneidiq	Timsâh, Ismâ'îlîya
I	1 Ibrâhîm	Matarîya
	3 Ismâ'îl Imbâbî	Imbâba
M	5 Mariam	Mustarod, Matarîya
	8 Matrâwî	Matarîya
	9 Mazlûm	Sharâbîya
	11 Muhammadî	Demardâsh
O	2 Oqbi = 'Uqbî	Mît 'Uqba
R	1 Rûbî	Fayûm
S	7 Sayyid el-Bedawî	Tantâ
	14 Shibl	Shuhadâ'
T	1 Takrûrî	Desert between Cairo and Suez
	2 Tartûrî	Hatîya, Mît 'Uqba
W	1 Wafâ'î	Alexandria

Notes:

1 Muharram 1359 = 9 February 1940.

The Moslem Calendar dates from the Flight of the Prophet from Mecca to
    Medina (622 A.D.).

Each month has either 29 or 30 days, being 11 short of the solar year.

1 Tût 1657 = 11 September 1940.

The Coptic Calendar dates from the "Year of the Martyrs" (284 A.D.).

The "little month", Nasi, consists of 5 or 6 intercalary days to complete the solar
    year, the other months having 30 days each.

In addition to these New Year's Days, there is a fourth recognised in Egypt: the
    Jewish, dating from the Creation.

1 Tishri 5701 (A.M. or Anno Mundi) = 3 October 1940.

1 Tishri 5702 (A.M.), Rosh Hashanah = 22 September 1941.

A 1 (vide Map of Delta)

'ÂRIF (SÎDÎ 'ÂRIF BILLÂHI SAYYID MUHAMMAD EL-GAMEL)

(سيدي عارف بالله سيد محمد الجمل)

I have no knowledge of this moulid beyond seeing it mentioned in one of the
Arabic papers in 1357 (1938), which indicates that it is of some importance. It was
to be held near Tîla in Manûfîya province (two stations from Tantâ on the main
line), from Friday, 9 to 16 Gamâd II 1357 (5 to 12 August 1938).

A 2 (vide Sectional Map VIII)

'ABD EL BÂSIT

(عبد الباسط)

This microscopic moulid seems to be always held at or very near the end of
Sha'bân. In 1355 it was 29 Sha'bân, the *waqfa* [eve] of Ramadân (14 November
1936).

It is about the smallest of a group of little moulids held together in a most
impressively picturesque bit of ancient Cairo, about the gates of the Eastern
side of Cairo, Bâb el-Futûh and Bâb el-Nasr. 'Abd el-Bâsit is about equidistant
from the two, and in the Shâri' el-Dabâbîya. Bus 12, between Beit el-Qâdî and
'Abbâsîya, passes the end of this street.

A 3 (vide Sectional Map X)
'ABD EL-DÂ'IM
(عبد الدائم)

I saw this very small moulid on Friday, 16 Muharram 1354 (19 April 1935) and on Friday, 16 Rabî' II 1356 (25 June 1937).

The little modern mosque of Shâri' 'Abd el-Dâ'im is very near Bâb el-Lûq Station, in Shâri' 'Abd el-Dâ'im, which runs parallel to Shâri' el-Dawâwîn, and joins Shâri' Qawâla and Shâri' Kubrî Qasr el-Nîl.

This is a very unpretentious moulid, with few or no secular attractions, but rather impressive from the devotional attitude of its votaries, who with their prayers and "zikrs" fill the mosque and the little street.

A 4 (vide Sectional Map VIII)
'ABD EL-KERÎM
(عبد الكريم)

One of the very small moulids held at or near the end of Sha'bân, in the region of the Babs Futûh and Nasr.

A 5
'ABD EL-QÂSID
(عبد القاصد)

Another small member of the Sutuhîya group, held in the district of the Bâb el-Nasr and Bâb el-Futûh, at or near the end of Sha'bân.

There is a tomb of a Sîdî Qâsid in Shâri' Dâ'im almost opposite the mosque of Shâri' 'Abd el Dâ'im and near Shâri' Qâsid (Bâb el-Lûq), at which I am told a small moulid is held. This I have not confirmed.

QENÂ

A 6 (vide Map of Upper Egypt)
'ABD EL-RAHÎM EL-QENÂWÎ
(سيدي عبد الرحيم القناوي)

This is one of the leading moulids of Egypt, and of provincial feasts I should imagine it to be second only to that of Sayyid el-Bedawî at Tantâ. Being observed at that very holy time, mid-Sha'bân, it clashes always with the moulids of Matarîya and Luxor, and with sundry smaller ones. For example, in 1356 (1937), the beautiful little Moulid of Sîdî Hârûn fell on the same night, but happily that has been avoided since.

Owing to the conflicting attractions of these synchronising feasts and its distance from Cairo, I had never witnessed Sîdî -l-Qenâwî until the year 1357 (1938), when by the hospitality of Dr. E. E. E-P[2], and a companion, who were studying the ways of the Thebans in the Thebaïd, I was enabled to observe its salient features during four full days. They had forsaken for the time their quarters, then an island near Qoft, and engaged rooms at the Hotel Dendara, Qenâ, looking on the main street with its little gardens and canal, through which passed streams of galloping donkeys and camels, music, processions of women, goats, etc.

Crossing the bridge to the vast *enceinte*[3] enclosing a splendid group of sacred buildings, with the shrines of ʿAbd el-Rahîm and el-Qureishî, it was depressing on the preliminary nights to feel at once that the atmosphere even here was somewhat chilled by the kill-joy *Zeitgeist*.

The illuminations were brilliant and beautiful, but the lights fell on "margûhas" [swings], which did not swing, goose-nests which did not turn, and the disappointed faces of many who had come hundreds of miles perhaps to give innocent pleasure and earn a little money; and others who were only too eager to patronise them, but were driven, after performing the religious observance, to just loaf about or visit one rather dull theatre and two or three stalls. Has it suddenly become a sin to watch a shadow show or a *hâwî*, a snake charmer, or a conjurer, *bahlawân*[4] [acrobat] or fire-eater? And poor *Qara Goz*, the Punch of the East, who has been a good Moslem here and in Turkey and elsewhere for hundreds of years! Has he turned heretic in his old age?

On Friday, 13 Shaʿbân, the dullness was relieved by the performance of beautiful horses and skilled picturesque riders, but only for an hour or so before sunset. Saturday, 14 Shaʿbân, the great night, was brilliant enough for minor entertainments to be little missed, and at last the swings and goose-nests performed their functions, though *Qara Goz* came not to life.

The shrines were thronged, and the groups about the numerous "zikrs" were immense and perfectly orderly. Why the good people who preferred to stand should have been coerced into sitting down by the gentle application of whips was not quite obvious, but it tended to silence and attention. I was greeted several times by the *magzûb*, the inspired one[5], whose hypnotic influence and powers

---

2 Evans-Pritchard
3 An enclosure.
4 bahlawân, from the Persian pahlavân, meaning "hero" or "strongman", generally known in the West through its cognate Pahlavi, the name of the former royal family of Iran.
5 Divinely entranced; more specifically, one who, through the shock of divine illumination, has left behind his rational faculties; in this sense magzûb is a dervish term.

Scenes from the Moulid of 'Abd el-Rahîm el-Qenâwî at Qenâ, a town on the Nile near Luxor. McPherson attended this moulid with Evans-Pritchard in 1938.

were so wonderful at the Moulid of Zein el-'Abdîn on 17 Gamâd II 1357 (13 August 1938), as described in connection with that celebration, but here each time I saw him he was just a simple unit in a *zikr*, attracting little interest – illustrating the scripture, "A prophet is not without honour save in his own country and amongst his own people."[6]

We were honoured by an invitation to a great *tashrîfa*, and excellent places, refreshments, etc, near H. E. the Mudîr [governor] of Qenâ, who presided. There were some eloquent speeches and quite brilliant rhetoric.

The *clou* [main point of interest] of the whole moulid was the great *zeffa* on Sunday, 16 Sha'bân 1357 (9 October 1938), which commenced about 9 and went on till sunset. It appeared at about 10.30 in the sacred enclosure; the usual music, dervishes with their banners and insignia, and their "khalîfas" mounted on fine steeds, then after cameleers with great brazen drums, flute players and the rest, came the *tûb*, a sort of *mahmal* in honour of Sîdî 'Abd el-Rahîm; then a repetition of this on a minor scale, in the form of a great number of "tâbûts" arranged like *takhtarawânât* [litters] on splendidly caparisoned camels, each honouring some notable sheikh or *walî*.[7] Amongst other groups the most impressive was a host of the *shurafâ*, waving green boughs and shouting paeons, most suggestive of a Palm Sunday procession at its best, when a multitude of children wave their palms and shout their Hosannas.

After a ceremony at the tent of *tashrîfa*, at which His Excellency was present, the *zeffa* and thousands of the crowd passed through the great necropolis and far into the desert, halting on the return, at the tomb of the Nebî -l-Lûsha, where a remarkable ceremony of rolling in the blessed sand, within the enclosure was enacted. It was highly reminiscent of the rolling women on Fridays at the tomb of the Sultân Maghrûri at the Bektâshî monastery under the Muqattam Hills.

A detail which seemed to us to somewhat discount the piety of the pilgrims and detract from the magnificence of the passage of the *zeffa* through the cemetery was the deplorable condition of this resting place of the dead – though perhaps this is unavoidable and a case of "necessity having no law" – hardly a square metre of the *campo santo* had escaped defilement by human deposits, and in many cases even the tombs had not been spared.

But the great shock and disappointment was the absence in the procession of the Boat[8], which has been a beautiful and distinctive feature of this moulid (shared

---

6 Matthew 13:57 and Mark 6:4.

7 tûb or tôb means "chest", "box". It is related to the word tâbût, "coffin" [E.W. Lane, Arabic-English Lexicon].

8 [McPher.] The boat, though not used, was to be seen. It is very similar to a Cantonese "Slipper Junk", as given in the Illustrated London News of 5 November 1938, p. 836.

Carrying the *tûb* at the Moulid of 'Abd el-Rahîm el-Qenâwî.

only by Sîdî Yûsef of Luxor) for centuries; for thousands of years, in fact, seeing that Egyptologists hold that it was adapted by Islam, as an integral part of this *zeffa* from the processions of Pharaonic times. It must date back to beyond the time of Ramses III for it is pictured on his temple walls at Karnac. I know not who or what caused the suspension of this time-honoured practice, but what a responsibility to tamper with a beautiful and venerable Egyptian custom, part of the very spell of Egypt which holds the admiration and draws the affection of the élite and cultured of the world! The Egyptians live in such a wealth of glorious antiquities, material and spiritual, that they barely realise their priceless worth and are so open-handed and free that they give away obelisks, allow ugly modernisations, suffer old customs to lapse, without realising the irremediable loss of each sacrifice, and that a fragment of the *Glory of Egypt* has departed.

It was well on in the afternoon when the shrine was again reached and circled seven times by the whole company which composed the *zeffa*, a ceremony fore-shadowed all the day by galloping crowds of cameleers, donkey riders and horse-men, a most attractive and exhilarating spectacle. Then it moved on through the town, in the direction of the *mudîrîya*, the good camel which bore the *tûb* showing practical disapproval of any deviation from the traditional route by summarily "baraking" [kneeling][9] and only consenting to rise when adjured by a chorus of cries — "By the Prophet, rise!".

At last, at sunset, arriving at the Mudîrîya, the great ceremony ended by the symbolic scattering of money amongst the crowd, and great was the eagerness to acquire one of the glittering *millièmes* and the *bărăkă* (blessing) attached to it. (Little boxes of these blessed *millièmes* were also given to some of the pious notables who took part, doubtless in order that the *bărăkă* might be extended to the people of their respective villages).

Qenâ is a treasure house of folklore and legend, much of which centres about pilgrims and the pilgrimages, for Qenâ is at the Nile end of the old pilgrim road across the desert to the port of Qoseir[10], and naturally Sîdî ʿAbd el-Rahîm el-Qenâwî is the hero of many of these tales. One of these, of which I heard sundry versions when on the spot has just been retold to me by my gardener, who himself is a "Qenâwî", and put baldly into English is as follows:

Sîdî ʿAbd el-Rahîm was not Qenâwî by birth, but rather because he sancti-fied Qenâ by dying there. When very old and feeble, he came from his home

---

9 bărăkă/yŭbrŭk (verb past/present) mean "to kneel"; but note the noun form bărăkă meaning "blessing" from the same root in the next paragraph.
10 Nearby Qoft (Coptos), just below Qena, is the Nile end of the caravan route.

somewhere remote in the South, and leaving the Nile at Qenâ he was well on his way to Qoseir, when his *nâqa*, [she-]camel, foundered and died. If he had companions, they went on, leaving him to follow painfully on foot. When his poor feet were worn to the bone he proceeded on all fours, till his hands were in an equally bad way. Rolling, crawling on his belly took him a little nearer Qoseir, and therefore his goal of Mecca, and then he tried to move forward by sitting on the sand and jerking himself along, but that only increased the abraded surface.

At length lying helplessly down, he called on the breeze – *"Yâ Sa'd,* go tell the Nebî (*sallâ Allâhu 'alayhi wa-sallam)*[11], that I have done my best, but can go no farther", and the breeze returned and whispered, "The Nebî takes the will for the deed and forbids you attempting more, but to return."

It was a wonderful thing to get a message from the Prophet though a disappointing one, for how was he to return. He did at length, however, get most painfully back as far as Qenâ, but only to die. On his death bed, the Nebî himself came and cheered him and said: "You made all the efforts that a mortal could, almost more, to come to me but could not, so I, the Prophet, have come to you and bless you."

If tales of a different and more material stamp are to be believed, the Qenâ-Qoseir district is a treasure house in quite a different way. There are more than traces of the mines the Romans worked for silver and gems, where now precious deposits of phosphates bring wealth to an Italian Concession and to a Scotch firm, Messrs. Crookson and Son and, I daresay, others; and everywhere (at Qoseir, Safâgâ, Qenâ, etc.) one hears tales of recent finds of precious stones. I know more than one wealthy family at Qenâ, who assure one, *sub rosa,* that their fortune is founded on emeralds the grandfather or some near ancestor lighted upon.

But to return to what is nearer the subject of this book, I recommend readers who desire an unique holiday without quitting Egypt, to voyage down the Red Sea, and having stayed long enough at Qoseir to enjoy its fascinations, to ride a camel to Qenâ, leisurely and with an intelligent guide. If by happy chance they be in Qoseir at mid-Sha'bân, as I was, they will see strange rites amongst the many tombs raised to those who died here on the way back from Mecca: Arabs on brilliantly harnessed and accoutred camels, with *takhtarawânât* (palanquins[12]) on their backs circling the most holy tombs, in the neighbourhood of the old castle. There is much in this suggestive of a moulid, but from what I understood locally,

---

11 *Blessings of God be upon him and peace.* [McPher.] an ejaculation customary when the Prophet is mentioned.
12 A palanquin is carried by men; a takhtarawân is an animal-borne litter.

the celebration was too general to be classed as such, anyway to justify me in attributing it to one particular saint.

Though the writer has paid many visits to the Theban region of Egypt, finding new beauties and interests every time during nearly forty years' residence, he will look back on this last experience of the moulid as something quite unique and recommends both Cairenes and visitors to do the same. The Nile, the blending of "the desert and the sown". the glorious monuments even in beautiful but obscure villages like el-'Uweidât, the hearty kindness and hospitality of rich and poor, the associations of such places in the immediate neighbourhood as Qoft, which gave its name to the country and to a great and ancient cult; and, in addition, this great moulid, and this year a flood forming a sea almost from the Libyan to the Arabian hills, all unite to produce a picture[13] not easily matched. It is only marred by the fear that the trimming down of this splendid moulid will go on till the clipping of the wings of this bright bird of history and tradition will take away all its beauty, but let us hope it will quickly rise again like the phoenix, and that without first being reduced to ashes.

A 7 (vide Sectional Map VI)
'ABD EL-WÂHID
(عبد الواحد)

The date on the one occasion on which I witnessed this moulid was Sunday, 25 Rajab 1355 (11 October 1936).

The *maqâm* is in a little garden on the W. side of Shâri' 'Abd el-Gawâd, the big Bûlâq street commencing in front of the Mosque of Abû -l-'Elâ, not far from where it is crossed by the Darb el-Nasr. Bus 15 passes it. It bears the superscription – "This is the tomb of 'Abd el-Wâhid".

This is a very small moulid hardly extending beyond the garden and a big cafe, in a rather rough and uninteresting neighbourhood. The people flocking about were not of the usual admirable type, but consisted mainly of *turpissimi pueri*[14],

---

13 [McPher.] The Nile Flood. Naturally, the time of the flood does not necessarily coincide with that of the moulid, whose date, mid-Sha'bân, recedes annually eleven days in the solar year. On the occasion described, 16 Sha'bân [1357] being 9 October [1938], about a maximum of land was under water. Mr Evans-Pritchard's quarters at Qoft were so isolated that a little raft of earthen pots bound together with osiers called a *ramûs* was in constant requisition for going and coming. This was pushed by one or two naked lads across a considerable stretch of water, seldom deep enough to necessitate swimming. Qoft, or Qobt, is the ancient Coptus, a city most famous in Egyptian history.

14 "very unpleasant boys" [Latin].

who showed undue interest in me and some English and Dutch friends whom I had brought.

A 8 (vide Sectional Map X)
'ABDULLAH
(عبدالله)

On each of five occasions when I have witnessed this moulid, it has been on a Friday, but the date has varied between 24 Rajab in 1353 (2 November 1934) to 21 Sha'bân in 1355 (6 November 1936).

The mosque of Sheikh 'Abdullah is very accessible not far from Bâb el-Lûq Station, off the Dawâwîn – trams 4, 7 and 12 and several buses. It is on the North side of Shâri' Rihân.[15]

A small moulid, but up to 1352 (1933) very bright – the mosque well filled, and a good *zeffa*; with a few stalls and a lot of people in the open space adjoining; and at a suitable distance *Qara Goz*, fire-eaters, etc. A pleasant feature was the singing in the little side streets, mostly arranged by private parties, often accompanied by simple music.

What gave rise to the savage attack in 1352 (1933), when the space by the mosque was cleared most summarily, even of women sitting under its walls? Certainly, it was not to keep the way open for traffic, for there is none through this sort of courtyard. It survived rough treatment in 1353 (1934), but it was nearly crushed out of existence in 1355 (1936), so that I did not go in 1356 (1937) but am told it appeared a vanishing quantity. In 1355, however, (and I daresay other years) there was a small *zeffa* between 10 and 11 in the evening, consisting of about half a dozen sections of the *tarîqa* Hâmidîya Shâzlîya. One singing party also had survived and proved very popular well away behind the mosque; but this also seemed to have disappeared in 1357 (1938), and about all I saw at the door of a nearly empty mosque was a man with a handcart and a disgruntled look, hoping to sell sweet potatoes.

---

15 [McPher.] Kemp, in his *Egyptian Illustration* gives a handsome wood-cut of the Tomb of Sh. Rihân, who doubtless gave his name to the street. I can find no trace of the tomb nor record of the Sheikh; both seem to have passed into the Ewigkeit [German for eternity] in recent times.

A 9 (vide Sectional Map XVII)
'ABDULLAH EL-HAGR
(سيدي الشيخ عبد الله الحجر)

This very small one-day moulid was held in the year 1357 (1938) on 29 Sha'bân
(22 October), the eve of Ramadân, about the *tâbût* of Sheikh 'Abdullah which is
outside his mosque. The superscription indicates that this saint is Huseinî (of the
line of the Imâm Husein).

Being close to Sayyida 'Aysha, trams 13 and 23 pass it. It seems to be mainly a
children's moulid and, being in a very attractive quarter, is a pretty sight.

The *zeffa* promised for the afternoon, as I was assured had been the case in
previous years, did not appear.

This year 1359 (1940), I found the moulid in action on the same date as in
1357, the eve of Ramadân, Wednesday, 2 October 1940. Its characteristics were
unchanged, that of being a children's moulid being decidedly emphasised.

A 10 (vide Sectional Map XVII)
'ABDULLAH KHAFÎR EL-DARB
(عبد الله خفير الدرب)

On each of the two occasions on which I witnessed this picturesque little moulid,
the date was 27 Sha'bân, the latter date being 27 Sha'bân 1354 (24 November
1935).

The *maqâm* of the sheikh is in a weird, rather fascinating spot behind the prison
behind *manshîya* Muhammad 'Alî and near the Tombs of the Mamelukes; but
though one feels rather out of the world there, it is a bare minute from the tram
track leading to Imâm el-Shâfe'î, tram 13.

It is a very small moulid, in one bright street, in which the *maqâm* is situated.
There is a very eager crowd, mostly of children, so that it takes the local sheikhs
all their time to prevent the holy gate being crashed. Over this is the inscription
"This is the *maqâm* of 'Abdullah Khafîr el-Darb". The only counter attractions
seemed to be a small amusement show and a big café.

A 11
ABÛ 'UMEIRA
(سيدي أبو عميرة)

This elusive little moulid near Kerdâsa requires considerable enterprise. This, I
am told, is rewarded by its general picturesqueness and the beauty of its position
between the desert and the sown.

Having been let down more than once by wrong dates, I succeeded at last in nearly reaching it by bus from the English Bridge[16], on Thursday, 11 Gamâd II 1353 (20 September 1934), but found myself separated from it by flooded land. I might have obtained a felucca, on the chance of finding a donkey at the moulid, to take me to Mena House, or possibly to Gîza, but preferred to return as I came, by the bus which brought me, as it was the last. It was then about 10 o'clock.

I think it would be better approached by donkey or camel from the Pyramids, but now that the basin system of irrigation is abolished, it should be approachable by bicycle or even by car via Bûlâq el-Dakrûr, Zenîn and Saft.

A 12
ABÛ ATÂTA
(شيخ ابو اتاته)

I cannot give an exact date for this moulid, as on the two occasions on which I have been present and noted it, the chief night was 17 Rabî' I 1348 (22 August 1929) and 6 Gamâd I 1353 (16 August 1934), respectively.

The tomb of Sîdî Abû Atâta is in a village called el-'Ezba -l-Gharbîya near the Gîza Reformatory, but on the other side of the level crossing over the railway and of the canal, about half a mile to the south.

It is best approached from Cairo by taking tram 14 or 15, or bus 6, via Zamâlek to the Gîza Mudîrîya, turning at right angles up Shâri' el-Brinsât, crossing the line at the end, turning left and following the canal. The road admits of a car.

It is a good typical country moulid with an earnest crowd about the tomb, and a merry scene in a field near-by, with *Qara Goz* and the usual shows, swings, &c., but I am told that it has lost much of its former vogue recently, and this year 1359 (1940) it appears not to have been held at all.

A 13 (vide Sectional Map XIII)
ABÛ 'AZÂ'IM (SÎDÎ MUHAMMAD MÂDÎ ABÛ -L-'AZÂ'IM)
(سيدي محمد ماضي أبو العزائم)

Sîdî Muhammad Abû -l-'Azâ'im is probably the most recent local saint to be "raised to the altars" of Islam, having died as recently as 1936 (1355)[17], about seven centuries later than, for example, Sayyid el-Bedawî.

It is reassuring and stimulating to find that the modern world can still produce a saint and recognise his sanctity, even to its *public* recognition by *moulid*, *zikr* and *zeffa*, and the other venerable dervish ceremonies. The writer deems himself

---

16 Kubrî el-Galâ', from the bottom of Gezîra to Duqqî.
17 McPherson offers two dates of death, 1936 and 1937.

very fortunate in having made the acquaintance of the little sect of the 'Azmîya and its present venerable head and *khalîfa*, the son of Sîdî Mâdî Abû -l-'Azâ'im, and that through the curious accident of a little vagary of the moon, which upset the calendar.

I was returning from the Citadel Mosque on Sunday evening, 10 September 1939 (26 Rajab 1358) according to the official calendar and others which I have seen, and therefore the *Leilet el-Isrâ'*, or *Leilet el-Mi'râg*, when the miraculous ride of the Prophet to Jerusalem and paradise is celebrated – for it had been ruled by the high authorities that the moon contradicted the calendar and that the following night was the true night of the "Ascension"; and minarets which had been lit up were put out and the ceremony at Muhammad 'Alî Mosque postponed to the Monday evening – and I was on my way to the Moulid of Tashtûshî to see if that had suffered the same postponement, when I noticed a great confluence under the Bâb Zuweila, with innumerable lamps and much chanting.

I think everyone who knows Cairo is acquainted with this wonderful city gate, hung with votive offerings of hair, teeth, scraps of clothing, &c., behind which the holy *walî* is thought by some to be concealed. I thought at first that the ceremony was exclusively in honour of the *walî* of the Gate, but noticed that a large *beiraq* (banner) was inscribed – "The Egyptian Order of the 'AZMÎYA" a sect quite new to me, and on asking the bearer of the *beiraq*, he told me that this was the Moulid of Sîdî Muhammad Mâdî Abû -l-'Azâ'im, and the *zeffa* had come from Sidna Husein and was on its way to the *tâbût* (shrine) of the dead saint. Going there too, I was most hospitably entertained by the living head of the order, the Sheikh Ahmad Mâdî Abû -l-'Azâ'im, sheikh of the Order of the 'Azmîya of the Valley of the Nile.

He told me that this was only the ante-penultimate night and invited me to the remaining celebrations, especially that of the final night, Tuesday, 28 Rajab 1358 (12 September 1939). The *tâbût* is in his palace in Hâret el-Farîq, between Sultân Hanafî and the *khalîg* –" Palace of the 'Azmîya Family".

Picking up the *zeffa* on Tuesday evening about 9.30, I was interested and impressed by the rites which preceded the "zikrs", the reading of an address by "the sheikh", punctuated by exclamations from the company of "God is Great", Allâhu Akbar, and in praise of the dead sheikh, and finally of "Long live the *khalîfa*, the Sheikh Ahmad Abû -l-'Azâ'im".

I should like to know what are the initial stages in the recognition of a saint, and what rites go to the making of a *walî*. The Vatican examines a "cause" usually over a period of many years, though occasionally, as in the case of Teresa, "The Little Flower" – whose cult at her basilica at Shubrâ is shared by Moslems and

Jews as well as by Catholic and Orthodox Christians – a few months proves sufficient. A "Devil's Advocate" is appointed to criticise the postulant's claims and advance anything that should preclude canonisation. Miracles must be proved, and in the *gradus ad altare*[18] a candidate is "venerable" and "blessed", before he is styled "saint". I have little doubt that the process is somewhat parallel in Islam, and crave *mehr licht* [19].

*

Since penning the above lines on this *Latter-day Saint,* the further light I desired has been supplied by the kindness and erudition of Dr. Evans-Pritchard, the sociologist. This information dissipates my assumption that Islamic saintship may result from hierarchical investment, for in this case at least it is clearly established by popular suffrage, more or less within the dervish orbit, for Sheikh Muhammad Mâdî began as an initiate of the sect of the Shâzlîya, making the "'Azmîya" an offshoot from that great *tarîqa.*

Sheikh Abû 'Azâ'im, as he came to be known, was born in 1870 at Desûq but settled in the village of Mutahharîya in Minyâ Province, Upper Egypt, which became the headquarters of his sect, the 'Azmîya.

He felt that he had the mission of a religious reformer, and his enthusiasm and, on the whole, mild and laudable Shazliyan tenets attracted many, especially minor officials in Egypt and the Sudan, during twenty years' service under the Egyptian Ministry of Education and the Education Department of the Sudan Government; but in 1915 his views and actions became so tendentious that he was discharged from the post he then held at Gordon College. His nightly "zikrs", secret meetings, and strenuous sermons brought him numerous disciples but created mistrust in official quarters, and he was sent back from the Sudan to Egypt.

There he voiced ideas which were on the one hand almost the stern tenets of the Wahhâbites, mixed with polemics against other sects than his own and political extravagances; and on the other liberal, even to alleged laxity, especially in the treatment of women. He is credited with having had a magnetic attraction for the other sex and accused by some of having acquired much of his considerable wealth by traffic in *hegâbât* (charms) and such like, not excluding the *poculum amoris.*[20] Some of his money went in the purchase of two printing presses, and at that time

---

18 "By steps unto the altar…" (*vide* Exodus 20:26 Vulgate).
19 "More light on the matter".
20 "Drinking cup of love", i.e., love potion [Latin].

his political activities included articles to *El-Akhbar* [newspaper]. This side of
his "mission" was most marked at the time of the entry of Turkey into the war[21].

His enthusiasm for a parliamentary career was damped by the antagonism of
students who actually stoned him on one occasion at least.

Later, except for occasional violent political articles, he reverted to the more
saintly character of his earlier years and was well known in Egypt as *fiqî*[22] and a
preacher until he died in 1937 (1356) amongst many devoted disciples and adher-
ents. His vogue in the Sudan was at one time remarkable, but after reaching its
zenith in the early twenties it has waned very considerably there.

On the other hand, he seems to be held in great and increasing esteem in Egypt,
especially in the Cairo district.

*

A 14
ABÛ BADÎR
(الشيخ أبو بدير)

This extremely small moulid is one of the many held at mid-Sha'bân; or such
was the case on the only date I have seen it, 14 Sha'bân 1352 (1 December 1933).

The tomb of the sheikh is in an '*atfa* [alley] of his name, off the Bâb el-Sha'rîya.
The entrance to the '*atfa* is passed by bus 12 from the Beit el-Qâdî.

A 15
ABÛ DEIF
(الشيخ أبو ضيف)

Reported as one of the Imâm el-Shâfe'î group, held in Sha'bân, but not so far
located by me.

A 16 (vide Sectional Map VI)
ABÛ -L-'ELÂ
(السلطان أبو العلاء)

I enjoyed the fine Moulid of Sultân Abû -l-'Elâ repeatedly early in this century,
well before the war of 1914–18. It was very big and popular, and extended not
only all around and about the mosque, but far into the little Bûlâq lanes on the

---

21 World War I.
22 In Egypt, a reciter of the Qurân. Otherwise, faqîh (with the "h"), an Islamic jurisprudent or
theologian.

other side of the main street. There was a sober brilliance about it; not many secular shows but many singing sheikhs in the shops and houses, and people were allowed to collect and listen and enjoy in peace – not irritated and hustled, and even beaten, as of recent years and goaded to a sort of perpetual motion.

Then came tragedy! A part of the mosque collapsed with tragic results. It was taken deeply to heart, not so much the loss of life and the expense of repairs, but the shock that so holy a place should fall down. "Why did not Sultân Abû -l-'Elâ intervene?" asked some pious simple souls. It was left to another to heal broken spirits, for the young King Farouk, soon after his accession made publicly his Friday prayer in the now restored mosque and, as it were, took away its reproach and set it gloriously up again. I have seldom seen in Cairo so large and enthusiastic a crowd as that which assembled in Bûlâq on that propitious day; nor people more joyous than some of the sheikhs who frequented the mosque. One remarked, "We have walked in darkness these twenty years, and now Farouk has brought light. He must be our *khalifa* as well as our King!"

This happy event was followed by the joyous renewal of the moulid on a generous scale, and immensely popular it was. The *apodosis* was on Thursday, 15 Rabî' II 1356 (24 June 1937), and it was repeated on Thursday, 10 Rabî' II 1357 (9 June 1938), and Thursday, 13 Rabî' II 1358 (1 June 1939).

This famous mosque is most easily found even by strangers to Cairo. It is about a hundred yards to the east of Bûlâq Bridge, in Shâri' Fu'ad el-Awwal, and is passed by trams 13, 14, 15 and 33, and buses 6 and 15. Tram 7 passes through the amusement park.

This collection of booths, tent theatre, the *piste à la mort* of Billy Williams, and innumerable stalls, is discreetly distant from the mosque where prayers, "zikrs", and "zeffas" are undisturbed, and is beautifully and picturesquely placed on the bank of the Nile; and a *ringa* and a *Qara Goz* and some other attractions exist in a small side street.

The popularity of the Sultân Abû -l-'Elâ is largely due to his being a local saint. 'Abd el-Wahhâb el-Sha'rânî in *el-Tabaqât el-Kubrâ* refers to the head of the sainted Abû -l-'Elâ being enshrined in Cairo, at Bûlâq near the Nile. Natives of the spot assure me that that is so, but that his "sir" keeps watch in the Nile, much as the spirit of another *walî* near Qoft (Sîdî Mas'ûd according to some, Sîdî Qenâwî to others, or, acclaimed at Minyâ, their patron saint Sîdî Fûlî) prevents any crocodile passing north. If it runs the spiritual blockade it is forced to turn belly upwards, becoming an easy prey. I have been asked why steamers blow their sirens in passing near Bûlâq Bridge. I have little doubt that it is in honour of Abû -l-'Elâ, though possibly the whole group of "maqams" in the vicinity of his mosque are considered also. These include Sîdî Muwaffaq who has his own moulid, as has Ahmadein, Hilâl who has, or had his *zeffa* and has a very beautiful little tomb, and Sheikh Mustafa, and others.

I am told by the Sheikh Abû -l-'Elâ Badawî of 'Agûza, that the reason why his mosque was allowed to fall into such a crumbling condition was a stern injunction against building or repairing laid by the *Sultân* himself. This is not a unique instance of such a veto: the Sultân Hanafî had the same fear for his beautiful mosque if tampered with, and put such a vigorous embargo on repairing, that until recently a part of the structure has been almost hidden by beams and wooden buttresses.

Floreas[23], Abû -l-'Elâ! May nothing but blessing rest in the future on your head, and your mosque, and your Nile, and your moulid.

In the war year 1359 (1940), Abû -l-'Elâ presented such an unusual aspect, that a special note is necessary.

The moulid was held on its day of predilection, Thursday, and at the normal date, 15 Rabî' II 1359 (23 May 1940), and its "zikrs" and religious side were nearly normal, except that I observed no procession of sufficient amplitude and solemnity to be regarded as a proper *zeffa*.

Italy had not then declared war, but there was a practice black-out whilst the moulid was developing, and throughout there was no trace of an amusement park in its usually charming site by the Nile and Bûlâq Bridge, probably owing to the special precautions and regulations concerning bridges. But an enclosure on the south side of Shâri' Fu'ad el-Awwal, two or three hundred metres east of the mosque[24] contained swings, some gaming and other tables and a considerable theatre. This ran for some weeks. I noticed that the dwarf who has been frequently referred to in these pages had found his duplicate, quite a promising *sosie*[25].

On the great night or rather afternoon there were very amusing attractions behind the mosque and in the region of Sheikh Muwaffaq, but these were scattered at sunset. There remained many singing groups and large "zikrs", and perhaps the most striking thing to a visitor, was the beautiful view of the interior from the immense doors at the back of the mosque, which had been thrown wide open. The great groups of worshippers, and the fine detail of the architecture and the decorations were colourful and impressive to a degree.

The most popular object by the tomb of Sheikh Muwaffaq was quite new to

---

23 "May you flourish" [Latin].

24 [McPher.] This small amusement park continued to function after the moulid.

25 A "double", someone of striking resemblance to another [Fr.].

me, and I think to moulids. It consisted of a large canvas globe blown up like an immense football, revolving slowly about a vertical axis (connecting its north and south poles) and painted in sections with the name of some country on each. Owing to the fading light, to the crowd, and to the fact that at this moment it was raided by the police, I only made out Germany, Italy and America. Stakes were laid on a board painted in corresponding colours.

BENÎ MAZÂR

A 17 (vide Map of Upper Egypt)
ABÛ -L-LEIL
(أبو الليل)
This is a Benî Mazâr moulid, held in 1357 (1938) in Gamâd I and said to be important, at least locally, but any definite information about it is lacking to me.

HELWÂN

A 18 (vide Map of Upper Egypt)
ABÛ -L-TARÂBÎSH
(أبو الطرابيش)
Though never there myself, English friends and others who were, on Sunday 10 Zû -l-Higga 1355 (21 February 1937), told me that it was a big and interesting moulid, in a picturesque desert setting.

It is just outside Helwân – an easy walk or donkey ride.

A 19 (vide Map of Upper Egypt)
ABÛ HAREIRA
(سيدي أبو هريرة)
I have come across a letter written several years ago to one of our leading anthropologists, covering so much of the ordinary moulid ground, on the secular side, that I append it verbatim. As the letter is to illustrate a specific cult of very ancient origin, it naturally does not emphasise the religious side. This, however, is by no means neglected, witness the meetings of the *turŭq*, the "zikrs", readings in the mosques, pilgrimages to the tomb, &c., and the dervish element rather dissociates itself from the kaleidoscopic charivaria[26] which included the "royal" car, and sundry others of lads dressed up as girls, in its elements. The

---

26 Noisy public spectacle, from *caribaria*, a headache [late Latin].

elimination of the more carnal parts has not, however, heightened the spiritual side, if one might judge from the dingy, dismal condition into which I found the tomb to have fallen when visited subsequent to the date of the appended letter, and the diminished number of pilgrims. It told of poverty and the need of some wealthy benefactors.

A visit at dawn on the great day of the moulid, which as I have pointed out, is also the most characteristically Egyptian feast of the year, Shamm el-Nesîm, reveals many people rising from sleep in the fields to greet the rising sun. That this is a remnant of the worship of Ra is evidenced by the fact that at the same moment, a host which has passed the night in the fields and roads about the obelisk at Matarîya is rising for the same purpose; this on the very site of the Temple of Ra and of the rising of the Phoenix.

In spite of the great veneration in which Abû Hareira is held, especially at Gîza, I have learnt nothing consistent or reliable about him by local enquiry.

If, as I suppose, he is the Abû Hareira chronicled by the Sheikh 'Abd el-Wah-hâb el Sha'rânî (*vide* Vol. I, p 22 of his "el-Tabaqât el-Kubrâ"), he dates back to the first century of the *Hegira*, as he is recorded to have died at Medina at the age of 78 in the *khilâfa* [Califate] of Mu'âwiya, and, as we know, Mu'âwiya opposed the Imâm 'Alî, and usurped the *khilâfa* from the Imâm Hasan, grandson of the Prophet, and was responsible for the great revolt in Egypt.[27]

It seems to be one of the many cases of the body of an associate or descendant of the Prophet's immediate family being brought to Egypt by the Fatimites – doubtless with a view to ingratiating the Egyptians in spite of their dislike for the Fatimite *heresies.*

Abû Hareira's humble, simple character, his love of poverty and of God's creatures, human or otherwise, and his excessive devotion remind one somewhat of St. Francis of Assisi. He was passionately fond of a little cat, loved to serve anyone, rich or poor, carrying bundles of faggots on his head or performing any menial act. He is said to have commenced his day by uttering twelve thousand praises to God,[28] and to have so disliked abating his thanks to the Creator that he divided the normal time of sleep into three periods, during one of which his wife was responsible for this observance, his black woman slave (*gâria*) for another, and he himself for the third.

---

27 If this Abû Hareira is the man chronicled by el Sha'rânî, the correct spelling of the name would be Abû Hurayra ("father of the little cat").

28 "He, may God be pleased with him, used to pray 12,000 times daily." McPherson's source is presumably the previously cited *el-Tabaqât el-Kubrâ.*

It is strange that he had a marked dread of death, and wept bitterly towards the end, saying "How can I know whether I shall wake in heaven or in hell?"

The Moulid of Sheikh Abû Hareira (Gîza)

The Professor of Sociology, Egyptian University.

Dear Professor,

When the other day we were discussing the lamentable lapse of old Egyptian festivals and picturesque ceremonies, and even the threatened suppression of the moulids, under present vandalistic and kill-joy influences, you were struck by my mention of certain phallic elements in the Giza *zeffa* of a quarter of a century ago. I did not realise that these had an anthropological and scientific value, but as you assure me that such is the case, I will put on record from memory what I witnessed with another Englishman (whom you know and who will confirm this) at the Moulid of Sheikh Abu Harera in or about the year 1908.

The *zawia* or tomb of the Sheikh is, as you are aware, close to the Giza Market, a vast space enlarged on this occasion to enable primitive horse races to be run. These, which I presume were the opening ceremony (apart of course from "zikrs" and other Moslem observances), were about to start when I arrived at about 10 a.m. and being mounted on a very swift arab I was rash enough to take part. Competitors were allowed to use a stick to beat their opponents' horses, or to baulk the riders, exactly as in the *Palio* raced at Siena on the Feast of the Assumption. After a little preliminary play to get used to these peculiar conditions, we raced and I won amidst vociferous and generous applause, partly because "El-Burâq" was better fed than the other horses and had had good practice at the Gezira Sporting Club, but more I think through the mild use they made of their sticks where I was concerned. My triumph was short-lived, for I was entirely out-classed in the management of my mount at the finish, they pulling up almost in a length and I committing some havoc in the crowd before I could stop. Riders and onlookers took this with the same chivalrous good temper. Even the people whom I fear I hurt, refused any compensation; but a picturesque vendor of *Qara Sus* or *'Erq Sus,* a drink made mainly of sarsaparilla, I fancy, was on the spot and I bought up his stock for the liquid delectation of *quicumque vult*[29]. As I rode away, I heard his cry, sibil Allah, ya

---

29 "Whosoever wishes"; also, the opening words in Latin of the Athanasian Creed.

'atshanin![30] (Fountain of the Lord, oh ye thirsty ones) and saw him thoroughly well-mobbed.

There was a great crowd about the tomb, with acrobats, conjurers, dancing girls and the rest; and the streets were so thronged that my progress was most difficult, and I had to take a short cut through the harlots' quarter, almost deserted at that early hour and out of the route of the *zeffa*. At the beginning of the *suq* [bazaar], the main street of the little town, further advance was impossible, and I was immobilised for quite an hour watching the pageant pass, and there I spotted W., another Englishman in the same condition. After the usual *turuq* [Sufi orders] with their banners, music, sashes and insignia, came endless carts bearing groups dressed up to represent some guild or some fancy, and others drawn by one horse or donkey and bearing thirty or more children and women in gala attire, then I noticed approaching a large cart with a raised platform at the front. At the centre of this was a throne, and before it was standing a very handsome lad of fourteen or fifteen, perfectly naked except for a little crown, and an open bolero of crimson stuff embroidered in gold, and bearing little epaulettes, through which almost invisible cords passed. Brightly coloured circles had been painted round his navel and nipples. A *wazir* in gorgeous robe adopted from *syces'* costumes stood on each side of the monarch, one holding a gilt chamber pot and the other a basin, which with low *obéissance* they presented to him at intervals. Musicians beat *tars*, *tablas* and *darabukkas*[31] on a somewhat lower platform behind. But the amazing thing was that the little king's virile organ was dancing to the music in seeming excitement, turning to the right and left, dipping down, and then flying up and down as though actuated by a spring. The royal car paused for a minute or more a few yards from where I was, and I could detect a fine cord attached to the anterior portion of this marionette of flesh and blood, passing under one of the epaulettes and descending from behind to the lower part of the cart, where obviously a string-puller was concealed.

I did not witness any of the subsequent proceedings, but as far as I am aware, they were such as are common to any moulid.

Though I witnessed the *zeffa* on two or three rather more recent occasions, but before the war, I saw nothing of the "royal" car. I do not know if it was officially suppressed.

The war 1914–18 nearly obliterated this moulid, though of recent years it

---

30 More correctly, "for the sake of God, O thirsty ones".
31 The târ is a tambourine. The tabla and the darabûkka are types of bongo-shaped Arab drum.

Mid-Sha'bân celebrations at Qoseir

Sword-dancing

Circling the tombs

has recovered some little of its ancient glory; as is also the case with the Giza weekly fair, *suq el-talat*.

It is worth noting that the Moulid of Sheikh el-Harera does not (now at any rate), follow the Moslem calendar observed by nearly all the others, but is held on Shamm el-Nesim, the Easter Monday of the Coptic and Greek Churches: and I suspect the *Zeffa*, with its phallic elements, dates back to pre-Islamic, and pre-Christian festivals in honour of Spring.

Yours,
J. W. McP.

QOSEIR

A 20
ABÛ HASAN EL-'ABÂBDÎ
(سيدي أبو حسن العبابدي)
Information is required about this, as I have heard it referred to in the Qoseir district and to the South of that Red Sea town, as of considerable importance but can ascertain nothing definite. Zû -l-Qa'da was mentioned as the month of the moulid, but this needs confirmation.

Dr. Evans-Pritchard who has studied the important Bedawin tribe of the 'Abâbda, which is met with mainly from Qenâ to Aswân, confirms the existence of a moulid which, he says, is unusual in those regions, except in the case of that of the Prophet (cf. Moulid el-Nebî), but cannot at present give me the exact date and place.

HELMÎYA

A 21
ABÛ QAFAS
(شيخ أبو قفص)
Though I have often heard this referred to as well worth seeing, my information has always been too late to enable me to witness it.

Dr.R..., who lives close to the Helmîya Station, says it is held under his windows, which fairly well locates it. I gather from what he and others have told me that the date is in or about Rajab.

ZENÎN

A 22
ABÛ QUREISH
(شيخ أبو قريش)

I made a rather stormy acquaintance with this moulid about 1348 (1929), as I arrived at about 9.30, just as the police raided it, pulled down tents and utterly stopped it. I believe this step was justified by the moulid having waited for no authorisation. It went smoothly enough on Thursday, 13 Gamâd I 1353 (23 August 1934) and again Thursday, 15 Gamâd II 1357 (11 August 1938).

It is situated at the village of Zenîn, and may be reached by the Kerdâsa bus from the English Bridge. In 1357 (1938) taxis at one piastre for a place were plying frequently between these two, long after the very infrequent buses had ceased to run. It may also be visited by motor by the way of Shâri' el-Brinsât crossing the line at the Brasserie des Pyramides and following rather rough country tracks. It is a simple country moulid, lively and picturesque, and well worth a visit, especially before the light has gone, and the beauty of Zenîn with its water and encircling vegetation can be appreciated.

On the secular side I saw no theatres in 1357 (1938), nor shows, though plenty of amusing and popular stalls, but was considerably surprised to find that all the big cafés had their music and dancing girls. There was a lot of merry feasting as eight camels had been slain earlier in the day.

As for the sheikh, Abû Qureish, I could elicit no information sufficiently reliable to put down.

A 23 (cf. Sectional Map VI)
ABÛ -L-SEBĀ'
(أبو السباع)

The date of this seems very erratic, but on each occasion when I have seen the moulid and noted the date, it has been held on a Thursday, but the month has varied from Rabî' I in 1348 to Gamâd I in 1353. In 1356 it was on 8 Rabî' II (17 June 1937).

The mosque of Abû -l-Sebâ' is at the Saptia end of Shâri' 'Abd el-Gawâd, the big new street of Bûlâq, a rather low district preserving some of the traditions of the old port of Cairo, and not singularly picturesque – bus 15 or tram 4.

Though much reduced, it is a big moulid with, on the secular side, theatres, *Qara Goz*, "ringas", &c, and in several recent years the famous *piste à la mort* of Billy Williams.

A 24
ABÛ ZEID
(أبو زيد)

Reported as one of the Imâm el-Shâfe'î group in Sha'bân, but not located.

A 25
'ADAWÎYA
(شيخ العدوية)

Reported as one of the small moulids in the Imâm el-Shâfe'î district and following that of the Imâm, in Sha'bân. I have not, however, been able to locate it.

A 26
'AGÂN
(سيدي محمد العجان)

One of the smallest of moulids, but gaily beflagged, held at mid-Sha'bân in a small street off Shâri' el-Khairât. Sayyida Zeinab trams 4, 7 and 12, and buses 3 and 9 pass this way.

Over the tomb is written, "This is the tomb of Sîdî Muhammad el-'Agân."

A 27 (cf. Sectional Map VI)
AHMADEIN
(سيدي الأحمدين)

Though present on Sunday, 30 Gamâd I 1353 (9 September 1934), and on one other occasion, whose date I omitted to note, I have not been able to hit the right day for several years, and if still held it must be at a widely different time.

The *maqâm* of Sîdî Ahmadein in a little street of the same name, off the new broad one in front of the mosque of Abû -l-'Elâ, is very easily reached, as it is only a couple of minutes' walk from that well-known mosque. Bus 15 passes it; and bus 6 and trams 13, 14 and 15, which all traverse Shâri' Fu'ad el-Awwal, stop by Abû -l-'Elâ.

The street is very picturesque with two tombs of sheikhs in addition to the mosque and *maqâm* of Sîdî Ahmadein, which last bears the inscription over its portal – "The tomb of Sîdî Ahmadein".

The secular side is almost nil, the great feature being the *zeffa* in the late afternoon. This comes from the Saptia direction, arriving at the tomb by the winding Shâri' Wagha. It is very peaceful and well attended, and I hope to find that it is still flourishing.

A 28 (cf. Sectional Map XI)
ANSÂRÎ

(سيدي محمد الأنصاري)

This beautiful little moulid has been held on each of the occasions on which I have been present in the last week of Sha'bân: on 26 in 1354 (23 November 1935) and 1355 (11 November 1936), and on 27 in 1357 (21 October 1938). In 1356 (1937) it was to have been on 26, but was put off owing to the death of a member of the family of Sheikh Madbûlî, who I understand is an Ansârî descended from the founder. This year 1359 (1940), it was on 26 Sha'bân (29 September 1940).

It is held in the tiny Hâret el-Ansârî, off Shâri' Muhammed 'Alî, a few minutes' walk from the 'Ataba[32] on the right. The *tâbût* is just within the main door of the house at the back of the *hâra*, where there is also ample space for praying and for "zikrs".

It is the fascination of moulids that, though one is liable to shocks and disappointments, there is the chance of witnessing scenes of amazing beauty or interest and of being carried out of this mechanised *blasé* age into the sort of oriental atmosphere one reads and dreams about. This tiny moulid has so delighted and impressed me that I venture to describe what I have heard and seen in some detail.

On Saturday, 26 Sha'bân 1354 (23 November 1935), I was enjoying another very pleasant and classic little moulid opposite the Court of Appeal in the Qantaret el-Amîr Husein, that of the Sheikh Nûr el-Dîn el-Marsafa, when we were visited by a singularly well-appointed *zeffa*, with *khalîfa* mounted with his little son on a richly caparisoned horse, and expert musicians striking huge tambourines above their heads as they danced. When they had well heated their instruments in the flames of the *mesh'al* which always accompany these processions, their unisons were so exact and so powerful that they suggested volleys of musketry. Leaving the underground Mosque of Sîdî Marsafa, I passed with the little party through the Street of the Thunderbolt (Shâri' el-Suwayqa), where the little Mosque of Sîdî Arba'în was duly saluted. This I noticed was be-flagged for a coming moulid. Then, crossing Shâri' Muhammed 'Alî, we were welcomed by a noble and venerable sheikh, referred to as the Sheikh el-Rifâ'î, at the door of the shrine of Sîdî -l-Ansârî. Over this is written: "The Moulid of Sîdî Muhammad el-Ansârî".

A religious service with *zikr* commenced at once, the patriarch presiding with a whip – and using it on any of the congregation lax in the observance of the

---

32 El-'Ataba 'l-Khadrâ Square, at Ezbekîya.

custodia oculorum[33], or falling into the sin of *admiratio populi*[34]. They took it in a humble and contrite spirit – except one impenitent who grumbled. He received a further flagellation and was cast out into "outer darkness".

Meanwhile, under the flags and lamps of the *hôsh* [courtyard], more and more musical instruments were brought, quaint and some of great beauty, particularly the *naqrâzân*, a lovely hemisphere of glowing copper, richly decorated at the rim, a most attractive form of kettle drum; or *tabl shâmî*. The genus drum was largely represented, ranging from the tiny *bâz*, to what was, I suppose, an immense *tabl baladî*, but which suggested a British military drum, and the species *naqqâra* was conspicuous in various forms and sizes, some of these *naqâqîr* (the plural) being of fine material and chaste workmanship, almost as decorative as the *naqrâzân*. Of tambourines (*târât*), I noticed not only the great shallow *târ*, so effective at the *zeffa*, called *bandîr qadrî*, but a deeper type, the *bandîr 'arûsi*, and also the little *riqq*. There were cymbals of brass, similar to but larger than those used in Coptic services, *kâs*; and of wind instruments, the little *sibs*, about eight inches long, and the *nay*, twice that length. This is sometimes called the "dervish's flute", because employed as on this occasion to lead the sacred orchestra.

The players seemed trained musicians, and their souls were in the music. The time and harmony were wonderful, and there was mystery in it, enhanced by the *mise en scène*. I have very rarely enjoyed such a musical treat. It will be noted that this fine effect was produced without any brass wind instruments, or any of the common forms of the *zummâra* and *arghûl*. Strings also were excluded, such as the *qânûn*, the *'ûd* and the *kamanga*, all delightful in their right places, but perhaps suggestive of *'awâlim*[35], or savouring of the theatre, or concert, or such as the *ringa* and *sistrum* of the *bûza* booth.

Looking forward to a repetition of this, I have been careful each year since not to miss this moulid, but have been disappointed as far as the music has been concerned. What I have heard has been quite banal. In 1357 (1938), for instance, there was a brass band at a *zeffa* without *khalîfa* and a few comparatively feeble performers on the *târ;* and so little prospect of much better things, that I deserted the little *hâra*, and made a round of other moulids, which like Bahlûl were working

---

33 The monastic tradition of "guarding the eyes", i.e., against letting them stray, staring at anything/anyone which/who will weaken the resolve not to sin.

34 McPherson clearly means here "admiring [other] people", although in Canon Law the phrase means causing others astonishment due to some peculiarity of oneself that catches their attention.

35 This word is the plural of 'âlima, the woman expert leading the zâr; and the plural of 'âlam, meaning "world". McPherson is, presumably, referring to the former.

up for the final evening, or actually consummating their last night. Of these were 'Abdullah near Bâb el-Lûq, 'Aysha -l-Tûnsî close to Sitna 'Aysha, and Darghâm and 'Amrî off Shâri' Muhammad 'Alî.

But passing in a tram about midnight I saw a much increased company in Hâret el-Ansârî, watching a whirling dervish. Getting off at the 'Ataba, and returning on foot, I found him still whirling and commencing to divest himself of his "seven veils" without interrupting his gyrations. He was succeeded by a bearded dervish of the Rifâ'îya, brandishing an alarming *dabbûs* who commenced a sermon such as I think has seldom been heard since the time of Peter the Hermit. His rhetoric was most powerful; likewise his voice, or rather his voices – for he had many, from a trumpet-call to a subtle whisper. He could roar, bark or growl; croon or rage; employ staccato; become hoarse or bell-like, and let his words fall like notes of music, over a gamut compassing falsetto and deep base.

His subject matter was both revivalist and philosophic, Sufic in the main. Suddenly without breaking off his discourse, he appeared to go berserker, spun round with his *dabbûs* at arm's length, its chains ringing and its dagger point glittering; then punctuated his sermon by jabbing it into his throat, under his beard. *Aposiopesis*[36] followed; one could have heard a feather fall, as he sagged, dropped on his knees, and his head jerked forward, throwing his weight on the point, with the spherical head of the *dabbûs* vertically beneath. Just as we half expected to see the point emerge from the back of his neck, an ancient dervish jumped lightly on his shoulders, and proclaimed the greatness of God, "who alone worketh great marvels", or words to that effect.

Certainly, there seemed to be forces at work beyond our human ken, for he rose again, waited a moment for the leading dervish to touch and magically heal the punctured spot, then in an even tone discoursed on the quasi-spiritual functions of the heart. He might have been quoting Gregory Palamas[37], or some hesychast of Mt. Athos.

But my eyes and attention wandered to a young man of our party, naked but for his *libâs*,[38] who was being converted into a living chandelier. Small sharp *dabâbîs* of sorts were being run through the flesh of his arms, chest and back, weighted at the lower end and fitted at the top with lighted tapers. The sermon over, a *dabbûs*, not unlike a sword was pushed through both cheeks, and whilst he held the blade in his mouth with his teeth, candles were adjusted and lighted at both ends, and he slowly revolved.

---

36 Sudden silence.
37 Prominent theologian and saint (1296–1359) of late Byzantine period.
38 libâs = undergarment

Cheek-piercing with the 'dabbous'
"As for the 'santons', a type of saint even more enthusiastic than the dervishes and of
an orthodoxy less recognised, we saw several who were piercing their cheeks with long,
pointed implements and so were covered with blood; others were devouring live serpents,
or filling their mouths with hot coals…"
(Gérard de Nerval, *The Women of Egypt*, Part 2, Ch. 11)

The youth was not excited, as might have been the case had he just emerged from a *zikr;* he was simply normal – if indeed it is normal to be normal under such abnormal conditions. He showed no symptom of pain or discomfort, nor of interest in the proceedings; not even when the burning candles keeled over onto his flesh. When the blessed touch of the ancient dervish had immuned him from bleeding or any ill consequences, he just took his place amongst the other lads, with no sign of self-consciousness. I leave it to others to explain these things: *hypotheses non fingo*[39]. I was not in a stall below footlights, watching happenings on a stage with managed curtains, mirrors, lamps and the rest, but at the closest quarters free to examine and to touch, and could get no material clue. I shall be grateful for any light on this mysterious *Candlemas.*

A 29 (cf. Sectional Map XI)
ARBA 'ÎN

(سيدي أربعين)

This very small moulid is held almost at the end of Sha'bân – in the year 1357 (1938) on 23 Sha'bân (17 October 1938). The small and most unattractive mosque is in Shâri' el-Suwayqa, almost opposite Hâret el-Ansârî of Shâri' Muhammad 'Alî not far from the 'Ataba end. The street and surroundings are not beautiful, its most interesting object perhaps being an enormous bottle of live leeches over a shop near the mosque. This is labelled [in French] *"Sangsues".*

A 30 (cf. Sectional Map XI)
'ASHMÂWÎ

(سيدي العشماوي)

This is one of the comparatively few moulids whose date is definitely fixed. It is now as it was in the days of Lane, over a hundred years ago, on the eve of the 11 Rabî' I, always the day before the great Moulid el-Nebî. It is equally easy to locate being the most central of all, in the Shâri' el-'Ashmâwî behind the Post Office and the Muskî *Caracôl* (Police Station), the little street which emerges in Shâri' 'Abdîn, not far from the opera. It is now, however, so reduced that it is easy to pass in the main streets on each side of it without noticing it.

One of the most fascinating parts of Lane's great book, *"The Modern Egyptians"*, is an account of a *zikr* at the *zâwiya* of Ashmâwi, the street being then known as the *Sûq el-Bakrî.* That was about 1830 when the palace of the *Sheikh el-Bakrî* was here, close to the little lake which is now the Ezbekîya Garden, and this

---

39 Famous phrase used by Isaac Newton: "I contrive no hypotheses".

part of Cairo was the site of the Moulid el-Nebî and of the *dôsah*. The Sheikh el-Bakrî of today dwells in the Shâri' el-Khronfish, and there is a disturbing rumour that his palace is marked for destruction.

Now, as then, the observances are of almost purely a religious nature, but a few years ago in addition to the "zikrs" and *zeffa*, there was some very pleasant singing by sheikhs and "munshids" in a little *zuqâq*[40] near the Shâri' 'Abdîn end, where stick play and innocent entertainments were held. Practically nothing of that remains, but I am told that the discontinued *zeffa* was renewed in 1357 (1938).

In 1351 (1932), I witnessed an extraordinary incident, strongly suggestive of a tale in the *Alf Leila wa-Leila*[41], of a *farouche* [shy] but fearless lad who bearded the "Commander of the Faithful" in such violent and stinging terms that, seemingly, the very excess of his language brought him forgiveness. *'Ashâ* (dinner) was provided in a tent to a great many poor, and when nearly over a tall boy of about fifteen, in rags, with wild black eyes and hair, burst unceremoniously in, and was as unceremoniously ejected. He took it ill and crashed in again, but was told very gently by a police officer that he had come too late, and was given to an *askari* to be removed. But he kicked, fought, and tried to bite, abusing the patrons of the feast in unmeasured terms. "I come for 'ashâ", he shouted, "and ye give me blows – a curse on such charity!" Again and again, attempts were made to lead him quietly away, but in spite of wonderful forbearance, his own violence soon reduced his rags to tatters, and there was blood on his face. At length a high officer (the *ma'mûr*, I think) and a couple of "ifrângîs" who were in the tent talked to him with all gentleness, calling him a *gada'* (a brave lad) and smiled at his intrepid fury, and someone kissed him on the head, and he was tamed at last. Then he was led in and a great dish of delicious *fath*[42] put before him. Such patience and kindness were doubtless largely due to the piteous plight of the undaunted and handsome young fury, but also from a wish to divert an evil omen from the feast.

I wish I had asked his name and watched his career. He had the makings of an Atatürk.

Lane, in describing an 'Ashmâwî *zikr* and the beauty of the music and the words sung by the "munshids", mentions the effect on a soldier and on an eunuch of "the Pâsha". The eunuch became very *melbûs*, wildly ejaculated "Allâh ! ...

---

40 zuqâq = lane, alley.
41 Thousand and One Nights.
42 Pronounced fat'h, with 2 syllables.

lâ ! lâ ! lâ ! ... Yâ 'ammî! ... Yâ 'Ashmâwî! ... Yâ 'ammî! 'Ashmâwî! (Oh ! my uncle 'Ashmâwî!), and finally collapsed in a fit. Had he, Lane, been at the moulid in 1356 (1937), he could not have complained of any falling off of the fervour inspired by the *zikr*. The floor of the *maqâm* of Sîdî Muhammad el-Beidek in the little street connecting Shâri' 'Ashmâwî with Shâri' 'Abd el-'Azîz was like a tiny battlefield at one time, as one after another became *melbûs* and then collapsed for a while. So far, so good, but in the little *zuqâq* already referred to, in which singing, stick play and such like had been suppressed, and in which for the first time a *zikr* was held instead, the scene was far from edifying, and, I think, showed the danger and inadvisability of repressing natural exuberance and desire for play as well as prayer. Two great lads insisted on cutting in roughly and with very improper language, much to the discomfort of the "zikeers", and quickly became violently *melbûs*. One subsided fairly quietly, but the other, a black youth, became so wild that it required several people to hold him, and he was ultimately carried away. By-standers said that the youth had been drinking. The next year when I went a little late, the *maqâm* of Shâri' Beidek was closed, the *zuqâq* empty, and mosque and street, compared with the past, rather deserted.

Allâh ! Allâh ! Yâ 'Ashmâwî! Oh, my uncle 'Ashmâwî! Oh, my uncle!

A 31 (cf. Sectional Map VI)
AWLÂD BADR
(أولاد بدر)

This little moulid centres about the mosques and tomb in Darb el-Sheikh Faraq, close to Darb el-Nasr and the big new Bûlâq street, Shâri' 'Abd el-Gawâd, and should be early in Sha'bân.

It is rather a rough district and moulids pay dearly for any disorderly behaviour (which happily is extremely rare). Anyway, I believe in 1353 (1934) it was suppressed altogether, and on going in 1354 (1935) to what should have been the chief night, 3 Sha'bân (31 October 1935), I found flags and all decorations being hauled down, and all celebrations (which included a *ringa* or two and some small shows) forbidden. There only remained the freedom of the mosque. I was told there had been a free fight. However, after this warning it was allowed to resume, and the final evening, 27 Sha'bân (24 November 1935), passed quietly.

A 32
AWLÂD SHU'EIB
(أولاد شعيب)

I have never located this little moulid, but Mûsâ, my reliable *murâsla* reported on Friday night, 28 Sha'bân 1355 (13 November 1936), that he had just assisted thereat, and had witnessed rather a fine *zeffa* in the late afternoon. It is for this reason that I include it, for *zeffas* are becoming rather rare.

The position was given as between Shâri' 'Abdîn, and Shâri' 'Emâd el-Dîn, in the Hâret el-Fawâla. If so, it may be traced on Sectional Map X, F 8 & 9.

A 33 (cf. Sectional Map XVII)
'AYSHA
(سيدة عائشة)

Although I only once witnessed this moulid, on Thursday, 16 Sha'bân 1356 (21 October 1937), I think it is held annually about the middle of Sha'bân.

The mosque is near the tombs of the Mamelukes, a few yards to the right of the tram track to Imâm el-Shâfe'î, behind a beautiful old city gate and amidst ancient unspoilt surroundings, well worth a visit, apart from the moulid. Trams 13 and 23 stop at the station of Sayyida 'Aysha.

It is a small but picturesque affair with little on the secular side beyond good stick dancing and playing, though there are cafés in the main road with dancing girls.

A feature when I was there was the blind Hâgg Husein preaching near the old city gate. He used very good Arabic and was gentle and restrained. After his discourse he repeated the ninety-nine names of God, and wrote the name of anyone so desiring on an illuminated text, of which he carried a sheaf.

This Sayyida 'Aysha was daughter of Ga'far Sâdiq, the 6th Imâm and therefore in the direct line of the Prophet and must not be confused with 'Aysha the daughter of Abû Bakr el-Siddîq and wife of Muhammad, whose tomb near Medina was destroyed by the Wahhâbis. She is described in the *Tabaqât el-Kubrâ* as singularly holy: one of her sayings quoted is, "I will trust God, even if He thrust me into the fire." Almost the words of holy Job who said, *Etiam si occiderit me, in ipso sperabo.*[43]

---

43 "Although he should kill me, I will trust in him" (Job 13:15).

A 34 (cf. Sectional Map XVII)
'AYSHA -L-TÛNISÎ

(عائشة التونسي)

A very small moulid very near that of Sayyida 'Aysha bint Ga'far Sâdiq, held in 1357 on Friday, 27 Sha'bân (21 October 1938).

B 1 (cf. Sectional Map II)
BADRÂN

(سيدي بدران)

I was present only on 16 Gamâd I 1353 (26 August 1934) and was told that it was a new moulid only inaugurated the previous year.

The Mosque of Sîdî Badrân is in Shâri' Masarra, off Shâri' Shubrâ, so that any Shubrâ tram and bus 8 serve, getting off at the station before Tawfîqîya school (if coming from town) and turning at right angles to the left. As, however, this involves a considerable walk along Shâri' Masarra, it is better to take bus 15 from Mîdân Ismâ'îlîya, as this after a pleasant run along the banks of the Nile and through the Gezîret Badrân district passes the door of the mosque.

This moulid was initiated on a considerable scale and promised well in 1353 (1934). The mosque with the shrine of Sîdî Badrân was thronged; and in the neighbourhood, but not too near, was a large tent theatre with the dwarf and fat strong man, and the muscle dancers and the rest. Also, a Punch and Judy show, and the *piste à la mort*, in which Billy Williams thrilled successive audiences with his intrepid motor-cycle riding on the vertical walls of his "bear pit".

Alas, for reasons quite unknown to me, the police showed unwonted ferocity, and it was a *sauve qui peut* for a disappointed crowd, and merriment and piety alike froze up.

As far as I know, poor Sîdî Badrân has never lifted up his head since, but we hope for better things.

B 2 (cf. Sectional Map XIV)
BAHLÛL (SÎDÎ SAYYID MUHAMMAD EL-BAHLÛL)

(سيدي سيد محمد البهلول)

On every occasion that I have been present on the big night, it has been the 29 Sha'bân, the "waqfa" of Ramadân, and therefore coincident with the *ru'ya*, the ceremony of determining whether the new moon has been seen, and therefore whether the month of fasting has begun.

The tomb of Bahlûl is near the Bâb el-Wazîr in Shâri' Muhaggar. It is best reached by bus 17, from Ghamra to Bâb el-Wazîr, passing through 'Ataba

-l-Khadrâ. Also, any tram to the Citadel serves, in which case one leaves the tram at the *manshîya*, and walking half up the little hill towards the Citadel, turns to the left, a few yards from the tomb.

It was a big moulid when I first discovered it in 1352 (1933), for though I had often heard of a great moulid "at the Citadel", I was always misinformed as to date, and failed to locate it. A sheikh (Abû -l-Sheit), who as a youth had helped me in Intelligence work in the *gabel* to thwart illicit traffic in arms, and who now appeared to be in charge of the tomb, insisted on introducing me into the Holy of Holies. An old woman more garrulous than anything I have ever met or imagined, was the only occupant, and though very friendly, so flooded the shrine with language, that it was difficult to even read the epitaph or be conscious of anything but her tongue.

Some people with whom I dined that evening, including an Egyptian who was *sharîf*, and an English Professor from the Egyptian University, were so interested in my account of Sîdî Bahlûl, that they asked me to conduct them there. The approach to the tomb seemed so changed, that I had difficulty in finding it and effecting an entrance, but no one opposed any obstacle or warned us that it was the ladies' hour. Too late we found that the tomb in the centre was entirely surrounded by devout women seated on the floor. I apologised and explained that a few hours before I had found the place empty, and they good-temperedly forgave our intrusion, but insisted, that since we were there, we must process round the tomb in the correct manner. This my *sharîf* companion said must be in the opposite direction to the hands of a clock. We performed the ritual but had the greatest difficulty in preventing it being of the nature of a *dôsah* (cf. Glossary), so closely packed were the votaries at the shrine.

I gather that this was once indeed a great moulid with important *zeffa* and bound up with procession from the Citadel to the Qâdi's Court and the *ru'ya*, hence its being always held on the eve of Ramadân. It has greatly dwindled, especially of very recent years, but happily in 1356 (1937) there were signs of revival and, though small, it was pleasant and very picturesque and unharassed by police. A feature was the eloquence of the blind Sheikh Husein.

B 3 (cf. Sectional Map VII)
BAHRÎ (MUHAMMAD EL-BAHRÎ)
(محمد البحري)

Present on Thursday, 8 Muharram 1354 (11 April 1935) and Thursday, 25 Safar 1356 (6 May 1937).

On the first of these dates, the moulid clashed with that of Sîdî Marzûq. It will be seen that it is held on widely different dates, but apparently it affects Thursday, as also does Marzûq.

The mosque is on the north side of Shâri' Bâb el-Bahr near Clot Bey, from which Shâri' Bâb el-Bahr runs off in the direction of Bâb el-Sha'rîya.

I have nothing but a sad tale to tell about this once brilliant moulid.

As late as 1354 (1935), the religious ceremonies were carried on with all decorum, in and about the mosque, and to a less extent in a house situated in a narrow alley to the north of the mosque. Providence had provided an ideal place for lighter entertainment out of sight and sound of the mosque though not many yards away, in a *terrain vague* between Shâri' Bâb el-Bahr and the parallel street of Bein el-Hârât, approached from the one side by the narrow alley by the side of the mosque, already referred to, and from the other by a small opening near the remains of the Fatimite Wall – which by the way is not easily found.

This enclosure sheltered theatres, Punch and Judy, "ringas", and innumerable stalls and places of entertainment, with plenty of room for "zikrs" at its peaceful east end. All went happily, far from politics and mundane cares.

In 1355, the moulid was suppressed on account of King Fu'ad's recent death. I doubt if his Majesty would have approved this mournful abstinence, but all gladly accorded this mark of respect and grief; but in 1356, with King Farouk gloriously reigning, supporters of the ancient moulid naturally expected to be allowed to do honour to the Sheikh el-Bahrî and commenced preparations; but on the night of the *apodosis*, 25 Safar 1356 (6 May 1937), I was surprised to find police guarding the entrance from Bein el-Hârât and disgruntled votaries of el-Bahrî forbidden to visit the mosque by this public way. I had no difficulty however in running the blockade, only to find nothing within but the most depressing melancholy: some singers and such like thrown out of their pleasure-giving work and a-hungry, and a dismal attempt at a *zikr*.

So, I took my way down the alley, towards the main street and the mosque, noting on the way that no sounds of the reading of the Qurân, no "zikring" proceeded from the now gloomy house, once echoing with religious joy and fervour – the typical languishing of the soul of a moulid when its body is oppressed. On nearing the end, my progress was stopped by a much more effective blockade than that at the entrance from Bein el-Hârât, and I realised that with a number of other victims I was imprisoned between two guards stopping public ways in time of peace and supposed rejoicing.

"Mamnû' el-murûr"[44], said an '*askarî* when I tried to pass, so feeling that tact

_____

44 No entry!

and patience were called for, I replied, "But, *onbâshî*, if both ways passing is forbidden, how am I to go home, or how are the poor people living here to reach their homes". (Applause from other victims). *Mush 'âref, Hadratak, mush shuglî* – "I don't know, your Honour, not my business!" "But why", I asked, "is the moulid crushed in this way?"

El-malik mât – "The King is dead", he replied.

"But that was over a year ago," I rejoined.

W'ana mâlî, huwa lissa mayyit – "What's that to me, he is still dead."

All the time I was manoeuvring a sidelong movement in the desired direction, and ultimately wangled an escape, [only] to find about the mosque few worshippers, no joy or enthusiasm, a few timid looking people, and an imposing array of police. "Surely", thought I, "Sîdî Muhammad el-Bahrî must be the Patron Saint of 'Bobbies', but they need not keep him so exclusively to themselves".

Still, curious to know what was really wrong with the Sheikh el-Bahrî, I enquired of a somewhat higher authority than the *'askarî*, and he gave as the reason "that the moulid obstructed traffic". A most irritatingly absurd reason, as the moulid was always held in the *terrain vague* where there is *no* traffic, and the policy now adopted, by driving everyone into the main street *does* obstruct traffic, if only by the plethora of police, and of people hanging about in vain expectation. This reason (sic) reminds one of some of the paradoxical absurdities in the police arrangements at home, where I recently wanted a few bottles of beer and was told I could not have them unless I bought a bottle of cognac at the same time; this, the shop-owner explained with a wry grin was to check drinking.

I went in 1357, in Muharram, in Safar and in Rabî' I, but the Sheikh Muhammad el-Bahrî, or at least his moulid, seemed to have been definitely crushed. A disappointed little sheikh who claimed some sort of spiritual descent from el-Bahrî exclaimed, "This is the work of the *djinn*". I thought of the last verse of *el-Qur'ân el-karîm* and went my way.

"Say, 'I take refuge with the Lord of Mankind ... from [the evil] ... of djinn and people.'"[45]

---

45 McPherson's less accurate interpretation of the first and last line (verses 1 and 6) of Sûrat al-Nâs has been replaced above with the corresponding (slightly amended) lines from the Arberry translation.

B 4 (cf. Map of Upper Egypt)
BARSÛM (ST. BARSÛM EL-'ARYÂN)
(مار برسوم العريان)

This being a Coptic moulid naturally follows the Coptic calendar, falling on or near the feast day of the saint, in the middle of the first month, Tût.

Amongst the dates on which I have been present are as follows:

Wednesday, 16 Tût 1651 = 26 September 1934 = 17 Gamâd II 1353
Sunday, 18 Tût 1652 = 29 September 1935 = 1 Rajab 1354
Saturday, 16 Tût 1653 = 26 September 1936 = 10 Rajab 1355
Wednesday, 16 Tût 1656 = 27 September 1939 = 13 Sha'bân 1358

It is held at the Monastery of Saint Barsûm el-'Aryân at Ma'sara near Helwân, and is therefore reached by train from Bâb el-Lûq to Ma'sara Station, where donkeys are waiting, not only on the great night, but during the previous week. If one prefers to walk, it is a pleasant stroll of about twenty minutes through the little village and over the canal bridge through the vegetation.

Coptic moulids have sadly waned, but this, the only one of note with which I am acquainted, remains big, popular and wonderful. No visitor to Cairo in the latter part of September (and for the matter of that, no resident) should miss it, if interested in pilgrimages and popular religious gatherings; and not only is the *apodosis* worth witnessing but a visit or two on the earlier and smaller nights also. I usually, especially if I have friends with me, combine a pilgrimage with a picnic, by going well before dark and taking a *sufrâgî* with me who lays an *al fresco* meal in the *durra* [corn]fields by the canal, whilst one is having a preliminary turn by daylight. There is unlimited time after as donkeys and trains seem to be always available, even hours after midnight.

I have never, however, ventured to take ladies on the last night, owing to the crush on the trains. These are invaded by window and doors with no respect for class, and, particularly on the return, one has to take a strong position on the platform and try one's luck in a good-humoured fight for a place. I have been mischievously amused to see a dozing magnate in a first-class carriage to himself, or an affectionate but high-brow couple, suddenly invaded, sat on, subjected to all manner of shocks and pressure, and snowed under by a boisterous jolly mass of humanity sufficient to fill several compartments. The pressure is soon relieved by a number of these occupying the luggage racks.

The fields in front of the monastery, from which the corn has been cut, are filled with "ringas", *cafés chantants,* shows, theatres and so on, on which none of the very modern Moslem restrictions press; but the fascinating sight is within the walls in the vast grounds of the monastery. There, several acres of orchard and garden have become for the time a village of tents and wattled dwellings. People have come from far and near, and are living here for the nonce, and have their beds, cook their food, and entertain themselves and their friends with dancing, music and singing, not forgetting the pious exercises, which the place and the occasion claim. Little streets are arranged, and a water supply, primitive drainage, and butchers' and other shops, and the scene is most colourful. There cannot be much privacy, but this seems to cause no annoyance, though the brilliancy of texture and hue in the little dwellings, and the picturesqueness of their occupants, tempts the passer-by to glance in unduly. The only reaction is a smile and a hearty invitation to enter and partake of whatever there may be. A gay and innocent freedom prevails, though if the whole truth must be told, I have known occasions when the honours of the little house have been proffered by a lady so fair, so highly tinted and scented, so dazzling with *kohl* and lipstick, and so *mouvementé* about the haunches, and so exiguously and exquisitely clad, that I have thought of Tasso's verses picturing Armida in her bower.[46]

At other Christian moulids and allied ceremonies, I have generally found the church doors open to pilgrims well into the night, so was surprised here to find them closed even on the last and great night. I suppose it is that pilgrims come here to stay, sleep in the sacred precincts, and hear mass in the morning. In 1653 (1936), the final night falling on a Saturday, I returned to Cairo in the early hours of the Sabbath morning and went to mass in the Church of St. Mercurius (Abû Seifein) in the *Deir* of that name near Old Cairo, and was impressed by hearing a reading about Barsûm el-'Aryân, and his commemoration in the *anaphora*. I had hoped for this and for more, as Butler in his *Coptic Churches*, declares the screen of Abû Seifein so beautiful that it alone is worth a visit to Egypt, and says that the church contains a little chapel of Mâr Barsûm in which service is held, once a year on his feast day.

I could not confirm this, but a young archdeacon kindly took me down into the cave (within the church of Abû Seifein) where he assured me Barsûm spent 25 years in company with a snake, as a variant to passing 30 years on the roof unprotected from sun and weather. He showed me an ancient picture of Barsûm and his snake, and a little devil the snake had vomited up. The casting out of this devil was the beginning of a long and happy symbiosis in the cave, very different from the

---

46 Italian poet Torquato Tasso (1544 – 1595); in the story Armida was an Arab sorceress and her lover Rinaldo, a crusader.

The Church of St. Mercurius (Abû Seifein) near Old Cairo

An icon of St Mercurius –
Abû Seifein (the father of two
swords) killing Roman Emperor
Flavius Claudius Julianus.

"Butler in his *Coptic Churches*
declares the screen of Abû
Seifein so beautiful that it alone
is worth a visit to Egypt…"

tragic companionship of Rodrigo, the last of the Gothic Kings of Spain, and his black serpent in the tomb.[47] I was assured by the Archdeacon and his friends, and others in the *Deir*, that Barsûm acquired from his snake knowledge which gave him power over all serpents, and that his name is still invoked in the district for the exorcism of such. (I have been told since by a high authority on such matters that this power should be attributed to a certain other saint, not to Barsûm.)

In any case, "May Anbâ Barsûm be exalted", as they say in the Coptic Liturgy...

Ⲡⲓⲛⲓⲩϯ Ⲁⲃⲃⲁ Ⲡⲁⲣⲥⲱⲙⲁ

It is characteristic of the tolerance of the Egyptians that this Christian feast is almost as popular with Moslems as with Copts. In fact, they gently appropriate Mâr Barsûm, and I have heard him referred to as Sîdî Muhammad Barsûm! What a truly blessed trait this is. Never have I found a place, where Christians of various sects, Moslems and others so honour one another's mosques or churches publicly, with graceful friendliness, apply for blessings at one another's shrines, and where the Prophet's words in the Sûrat el-Baqarah are so practically observed:

"Surely, they that believe, and those of Jewry, and the Christians, and those of the Sabaeans, whoso believes in God and the Last Day, and works righteousness – their wage awaits them with their Lord, and no fear shall be on them, neither shall they sorrow."[48]

B 5 (cf. Sectional Map VIII)
BAYÛMÎ (SÎDÎ 'ALÎ -L-BAYÛMÎ)
(سيدي علي البيومي)

Though always on Thursday, I found the date most baffling, for it ranged from Zû -l-Qa'da in 1351 (1932) to Safar in 1359 (1940), falling intermediately in Zû

---

47 Rodrigo was the last Visigoth king of Spain when that land was conquered by the Moors. According to legend, he saved his life by running away from the battlefield. A hermit told him he should, in penance, retire to a tomb full of snakes, where he survived for three days and nights, but then was bitten and died, thus atoning for his sin.

48 Arberry translation of verse 62, Sûrat el-Baqarah.

[McPher.] That the moulid of 27 September 1939 (16 Tût 1656 / 13 Sha'bân 1358) should have been enhanced in every way, rather than the reverse, by the fact of war having broken out, whilst the Islamic moulids at the same period were most adversely affected, is so significant that it is specially commented on in my Preface. I am indebted for the photographs to Miss Barbara Fry, an authority on the Eastern Churches, who accompanied me to the church on a different occasion. [Editor's note: Barbara Fry founded *The Eastern Church Review* in 1966; she died in 1968.]

-l-Higga in 1353 (1934) and Muharram in 1355 (1936). The advantage of noting both Islamic and Christian dates over a number of years is exemplified in this case, for all of these widely differing *lunar* dates fall in March, between the 8th and the 28th. This points strongly, though empirically, to the feast of Bayûmî following the solar calendar, and leads to our expecting it in March, or by the Coptic reckoning, in the month of Baramhât. I have recently found confirmation of the first of these conclusions in Murray's "*Egypt*". I will quote his paragraph on the subject *in extenso* as it shows that important changes have taken place since he wrote in 1888.

The Moolid el-Beiyoomee – This is a very extensive and remarkable fair and dervish festival, which is held annually in the early part of October. The scene of the fête is the portion of the desert bordering on the Abbasseeyeh road, immediately N. of the Bab el-Hassaneeyeh. It is in honour of the Seyyid Ali el-Beiyoomee, founder of the great sect of Beiyoomeeyeh Dervishes (a branch of the Ahmedeeyeh), whose memory is much respected in Egypt. All the characteristics of the Moolid en-Nebbee, are here repeated.

It will be noted that it was then a desert moulid and that the date was October. Possibly there was a second celebration in March not mentioned by Murray, as in the case of the parent feasts of Sayyid el-Bedawî about March and October (with yet a third).

It is curious that almost the only other Cairo moulid which goes by the seasons and not by the moon, is that of Sîdî Ismâ'îl Imbâbî who was a Tantâwî and sent from there to spread the Ahmadîya tenets. To quote again from Murray it appears that there was yet another which followed the sun by following Bayûmî, that of 'Afîfî – which I have failed to trace and fancy no longer exists.

The Moolid el-Afeefee – This is also a remarkable festival, always celebrated immediately after that of Beiyoomee. The scene is the E. district of the Tombs of the Circassian Memlooks, in which is the tomb of Afeefee, the founder of a large sect of Cairene dervishes. Here amongst the tombs are pitched innumerable tents, and country people from all parts of Egypt, including many Bedaween, encamp around. The moolid lasts as usual 8 days, and is of the usual festive and semi-religious kind.

The Moulid of Sîdî Bayûmî is now held at his mosque and tomb, in the street of that name, to the North of the Bâb el-Futûh, and is therefore best reached by bus 11 which, plying between 'Abbâsîya and Beit el-Qâdî, passes the mosque both ways. As its secular attractions are on a *terrain vague* between Shâri' el-Bayûmî and Shâri' Farouk, and very visible and audible from the latter street, any tram going in the 'Abbâsîya direction up Shâri' Farouk may be used, descent being made before Hasanîya.

It is, when given a fair chance, a very fine event, perhaps the nearest to what moulids were in bygone days – by no means the biggest or the grandest, but singularly satisfying in its very primitiveness.

The *zeffa* from Sidna Husein to Bayûmî in the afternoon should by no means be missed. It is easily the finest to be seen in Cairo nowadays, at least as far as my knowledge goes, for an unfortunate predilection for siestas may have robbed me of marvellous manifestations about the time of the *'asr* [afternoon prayer].

The gathering of the *tŭrŭq* in the early afternoon, in the courts of Sidna Husein is a brave sight, and the crowd displays a happy mixture of gaiety and piety, as the *khalîfa* mounts his steed, and the procession with banners, insignia, and music proceeds in peace. The Alexandrine *balawânîs* in their picturesque boleros and other garments, their long *mesh'al* and their quaint musical instruments have already set out and indicated to the crowds, who line all the way from Sidna Husein to Bayûmî, that the *khalîfa* is coming with his dervishes and varied following, and all the people are agog in expectation.

These *prodromoi* fill up any delay with balancing tricks and other performances and expect a few *millièmes* from the bystanders, the only time throughout the moulid that anyone is asked for money (except of course in the enclosed shows and cafés, where the charge may vary from a *millième* to a piastre). This is a pleasant change from the days about which Lane wrote, when every phase of every ceremony seemed to be accompanied by customary donations.

Descending to the Nahhâsîn, the *zeffa* passes that glorious group near the Beit el-Qâdî which includes the great mosques of Qalâwûn and Barqûq, then continuing on the main way to the Bâb el-Futûh past the *sebîl* and some dear old mosques, and passing under the Bâb, it struggles on through an immense crowd to the mosque and shrine of Bayûmî, where the proper devotions proceed, quite uninterrupted by the lively assembly in the *terrain vague,* a short but sufficient distance removed.

There are usually at least two large tent theatres and smaller shows, and "ringas", and of course the ubiquitous Punch, and "zikrs" are held and "fiqîs" employed in many houses in the neighbourhood. This moulid is usually unmolested or nearly so, because mainly there is no traffic route through the waste bit of ground, but in 1352 (1933) the interference amounted to something like persecution. Some eminent professors had accompanied me and were enjoying the merry sights and the tonic atmosphere of the happy orderly crowd, when for some reason unknown (and indeed inconceivable to us, for no one was in anyone's way), we were charged by a lot of '*askaris*, and scattered utterly, with the greatest difficulty keeping our feet in the stampede. The forceful way these police soldiers scaled the heights and laid about them was worthy of a real and important cause. My poor friends had the shock and surprise of their lives.

After King Fu'ad's lamented death in 1355 (1936) most moulids were *en deuil* long after court mourning had officially ceased, but in 1356 (8 April 1937), the moulid was surprisingly fine. Some minor incidents indeed happened, as for example, at the congestion incident on the stopping of the *zeffa* on arrival and the pressure of those behind, a mounted '*askarî* herded a gang of us in the little '*atfet*[49] Abû -l-Elâ just beyond the mosque, to relieve pressure in the main street. So far so good, but another, ignoring the fact that the '*atfa* is a cul-de-sac, and pretty full of women, children and carts before we were driven in, attempted to ride in and force us through. One boy was badly injured but no general harm done. Also, the manoeuvre of storming the heights was repeated, but in such a comparatively mild way that only youngsters were in danger. As these scampered under carts, into holes or anywhere for safety, a motherly soul near me appealed to the "'askarîs" in moving tones, "For the love of the Prophet, spare the rabbits."

There are places about this moulid and some others, where little "rabbits" can go with impunity, but grown up "bucks" at their peril. This I found to my discomfiture when exploring curious little "zuqâqs", and cave-like entrances to ancient half-ruined mansions, from which came light and sight or sound of "zikring", or of music and dancing. Attracted to one of these by the *zaghârît,* that curious wavering tongue-trill that one hears at "farahs" [wedding feasts] and many ceremonial occasions, I ventured in to find, too late, that I was intruding at some purely feminine function suggestive of a *zâr*. Confronted by a lot of indignant and threatening women, I was more than alarmed, but happily had the inspiration to exclaim, "Illi tuhibb el-nebî tuzaghrid" – Let her who loves the prophet warble!

For a moment I feared I had made matters worse, but I had put them in a dilemma and, I think, rather appealed to their sense of humour, and my punishment was nothing worse than to be chased out with a chorus of *zaghârît*.

The Mosque of Bayûmî had long called for repairs, so without risking a tragedy such as befell Abû -l-'Elâ, these were taken in hand in 1356 (1937) and continued for about two years, during which time no moulid was held.

---

49 'atfa = blind alley, dead end.

In Ramadân 1358 (1939), the King assisted at the ceremony of re-inauguration, a most popular occasion somewhat similar to that on which he restored Abû -l-'Elâ to its high prestige. As also in the case of Abû -l-'Elâ, this was followed by the renewal of the moulid, and on Thursday, 5 Safar 1359 (14 March 1940), in spite of the depression of moulids (where there was not actual repression) ascribed to war conditions, Sultân Bayûmî was honoured almost in the fine old style. The *zeffa* had lost nothing of its essential elements and showed the greatness of the Bayûmîya, for the red banners and insignia of this branch of the Ahmadîya stretched in the afternoon *zeffa* perhaps a mile or more.

The amusement park on the *terrain vague* was considerably reduced by building, which has been and is still going on, but during an hour or two that I was there all was peaceful and happy, and the affluence at the shrine correspondingly satisfactory.

B 6 (cf. Sectional Map VIII)
BENHÂWÎ
(سيدي البنهاوي)

I heard of this moulid for the first time in 1353 (1934), and then too late to assist at the principal night, 13 Gamâd I, and saw only what small celebrations and decorations remained the following day, at the *khatma*, Friday, 14 Gamâd I (24 August 1934). It was definitely not held in 1354, and I have not been able to ascertain if it has been celebrated since.

I include it mainly because the little mosque is in a nice old street, in one of the most beautiful and unspoilt parts of Cairo, close to the Bâb el-Futûh. It is best reached by bus 12, which plies between Bâb el-Hadîd and Beit el-Qâdî, and passes through Shâri' Benhâwî on the way to the Beit el-Qâdî, but not on the reverse journey. Or bus 11 between 'Abbâsîya and Beit el-Qâdî can be used as that passes through Bâb-el-Futûh both ways, and Shâri' Benhâwî ends at the bâb on the north side.

It must have been a primitive little moulid, but attractive from the situation and its very simplicity.

D 1 (cf. Map of Delta)
DAMIÂNÂ (SITNA DAMIÂNÂ)
(القديسة دميانا)

I regret never having seen this great Coptic moulid, nor even the celebrated convent of St. Damiânâ, which Marcos, a Roman Governor and her father, erected as a retreat and protection for her and her maids, who, however, were

The Convent of St. Damiânâ (a 4th century Coptic martyr) at Belqâs in the Nile Delta.

all martyred because they refused to apostatise at the time of the Diocletian persecutions.

The convent is to the north of Belqâs in the Beheira province, in the direction of Damietta. Belqâs is on the E.S.E. not far from Shirbîn, but I do not know how far from the Convent.

My old friend Kemp[50], who explored the desert and the Delta alone more thoroughly and more lovingly than anyone I have met, gives an interesting account of his very rough and bumpy journey of forty miles on a mule, with a woodcut of the convent – but that was nearly half a century ago, so perhaps the railway arrangements were then very different from now.

Kemp does not describe the moulid but gives the date as 12 Bashans. That date is still observed, for several newspapers announced it for "from the 12th to 20th May 1938" – the 20th being 12 Bashans – and "for Monday, 12 Bashans 1656" (20 May 1940, 13 Rabî' II 1359).[51]

ALEXANDRIA

D 2 (cf. Map of the Delta)
DANYÂL (EL-NEBÎ DANYÂL)
(النبي دنيال)

I have been assured that the Nebî Danyâl has his moulid at Alexandria, and understand that it centres about the mosque of his name, but beyond that am lamentably ignorant, not having been able so far to connect it with or disconnect it from the remarkable Nubian procession that takes place on the 10th Zû -l-Higga, the first day of the Qurbân Beiram.

Judaic and Byzantine elements are so conspicuous in the *zeffa* which goes from the Mosque of Nebî-Danyâl to that of Sîdî Mîrghânî, that they support certain

---

50 Walter Gustav Kemp (1854–1920), engineer, archaeologist and illustrator.

51 [McPher.] Two articles on this subject are contained in his book, *This and That of Egyptian Illustration*, a book not only written and illustrated by him, but printed, woodcuts and all, by himself here in Cairo.

The same is true of another book of his with which he presented me – a collection of his poems commencing with one entitled "The Bashful Earthquake".

Further Note —

There is an excellent note on Sitna Damiana (or Dimiana as he calls her) in *The Oriflamme in Egypt*, by Dean Butcher of Cairo, a charming book about the battle of Mansura, &c. His wife points out in her "Story of the Church in Egypt" that there is considerable confusion between the two Saints Catherine and Damiana, particularly as regards their ikons.

curious theories concerning the religious history of the once powerful nation of the Nubians.

My attention has been drawn to an article in which this thesis is developed by Dr. Pappalexis – so significant in some of its points, that I reproduce the part bearing directly on the *zeffa*, regretting that the length of the entire article precludes my adding his further suggestive and illuminating information on "La Grandeur et Décadence des Nubiens".

(The extract in my possession is not dated, but I imagine was written three or four years ago.)

A Curious Religious Survival

(*From our Editorial Staff in Alexandria*)

Were the Nubians, successively, practising Jews and then Christians before their conversion to Islam?

This hypothesis actually seems possible when one compares the religious procession favoured by the Nubians on the first day of the Greater Bairam ['Eid el-Adhâ] with those of the Jews of King David's time, and with the Byzantine litanies preserved in today's Greek Orthodox Church.

Our fellow-countryman, Dr C. Pappalexis, has, in this regard, described in the Hellenic journal "*Pan Egyptia*" (issue of 20 January last), a procession of Nubians in Alexandria, which is absolutely unlike any other you might see in this country's many Islamic festivals.

As observed by Dr Pappalexis, this procession begins at the Nebi Daniel Mosque and finishes at the Marghani Mosque, the latter of which is especially designated for the religious needs of the Nubians.

As for Nebi Daniel Mosque, it is universally known, since the area of its crypt is generally accepted as being the likely final resting place of Alexander the Great.

The Nubian Procession lacks the simplicity found in other Islamic festivals; it has instead more of the pomp and ceremony of the Byzantine Church, and if it were not for the many tarbouches and galabiyas following along, one would think the whole spectacle was Greek.

First of all, the clergy who form the main part of the cortege are dressed just like Greek deacons, lacking neither the colourful Roman-type tunics, nor the stole – or rather the "sticharion" – which is a long, wide sash wrapped round the waist, then up the back and over the shoulders, coming down the

front to the knees. Then, we see all the incense with censers of all types, some
simple, others luxuriously worked, burning an incense exactly the same,
judging by its scent and colour, as that used in Greek churches. But what
really attract the attention are the numerous silk banners, displayed in long
series between the ranks of flags, and held up high – each with embroidered
inscriptions in gold on a background of red, blue, green, or some other colour.
If the participants were only carrying candles and wearing different headgear
– for example, Persian-style mitres – this would be the very image of a
Christian litany. But the festival took place during the day, so candles would
have been out of place.

This Alexandrian festival also brings to mind that of ancient Israel, or
at least the one where King David transfers the Ark of the Covenant to
Jerusalem, his new capital. At the head of the cortege there marches a choir
accompanied by drums like ancient Greek tympanons. The participants are all
"ephebes", that is, young people in their late teens. They begin the procession
as did priests of antiquity when they accompanied the idol of their god, or the
Levites when they transferred the Ark.

There are not many dancers, three or four at the most, and they dance to
the rhythm of the tympanons, as beaten by the ephebes. Following them, is
another group of "the faithful", led by more young people, richly dressed and
carrying flags and banners, while others among them sing hymns. Behind this
second group is left a rather large space, wherein those carrying censers can
freely move about to spread incense among the crowd. This arrangement is
then repeated *ad infinitum* – more singers, dancers and banners; then another
space, and so on… Order is maintained by older men especially designated to
keep an eye on the crowd. They walk ahead of each series in the procession,
taking care, in particular, that the successive open spaces are properly
maintained. The music sung during this spectacle is analogous to that of the
Byzantines, i.e., oriental.

D 3 (cf. Sectional Map XI)
DARGHÂM
(سيدي درغام)

This very pleasant little moulid is held near the end of Shaʻbân. I witnessed it in
1355 (1936), and again on Friday, 27 Shaʻbân 1357 (21 October 1938), when it
seemed to have developed considerably.

It is in a *hâra* of the same name as the mosque, off Shâriʻ Muhammad ʻAlî,
on the right going towards the citadel, and not far from the ʻAtaba end. It is just

beyond the *hâra* and Moulid of Ansârî. It has no secular side. In 1357 (1938), in addition to "zikrs" there was a whirling dervish late in the evening.

D 4 (cf. Sectional Map VIII)
DASHTÛTÎ (SÎDÎ 'ABD EL-QÂDER EL-DASHTÛTÎ)
(سيدي عبد القادر الدشطوطي)

The Moulid of Tashtûshî (as he is usually called) is one of the few limited to a definite date, being held on 26 Rajab, coincident with the *Leilet el-Mi'râg*, or *Leilet el-Isrâ'*, the night of the miraculous journey of the Prophet on the winged horse Burâq to the Seventh Heaven. In 1356 (1937) when, presumably owing to some ambiguity about the moon, the celebrations of *Leilet el-Mi'râg* were on Saturday evening, 27 Rajab (2 October 1937), both in Alexandria and at Sultân Rifâ'î in Cairo, instead of Friday, which according to the official calendar was the true date, the Tashtûshî moulid was correspondingly put off from Friday to Saturday. (This coincidence is probably due to one of the *Sîdî's* reputed miracles being intimately bound up with the miracle of the *Mi'râg*, as described below.)

The Mosque of el-Dashtûtî is easily reached from the 'Ataba by any tram going up Shâri' Farouk to where the *khalîg* crosses the track. A few minutes' walk to the north, along the *khalîg*, or via Shâri' el-'Adâwî, parallel to it brings one to the site of the moulid. Or, of course, a *khalîg* tram serves, in which case one gets down at the first tram station north of the crossing. Also, bus 12 from the Station to Beit el-Qâdî passes through Sikkat Baghâla which is close to Tashtûshî.

Tashtûshî was a most popular and celebrated Saint, and his moulid one of the biggest and most solemn events of the Moslem year in Cairo. He was essentially a Cairene, associated with Ma'âdî, Gîza, Ghamra, and particularly with the district of his mosque, where a street bears his name.

'Abd el-Wahhâb el-Sha'rânî who met him on 1 Ramadân 912 (1507) gives a long account in his *Tabaqât*, of Tashtûshî's affectionate relations with great and small, and of the miracles he wrought. He groups him with the *magâzîb*, a term now used, like *magânîn* for fools, but really meaning those divinely entranced. Indeed, the singular of this word, *magzûb*, was the name of many eminent sheikhs, such as Sheikh 'Alî -l-Damîrî -l-Magzûb, Khalîl el-Magzûb, 'Amr el-Magzûb, &c.

He neither wore hat nor shoes, even on his pilgrimage to Mecca, and had already acquired a reputation for holiness at Medina, and there on arrival, he was too humble to enter the *sanctum sanctorum*, but laid his head on the threshold of the Bâb el-Salâm and slept.

The Sultân Qâitbâi held him in great affection and esteem, and on one occasion obeyed a summons to the grave where Tashtûshî then dwelt, and acceded to his demand for ten thousand dinars for the poor. And the poor got it, for the saint brooked no false claims, and no peculation by his almoners, and regarded a *waqf* as a very sacred trust. One who lapsed is said to have paid for his cupidity with his life.

When the *gazb*, the Spirit of the Lord, came upon him, his life was profoundly modified, much as were the lives of St. Francis and the other saints who received the stigmata. He is reputed to have fasted from all food and drink for forty days, and when his disciples suggested that he had given up praying he could hardly be sure whether indeed he had prayed, or at any rate in the accepted manner, so exalted had been his ecstasy.

Then rumours of amazing miracles spread abroad. It was declared that he slept at the home of two different persons during all the same night in different places, and the Sheikh el-Islâm and the Sheikh Galâl el-Dîn el-Suyûtî investigated and confirmed this. When Qâitbâi hesitated about journeying from the Nile to the Euphrates, and consulted Tashtûshî, and was told to go in peace and safety, he and his companion, the Amîr Yûsef, were surprised at repeatedly seeing him at the head of their party, but disappearing when they dismounted to accost him, but much more surprised on arrival at Aleppo to find him there, and in bed ill, where he had been for many weeks according to the neighbours.

Lane, in his "*Modern Egyptians*" tells of another miracle, which suggests in an interesting way the close association of Sîdî Dashtûtî with the *Leilet el-Mi'râg*. An unbelieving Sultân whilst playing chess with his *wazîr* in a public place, scoffed at the miracle of the Prophet's ascension, on the ground that Burâq, the winged horse, could never have carried Muhammad to Jerusalem, and then to Heaven, and back again to Mecca so quickly that the Prophet's bed had not had time to cool. Tashtûshî, who was hard by, shortly after offered to take on the Sultân at *shatrang* (chess), stipulating that in the event of his winning, he was to be obeyed in a little matter.

The expert Sultân, seeing no possibility of being beaten by the sheikh, willingly agreed, and when in effect he found his king checkmated,[52] he obeyed Tashtûshî's order to plunge in a tank. On entering the water, he found that he was in a royal palace, had changed his sex and was a fair long-haired maiden, who married a prince and brought up three children. When at length he came out of the palace, he also emerged from the water, and was amazed to find his *wazîr*, Tashtûshî, and the rest around the chess board, and on realising that, as they assured him, he could

---

52 [McPher.] *shatrang*, or chess, is of course an ancient Eastern game, whose origin appears in such terms as "checkmate" or *el-sheikh mât*, "the Sheikh is dead".

not have been under the water a single minute without drowning, he recanted his unbelief in the miracle of the *mi'râg*, and became a good Moslem.

Tashtûshî built several mosques and converted many to Islam. When once his scandalised followers blamed him for going to the Christian quarter, and sleeping at the home of a youth who was *nasrânî*[53], he put himself again into good odour by assuring them that the youth was no *nasrânî* – for he had converted him, and had made an excellent Moslem of him.

When he felt a presentiment of death, he ordered the builders of his tomb to hasten with its completion, and to so construct it that no one could share it with him. Then he wept and died in the year of the *Hegira* 930 (1523), and all the great ones of Cairo and many from afar came to do honour at his grave, and amongst them Mâlik el-Amîra, Kheir Bey.

It is no wonder, then, that Lane, writing a hundred years ago, and describing barely half a dozen of the very greatest moulids, should include that of Tashtûshî in this select few. Besides the solemn inauguration of the moulid, the Sheikh el-Bakrî took up his residence on the spot some days before the *Night of the Mir'âg*, and entertained poor and rich most with a hundred dervishes, and then when with many others they had prostrated themselves before the mosque, he rode over their closely packed bodies – he alone being reputed to have the power of performing the *dôsah* to the benefit of souls and without injury to bodies. Then the moulid *battait son plein*[54], until late on the 27th, when, after the *khâtima* [final prayers], the Sheikh el-Bakrî returned in procession.

Alas, what a drab and trumpery affair the moulid has become, under the wet blanket of the modern outlook, and kill-joy restrictions which *pari passu* slay also religious fervour. Even a few years ago the mosque was thronged, and eagerness shown to join in the "zikrs"; in the lively streets, stalls were raised for singing sheikhs, and the cafés were full of mirth, and the band of the Reformatory was a bright and tuneful spot opposite the corner of the mosque, and children could enjoy swings on the tiny hill by the *khalîg*, and even watch the antics of *Qara Goz*.

The year of the Prophet 1356 (1937) saw the "apocolocyntosis"[55] of poor Tashtûshî; no sheikhs sang, no children swung, no band played, few people prayed in the mosque whose outer wall showed a line of police "'askarîs", as the one bright spot. The only thing to interest the multitude was a prison van, like a mighty cage from the zoo, in Shâri' el-Dashtûtî, into which offenders were popped to be

---

53 nasrânî = Christian.
54 *"was going full swing"*.
55 "Gourdification".

jeered at or pitied through the bars. A good thing indeed to immobilise the rare disturbers of the moulid's peace, but why depress and disappoint a host of poor and worthy people; why trample on fine old traditions, and treat the memory of the great miracle worker, and illustrious Cairene with such a miserable simulacrum of the old glory.

I think it was in 1357 (1938), that an English visitor to Egypt accompanied me to this moulid, but remembering a dinner engagement, had only time to locate the mosque, and note the decorations and a few circumcision booths and such like. Having read Lane's account, these seemed promising, and he asked me to meet him there at 9.30. This I did, but he had brought the whole dinner party, an English professor, and three foreign diplomats, all in evening dress with tall hats or Opera caps. We proved an immense attraction, and were joined by great numbers who evidently regarded us as the best show of the evening, and as the nucleus of an up-to-date procession, till a much-worried police officer "besought us to depart out of their coasts".[56]

D. 5 (cf. Map of Delta)
DESÛQI (SÎDÎ IBRÂHÎM EL-DESÛQÎ)
(سيدي إبراهيم الدسوقي)

It may seem a little out of place to include this in the Cairo moulids, as of course the great celebrations are at Desûq in the Delta where Desûqî was buried in 1278 A.D., but it is interesting to know that at Sâqiyet Mecca, close to Gîza (and therefore to Cairo), we have representatives of the illustrious line holding, I am told, the diploma (sanad) of the tarîqa Desûqîya. These hold "zikrs", readings, and quiet ceremonies in honour of their founder, though he has not even a cenotaph there.

I have never been, but sent two reliable "murâslas" to it Monday, 17 Gamâd I 1353 (27 August 1934); and in 1357 (1938), it was reported to me as held on Sunday, 18 Gamâd II (14 August 1938), the same day as Sîdî 'Uqbî, which he said was the case each year. I know of no reason for this synchronism.

Though Egypt justly claims Sîdî Ibrâhîm el-Desûqî, he is far from being a merely local saint. His cult in Palestine, Syria, and some other places perhaps exceeds that in this country. With the "walîs" 'Abd el-Qâdir el-Galânî, Ahmad el-Rifâ'î, and Ahmad el-Bedawî, he is said to "hold up the earth". These four great founders of mighty dervish orders – tŭrŭq – are therefore known as the "poles". They are deemed as pre-existent in the spirit of Muhammad, and as trees of which the other tŭrŭq are the branches. It will be noticed that of these "four poles",

---

56 Matthew 8:34.

Egypt can boast also Ahmad Sayyid el-Bedawî, buried at Tantâ, and honoured by perhaps the greatest moulid known, and though Ahmad el-Rifâ'î lies at Baghdad his cult in Egypt is immense.

E 1 (cf. Sectional Map XI)
EMERY I = 'AMRÎ I

(سيدي عمري)

Present on Friday, 20 Sha'bân 1352 (8 December 1933), 15 Sha'bân 1353 (23 November 1934), and 18 Sha'bân 1354 (15 November 1935) – in each case the third Friday in Sha'bân.

The little mosque is very near the *khalîg*, between it and Shâri' Muhammad 'Alî. Any tram from 'Ataba -l-Khadrâ going in the direction of the Citadel will serve. Leave the tram at the first stop after Bâb el-Khalq, and proceed for a few minutes up the little street to the right.

It is a small and squalid moulid, attended sometimes by dirty, officious, offensive people, especially of the hooligan class, and the immediate surroundings are not very attractive. There are no secular attractions beyond a few cafés and singing groups near the mosque, and it is one of the very few moulids not much to be recommended to visitors.

E2 (cf. Sectional Map XVI)
EMERY II = 'AMRÎ II

(سيدي عمري)

Present on Friday, 21 Sha'bân 1355 (6 November 1936)

The small rather modern mosque of Sîdî 'Amrî is in the *hâra* of that name off Shâri' Ibn Tûlûn, near the great mosque of Tûlûn, and between it and the *gabel*.

Bus 4 which can be picked up at the Gezîra, English Bridge, Bâb el-Lûq, etc., takes one to Tûlûn; also bus 13 from Gîza to the mosque of Sayyida Zeinab, and any tram to Sayyida Zeinab leaves one a short interesting walk, but the best way is by bus 18 plying between Darâsa and Sitna Nafîsa, via 'Ataba -l-Khadrâ, in which case it should be left at Shâri' Ibn Tûlûn, and that street followed past the big mosque.

It is a tiny moulid, and perhaps mainly interesting from its position near Tûlûn. In 1355 (1936) a great sheikh from Sultân el-Rifâ'î attracted many in the evening.

F 1 (cf. Sectional Map I)
FARAG
(سيدي فرج)

On one of the two occasions on which I saw this moulid I noted the date – Thursday, 7 Rabî' II 1353 (19 July 1934) – but have not found it at or about that time since. According to informants on the spot, it can only be held when the piece of almost waste land in front of the mosque on which it is kept is free from crops. (Several other moulids, especially provincial ones, have their dates more or less dependent on the cultivation.)

This spot can be reached by car via Gezîrat el-Badrân, or by a walk of about 10 minutes from the level crossing in Shâri' Saptia, to which tram 4 takes one, or by a rather longer walk from the Rôd el-Farag track, tram 13, leaving the tram at the raised part shortly before the site of the Moulid of Sîdî Hillî.

It is a pretty and jolly moulid, or was when I saw it, with "zikrs" about the mosque, and theatres, Punch and Judy, performing dogs and the rest away in the patch of land.

ABÛ TÎG

F 2 (cf. Map of Upper Egypt)
FARGHÂL
(سيدي فرغال)

This is one of the important moulids of Upper Egypt and is held at or near Abû Tîg in Rabî' II.

F 3 (cf. Sectional Map XIV)
FÂTIMA -L-NEBAWÎYA
(ستنا فاطمة النبوية)

This important moulid is usually held on the last Monday of Rabî' I. Anyway, this was the case in 1351 (1932), 1353 (1934), 1356 (1937), 1359 (1940) on which four occasions I was present, but in 1348 (1929) I think it was on a later date, and in 1357 (1938) the great night was Monday, 7 Rabî' II (6 June 1938), and in 1358 Monday, 3 Rabî' II (22 November 1939).

The little mosque is in the Darb el-Ahmar district, one of the least spoilt and least known bits of Cairo, though not far from Tabbâna and the popular mosque of Âqsunqur (the Blue Mosque), but away to the East towards the *gabel*.

Though as a function the moulid has dwindled, a ramble is well worth while, through the narrow streets beneath mighty buildings, whose stones in places are so

Dr Mahmûd 'Enâyet Allâh, Doyen of Circumcision
(at the Moulid of Fâtima -l-Nebawîya).

immense that one's attention hardly strays beyond them. *Quand les pierres disent de telles choses, on oublie les édifices.*[57]

It is easily reached by bus 17 which on its way to Bâb el-Wazîr passes the entry to sundry gaily be-flagged little streets on the left, either of which leads in a very few minutes to the heart of the moulid.

Whether I had been extraordinarily unobservant in previous years, or whether 1351 (1932) was an epoch in Egyptian moulids, I do not know, but I rarely, if ever, noticed either public circumcision booths or Sudanese music and dancing before that date. In 1351 (1932), the former were most conspicuous at Fâtima -l-Nebawîya, and the latter, though too far from the mosque to call attention, were big and numerous in a side street.

The booth of Dr. Mahmûd 'Enâyet Allâh, the doyen of this guild was at the door of the mosque, and those of Dr. Nâdî and others in Hâret el-Nebawîya and the *shâri'* of the same name. Each booth had its large framed picture illustrating the operation. An European doctor to whom I mentioned this, and who was in the habit of charging L. 5 to parents desiring to mutilate their offspring, greatly mar-velled that anything so delicate could be achieved so summarily for nothing or a few piastres, with results enviably satisfactory and safe; and desiring to witness the technique accompanied me on the penultimate day of the moulid. Though these medical gentlemen showed no desire to conceal the secrets of their skill and were most obliging, we had come at an off-time, when there were few patients, and only one operation, that on a little girl, in action. As my companion was only remaining a day or two in Egypt, he expressed his willingness to pay for anyone the small customary fee, and 5 piastres over to the patient. The response was surprising, and one of the volunteers was an old gentleman who looked about seventy, to whom it was explained with difficulty that certain things can only happen once in a lifetime.

In 1353 (1934) moulids seem to have reached their zenith, for modern times, as witness a notice in the Arabic papers of that date, which reads:

Moulid El-Sayyida Fâtima

The Ministry of Interior has authorised the observance of the Moulid of El-Sayyida Fatima El-Nebawiya by the people of the Darb el-Ahmar, Cairo, for a period of fifteen days beginning today and ending Monday evening, 9

---

57 "When the stones say such things, one forgets the buildings!" Source unknown.

At the Moulid of Fâtima -l-Nebawîya, "an adjacent tomb of
considerable sanctity". The person to the left is Muhammad Mûsa,
McPherson's *murâsla* (a military term meaning "orderly").

July 1934, and H. E. 'Abd el-Maqsud Khadr, Naqib el-Sada el-Ashraf of Giza
Mudiria, has undertaken the decorations and ceremonies in honour of the
night of commemoration of this majestic moulid.

It should be mentioned in this connection that the full title "Naqîb el-Ashrâf"
is a very eminent one in Islam, being at least as high as 'Patriarch' in Christendom. The *Naqîb el-Sâda* or *Sheikh el-Sâda*, is the lineal descendant of the *khalîfa*
'Alî, and "occupied the carpet" of that great Founder, the spiritual throne. There
is another who "occupies the carpet" of the *khalîfa* 'Omar, and yet a third, the
greatest of all, and ruler of all Cairo dervishes, whose "carpet" is that of the first
khalîfa, Abû Bakr. He, of course, is the Sheikh el-Bakrî, Naqîb el-Ashrâf, (chief of
the "sharîfs"), who figures largely at the Moulid el-Nebî, and other great moulids
and Islamic functions.

(These *Naqâ'ib* are commonly credited with supernatural powers. Early in
the century, for instance, I was assured in the palanquin of the last named, that
the Khedive 'Abbâs Hilmî had been smitten by a dreadful infirmity for speaking
disrespectfully about him, but on humbling himself in the dust before the representative of Abû Bakr, he was miraculously cured.)

Three years later, 1357 (1938), when I went with Eric Gill the sculptor and
other visitors, the moulid had still much of its old charm and characteristics, and
they were edified and deeply interested: but on 7 Rabî' II 1357 (6 June 1938), an
unpleasant air of insincerity had crept into the moulid, demonstrating convinc-
ingly the ill results of restraining the natural expression of the people's piety and
emotions. Going in the afternoon to see the *zeffa* disappointed people told me
there was not to be one, and I was presented to a forlorn-looking sheikh whom
they had expected to mount as *khalîfa* and follow to some shrine.

Whilst talking to him I was greatly puzzled at hearing music, rather blatant
from some brass instruments, and seeing a little crowd escorting a turbaned
rider. A *zeffa* after all, I thought, but some rival *khalîfa*, and straightway followed. My first shock was when we were about to emerge by the side of a
beautiful mosque detached on all sides, into the main road near the *caracôl*;
a carter blocking the way made no effort to make room for the *khalîfa*, and
addressed that dignitary in language worse than flippant, to which he replied in
terms I cannot put down, starting a duel between the two of coarse *badinage*,
and to increase my amazement the people laughed and chaffed. We ultimately
halted in the court of a large private house, where the *khalîfa* in response to
requests from the windows above descended from his horse, did a comic dance
and held up his garment to catch coins which they were throwing down. "What

manner of holy man is this?" I asked. "Oh, he is a *magzûb*"[58] was the reply: "Isn't he funny?"

So, I was no longer assisting at the ancient picturesque devotion of the *zeffa*, but at a mockery. I came away.

Sitna Fâtima -l-Nebawîya was no less a personage than the daughter of Sidna Husein, and great-grand-daughter of the Prophet. She was therefore great-aunt of the other Fâtima -l-Nebawîya, bint Ga'far Sâdiq, the Sixth Imâm. (The moulid of this namesake is held on an early Tuesday of Sha'bân in a street of the same name (Nebawîya) near Bâb el-Khalq, behind the Appeals Prison.)

May Allâh see that the great-grand-daughter of His prophet has a *zeffa* this year worthy of her lofty state, and not a vulgar clown to usurp so honourable a position.

It is painful to have to add a note on the moulid of Monday, 28 Rabî' I 1359 (6 May 1940) within the war period, but before that had assumed alarming proportions. In point of fact, I could not ascertain any connection between the war and the happenings about the shrine of the grand-daughter of the Prophet.

This is referred to in the Preface, in striking contrast to the happy peaceful evening enjoyed by the people in the royal square, for this was the occasion of the King's accession.

I had seen the moulid timidly working up on two of the preliminary evenings, and though late after the royal entertainment (after 10 perhaps), went to the great *dénouement*. The usually bright Tabbâna district was gloomy, and on turning up one of the streets towards the mosque I was stopped by an '*askarî* and told that it was forbidden to go there. Though this was repeated elsewhere, I finally arrived by a roundabout way, to find sheer desolation. I enquired the cause of sheikhs, residents, police (including an officer) and visitors, and elicited no reason. One, indeed, gave me in lieu of valid reason, that there had been loose women in the neighbourhood, and took me to the place where these had offended, and in truth I needed a guide, it was so far from the afflicted shrine. All whom I spoke to, and those I did not, seemed distressed – except perhaps one Italian-speaking visitor, who remarked, "You are too late for the raid: except for the costumes, how splendidly it would have filmed – as a ghetto in Warsaw with the Gestapo at work!"

---

58 [McPher.] Magzûb, which in its original meaning is "entranced", "carried away by God", is commonly used, as in this case, for a fool or buffoon.

F 4 (cf. Sectional Map XI)
FÂTIMA -L-NEBAWîYA BINT GA'FAR SÂDIQ
(السيدة فاطمة النبوية بنت جعفرصادق)

Always held on a Tuesday early in Sha'bân: in 1355 (1936), 1356 (1937) and 1358 (1939) on the first Tuesday; in 1354 (1935), 1357 (1938) and 1359 (10 September 1940) on the second.

This must not be confused with the Moulid of Fâtima -l-Nebawîya held in the month of Rabî' I in the Darb el-Ahmar district (which see). They are both in a street called by the same name, el-Nebawîya, but the tomb of Bint Ga'far Sâdiq is behind the Governorate and Appeals Prison, and therefore reached by any Citadel or *khalîg* tram or bus.

This is clearly the daughter of the Sixth Imâm, 'Abdullah Ga'far Sâdiq, the inscription over the door of the shrine being: "This is the *maqâm* of Sayyida Fâtima -l-Nebawîya bint Ga'far Sâdiq".

She is, therefore, the grand-daughter of Zein el-'Abdîn and descended directly from the Prophet through Husein, and is sister to Sitna 'Aysha and Sitna Sakîna, both of whom, as well as Zein el-'Abdîn, have moulids in Cairo.

It is, or was, a small but lively and attractive moulid, and the shrine well worth a visit; but it has changed character in a curious way. When I first saw it in 1353 (1934), the very numerous "zikrs" dominated everything. They were very weird and earnest in the cave-like *sous-sol* (underground) chambers of the *sikka* (lane), and throughout the range of the moulid. In 1354 (1935), more than one of these caverns had become cafés of sorts, and two others presented strange sights. In one, youthful dervishes, or would-be dervishes, were whirling, and in the other, was a boys' *zikr*, conducted so sedately and with such apparent seriousness, that I did not see any one of the little chaps rebuked by his elders.

But the really curious change came in 1355 (1936), when, except in the tomb, it was difficult to find a *zikr*, and, on the other hand, the street under the prison windows was full of little gaming stalls and amusements of all sorts, to the great delight of the occupants of the cells who joined in vociferously from their windows. This modification was quite paradoxical as it came just when the *mot d'ordre* was to raise the spiritual and religious side of moulids at the expense of what was considered profane. In effect, exactly the opposite came about; but all was orderly and happy, and nothing to shock the gentlemen up at their windows.

Another thing in 1355 (1936), which to me was new and peculiar, was the observance of the *subû'*, octave, of the great night on 11 Sha'bân, the official consummation of the moulid having been on the fourth. That, however, took an almost exclusively religious form.

I have never seen a *zeffa* there, but this is probably my own fault in coming late, as I was assured on arriving after sunset in 1356 (1937) that there had been a very fine procession with mounted *khalifa* in the afternoon.

The daughter of the great VIth Imam was one of the first scapegoats of the war. Her moulid fixed for Tuesday, 5 Sha'bân 1358 (19 September 1939) was simply crushed, and her shrine forsaken. Enquiring the reason at a cigarette shop near the end of the Shâri' el-Nebawîya, I was taken for an official and informed in tones of horror that some wretch had had the audacity to play on an *arghûl* in the street under the prison. I wonder what his fate was and why this dear instrument, with its immensely long reed and deep base notes, almost peculiar to Egypt, the delight of visitors and the pride of music-loving Egyptians, should have fallen under a ban. I looked up at the prison windows, generally full of happy faces enjoying an annual treat. Not a face! Poor things, they doubtless found their cells more cheerful than the look-out.

Finding a café open, I called for a *qirfa* (cinnamon tea) and an Arabic paper. In that I read an exhortation from the ancient university to cheerful acceptance of the situation that might follow from the war, and to carry on as usual. Other equally harmless platitudes followed but the whole tone was so depressing that I felt it should be read aloud in the perfect staging of this little corner of dejection, like Mark Antony's oration in the Roman Forum.

F 5 (cf. Map of Upper Egypt)
FÛLÎ
(سيدي فولي)

I have no information about this moulid except that it is of local importance in the Minyâ district of Upper Egypt.

Sheikh Fûlî is generally credited with being the *wali* who protects us from crocodiles, by preventing their passing north of Minyâ, but this is contested by the votaries of certain other "walîs" by the side of the Nile further South.

G 1 (cf. Sectional Map I)
GALÂDÎN
(سيدي جلادين)

This I saw on 27 Sha'bân 1355 (12 November 1936), but on going more recently about that date I have been informed that I am too late.

It is in a street of the same name in the Bûlâq district, off the Sûq el-'Asr, and adjoining the Hâret el-Kurdî, where the moulid of that name is celebrated (cf. Kurdî).

It is small and bright, without any shows, and centres about the mosque of
Galâdîn. A conspicuous inscription in the mosque is "Fear of the Lord is the beginning of Wisdom".[59]

G 2 (cf. Sectional Map III)
GALÂL
(سيدي جلال)

Held on Sunday, but the day of the month and the month itself varies. It was on 4
Muharram 1354 (7 April 1935) when I first discovered it through my *murâsla*, 20
Muharram in 1355 (12 April 1936) and 21 Safar in 1356 (2 May 1937).

It is in the Sharâbîya district behind the railways, about half way between the
Station of Kubrî Lîmûn and the site of the Moulid of Mazlûm (which see). There
is no way of reaching it, as far as I know, except by walking (about half an hour),
riding or driving. One misses the good old donkeys when going, and still more on
returning, as a cab easily obtained at Kubrî Lîmûn to go there, generally fails to
return for one late in the evening.

There is one theatre and a few shows in a long squalid street, and it is hardly
worth a visit. I suppose there is a mosque or shrine, but have not found it. It boasts,
however, a fair *zeffa* in the afternoon.

ASYÛT

G 3 (cf. Map of Upper Egypt)
GALÂL EL-DÎN EL-ASYÛTÎ
(سيدي جلال الدين الأسيوطي)

Being in this most ancient city of Lycopolis in the middle of June 1936, I had the
good luck to see the big provincial moulid in full swing. The great night was on
28 Rabî' I 1355 (18 June 1936).

Its features, both religious and secular, were on the whole those of a typical
moulid, but being a rare occurrence in these parts, there was more excitement
and intensity than is usual at a Cairo moulid. A zeal amounting almost to fanaticism animated a group of dervishes, as a party of English friends of mine butted
in. These were solemnly warned off the pitch by a venerable turbaned sheikh,
to whom their bare or billy-cocked heads and very *ifrângî* gait was evidently a
shock, I think, quite understandably so, but what repelled him and his associates
proved an irresistible charm to a multitude of youngsters who formed a moving

---

59 Identical wording is found in Proverbs 9:10.

entourage whithersoever they wended. Staying on in my inconspicuous *tarbûsh*, unchallenged and in peace, I marvelled for the umpteenth time at the peculiar insular complex still rife which prevents many from appearing in the Egyptian head-dress except when obliged to by their official functions.

The number of sugar figures, "'arûsas", great at all moulids, was here enormous, and many of them of a type no longer seen in Cairo except rarely, suggestive of Tanagra,[60] or of Pompeian figurines, groups representing the loves of the animals, human and otherwise: of much interest, I am told, anthropologically. Lycopolis was of course a great centre of the animal cult, mummies of which are still abundant, so that the excess of these figurines here is suggestive.

G 4
GAMÂL EL-DÎN
(سيدي جمال الدين)

A small moulid reported as held on Thursday, 17 Gamâd II 1358 (3 August 1939) at Kafr Turmus near Saft.

G 5
GAMÎLA
(ستنا جميلة)

Reported as one of the Imâm el-Shâfe'î group, held in the tombs about the middle of Sha'bân.

G 6 (cf. Sectional Map VIII)
GAMÂL (SÎDÎ MUHAMMAD EL-GAMÂL)
(سيدي محمد الجمال)

A member of the group of small moulids held at the end of Sha'bân near the Bâb el-Nasr. The very pretty tomb of the Sîdî is in the Hâret [Bîr] Guwân.

G 7 (cf. Sectional Map XIV)
GÂNIB
(سيدي جانب)

I was conducted to this on its penultimate night, on Saturday, 28 Sha'bân 1357 (22 October 1938), by a dervish with whom I made friends at the little Moulid of 'Alî -l-Gîzî in the tombs of the Fatimite "khalîfas", but to our distress found that for some reason the police had actively discouraged it by moving on the people

---

60 Boeotian town in Greece famous for its figurines.

who were sitting about in the Sarûgîya [district] where the tomb is situated, even those recessed back from the road. I did not go the next night so that I cannot tell to what extent it was observed. The district is not nearly as well-known as it deserves, though it is very accessible, between Bâb el-Mitwâllî and the Mosque of Sultân Rifâ'î in Shâri' Muhammad 'Alî.

G 8
GHARÎB (SHEIKH EL-GHARÎB)
(شيخ الغريب)
One of the three little moulids held in the village of Mît 'Uqba, the others being Sîdî 'Uqbî and Sheikh el-Lâshînî.

I do not know if it is always the case, but in 1358 all three were held on one evening, Thursday 24 Gamâd II 1358 (10 August 1939, cf. 'Oqbî/'Uqbî).

G 9 (cf. Sectional Map XVIII)
GIRGIS (MÂR GIRGIS OR ST. GEORGE)
(مار جرجس)
This Christian moulid, observed by Copts and Orthodox Greeks principally, is naturally held on or very near the Feast Day of the Saint. This being according to the Latin calendar on 23 April, and the old reckoning being 13 days later, the observance is at the beginning of May. In 1937 it was 2 May, that is 24 Barmûda 1653 (21 Safar 1356).

It should not be missed, for the old fortress of Trajan in which the Church of St. George, and a Chapel beneath belonging to the Copts are situated, is a picture of light and life. The circular galleries and every part are full of people, visiting the shrine or sitting about meditating or engaged on more social intercourse; and a curious woman's ceremony is observed now as on certain other occasions of circling the head with a mighty and ancient chain. Outside the barbican all is light-hearted enjoyment at the tent cafés and little shows, most of which are just on the other side of the level crossing. Inside the fortress of Babylon too there is unusual animation and light, but the sombre majesty of this classic *enceinte* with its ancient Coptic churches, synagogue and buildings seems only to become more striking.

Let us hope that this Feast will not go the way of those of St. Mercurius (Abû Seifein), and St. Sergius (Abû Sarga), which according to Butler's notes were brilliant in his day, and now alas, as far as I can ascertain almost vanishing quantities!

I am told there are considerable observances at Asyût.

G 10 (cf. Sectional Map XVII)
GÎZÎ (SÎDÎ 'ALÎ EL-GÎZÎ)

(سيدي علي الجيزي)

At 9 o'clock of the evening of 28 Sha'bân 1357 (22 October 1938), I accidentally came across a small zeffa with the usual lanterns and tambourines, and the dark banners of the Rifâ'îya approaching the tombs of the Fatimite "khalîfas"; and joining it, we soon arrived at a tâbût, that of Sîdî 'Alî el-Gîzî, where a religious service commenced leading up to a zikr.

The weird surroundings, and the zeal of a wild-looking, earnest and picturesque little crowd gave a romantic air to this small and obscure moulid.

Its position is just off the track of tram 18 to the west, near the beginning of the tombs.

MINYET EL-QAMH

G 11 (cf. Map of Delta)
GÛDA

(الشيخ جوده)

I am told reliably that this is a big and important moulid, and was held in the year 1358 on Thursday, 25 Gamâd I (13 July 1939).

Minyet el-Qamh is on the main line between Benhâ and Zagâzîg [Zaqâzîq], and about half way between the two. I should like to know whether the name of the next station given on the railway map as el-Gûdaiyida has anything to do with Sheikh Gôda (or Gûda).

H 1 (cf. Sectional Map X)
HAMZA

(شيخ حمزه)

Sheikh Hamza favours a Friday for his moulid, but seems thankful in these days for any date he can obtain, since he is under a sad cloud. In 1351 the chief night was that of Friday, 14 Gamâd II (14 October 1932), in 1353 Friday, 28 Gamâd I (7 September 1934), and in 1354 the date at first fixed, Friday, 15 Gamâd II (13 September 1935), was changed to Sunday, 18 Sha'bân (15 November 1935). Since then, it has been quite irregular. In 1359 it was on Friday, 29 Gamâd I (5 July 1940).

The tomb is at the junction of Shâri' Balaqsa and Shâri' el-Qawâla, the latter being the street at right angles to the old front of Bâb el-Lûq Station: the mosque is a little up Balaqsa which opens up at the other end in view of 'Abdîn Palace, and is near and parallel to 'Imâd el-Dîn.

The secular attractions were of the simplest, not going beyond vendors of biscuits which might or might not contain a prize varying from a *millième* to a *barîza* (10 piastres), and the quaint sellers of equally quaint articles to a chorus of *ma'lûm* from the youngsters. Its great feature was the *zeffa* from the mosque of el-'Ashmâwî, which attracted an enthusiastic concourse, but 1351 (1932) was the beginning of sorrows, for the pressure and excitement of the people was such that on entering the narrow Balaqsa, the old infirm *khalîfa* fell from his young and frightened horse. Not that he was physically hurt for his supporters caught him before he reached the ground and carried him to the shrine, but many looked on this as an evil omen. This superstition gains support from the fact that things have never gone well since; the moulid has been put off or the *zeffa* forbidden, and in a recent year someone must have been deemed to have sinned against "morals and religion", and the moulid was afflicted in consequence. I had returned with friends from Ma'âdî, and we were walking down Shâri' el-Qawâla ignorant that it was Sheikh Hamza's day, until we were suddenly swept nearly off our feet by a rush of terrified votaries pursued by "'askarîs" with canes, and the "purge" extended to the walls of the tomb where women were sitting in supposed sanctuary. Disgruntled souls assured us that 'Abdîn *caracôl* was like a concentration camp for the nonce. My poor friends, who had long wanted to see a moulid, are cured of that yearning, and have carried away the idea that such is a pious observance, from which a blessing is looked for through flagellation.

It sometimes happens that an early minor night is more edifying and enjoyable than the final. That was the case on 10 Sha'bân 1354 (7 November 1935), three days before the *apodosis*, when I went through Shâri' Balaqsa with the Professor of Anthropology of the Egyptian University and his wife, and finding things very dull, we were about to move on to the Moulid of Sîdî Muwaffaq behind Abû -l-'Elâ. But suddenly a whirling dervish appeared, with the accessories of music, etc., and his performance and endurance were wonderful, and the whole scene impressive.

Resurgat Hamza![61]

H 2 (cf. Sectional Map XIII)
HANAFÎ (SULTÂN HANAFÎ)
(سلطان حنفي)

On each of seven occasions that I have been present, the main day has been the first Wednesday after mid-Sha'bân, so that this is one of the moulids whose date

---

61 May Hamza rise again!

can be calculated and relied on. It is also an example of the utility of noting the day over a series of years, and establishing one's formula, so to speak, in preference to empirical information about the expected time. Sultân Hanafî runs officially for seven days, but decorations are up for nearly a month, and I have again and again been given a wrong and unduly early date, and should have had a journey in vain, but for preferring the above generalisation.

The two great contiguous mosques of Hanafî and Sâleh are in a little known region between 'Abdîn and Sayyida Zeinab, worthy of far better acquaintance. For those not familiar with the intricacies of the district, they are best reached by tram 17 or bus 18, getting out where one leaves Shâri' 'Emâd el-Dîn at Shâri' Sheikh Kilyân. By walking straight on the small remainder of 'Emâd el-Dîn and turning down to the left, one is on the spot in a few minutes.

There was a great charm about this moulid, now unhappily lost. There never were (in my time) theatres, "ringas" and such like, but in the little side streets the people brought out chairs and musical instruments, and a table decorated with lighted candles and flowers, and the singing and playing had a most pleasant effect, and was often really good, a graceful supplement to the more austere ceremonies at the mosque. Then a little south of the mosque, on the other side of the road, and well out of sight and sound, a mighty stone gateway and an arched passage leading to a great space amongst old palaces revealed a merry host of youngsters on swings and goose nests, or enjoying the quaintest of Punch and Judy shows and shadow pictures. That survived until 1357 (1938).

Circumcision booths with their great framed pictures are still plentiful, and I am glad to say an innovation of hanging huge banners across the street bearing an inscription offering free treatment, survived only one year, 1351 (1932).

A dramatic incident occurred the next year not easily forgotten. A most peaceful evening was suddenly marred by the apparition of a mad woman, blaspheming and attacking anyone who tried to restrain her, with teeth and nails. Holy men who tried to quiet her regretted their temerity, and police and people were puzzled how to deal with such a fury, whose strength seemed almost supernatural. When even gallant "'askarîs" recoiled before her fangs and claws, suddenly a merry handsome lad cut in, laughed cheerily in her face, chaffed her, and ultimately led her quietly away, joking her as they went. He soon returned and I asked him if he knew her? "O, no", said he, "but she's all right!" I have seen and heard of the youth several times since, Mahmûd 'Alî by name, and was recently told that he is with the RAF, a fine boxer and in the running for Olympic honours.

In 1354 (1935), the ancient zeffa was suppressed in the afternoon. In the evening there was a little one to a shrine in a neighbouring street. In that year the

Sheikh el-Khûlî, of some local importance, showed me remarkable old buildings in the neighbourhood of the Punch and Judy enclosure referred to above, one immense place suggestive of the well-known Beit el-Qâdî. He also offered to show me a treasure worth L.10,000. The Sheikh Abû -l-'Elâ of 'Agûza showed me much of interest about the mosque and explained the enormous wooden buttresses and supports which disfigured it as the result of Sultân Hanafî's injunctions to his followers against tampering with his mosque by any sort of repairs. That too implicit obedience to such exhortations is dangerous has been demonstrated by the tragedy of Abû -l-'Elâ, amongst other cases, so the authorities have wisely taken the matter in hand and effected considerable repairs to the stone work and removed the timber. As I write in February 1939 (Zû -l-Higga 1357), King Farouk is expected shortly to inaugurate the restored mosque. God save the King, and restore the dilapidated moulid!

Since penning the above I have seen two moulids under war conditions, and in spite of having to fight against these and more destructive foes at home, they *did* show favourable symptoms, and at the moulid of Wednesday, 22 Sha'bân of this year 1359 (25 September 1940), old Punch had come to life again, and was very actively pugnacious in attacking powers of evil new to him in the persons of Hitler and Mussolini. But a sick moulid takes a lot of healing. Let us hope Sîdî Hanafî has kind and pious friends to nurse his feast back to vigour and beauty.

The date of the first Wednesday after mid-Sha'bân was strictly adhered to on both of these occasions.

H 3 (cf. Sectional Map XIII)
HÂRÛN (SÎDÎ HÂRÛN EL-HUSEINÎ)
(سيدي هارون الحسيني)

In these days when even old-established moulids are struggling for existence, and in some cases, as in that of Dashtûtî, fallen from the eminence and magnificence of a national and Islamic celebration to a parade in front of a more or less neglected shrine under police supervision, it is a high pleasure to be able to record the revival of an ancient moulid, which had not been observed within the memory of this generation until its re-establishment a few years ago by, the writer is proud to add, the instrumentality of one of his own countrymen – one, too, who has breathed in all that is best of the atmosphere of Egypt, whose taste and judgment in such Oriental matters is above all attack, the springs of whose actions are purely a love of Egypt and the Egyptians, and all that is venerable and beautiful in the valley of the Nile and elsewhere.

Sîdî Hârûn, spoken of as Huseinî owing to his close relationship to Sidna

Husein and therefore to the Prophet, has his *maqâm* at the corner of the great *enceinte* of Ibn Tûlûn. It forms part of, perhaps, the most beautiful old house in Cairo, rendered more so by the lovely antiques introduced by its occupant. He has put the tomb in order, lighted and adorned it, and established there an ancient sheikh, Sheikh Suleimân el-Kreitlîya, of the family associated for generations with the shrine and the house, and who boasts his *sanad* connecting him with the *walî* whose tomb he watches over.[62]

The new lease of life commenced in 1354 (1935), so that the great celebration on 23 Sha'bân 1357 (17 October 1938) was the fourth. Each year it has been in Sha'bân, though the day of the month has varied from the 11th to the 26th.

It is best reached from the 'Ataba by bus 18, getting down at Shâri' Ibn Tûlûn, from which point it is barely two minutes distant. Bus 4 also passes near, and it is quite a short walk from the Citadel and from Sayyida Zeinab, to both of which sub-centres many trams and buses run.

Sîdî Hârûn is a very colourful and tuneful little moulid. It has its *zeffa*, with visits to the tomb, followed by *zikrs*, and the usual ritual, and a great feature has been a dervish of the Rifâ'îya whose mastery over fire can hardly be explained on natural lines. He also fascinates all present by the use of his *dabbûs*, a straight dagger headed by a ball to which are attached a number of short chains terminating in pieces of metal, to produce a musical effect, enhanced sometimes by objects contained in the ball, which is in that case a kind of sistrum. The *dabbûs* is thrust freely through his face or into his body without any appearance of pain or flow of blood. A whirling dervish and a *hâwî* add also their quotum.

The tomb, over whose dome floats a mighty gonfalon in the colours of the Rifâ'îya, besides numerous smaller banners and the processional *bawâriq* has a little window looking on to a picturesque corner garden known as the "Dorotheum", which on these occasions is very full of visitors, only lightly separated from the *zikr* enclosure. The overflow take up a commanding position on the roof of the Beit el-Kreitlîya, or at the *mashrabîya* embrasures, or at the door of the tomb with the old Sheikh and his pious companions, initiates of the Qâdarîya, Rifâ'îya, Shâzlîya and other *tŭrŭq*, "murîds" and "tâlibs", "nâ'ibs", "khalîfas" and the rest – a goodly company.

These are not a whit disturbed by the proximity of non-Moslems and Occidentals, for happily the virtues of tolerance, mutual regard, and sympathy are the

---

62 The occupant referred to is Irish-born aesthete, art collector, soldier and former Oriental Secretary to High Commissioner Field Marshal Viscount Allenby, Robert Gayer-Anderson (1881–1945).

Beit el-Kreitlîya, home of McPherson's friend, "John" Gayer-Anderson. Now the Gayer-Anderson Museum. Beit el-Kreitlîya means "the house of the Cretan woman", referring to a lady who is said to have owned the house in the late 18th or early 19th century.

blessed order of the day in Egypt, and indeed they soon become so absorbed in their mode of throwing off all earthly shackles, that they are rendered oblivious to all visible surroundings.

This meeting and blending of East and West in the home of an ex-Oriental Secretary is a heartening sight, and the names or functions of a few of the people I have met at this Moulid of Sîdî Hârûn will show what varied types of Anglo-Egyptian society have been represented, by no means excluding those also of other nationalities. I have seen leading members of the British Embassy there, and Baron de Bildt and other representative diplomats, also the Commandant of Police[63], with Lady Russell,[64] and sundry distinguished Egyptian Officers. It is not, perhaps, generally known that Sir Thomas is an authority on dervish lore and *persona grata* with the *bâbâ* and monks of the Bektashi *tekîya*[65], at the "Maghrûrî" under the Muqattam Hills, and (so the *bâbâ* informed me with great satisfaction) is writing a book about their Order. One of the officers referred to, Yuzbâshî 'Abd el-Rahmân Zâkî,[66] showed me the second volume of his work on Cairo, *El-Qâhira*, beautifully introduced and illustrated. Other writers present of authority and renown on the monuments of Islam were Mrs. Devonshire[67] and Prof. Creswell[68]. In the Poets' corner was Prof. Scaife[69] of the Egyptian University, whose beautiful *qasîda* on Sayyid el-Bedawî was read by himself in these most appropriate surroundings not long ago. Also, the poet and writer, Mr. S. F. A. Coles,[70] who, by the way, introduced a picture of the tomb of Sîdî Hârûn into his account of the Beit el-Kreitlîya, in the *Sphinx*, 9 November 1935.[71]

---

63 Sir Thomas Russell Pâsha (1879–1954), Commandant of the Police in Cairo.
64 Author of *Medieval Cairo and the Monasteries of the Wadi Natrun: A Historical Guide* (London, 1962).
65 An architectural term referring to the hall of assembly in a Sufi "monastery", though McPherson is presumably using it to mean the monastery itself. See Glossary: tekîya.
66 No information available.
67 Henriette Devonshire (1864–1949), author of *Rambles in Cairo* (Cairo, 1917).
68 Professor Sir Keppel Archibald Cameron Creswell (1879–1974), distinguished historian of Islamic Art.
69 Christopher Scaife (1900–88), poet. He worked as assistant editor of *The Egyptian Gazette* (Alexandria, 1927); also, senior lecturer in English (1928), assistant professor (1937) and acting professor in charge of the English Department (1939–40) at Fu'ad el-Awwal University.
70 Poet and writer on Spain (1896 - ?).
71 [McPher.] Pictures of the tomb and the house also appeared in *Egyptian Radio* of 27 February 1937; and one of the "Miraculous Well" in the *hôsh* [courtyard] in the issue of 22 January 1938. See also *Country Life* of 13 December 1931; also, a series of twelve tales told by Sheikh Suleiman el-Kreitli, which came out in the *Sphinx* from December 1939 to May 1940.

Amongst military leaders, Spinks Pâsha,[72] with Lady Spinks, and General Macready[73] were there, and at least one Egyptian *lewâ'* [74].

An interesting and appropriate guest on each occasion has been the Sheikh Deif el-Khudeirî, descended from the founder of the neighbouring mosque of the same name, who rides *khalîfa* in the *zeffa* of his own moulid. Amongst other "sons of the Prophet" were *ashrâf*, whose "sanads" (diplomas) show a *silsila* proving not only their descent in a clear line from the founder of Islam, but even going back much farther, till the old parchment reads like a chapter from the Book of Numbers.

Amongst the guests of great good omen were several members and the president himself of the Society for the Preservation of Ancient Monuments against the attacks of material vandalism, which have, alas, irreparably reduced the great beauty of Cairo, even in places to utter uglification. This Society had, I believe, much to do in the rescue of this very Beit el-Kreitlîya, and we know not how much we all, and Cairo itself, have to thank it for. There is, moreover, the Society for the Preservation of Coptic Art, also represented at the Moulid of Sîdî Hârûn, and doubtless other groups engaged on this splendid work, but I am not aware of any concerted effort to save priceless old Egyptian customs from an equally deadly wave of *spiritual* vandalism. Is it too much to hope that committees similar to the above will be formed to defend Egypt's dear old customs, before it is too late? Perhaps the germ of this lies in the moulid meetings at the Beit el-Kreitlîya. May Sîdî Hârûn, to whom miracles are ascribed by his votaries, be propitious here, and interpose to save us from what Pierre Loti termed "La Mort du Caire".

BETWEEN THE LINES[75]

A Private Mulid

It is not everybody's privilege to have a Sheikh's tomb attached to his home, and to have, as it were, his own private *mulid* once a year at his very gates. It is one, however, enjoyed by Major Gayer-Anderson, the owner of the

---

72 Major-General Sir Charlton Watson Spinks (1877–1959), the last Sirdar of Egypt serving from 1924 to 1937. His predecessor Sir Lee Stack was assassinated while being driven through central Cairo.
73 Lieutenant-General Sir Gordon Nevil Macready (1891–1956), head of the British Military Mission to Egypt in 1938.
74 Brigadier-General.
75 [McPher.] This appeared in *The Egyptian Mail* of 19 October 1938. Thanks to the unknown writer for the appeal for the more liberal treatment of Moulids!

beautiful old Arab house overlooking the Ibn Tulun mosque, which he has filled with all the treasures of Arab art, and which must be quite unique of its kind. Attached to his house is the little white-domed tomb of Sheikh Haroun, reputed to be a relation of the Prophet, whose *mulid* is a strictly local affair, celebrated by the people of the quarter.

THE FIRE-SWALLOWER

The guests whom Major Gayer-Anderson invited to watch the festivities from his house on Monday night were lucky; in addition to the usual *zikr* there was a dancing dervish and a ragged performer who licked red-hot knives, swallowed fire, walked on burning ashes, and stuck skewers through his cheek and tongue, all with the utmost *sang froid*. With the man standing less than a yard away, it seemed indisputable that the skewer was really sticking through his check, though there was no hole and no blood when he withdrew it, but no one present could explain how it was done.

Such Performances are getting rarer every year. There are always *zikrs* at every *mulid,* but few dancing dervishes can be seen, and you have to go fairly far afield to find a fire swallower. The authorities unfortunately frown on the purely secular side of a *mulid*; they have gone so far as to sweep away the fairground which used to be a feature of the *Mulid el-Nebi* at Abbassia, and it seems likely, unless someone can persuade them to a more liberal point of view, that in a few years' time all the fun of the fair will be gone.

In Ch. II, under the rubric of "imponderable influences…, which sometimes determine the date or ensure the observance of the moulid", the case is cited of the apparition of Sîdî Hârûn to the old Sheikh Suleimân el-Kreitlî, guardian of his tomb, warning him that nothing must be allowed to deprive him of his moulid rites and rights.

In this thirteen hundred and fifty-ninth year of the Prophet, and second of the war, the person referred to in the above connection as the Fairy Godmother, who caused the vision to materialise, mentioned to me that though Sha'bân, the last moulid month, was far advanced, Sheikh Suleimân had not reported any such vision as the previous year, nor even broached the subject. This I found on a quiet visit to the tomb was in no way due to apathy, but to a perfect confidence that the Fairy Godmother would hold the moulid *motu proprio*[76]; that were it otherwise,

---

76 Literally, "on one's own impulse" or "of one's own accord"; so here, that of the fairy godmother.

there would have already been voices from the penetralia of the shrine. This faith was rewarded by a small but excellent celebration on the first Thursday after mid-Sha'bân, at which piety and joy were most pleasantly mingled. At the tomb was a continual *va et vient*[77], and a striking feature was the earnestness with which a great number of young lads joined the mature dervishes in the "zikrs". There was at the opening a *zeffa*, at which "tars" and "tabls" observed impeccable time. Later, a red-robed Maulâwî gave us the whirling dance of the *samâ',* and then some marvellous dervishes of the Rifâ'îya demonstrated the supremacy of the spirit over matter, over pain and the usual physical limitations, in a way that could neither be explained nor explained away, culminating by defying the dagger point of the mystic *dabbûs,* and the edge of the sword, and submitting to the *dôsah* on a small scale, a rite so rarely seen these days.

Old Sheikh Suleimân, leaning on his stick and his son's arm, though bent double, paid a visit to the Beit el-Kreitlîya adjoining, and received a return visit. He looked ecstatically joyful, and his lips moved as if muttering a "Nunc Dimittis".[78]

H 4 (cf. Sectional Map XV)
HASAN EL-ANWAR
(سيدي حسن الأنور)

Originally the date of this moulid appears to have been 7 Rabî' II, at least this was the case in 1348 (1929) and 1351 (1932), but since then it has suffered from chronic postponement. I think that it has always been held on a Tuesday. I have been present and noted the date on Tuesday, 9 Gamâd II 1353 (18 September 1934), Tuesday, 22 Gamâd II 1355 (8 September 1936) and Tuesday, 3 Sha'bân 1357 (27 September 1938). It is on the fringe of the *gabel* beyond the *salakhâna* (slaughter house) and reached by *khalîg* trams 5 or 22. One goes to the end of the track and walks on through the broken mass of Muhammad 'Alî's aqueduct, then between groups at stick play and divers diversions on the right, and theatres, "ringas", and other shows on the slope of the *gabel* on the left, and reaches the mosque of Hasan el-Anwar situated in the square of a sort of suburban village, a few minutes after leaving the tram. Sometimes I have seen the egregious Billy Williams there with his wonderful *Piste à la Mort.*

The mosque and the square are full of "zikrs" and groups of sheikhs, and the amusement place, sufficiently removed, is a weird, attractive sight in its setting of ruined aqueduct and rugged desert.

---

77 "coming and going".
78 "Lord, now lettest Thou Thy servant depart in peace…"

Hasan el-Anwar had bad luck in 1353 (1934), for after repeated postponements, torrential rain burst many city drains, and on the last night, the column of
sewage carts coming through was obstructed by the crowd which the police could
not keep to the sides, and the local authorities broke it up.

I was told in 1357 (1938) that I had missed a good *zeffa* at 5 o'clock.

H 5 (cf. Sectional Map VI)
HILÂL

(سيدي هلال)

I have included this microscopic moulid which I lighted on by chance on 6 Gamâd
I 1353 (16 August 1934), the final day of the big Bûlâq Moulid of Abû Sebâ'
(though I am not certain that it was anything more than the destination of a *zeffa*
from the bigger mosque), because of the beauty of the little shrine in a delightful
court easily visited and worth the visit. It is just off the big new street, Shâri' 'Abd
el-Gawâd at right angles to the façade of the mosque of Abû el-'Elâ, a minute from
that mosque on the left between the Fu'ad el-Awwal end and the Shâri' Ahmadein,
the scene of a moulid and the site of many shrines (cf. Ahmadein).

The *zeffa* came at about 5.30 in the afternoon, but I do not know if it is a regular
institution.

H 6 (cf. Sectional Map I)
HILLÎ

(سيدي حلي)

Both the day of the week and the date vary greatly. I first saw this moulid on Saturday, 17 Safar 1352 (10 June 1933), but when I went early in Safar the following
year, I was told it was over. I missed it also the three following years, but was
assured that in 1356 it was held on Thursday, 7 Gamâd I (15 July 1937). Going
early in Gamâd I in 1357 I found it in full swing, and witnessed the big night on
Tuesday, 7 Gamâd I 1357 (5 July 1938).

It is situated between Bûlâq workshops and Rôd el-Farag and trams 7 and 13
pass literally through it for the little mosque, and the "zikrs", &c., are on the west
side of the Rôd el-Farag road, but the amusement park on the east, in the road
which becomes Shâri' Ma'sara and emerges in the Shubrâ Road, a little south of
the Tawfîqîya School. Tents, swings and shows spread into the *terrain vague* on
each side of the road. Anyone missing the last tram (about 11. 30) to Cairo can of
course obtain tram or bus by walking along the road mentioned to Shubrâ.

Sîdî Hîllî is a strange moulid, the secular side being relatively more pronounced than that of any other that I have seen, except perhaps Abû Hareira,

the great Shamm el-Nesîm moulid held at Gîza. I had difficulty in re-finding the mosque, several good people whom I asked being equally ignorant, and could obtain nothing the least reliable concerning the history of the saint. I fancy this, like many Christian local feasts, is a religious graft on some ancient fair or perhaps pagan ceremony. I am sure there is scope here, as at Gîza, for a student of folk lore, anthropology, and ancient customs.

When I first discovered this moulid in 1352 (1933), some evenings before its *apodosis*, I was *intrigué* by the action of three girls of perhaps 13 to 16, in the rubbish heaps and holes well away from the crowd. They appeared in the fading light to be girding two of their party with *ceintures de chastité;* but their subsequent behaviour indicated clearly the reverse, and so absorbed were they in a "game" in which two of them affected the part of boys, that I was able to approach near enough to see that the anterior part of each girdle was armed with a phallus apparently of tin, but perhaps of cardboard, length about 6 or 8 inches. A scream of pain only partially suppressed from the third, brought a real lad on the scene, who spake winged words to the accompaniment of strokes of an *aluba* (a five-millième cane sold at all moulids), and drove them towards the houses. There was nothing apparently to connect this with the moulid, yet so unusual a sight on this spot at such a time seems to suggest the possibility of the tradition of some ancient phallic observance.

Hillî is fortunate in being one of the few moulids in crescendo. In 1352 (1933), it was indeed big and popular, but in 1357 (1938), a year of the suppression or reduction to a minimum of many great feasts, Hillî flourished exceedingly. I noticed two big tent-theatres, a *Qara Goz*, a tent for the display of the dwarf Zubeida, a Sudanese *ringa*, stick combats, Aunt Sallies[79], and endless stalls and side shows; and on the mosque side many more groups, some more sober and sedate than on the amusement side, some less so.

LAKE TIMSÂH, ISMÂ'ÎLÎYA

H 7 (cf. Map of Delta)
HUNEIDIQ
(سيدي حنيدق)

About the end of the war,[80] I was camped for a short time with the RAF near Lake Timsâh (the Lake of Crocodiles) and heard of a strange Bedouin moulid, with

79 A game in which players throw sticks or balls at a wooden dummy.
80 WWI.

wonderful horseraces, in the desert nearby. We saw nothing of it and indeed it was probably suspended in war time – and there was plenty to occupy us in the way of fancy flying, looping the loop and such like, and a sport new to me, duck shooting from aeroplanes over and about Lake Timsâh, in which to my surprise few birds were lost, for Arab boys retrieved them from the sand or the water and received a piastre a head. I have enquired about it often since, but could never get definite information, as regards place or time and could find no Englishman or European who knew anything of it, nor Egyptian, for the matter of that. Then in 1357 (1938), my *murâsla* got definite information from relatives of his little Bedouin wife, who had settled at Birket el-Gamûs (Buffalo Pool), quite near the site of the moulid. So, I took him and his wife and youngster with me to Ismâ'îlîya, where a lot of her tribesmen met us, and Mûsâ went on with them to arrange anything necessary – horse, tent, &c, whilst I took a room at the Locandet el-Sharq as a *pied-a-tèrre*, close to the lake. That was on 9 Gamâd I 1357 (7 July 1938), and there were to be two big days, Saturday and Sunday 11th and 12th Gamâd I, the second date being that of the *khâtima* and the horse play and races. On enquiring at the jetty if it were possible to sail to the moulid, I was told that steam launches were being specially run, and that big steamers would ply the final nights.

I took the first launch that went, and had a most picturesque hour's run, in the light of the stars and a half-grown moon, across the lake, and then along the canal, till the lights of what might have been a town appeared at the foot of a desert hill crowned by the shrine of Sîdî Huneidiq. From the height of that I saw that we were on a tiny stretch of land, its shores bathed by another lake, the moon glitter broken in places by palm woods. Except for swings and a few shooting galleries, and such like, and of course the mosque itself, the moulid was far from typical: streets and streets of wattled huts and stalls made it more like a fair, and toys, trinkets, garments and all manner of things were changing hands. Most trade was done in melons, of which camel loads were constantly arriving, the celebrated melons of Huneidiq, big as the head of Goliath and going at half a piastre.

When I landed, I hardly noticed that I had done so across a plank, long, and less than a foot wide, but on returning to the launch, I was very aware of it and disliked it very much, for it was not quite level and was swaying; and gazing down into the deep dark waters of the Suez Canal, they seemed to be swirling past, and what looked like the flukes of an old anchor were projecting just above the surface. There seemed to be a spot of murder going on in the launch, for a little man was attacking an enormous fellow with a key such as they start cars with, and had already torn his clothes off and had got him down. But the giant rose again, grim and gory, and the little one sprang over the side. This did not tend to the stability of launch or plank, nor to the prospects of a happy voyage, as presumably these pugnacious gentlemen were our able mariners.

Hesitating whether to *walk the plank* and descend *dans cette galère,* I noticed that the launch was moving out *motu proprio,* so to speak, and fearing it might be the last for the night, I made a sort of hop, skip and jump, landing on an upper story of the colossus, and sliding down his naked and bloody body into a seat. Someone took effectual charge of the navigation, and all went well. Before reaching the open lake, we met two enormous liners, whose searchlights transformed the sand and rocks of the canal banks into snow and icebergs, luminous, glittering, and seemingly transparent, a weird and beautiful sight.

When I went again two days later, I was decidedly glad to find that a gangway and excellent landing arrangements had been made. Several people had slipped in, and there were some drownings, but whether the planks were responsible or not for these I do not know. There was a great concourse on the Saturday, but many were complaining that the moulid had been wet-blanketed the past few years and had lost much of its *éclat.* And that in spite of the fact that the old difficulties of approach by riding or walking only, are now removed not only by the launches but by a motor track from Ismâ'îlîya. There was a row of tents at the moulid for parking private cars, but what seemed a very cruel regulation was made on the big night, that only private cars, no taxis might use the road after 6 o' clock. I suppose there must have been some reason for this, but it was indeed hard that the desert people, old votaries of the shrine, and the many people of Ismâ'îlîya and the villages who could have raised the money for a taxi for the occasion, but could not buy a car, had either to come and go in the blaze of the sun and leave before the best part, or pass the night in the sand with the privilege of watching any *flâneur,* dilettante, or Saturday evening pleasure-seeker with a car enjoy the freedom of the road and of the parking tents. My *murâsla* had come late in the afternoon with his wife and a party of her friends in a taxi from Birket el-Gamûs, and found themselves marooned, so to speak. They would have had to sleep *sous la belle étoile,* and thank Allâh for soft sand and warm air, but that Mûsâ, who had heard of the launches from me, had enough money and *nous* to put a harem of nine including his wife, and also three children into a launch and squeeze the lot into one taxi at Ismâ'îlîya for Birket el-Gâmûs. Hundreds of others of both sexes either slept in the sand or tramped their weary way, if indeed there was no regulation forbidding pedestrianism. The sufferers from this seemingly arbitrary action blamed the Canal Co. rather than the police authorities.

The *clou* of the moulid was the horse racing and equestrian sports on Sunday afternoon, which alone was well-worth coming from Cairo to see; and when the riders, about a dozen of them, fell to quarrelling through the fault of one of the onlookers, and fought on horseback with whips, sticks or anything they had, nothing could have been more picturesque, even back in mediaeval times. And what a setting of desert, lake, and a city of wattles, with an unclouded sun!

I have gone rather fully into this little experience, as I think, even apart from the moulid, that Ismâ'îlîya and its lake and surroundings are not appreciated as they deserve. There is fine fishing, bathing and sailing, good accommodation, nice gardens, and lovely walks, some of them in the richest of vegetation, and the builders of the attractive little city have shown, as those who built Heliopolis, that new buildings need not necessarily be hideous. Its climate too is good, and it is very accessible.

I came on to Port Sa'îd in time for the French fête of *XIV Juillet*, with its fireworks on the breakwater; and flew here, Haifa, the next day, in time for the Feast of Our Lady of Mt. Carmel on the 16th July, and that of Mâr Elyâs on the 20th, and tomorrow go on to Iskanderun, and wonder if the Sanjak will have a little moulid on, though I regret leaving this delightful and hospitable place, Stella Maris, on the Holy Mountain.[81]

As regards the sheikh Huneidiq, my purely local information is vague and unreliable, but he seems definitely regarded as a "patron of the Canal" and waterways, and this is supported by a tablet at the door. People about the tomb told me that it is subsidised by the Suez Canal Company. He is generally supposed to be Arab, though there is an idea with a few that he was a Frenchman. Why not?

H 8 (cf. Sectional Map XII)
HUSEIN

(الحسين بن علي بن أبي طالب)

Always a Tuesday in the latter half of Rabî' II after a fifteen days run. Anyway such was the case over a hundred years ago, as Lane recorded a visit on Tuesday, 21 Rabî' II 1250 (1834), and equally so during the present century on the many occasions I have been present. In 1357 (1938), it occurred on the 20th of the Arabic month, but in all previous years that I have noted, it was on the last Tuesday. This was also the case in 1359 (1940).

The position of the great mosque behind the Khân el-Khalîlî is too well known

---

81 [McPher.] This is a copy of a private letter written home, which at the time of writing I had no idea of ever publishing.

to require description. It is best reached from the 'Ataba by bus 18 which passes through the moulid, or by tram 19 to Al-Azhar, which is on its fringe. (Bus 3 from Sayyida Zeinab and buses 11 and 12 from the Station and 'Abbâsîya respectively also serve.)

Two of the features Lane emphasised and which greatly enhanced the *éclat* of the moulid, and still observed at the beginning of this century, were the brilliant lighting of the contiguous bazaars with chandeliers, and the singing sheikhs in shops and houses in these bazaars, in the Nahhâsîn and other places. Dancing girls which Lane calls "Ghawâzee"[82], and which he says were of a distinct tribe, seem to have been much in evidence, and their modern successors (whether tribal "Ghawâzees" or not, I cannot say) had a meteoric revival in recent years, reaching their zenith in 1353 (1934), when, however, they did not perform nor accost pilgrims and visitors in the precincts of the mosque, but were in "ringas" and other dancing booths, in a mile-long line of tents, beginning at the end of the Shâri' el-Gedîda, and skirting the *gabel* towards 'Abbâsîya. Other tents in this row housed theatrical troops and all manner of shows, and the line was interrupted by open spaces for stick play, horsemanship and *zikr* groups, though these last were of course much more prominent near and in the mosque. Previous to 1353 there had been a few little shows in the rubbish heaps at the end of Shâri' el-Gedîda, the continuation of the Mûskî, with a "telegraph" – a long wire stretched across space, with pulley wheels and nooses by which lads swung and traversed to the other end of the wire.

This sort of fair in the *gabel* had disappeared in 1355 (1936), and the "Ghawâzee" stars had fallen as rapidly as they rose, and all I saw of the diversional side then and in 1357 (1938) were a few little shows and gambling carts in a bit of waste land in Darâsa (beyond the mosque to the right). In 1359 (1940) only a big and good circus survived to the final night.

The *peritomists* are busy as in Lane's day, Dr. 'Enâyet Allâh, the *bâsh-prépucier*[83] informing me that he had already circumcised over a thousand infants, some days before the end of the moulid. He has a wonderful erection with towers and boats quite near the mosque by the main road.

To refer once more to Lane, his account in "*Modern Egyptians*" should be read. It is full of vivid detail, from the crush about the tomb and the utterances

---

82 s. ghâzîya, pl. ghâwâzî.
83 A Turkish-French concoction by McPherson meaning Chief Circumciser. "Peritomist" is another concoction by the author, from the Greek word for circumcision.

By the Bâb el-Akhdar at the Moulid of Sidna Husein.

of the *zikâkîr*[84] to the manners of the "ginks". These were Greek singing boys, with effeminate ways, flowing manes, and often impudent manners. In contrast were the Moroccan dervishes of the 'Îsawîya sect, followers of Sîdî Muhammad Ibn-'Îsa, whose wonderful fire-eating feats when in a state of spiritual exaltation, almost beyond belief, are equalled to this day, though not so freely before the public.

Murray, writing half a century ago, says that the Khedive went always in state, and describes his passage on foot through the Khân el-Khalîlî, over rich Persian carpets, spread for the occasion.

Lane's long account of his personal experiences at the head of Husein emboldens me to mention my brief imprisonment in the mosque the first time I ventured in under the *aegides* of Sidqî (RIP) a brother of Hâmed Bey Mahmûd, Minister of Hygiene; and the now well-known doctor, then pupil, Ibrâhîm Zakî Kâshif.

With youthful thoughtlessness they chose the time of the midday Friday prayer, and, though the worshippers showed no sign of resentment at their prayers, on our trying to go away, every exit door was barred. Presently Sidqî and Zakî were taken off in terror, whilst I was left within a ring of silent sheikhs, near the shrine containing the sacred head, which I had plenty of time to observe, for, as I was told later, the lads' wrists had been examined for the Coptic cross, and then retaining Sidqî as hostage, Zakî had been taken under escort to his home at Qasr el-'Einî. Happily, his sainted father was at home, who assured the sheikhs that all our intentions were of the best, that the *Englishman* regularly came to his house to hear the *fiqîs* read the Qurân (which was exact), and that he unequivocally guaranteed us.

(There endeth my first lesson in mosque gate-crashing; the second lesson appears under the account of the Moulid of Sayyida Zeinab).

Of course, all centres round the head of Husein, believed to be enshrined in this mosque, the most sacred Islamic relic in Cairo. Its authenticity has been questioned through the centuries, but found much support in the vision of a very holy man, Muhammad el-Bahâ'î, who was assured by the Prophet himself that his grandson's head was truly there.

'Abd el-Gawâd el-Sha'rânî in his *Tabaqât* is very definite in the affirmative. He says *inter alia*:

He (Husein) was born in the year 4, and made the pilgrimage twenty
five times on foot…was slain a martyr on Friday (yôm el-'Âshûrâ), 10th
Muharram in the year 61 at the age of 56 … his sister Zeinab, buried in

---

84 A plural form of *dhakkīr*, one who practises *dhikr*.

Cairo...sang lamenting him, raising her voice and baring her head; ...then the
head was borne to Cairo and buried in the famous mosque...

The chronicler is a little misleading in the last passage quoted, which seems
almost to imply that the sacred head was taken to Cairo shortly after Husein's
death. This, of course, is far from being the case. He lived and died in the first
century of the *Hegira*, and it was not till the Fatimite Amîr el-Guyûsh[85] was
warring in Syria at the end of the fifth (by the Christian reckoning the eleventh),
that the head was found by him at Ascalon, and suitably enshrined. Owing to
the Crusades, fears were entertained lest it might be desecrated by the Christians, which may account for its having been kept for a time in Damascus, as the
Damascenes allege, and for its ultimate transference to Egypt in 549 A.H. (1154
A.D.), in the time of the Fatimite *Khalîfa* Fâ'iz. There, after lying for a time in
the mosque of Sâleh bin Râziq, it was placed magnificently in a mausoleum in
the royal palace, the Qasr el-Zumurrud[86], the site subsequently of the mosque of
comparatively recent date, where behind one of the "qiblas" (for there is another
to Husein's brother Hasan) it is still enshrined.

Reference above to the 'Âshûrâ renders it advisable to add that a second great
ceremony centred about the head of Husein up to about the time of the 1914–18
war, on 10 Muharram. After mourning at the tomb, a procession mainly of Shî'a
dervishes, proceeded to the Persian *tekîya*, slashing themselves with swords and
crying, Yâ Hasan! Yâ Husein! These, when I witnessed the threnody, were led
by a boy in white on a white pony, pathetically eager with voice and sword. Both
horse and rider were crimson as were indeed the streets before the *tekîya* was
reached. Considering how bitter the feuds have been between Sunnis and Shias in
many parts of Islam, and that the great majority of Cairenes are Sunni, it is a great
tribute – one of many – to Egyptian tolerance that the Sunnis and Shiites are united
in one bond in the mosque, and nothing but sympathy shown at the procession.

The 'Âshûrâ is still observed in many Muhammadan countries, and in Persia
it is perhaps the greatest ceremony. Let us hope the recent union of the royal
houses of Egypt and Iran[87] will bring about the revival of this august and ancient
observance.

Oh Hasan! Oh Husein!

---

85 Commander of the armies.
86 Emerald Palace.
87 Princess Fawzia, daughter of King Fu'ad of Egypt, married Muhammad Reza Pahlavi in
1939. The latter became Shah of Iran in 1941. They were divorced in 1945.

MATARÎYA

I 1 (cf. Map of Delta)
IBRÂHÎM

(الشيخ إبراهيم)

This moulid, like that of Tashtûshî, is held on the *Leilet el-Mi'râg*, 26 Rajab, or at least that has been the case on three out of four occasions when I was present. The fourth occasion, it was on Friday, 27 Rajab 1356 (1 October 1937), that is the eve of the 28th, instead of the 27th. Tashtûshî was also held a day late according to the official calendar, and also the *mi'râg* celebrations at Sultân Rifâ'î, and a minor ceremony at Abû -l-'Elâ in honour of that miracle. I suppose the moon was in some way responsible for this seeming exception.

It is held at Matarîya, but must not be confounded with the great moulid of Matrâwî, always held at mid-Sha'bân. The little mosque and shrine of Sheikh Ibrâhîm are well behind the great mosque, and in the heart of the ancient village. Quite near is a holy tree on which people, particularly women, hang all sorts of votive offerings of an intimate nature. Quite early in the century, at which time I had a chalet and garden at Matarîya, I frequently saw many women visit the tree and then the tomb of Shâri' Ibrâhîm, but I have not been able to ascertain what relation there is between the two, if any, nor indeed have I been able to gather anything reliable or consistent about the sheikh.

Though obscurely placed, so that one might pass up and down the adjacent main road, without detecting its existence, this moulid is very well attended, especially by Bedouins; and the village streets as well as the mosque and the "ringas", cafés, etc., intensely crowded, presenting a very colourful and picturesque sight.

If visited by rail, there is a considerable walk from Matarîya Station to the site of the moulid, past the garden in which is another Holy Tree, that of the Blessed Virgin Mary, and the spring and well of the Virgin. It is therefore easier of approach by means of a Matarîya bus from Cairo, getting out immediately after the big mosque and turning down a dark and narrow street to the right. (The Matarîya bus 16 now starts from the Station Square, Cairo.)

I had a curious experience there in 1354 (20 October 1935), when feeling was running strong against Italy, and great resentment felt because of the aggression in Abyssinia. On my way to the moulid, I had visited some Italian friends in Matarîya, and one of these had accompanied me as far as the lane by the mosque referred to above, but left me there with salutations, to which I reciprocated in Italian, in the hearing doubtless of a good many people. Almost at once I noticed that I was persistently dogged by a little group, including the black servant of the Italian family I had visited. They regarded me and discussed me with great obvious interest, and presently one of them, whom I had seen at the Sporting Club, and who seemed to recognise me, saluted me politely and said "Buona Sera, Signore! Scusi tante, che ora è?" Falling into the trap, I replied, "Nove meno dieci." He turned triumphantly to his companions, saying, "What need have ye of further witnesses?" or words to that effect, and instantly there commenced a chorus of highly uncomplimentary remarks about Italy, the Italians, and Mussolini – "Et-Talyânîn wilâd kalb. Yasqut Mussolini ibn kalb, harâmî" (The Italians are sons of dogs! Down with Mussolini, son of a dog, brigand.)

Though they could not hurt my feelings by the worst things they might say about the master gangster, I felt that I was in danger of becoming his innocent scapegoat, and tried to beat a dignified retreat, but bigger louts joined my young tormentors and I soon had to defend myself with my stick. This broke, but an enterprising seller of "alubas" instantly handed me a tough cane which I bought and used. The sheikhs and people generally took an academic rather than an active interest in the conflict, but when they acted at all they helped me rather than the hooligans, and a party of police "'askarîs" coming up, so vigorously clouted my adversaries that they recoiled long enough to enable me to pass unscathed through the dark and dangerous lane into the main road. There, in supposed security, I awaited a bus. Suddenly, the gang appeared again from I know not where and attacked, this time, with real viciousness and, but for a stalwart young giant in khaki, who was passing and took my part, I could hardly have fought my way to the café, where at once *cafetier*, staff and customers put the pack to route. Drinking coffee and smoking cigarettes with these good people, I could see shadowy forms in the distance both ways, like wolves hanging about a camp, so when a bus was passing and I jumped on without stopping it, I was prepared for their raiding this. And they did, but the conductor rose to the occasion, and when I wished the ringleader "buona notte", he was on his back in the road.

I went again the next year, curious to know what would happen, but took the precaution to have my garden boy, *murâsla*, and one or two of their friends within rescuing distance, but nothing whatever of an untoward nature happened; so I went alone in 1356 (1937) and was surprised to find that I was recognised. But this time I think they realised that I was *Inglîzî* and not *Talyânî*, and though a little troublesome there was no attempt at violence. I hope that this personal explanation is the correct one, and that they have in no degree abated in their wholesome ferocity towards the arch brigand.

I 2 (cf. Sectional Map XIV)
IBRÂHÎM
(سيدي إبراهيم)

This is only the ghost of a moulid. I never saw it, and now certainly never shall. Its story, tragic and pathetic is perhaps worth recording.

I had heard more than once of the shrine of a holy man named Ibrâhîm, in the region of the *Sûq el-Silâh*, and being assured by a dervish friend that its moulid was on 27 Sha'bân, I gladly accepted the offer of his guidance in 1357 (1938), but a long tiring search was in vain. I mentioned my fruitless quest to a resident, a *mîrâlâi*, formerly of the Egyptian Army, whose knowledge of the intricacies of native Cairo is unique, particularly as regards the *Sûq el-Silâh* district. I had lit on the very person who could give me a first-hand account – not of the moulid – but of the little shrine. He said:

"Useless your searching! That seems to be the little *qubba* that stood on a property of the Yeghen family, at which time Sîdî Ibrâhîm was duly honoured; but the land was sold to a Hebrew in the belief that he at least would realise the sacred nature of the shrine and respect it. But the purchaser finding it in the way of some modernisation he proposed, blew it up with dynamite. I saw the beautiful little dome lying like a broken eggshell, near the shattered *tâbût,* and the turban of the sheikh on the ground".

Sic transit!

Recently (in 1940), the *mîrâlâi*, my informant, kindly showed me the spot. A great number of houses (over 60 I believe) now stand on the site of the vast Yeghen Palace. With difficulty and with the help of some residents and a sort of local *ghafîr* (watchman) we located the scene of this appalling act of vandalism, and the *ghafîr* (or whatever his office was) glibly recited what appeared to us a well-taught and oft-repeated tale, in quasi-explanation of the destruction of the *qubba*. He said, "It was no true sheikh buried there, but a false prophet, whom foolish people regarded with superstition, believing that money buried under the *qubba* would increase by magic, and so they came and hid their savings. The only way in the interest of pure religion was to strike at the object of such gross superstition."

This yarn had by no means the ring of truth, and the *ghafîr* was annoyed when I asked him "how much money was revealed when the tomb was blown up?"

If there be any truth in this version, it seems to suggest a worse and more sordid reason, than mere vandalism, for the sake of clearing the ground for building.

I 3 (cf. Map of the Delta)
IMBÂBÎ (ISMÂ ʿÎL IMBÂBÎ)
(سيدي إسماعيل إمبابي)

The Sheikh Imbâbî was one of the apostles of Sayyid el-Bedawî, or of his great
disciple ʿAbd el-ʿÂl, and his moulid which was probably established soon after
his death is therefore one of the oldest in Egypt, before it became the custom to
adopt a date from the Moslem calendar corresponding to the birthday of the saint
honoured. Like those of Tantâ, Desûq, and Damanhûr, and of Bayûmî in Cairo
(which last, as founder of a branch of the Ahmadîya dervishes, comes into the
orbit of Ahmad Sayyid el-Bedawî), Ismâ'îl's moulid is fixed by the season of the
year, not by the lunar calendar. It is or should be always held on a Thursday, a
little before midsummer near 10 Ba'ûna (16 June), absorbing and superseding an
ancient festival of Isis, of which traces exist till this day. This was the *Leilet el-
Nuqta,* when once multitudes, and considerable numbers until recently watched
for the falling of a precious tear of Isis into the Nile near the spot where the moulid
is now held – a tear of grief for her dismembered husband which the river refused
to yield up in its entirety.[88]

Sometimes agricultural conditions, and once the prevalence of cattle plague,
and now the war, have prevailed over the traditional claims of the "Night of the
Drop", so that the date is becoming more and more erratic, and early enquiries as
nearly as possible on the spot are desirable.

The village of Imbâba is on the Upper Egyptian line, and the station is close
to the mosque and the centre of the celebrations, but stopping trains are none too
numerous, and there are none after 9 o'clock either way. The most serviceable
tram is 33, which runs to the village, but that leaves a walk of nearly a mile to
the mosque. Tram 15 and buses 6 and 7 which cross Zamâlek bridge are nearly
as useful. The spot, opposite the Gezîra is well known to Cairenes, especially to
votaries of the cat-goddess Bast, to whom – judging from its name "Kit Kat" – a
modern *temple* has been erected.[89] Such have only to urge their cars a little further
along a rough road, crowded with all manner of animal and vehicle, to arrive at,
to the visitor, the most picturesque part of the moulid, its celebration on the Nile
banks, and on the river itself. They would do well to take a felucca or other boat
and join the laughing, singing throng on the water and, more consciously than

---

88 [McPher.] See Introduction.
89 An ironic reference to the Kit Kat Club in Imbâba, which had a notorious reputation in the
1930s and 1940s.

most of these, keep up a more than millenial custom in honour of Isis, the inventress of the sail and patroness of boats and boatmen.

I have seen fine "zeffas" in the late afternoon, and beautiful horses, and displays of horsemanship. These horses are frequently for sale, and in several ways this moulid has characteristics of a fair, as is so often the case with village and desert celebrations of the local saint.

It is well to remember that carriages, taxis, and even donkeys are difficult to obtain late at night, and the weary pilgrim may have to walk, at least to the tram, or share an open car, with a score and more of men, women and little children.

I 4 (cf. Map of Upper Egypt)
'ITMÂN[90] *or 'UTHMÂN*
(سيدي عثمان)

Though a small moulid, that of Sîdî 'Uthmân is perhaps better known to visitors and European residents than any except the three great ones, el-Nebî, Sidna Husein, and Sayyida Zeinab, the reason being that it is held under the Pyramids near Mena House in the village well known to those who go to the Pyramids, Nazlet el-Simân.

Somehow, I have always missed it, which is the more strange seeing that for some years I kept a couple of tents and a horse-shelter in the desert quite near. I was kindly invited by a local notable, the Sheikh 'Abd el-Salâm, to the moulid and a banquet at his house on Tuesday, 10 Rajab 1354 (8 October 1935), but to my regret was unable to go. Professor Sencourt[91] of the University and other guests on that occasion described it as highly picturesque and interesting, especially the equestrian performances in the afternoon. Previous and subsequent moulids have been reported in similar terms.

---

90 'Itmân being a local pronunciation of 'Uthmân.
91 Robert Sencourt (1890–1969), critic, historian and biographer. Sencourt was Professor of English at Cairo University from 1933 to 1936.

SHUBRÂ

K 1
KHALÎL
(شيخ خليل)

I had never heard of this moulid till Tuesday, 9 Muharram 1358 (28 February 1939), the eve of 'Âshûrâ Muharram, and not being free sent a *murâsla*. He went by Shubrâ tram 8 to the terminus and walked on over the little bridge to Shubrâ village and found that it was the final night. He reported it as quite small, saw no "zikrs" or ceremonies outside the mosque; a little theatre and a few stalls in the adjoining village street.

K 2 (cf. Sectional Map VI)
KHASÛSÎ
(الشيخ خصوصي)

An insignificant moulid of most indefinite date, Thursday, 21 Sha'bân in 1353 (29 November 1934), Wednesday 26 Rabî' II in 1355 (15 October 1936), centring about a very unattractive mosque in rather a fine old district, the Darb el-Nasr, Bûlâq.

K 3 (cf. Sectional Map XIII)
KHUDEIRÎ
(الشيخ خضيري)

A small private moulid in Sha'bân when held, but this has been seldom in recent years. It is not, however, abandoned, as I am invited to it when next held, by Khudeirî Bey, the *genius loci* of the mosque of his name, who himself rides in the *zeffa* as *khalîfa*. It is in the Shâri' el-Khudeiri, the continuation of Shâri' Marâsîna, and part of the street which joins Sayyida Zeinab to the Citadel, the mosque almost facing Ibn Tûlûn. Bus 4 passes the mosque and bus 18 crosses the street quite near it.

K 4 (cf. Sectional Map I)
KURDÎ or EL-KURDÎ
(سيدي الكردي)

On each of three occasions when I have been present on the final night, it has been a Sunday, but the day of the month and even the month itself is very vague. In 1352 (1933) it was 8 Sha'bân, in 1353 (1934) the 3rd of that month, and in 1354 22 Rajab (20 October 1935). I was then looking for the little Moulid of Wâstî in the same district, and lighted on that of El-Kurdî by chance. Since then, I have been on probable dates but have been much too late or too early.

Also, it is by no means easy to find, unless one is acquainted with the Sûq el-'Asr district of West Bûlâq. It is in a *hâra*[92] called Hâret el-Kurdî, off Darb Galâdîn; the entry is very narrow, but the way opens out somewhat near the Tomb of the Sheikh, which is a handsome little structure.

It is perhaps best reached by tram 13 or 7, getting out just before the Bûlâq workshops, and turning up to the right, and again to the right at Shâri' Sûq el-'Asr. Or, the new main road in front of the Mosque of Abû -l-'Elâ may be followed about two thirds of the way to Saptia, turning to the left down Shâri' el-Ansârî. Or tram 4 to Saptia may be employed.

Though small, there is a good attendance and notable "zikrs" near the tomb. In 1353 (1934), I was accompanied by an English lady, and we were both amazed and fascinated by a remarkable whirling dance, preceding a *zikr*. It was executed, not by a dervish, but by a young man clad in a *gallâbîya* who seemed immune from giddiness, for certainly he spun at great speed, and with easy grace, without a pause or turn in direction, for a period which could not have been much less than a quarter of an hour.

There is usually a primitive theatre in a kind of cave, a *Qara Goz*, some music, dancing, and a number of stalls with various attractions; and the moulid is greatly patronised by women and children.

The district is very old and unspoilt, and near el-Kurdî is the line mosque of Galâdîn in the street of the same name. This, owing to the very limited space about the tomb of el-Kurdî, is invaluable as an overflow for "zikrs", Quranic readings and so forth. Galâdîn has his own moulid in Sha'bân, and the mosque is well filled, but on the whole that moulid is not nearly so popular as that described above.

L 1 (cf. Sectional Map XIX)
LEITHÎ (IMÂM EL-LEITHÎ)
(امام الليثي)

This is one of the comparatively few moulids whose date can be relied on, for on the many occasions that I have enjoyed it, the final day has always been the Friday close to mid-Sha'bân, nine days after the vastly greater Moulid of Imâm el-Shâfe'î, which also has a fixed day, the first Wednesday in Sha'bân.

The ancient mosque is in the tombs behind Imâm el-Shâfe'î about a kilometre's walk from the terminus of tram 13.

Some years ago – it was Friday, 15 Sha'bân 1353 (23 November 1934) – I

---

92 City quarter.

called on tourist friends at their hotel and found them rather disillusioned. Even the pyramids had been spoilt by hideous photo kiosks and the banal cackle of guides and others, and they had never succeeded in getting quite away from jazzy American horrors, and aggressive modernisations. "Can you not take us somewhere with a purely unspoilt Egyptian atmosphere?" they asked me rather plaintively. "It need not be pyramidal, monumental – simple as you like, but that will give us back the dream of mystery that was our Egypt before we came." "I promise you your dream back," I replied, "but no cars, which most of you visitors dash round the beaten tracks in, seeing rather more than if they were in a coffin and rather less than in a hearse, and we might begin this evening by a walk in the tombs and a moonlight moulid in their midst, if you will take the remote sporting risk of being murdered."

The many mosques *en route*, Sultâns Rifâ'î and Hasan and the rest with the citadel flood-lighted by the moon, the ancient city gate near Sayyida 'Aysha, and much else were passed in the tram; and then on foot going behind Imâm el-Shâfe'î down a narrow way to the right the lights and voices of Imâm el-Leithî guided us to what must once have been a stupendous building. Its minaret now stands far away from what remains as a mosque, at the corner of what is now a sort of courtyard, which we reached from the mosque door by a tiny alley. In that I was rejoiced to see re-enacted a strange kind of ritual leapfrog, for it seems to have some connection with the moulid. At least I have never seen it at any other time. Youngsters and big lads, all experts, treated the spectators to most complex and graceful variants of the ancient game, even to leaping with another on the shoulders over three at once. Others indulged in whirling worthy of a dervish *murîd* (initiate). Taking my companions up a yard or two of rubbish by the minaret, a truly weird and lovely prospect charmed us. The vast rocky desert glittered white, and across it were the lights of Babylon and Old Cairo, and nearer the minarets of one or two mosques in the wilderness silhouetted against the sky. The son of Dr. 'Enâyet Allâh, whose circumcision kiosk was at the door of the mosque, had seen us, and with him some Bedouin notables. They led us back by a way that took us into the mosque itself, showed us the tomb of the Imâm and much of beauty and interest, and introduced the women of my party to a number of their own sex sitting demurely near the shrine. These were pious women leading almost the lives of nuns. They were mostly of high families, and some of them conversed freely and pleasantly in French to my delighted visitors. When we took our leave, we passed down narrow vaulted ways, almost subterranean, to the warm Springs and baths of 'Ein el-Sîra and the quarries and sheikh's desert tomb; then cutting again into the City of the Dead, traversed it – a matter of more than a mile – to Sitna

Nafîsa, passing the little Moulid of Sîdî Samân celebrating its *khâtima*, the final rites, an oasis of light and life, in the gloom and silence of the sepulchres.

My tourists confessed that I had kept my promise and left Egypt with their dream at least good in parts.

Go and do thou likewise![93]

A note must be added concerning the celebration on 11 Sha'bân 1359 (13 September 1940), as it was rendered a red letter day by the King having elected to hold his *salâmlek* (as the Royal Friday Prayer was always termed in Turkey, in the days of the Sultâns) at the mosque of Imâm el-Leithî. His sympathetic and kindly attitude toward his country's moulids was shown in a practical and generous way by his insisting on paying all the expenses of the Imâm from his own private purse.

The writer was on the spot, and can answer for the heartening and exhilarating effect on the people, and their appreciation.

The newspaper extract adjoined is from *La Bourse Egyptienne* of the same evening.

A FINE GESTURE ON THE PART OF HIS MAJESTY THE KING

As mentioned elsewhere, His Majesty the King attended prayers this morning at the Mosque of Imam el-Leithi. Upon arriving there, the Sovereign learned that a moulid was being held in celebration of the birthday of Imam el-Leithi. Thereupon, the Sovereign immediately ordered that all expenses incurred relating to the celebration be paid out of the royal privy purse. The inhabitants of the quarter are deeply moved by this gesture of royal generosity.

Certain incidents of this "Salâmlek" are faithfully recorded in a letter, signed "El-Hag Abu Masaud", which has appeared in today's *Egyptian Gazette*, and as this bears on the moulid of the Imam, and on our subject generally, it is quoted *in extenso*:

---

93 Luke 10:37.

"SALAMLEK"

The Editor,
The Egyptian Gazette

Dear Sir,

Now that Stambul has lost the traditional ceremony of the "Salamlek" – the Friday noon prayer attended by the Sultan – it is a great thing that it should be kept up by royalty here in Egypt. It is, moreover, exceedingly popular, as the enthusiastic crowds prove which line the streets between the palace and the mosque chosen each week by the king. It is one of the few bright occasions left for them, now that their moulids are so crushed, and the old public festivals dying out or at least suspended in the main, though we must gratefully remember the splendid thought of someone in these drab days to relieve them by the exhibition of Italian trophies in Ismailia Meidan, a move most highly appreciated by all the populace, besides being the best bit of propaganda so far.

On the Friday before mid-Shaaban, when the moulid of the Imam el-Leithi is held, the king chose the mosque of the Imam for his "Salamlek". The vast space before the mosque was entirely enclosed by tent work, somewhat inartistically, I thought, concealing the beautiful old building, and what was much more to the point – or so the local people thought – concealing all view of the brilliant scene before the mosque, and the advent of the royal party. When I arrived after a Sabbath day's journey from many miles on the other side of the Nile, and across the desert which lies between Old Cairo and Ein el-Sira, and through a weird and fascinating corner of the great necropolis on the south of Cairo, I found one little opening onto a wilderness of tombs which gave standing room to a small but eager little party, but this being promptly cleared by the police, there would have been absolutely nowhere to stand or sit even in the sun, but that the leading circumcision "doctor" had his little operating booth in the corner, as always at moulid time, and promptly gave me a chair under a welcome awning, over which was an immense gonfalon inscribed with "Long live King Farouk." His own name and profession – "Mahmud Enayet-Allah, Free Circumcision" – was on a small sign below the royal welcome. Many other visitors arrived, and all were given chairs, coffee and cigarettes by the doctor, till presently an officer, with a *crown* up, came and ordered him to take his sign down. The doctor pleaded in vain and, the *sagh*[94]

---

94 The officer in question is an Adjutant-Major (*Saghkolaghsi*). Turkish military ranks were

becoming peremptory, lost his habitual urbanity, and declared, "Never will I take my own sign down; Mahmud Enayet-Allah is an honourable name! My sign is my ensign! If you tear it down by force, I cannot prevent you, but never will I commit sabotage!" To which the gentleman with the *crown* said, "Then you will pay for this, and dearly". The dean of the faculty of circumcision, still undaunted, exclaimed – "I care not a *prépuce* [foreskin] what I pay or what I suffer, but tear my sign down, *abadan! abadan!"*

A brass band, paid for, I was told, by the doctor, then arrived, and a picturesque group of women at the only window, thinking the royal party near, began to trill a warble of welcome. This was instantly suppressed by horrified ejaculations of "mamnua" (a word I need not turn into English, as it is heard here now almost as often as "verboten" in Germany), for emancipation of women is not consistent with such indulgences as *wailing or warbling,* albeit sanctioned by the custom of about forty centuries.

But now the supreme moment arrives; the guard springs to attention; the doctor's band plays the royal salute; the king is received with due honours and enters the mosque.

Relative silence reigns without, till a distant bleat breaks it. Excited whispers that two sheep are being brought for slaughter in our corner – for the poor – reach my ears, and someone adds, "and two fat oxen". Someone else suggests that that also is the doctor's largesse, but he will not own to it (from modesty some say), and further enquiries are checked by a prudent member of our little party holding up a warning finger and saying, "mamnua el-kalam". So all shut their mouths though continuing to lick their lips.

Then a bomb fell! Not a mere bomb from an aeroplane, but a prohibition, by the same sagh, I understood, against bringing beasts there for slaughter, as "the sight of blood might upset the king". Not that there was any reasonable chance of the king seeing it in that corner, which was not on his route, and if he had, I can imagine his indignation had he known that he was brought into a *pretext* that might do the poor out of their feast.

We came away at that, hoping that this prohibition would be overruled as the attack on the "ensign" had been (!), but the trams being suspended and not being able to get a cab till after two, we sat and chatted to the people in a café near the mosque of Imam el-Shafei. The rumour seemed already to have arrived that the donors of the beasts might withhold them altogether under the

---

officially used until the Revolution of 1952, and some of the old terminology could still be heard for a decade or more afterwards, particularly in the police force.

circumstances, and there were some dour and glum faces, but presently all brightened up at a new rumour that the king had expressed great interest in the moulid, and intended to defray (from his private purse) all the expenses. A dervish of the Rifaiya told me they would have a fine zeffa in the evening, in which Qadiriya, Shazliya, and other orders would take part, and begged me to come (which only tiredness prevented me doing). As I came away, the last ejaculation I heard was remarkably like Shakespeare's

"Now is the winter of our discontent,
made glorious summer by this son of Fu'ad'."

Yours faithfully,
(El-Hag) Abu Masaud

M 1 (cf. Sectional Map X)
MA'RÛF
(سيدي معروف)

Though always on a Friday, the date has varied on the six evenings I have seen it from 21 Rajab in 1352 (1933) to 7 Sha'bân in 1355 (1936). The Moulid of Sîdî Ma'rûf coincided with that of 'Abdullah on 4 Sha'bân 1351 (1932) and on 24 Rajab in 1353 (1934).

This is essentially the moulid of the Berberines, in their district of Ma'rûf, and lies between the Mixed Courts and the Museum, close to Shâri' Champollion. Trams 17 and 12 pass within sight and sound of it.

It is rather a squalid unattractive little moulid. The best thing I have seen there was a *zeffa* at 11 o'clock at night on 7 Sha'bân 1355 (23 October 1936).

M 2
MADRÛS
(سيدي مدروس)

This minute moulid in the Bâb el-Sha'rîya district was seen by me once only on Friday, 27 Sha'bân 1352 (15 December 1933). It is passed by bus 11 which plies from the Beit el-Qâdî to the station.

M 3 (cf. Sectional Map X)
MAGHRABÎ
(شيخ المغربي)

I have never witnessed this moulid, but am informed by Major G-A who had a house in Shâri' el-Maghrabî, almost opposite the little shrine, that he saw it some

The Tomb of Sheikh Maghrabî
In McPherson's era, it was adjacent to and a landmark for
the Turf Club where McPherson was a member.

six years ago. It was a very small private moulid organised and financed by some local people.

The time of the year seems to have been about Rajab. The tomb is very central and well known and is beside the Turf Club, and a considerable piece of that district is said to have once belonged or to have been controlled by the Sheikh Maghrabî.

This moulid is included here, though apparently fallen into disuse, as it is not rare for a moulid to be dormant for years, and then to be revived. (This was the case with Abû -l-'Elâ, and an extreme instance is that of Sîdî Hârûn which was dormant almost from time immemorial, until revived a few years ago.)

The name of the street has recently been changed, in accordance with an invidious innovation that causes endless confusion, dislocates local history (a great pity in Cairo, where the names of streets and places were full of significance), and raises delicate problems, as for example: Does, in this case, the tomb also change its designation? Will the moulid, if revived, be that of Sîdî Maghrabî or Sîdî 'Adlî? And which of these saints should pious members of the contiguous Turf Club regard as *Genius Loci,* to be appeased by libations and revered as Patron?

M 4 (v. Sectional Map VIII).
MANSÎ

(سيدي المنسي)

This moulid, since I have known it, some six years, has varied but slightly in date, from 23 Sha'bân in 1354 (1935) to 21 Sha'bân in 1355 (1936), and has been quite independent of the day of the week.

The tomb is in the el-Zâhir district, near the intersection of the Khalîg and Shâri' Farouk, and therefore easily reached by trams 3, 5, 7, 22 and 33, or by following Shâri' Mansî from the point of intersection of the Khalîg and the 'Abbâsîya Road.

It has been the victim of diverse vicissitudes. It was lively and popular with a rather pronounced secular side up to 1354 (1935), and I took a good many European visitors who found the theatres and shows and the very mild scale gambling interesting, and the confluence at the shrine picturesque and impressive. In 1355 (1936) it was dismal to a degree, reduced almost to nothing, but in 1356 (1937) it rose again, had a fine *zeffa* at 5 in the afternoon, from the *sebîl* (fountain) near the Huseinîya, and gave edification and pleasure to a large crowd in the evening. I do not know what happened in 1357 (1938) but when I went in the evening, sheikhs and others were sitting in the waste land between the now almost deserted shrine and Shâri' Farouk, more dismally sad than if they had been amongst the tombs, and all music had been silenced. What had Sîdî Mansî done?

Hearing this year, 1359 (1940), that Sheikh Mansî's Feast was to be observed on the last Sunday of Sha'bân, I went on the Wednesday previous to this, to confirm the alleged date and to enquire about the prospects of a *zeffa*. A *zikr* was in progress in the *maqâm*, very impressive and colourful, amongst the lights and decorations, and the rich covering of the *tâbût*. The sheikh, guardian of the tomb, recognised me, and informed me that no *zeffa* would be attempted, but that on the Friday night there would be a great *zikr* by the Nubians, and on the Saturday night by the dervishes of the Rifâ'îya, and some others, who would do many marvellous things, and that possibly this would be repeated to some extent on the next and final night, Sunday.

I went on the Sunday, but only for a short while, as this was also the main night of the moulids of Sîdî el-Ansârî and of the anchorite Marsafa, and found even the tomb nearly deserted, and nothing but a few gambling tables and a café in the waste patch of land that used to be so merry. I was assured however that the programme for the earlier evenings had been carried out.

I mention this as it is becoming rather frequent for some of the preliminary nights to go better and more smoothly than the last, if indeed the moulid survives to the end.

It seems a little pathetic that fear of interference or repression gives rise to little manoeuvres and subterfuges in order to ensure the performance of rites which have been customary and approved. It reminds one, but happily in only a remote way, of the Christians in ancient Rome going underground for the peaceful conduct of their services. Here the dervishes are handicapped by having no catacombs to use as a last resort.

MUSTAROD

M 5 (cf. Map of Delta)
MARIAM
(ستنا مريم)

This Coptic moulid in honour of the Assumption of Our Lady is always held on or very near the date of that feast, Coptic reckoning. I saw it on 16 Misrâ 1650 (22 August 1934), a Wednesday, and also on 16 Misrâ 1652 (22 August 1936 or 5 Gamâd II 1355), a Saturday.

It is not easy to get at, and still harder to return from, but well repays the trouble. There is now an occasional bus from Matarîya station to the ferry near

Mustarod, leaving the ferry crossing and a short and pleasant walk along the canal bank.

Before the war, at which time I had a chalet at Matarîya, though I knew nothing of the moulid, I often took riding parties to the little village, for the sake of the ride past the Obelisk and over the site of On, the ancient Heliopolis, and the beauty of the position of the ancient Coptic church in the Land of Goshen, and its own priceless icons and other treasures. There was no bus in those days, but the whole distance could be done on horseback as the quaint ferry carries man and beast. The priests were and are always most kind and willing to show their precious things.

The moulid is an extremely pretty sight, particularly if there is a full moon, though there is little but a few small shows and a large tent for singing, dancing, and light refreshment, on the canal bank, and of course the church into which a stream of pilgrims passes till well on in the night. Across the canal is a palace much favoured by the Khedive 'Abbâs Hilmî in his day.

The buses stop at about nine. I have been lucky in spotting a cab at the ferry which has brought night visitors and would have returned empty to Matarîya. Otherwise, it means an hour's walk.

This is not a moulid in the typical sense of a celebration at the shrine of a local saint, but is rather of the type of Christmas or the Moulid el-Nebî, not connected with the locality except perhaps by a relic or icon, but is included here as being popular and open to all, and the goal of a pilgrimage; and also as being an example of the numerous Coptic feasts held at this time in honour of the Assumption of Our Lady. These are all, as far as I know, held by the *Orthodox* Copts.

I was invited to a moulid to be held in the village of Daqdûs, near Mît Ghamr, on 14 August 1940 (8 Misrâ 1656), the eve of the Assumption with all Catholics, Eastern or Western, so concluded that I had at last hit on a Coptic-*Catholic* moulid, but on going with my host and informant on that date, it was evident that his carefully acquired and sifted information was not exact, for instead of the final night of a Catholic Feast it was the opening of an Orthodox celebration whose great night was to be on the octave, 21 August (15 Misrâ). The local priest showed us with great urbanity and pride the old icons and other treasures of his church.

The beating of tom-toms and other merry noises, mainly children's voices, called us to the canal banks in front of the church, where Punch and Judy, and other little shows were already inaugurated.

I am told that Our Lady is honoured in many parts of Egypt by moulid-like feasts also at or about the date of the Annunciation, 6 April (28 Baramhât), that is thirteen days after the vigil of the feast by the Western reckoning, 24 March.

The public observance of these two Holy Days of the BVM, the annunciation

Mustarod Ferry
In McPherson's era, Mustarod lay on the northern edge of Cairo.

by the angel Gabriel, and her translation into heaven, is common throughout Coptic, Orthodox and Catholic Christendom, the second being, I think the more general and popular. I have already referred to the beautiful celebrations of that at Siena and Cremasto. My readers will at once think of the foul crime which emphasised the pilgrimage to Tinos in August 1940, the torpedoing of the *Helle*, and subsequent bombing of the injured. That island is thronged at both of these feasts.

But what a blessed country where the first care of the authorities was to protect the moulid and those who attended it, and to see that the *zeffa* and all proceeded in peace, *malgré tout!* And what a difference from the attitude here! One might ask, "But why this difference?" to which the obvious answer is, "Because there the enemy was from *without,* here the enemy of moulids is *within*".

But the lesson of the Tinos crime, a material loss but a moral gain to the Greeks and to Greece is brought out in a letter before me in *The Egyptian Gazette* of 4 September 1940, which is so full of important truths bearing on our subject, and on the welfare of this country and its people that I have quoted it *in extenso* in the Introduction (which see).

M 6 (cf. Sectional Map XI)
MARSAFA

(سيدي علي المرصفة)

The Moulid of Sîdî 'Alî el-Marsafa has been held on the last Saturday of Sha'bân, each of six occasions on which I have noted the date, though in 1355 (1936) when I was not there it was reported as being held on Monday, 24 Sha'bân (9 November 1936). This year, 1359 (1940), it was on the last Sunday.

The little street in which the saint lived, died and was buried, Qantaret el-Amîr Hussein is just off the Khalîg in front of the Parquet (Court of Appeal), or it may be reached from Shâri' Muhammad 'Alî by taking a walk down Shâri' el-Suwayqa. The little underground mosque, however, may easily be missed as only the door is on the level of the street, and quite inconspicuous with its pots, pans and people to be seen inside, but for the *epitaphion* over it, "The mosque of Sîdî 'Alî el-Marsafa".

It is a small private delightful moulid unspoilt by police interference though so near their headquarters; anyway, that was the case up to 1355 (1936), but I fear it has been on the decline since. Apart from the religious ceremonies down in the mosque and in buildings opposite, the residents in the Qantara and an adjoining little street make up most pleasant little singing parties with a few comical characters entertaining the people innocently. A few years ago, I saw a rare and

beautiful sight, which it delights me to record: a large car containing police officers dashed into one of these narrow streets in which one of the entertainments
was proceeding, and in which the way was confessedly obstructed, if not blocked,
by performers, onlookers and chairs. An awful pause and frantic efforts to clear
a way, when an officer called out cheery salutations, and an injunction *not to
disturb themselves,* and the car backed out and went off. The singers were speechless for a moment and then their voices warbled forth the praises of God and the
Hakîmdâr[95].

The chronicler el-Sha'râni who calls our Saint "Nûr el-Dîn el-Marsafa" records
that he died about 930 (1524), and was buried in his corner *zâwia* in Qantaret
el-Amîr Husein, where his tomb is to be seen.

M 7 *(cf. Sectional Map XII)*
MARZÛQ
(سيدي مرزوق)

Though always on a Thursday, this moulid in the years I have known it has varied
in date from 29 Zû -l-Qa'da in 1352 (15 March 1934) to 4 Safar in 1356 (15 April
1937). In some way it is dependent on the greater moulid of Bayûmî, having
always followed this by either seven or fourteen days. This curious sort of symbiosis appears from the following dates:

1352 Bayûmî	22 Zû -l-Qa'da (8 March 1934)
1353 Bayûmî	23 Zû -l-Higga (28 March 1935)
1354 Bayûmî	Abandoned
1355 Bayûmî	3 Muharram (26 March 1936)
1356 Bayûmî	26 Muharram (8 April 1937)
1357 Bayûmî	Abandoned
1358 Bayûmî	In the hands of God at time of writing, Muharram 1358 (1939).
1352 Marzûq	29 Zû -l-Qa'da (15 March 1934) (7 days)
1353 Marzûq	8 Muharram 1354 (11 April 1935) (14 days)
1354 Marzûq	Abandoned
1355 Marzûq	17 Muharram (9 April 1936) (14 days)

---

95 The title of the officer in charge of a police station.

1356 Marzûq   4 Safar (15 April 1937) (7 days)

1357 Marzûq   Abandoned

1358 Marzûq   Likewise in His hands.

The Mosque of Sîdî Marzûq is situated in a beautiful so-far unspoilt bit of Cairo, in Qasr el-Shawq, near the *Sâgha* (Assay Offices)[96], Gamâlîya district. It is quite near Sidna Husein and the Beit el-Qâdî. Perhaps the easiest way of reaching it is to take bus 18 from the 'Ataba and, descending at Sidna Husein, to walk past the great door of that mosque and as far as possible straight on for a few minutes.

Behind the mosque there is a long *cul de sac* full of attractions of a varied nature; still nearer and possibly a part of the mosque premises, a hall for a sort of *tashrîfa* (reception) at which a band plays; also, in the neighbourhood Punch and Judy, booths for circumcision and spaces on the ground for tattooing, and occasionally whirling fire-eaters, but the great feature is the beautiful *zeffa*, the best, I think, after Bayûmî to be seen in Cairo. In 1356 (1937) I watched this from the collection of its elements outside the Bâb el-Nasr at about 3 in the afternoon, a splendid sight in a majestic spot, to its arrival after 5 at the mosque. The various companies of dervishes, with mounted *khalîfa*, music, banners and the rest, after a preliminary march into the desert, processed to the mûskî, rounded Sidna Husein, and past the *Sâgha*, every inch of the way attractive, especially that glorious group of Qalâwûn, Barqûq and other mosques and buildings at the end of the Nahhâsîn.

The above short account of Sîdî Marzûq, written in Muharram 1358 (March 1939) begins with a comparison of dates with those of "Sultân" Bayûmî, and it will have been noticed that though these dates advanced through Zû -l-Qa'da, Zû -l-Higga, and Muharram in the lunar calendar, they only passed from March to April in the solar. When then in 1359 (1940) Bayûmî was revived after being dormant for three years owing to mosque repairs, his date had advanced yet a lunar month to Safar, but returned to March, it was almost conclusively evident that Sîdî Bayûmî actually follows the seasons, and that his symbiote as regards date must do the same. This conclusion as regards Bayûmî was made quite definite by an account I found in an edition of Murray of 1888 stating that his moulid was fixed by the season, not by the lunar reckoning.

That the same is the case with Marzûq I have little doubt, but unhappily when I looked for the final proof in the moulid of Marzûq being renewed in March 1940, a week after Bayûmî as was expected also by the people of the district, it was said

---

96 Also, the gold market area.

to have been postponed, and now six months later we are still waiting and trusting that it is still in the hands of Allâh, and that He will prevail.

It is curious that all the Moslem moulids which follow the seasons like Sayyid el-Bedawî's are, as far as I know, his dependents directly or indirectly, for to take those in Cairo alone, Imbâbî was Sayyid's apostle, Bayûmî's sect of the Bayûmîya is a branch of Sayed's great *tarîqa* of the Ahmadîya, and Marzûq seems a filial of Bayûmî.

Writing on the eve of Ramadân 1359 (1940), a sort of *stop-press* postscript, and referring to the last clause but one, I am able to add, that He did prevail, and here are the details.

The vicissitudes of the moulid of the great Saint Marzûq of recent years, its abandonment on more than one occasion, and particularly its failing to follow that of Sîdî Bayûmî according to immemorial custom, now that the latter has come again into honour, raised dismal forebodings. Happily, these were dispelled by an announcement that the moulid and the ancient *zeffa* would take place on the last Thursday of Sha'bân of this year 1359 (26 September 1940). The news was as welcome as it was unexpected, for, as has been indicated above, it should fall about the beginning of April (Baramhât), thus being nearly half the year late, and there only remained a few days before the advent of Ramadân would close the moulid season for some months. The tidings reached me on the day itself about the time the *zeffa* was to start from the Bâb el-Nasr, 3.30 in the afternoon.

As it took some hours to reach Qasr el-Shawq, where the mosque and tomb are situated, deviating as usual through the Nahhâsîn and Mûskî to visit the shrine of Sidna Husein, it was about sunset when the banners were furled, and a friendly dervish led me into the ancient mosque, and showed me the green stone which bears the impress of the Prophet's feet, and of course the *tâbût* above the saint's body.

The mosque was very full of worshippers, including many distinguished people, and I much appreciated the privilege of entry at such a time, and the friendly attitude of everybody. My dervish's information was fascinating, though largely apocryphal, especially as regards the visit of the Nebî to the mosque, and his relations with Sîdî Marzûq on the occasion of the *impression* of the sacred foot. He confirmed what I have long felt sure was the case, that the relations of Marzûq and the great Ahmad Sayyid el-Bedawî were very intimate, though I think the assertion that he was Sîdî Ahmad's son also apocryphal.

A door in the side of the mosque led us into the hall of *tashrîfa,* where a band of young musicians who had enhanced the *zeffa,* were giving pleasure to a considerable company.

The *zeffa* I need not describe, as it was on its own traditional lines, and those of Sîdî Bayûmî, and of course the dominant colour was the red of the Ahmadîya and the Bayûmîya. The allied *Order* of the Awlâd Nûh was well represented, and was as picturesque and popular as ever.

It was reassuring to see this very ancient and venerable moulid shared and protected by high official personages, and the *Khalîfa* in the *zeffa* a lineal descendant of the great *Khalîfa* Abû Bakr, father-in-law of the Prophet, in the person of the Sheikh Muhammad Shams el-Dîn el-Bakrî. He was hailed by the crowd as *Sâhib Sigâda*[97] – *Naqîb el-Ashrâf.* This is not strictly correct, though I understand he comes very close to El-Sayyid el-Bakrî, who recently succeeded to his father's supremely high position as Sheikh el-Bakrî, which carries these titles.

It was a little unfortunate that this belated moulid was assigned to the same date as those of Mâr Barsûm el-'Aryân at Ma'sara, and Sîdî Muhammadî at Demardâsh, but that is vastly outweighed by the moral support its official recognition lends to Egypt's traditional customs in this hour of their depression.

MATARÎYA

M 8 (Map of Delta)
MATRÂWÎ

(سيدي المطراوي)

This moulid, almost unrivalled for the beauty and fascination of its position and associations, is one of the most easily accessible, for, unlike most others, its date can be relied on, always 14 Sha'bân, and bus 16 passes through it and past the doors of the Mosque of Sîdî Matrâwî. Or the train may be taken to Matarîya, and a walk of about a mile enjoyed past the Jesuit gardens, and the Holy Tree and Well of the Virgin, and that in the light of the full moon. Those who wish to combine the moulid with a visit to the Holy Tree and Well should, however, go before sunset, lest the gate be found locked; and then retrace their steps a little, before they become absorbed in the Feast of Matrâwî, to see the obelisk on the site of the Temple of Ra, and the ancient city of On, as the Sun-God goes to rest and the great full-moon of Sha'bân comes up. This is the home of the Phoenix; and I think there must be something of the Phoenix about Sîdî el-Matrâwî, for before the war for many years I had a *pied à terre* at Matarîya (the original Heliopolis) and passed the mosque constantly and through the present place of the moulid, and I never

---

97 Title of leaders of certain dervish orders based on their being owners of the founder's prayer rug.

saw it nor heard of its existence. Once certainly, about 1321 (1903), the mosque and the cafés were crowded, and there was an unusual concourse of Bedouins and others, but I have no direct reason to associate this with the saint.

I saw it first in 1351 (1932), a first-class moulid: a crowded mosque on one side of the road, and on the other so gay and happy a crowd that it did one's heart good; picturesque also to a degree. Prof. E-P of the University had motored me there, and as we flitted from attraction to attraction, we halted where a crowd was watching a strength contest – pushing a cannon, with ever increasing load up an incline till it rang a bell. Some hero had achieved great things, when my companion cut in. I heard amusing comments – "He can't be very strong... I don't suppose he has ever had a *fâs* in his hand in his life." When E-P beat the record, there was most generous applause, and I confess I was surprised, for the Egyptians are the most powerful people muscularly that I have ever come across. Three years later I was asked by a Bedouin at the moulid "Where is your friend who rang the bell with top weight on?"

I think the moulid reached its zenith in 1353 (1934). The following year the police, in clearing the road for traffic with excess of zeal, drove the crowd back and away from the road till there was a considerable mix up with the guy ropes of the show tents; but a *mulâzim awwal*[98] coming along told them to keep to their orders and maintain a way for traffic only. They obeyed absolutely, and all went happily, but I was much amused at a swing of the pendulum to the other extreme. A doddering carter came along, swung cart and donkey athwart the road, and gaped at the show, till an '*askarî* came to him and in honeyed tones said "Have the kindness, oh my uncle, to move on just a little, and no offence".

At the beginning of this short account of the Moulid of Matrâwî, I mentioned some of the sights which render Matarîya one of the most fascinating spots in Egypt, which could be easily visited at the same time. There is much more to be visited and studied which requires rather more time. For example, in addition to the Holy Tree of the BVM, there are at least two other trees sacred to local Islamic saints, hung with votive offerings of a very simple nature, unless they have gone in recent years like the beautiful *sebîl* and grove of fig trees near the obelisk, and the avenue of mulberry trees which connected them. One of these is at the back of the old village behind the mosque. The other is about a mile in the direction of Marg, near the railway, where the canal is crossed by a bridge. I had the temerity to photograph the first of these one Friday morning, in what evidently was the ladies' hour, and incurred considerable displeasure. Excusing myself on the ground of a

---

98 First lieutenant.

shocking cold in the head, and the desire to hang up my handkerchief and obtain the benefit of the sheikh's intercession for my cure, I was ultimately forgiven and allowed to perform this *act of faith*. This is not fundamentally as incongruous as it may seem: many Moslems come to the Coptic relics of Mâr Tadros in the hope of cures or blessings, and hundreds of non-Catholics, largely Moslems, to the Catholic shrine of St. Teresa at Shubrâ, bearing their votive gifts. Very numerous similar cases could be cited, and cases reciprocally where Christians seek cures or blessings at Moslem shrines.

Going this year 1359 (1940) on 14 Sha'bân according to the official calendars somewhat after the time of the '*ashâ*, I was not surprised at finding the recreative side much reduced, but distinctly so at a closed and unlighted mosque. On enquiring the reason, I was assured that the calendars were all wrong, and for *lunar* reasons this was decreed to be the 18th, and tomorrow night the eve of the 15th – mid-Sha'bân.

This information was correct, as the lit-up minarets and the celebration at the mosque of Muhammed 'Alî, and other indications showed, but I was unable to repeat my visit to Sîdî Matrâwî, so cannot report on that.

The importance of fixing the date exactly at this time of course arises from the peculiar solemnity of the eve of mid-Sha'bân – *Leilet el-Nisf min Sha'bân*; for on this night is shaken the Lote Tree of Paradise, *"el-sidr"*[99], the Tree of the Extremity, as it is called in the Sûrat el-Nagm, the 53rd of the Qurân, and each leaf which falls bears the name of one who is to die in the ensuing year.

My little neighbours, and children elsewhere make tiny processions, and sing:

"Lord, keep our leaves
Firm on our trees,
For we're Thy little kiddywees."

Amen.

M 9 (cf. Sectional Map IV)
MAZLÛM
(سيدي مظلوم)
A short account of Sîdî Mazlûm will, I hope, convince those addicted to sedentary forms of worship and amusement, that if the non-Moslem and uninitiated cannot

---

99 A variety of Christ's thorn (Zizyphus spina Christi); in Qurân 53:14, the "Lote tree" marks the end of the Seventh Heaven.

expect the maximum of edification, he can at least look forward to movement and excitement, life and colour, apart from the interests of anthropology, folklore and the like; and the great tonic of an atmosphere free from boredom and feigned interest and enjoyment, where fun and piety are equally whole-hearted.

The great night seems always to be a Sunday, but has varied in the five years 1353 (1934) to 1357 (1938) from 22 Muharram to 27 Rabî' II. Its date depends somewhat on the state of cultivation on its site, as is the case with Imbâba, Farag, and doubtless others.

The *maqâm* is in the fields beyond Sharâbîya, past the shrine of Sîdî Galâl, who also has a moulid; and unless you have at your disposal a car built for rough roads, the best way is to take a cab outside Kubrî el-Lîmûn Station. But do not rely on the cabby's promise to fetch you back at night. You must be prepared for a walk of two or three miles, or a rough mount, or a place on a cart of sorts.

I made the acquaintance of Mazlûm in 1353 (1934), some evenings previous to the big night, and found a circle of tents, theatres, "ringas", *Qara Goz, khayâl el-zill*, conjurers, performing dogs, push-cannon, "Aunt Sally", shooting galleries, and all manner of shows and games surrounding a group of trees picturesquely enshrining the *maqâm* of the Saint. There was an outer circle of stick players, performing horses, *hâwîs*, &c. &c, but having at the time an injured leg, I could do little but sit near the shrine, at the Café of Amîn, a well-known character, and enjoy the *va et vient* of the pilgrims to the *maqâm*, a colourful, and impressive sight.

My cabby failed me, and I much regretted the army of donkeys and donkey boys of a few decades past, available almost anywhere – a picturesque and useful asset to Egypt, brutally crushed out, alas, by the rage for mechanisation. I was in luck, however, for a Bedouin of quality pressed on me his horse which had been performing early in the evening. A lovely beast, but with a difficult mouth, and prone to dance when we met a *zeffa* with tambourines, and anxious at times to show me how neatly he could lie down and pretend to be dead!

I came again the next day, and early, bringing a *murâsla* with provisions in the cab, and much enjoyed a picnic dinner in an adjoining field. I had taken the precaution of withholding the fare, promising a big one on return, but the cabby did not appear. At least not then, for he accosted me in town days after, swearing he had come but was commandeered by a group who made him drive them back. The *murâsla* sought for a donkey in vain: donkeys indeed were still alive but the enterprise of their owners was dead, and they missed a chance of *coining* money. Ultimately, he produced a colossal mule, surmounted by a pyramid of leather and brass. What a mount, and what a time he gave me and my groggy leg! His owner was not to be seen, as arranged, at *Pont Lîmûn*, but my despair at having his sumpter mule left on my hands was soon dissipated by his arrival.

On the last and great night, I had the advantage both ways of Prof. E-P's car, but his desire, as Professor of Anthropology, to see a typical moulid was hardly fulfilled. The skeleton at the feast appeared soon after sunset, in the form of a huge veiled Arab, who caused intense annoyance by his freedom with the women, and the audacity with which he helped himself at anybody's stall. He was soon shadowed by two police agents in plain clothes, but finding his movements hampered, and their questions awkward, he suddenly produced a murderous file and laid one of them out. The law-abiding crowd immobilised and unveiled him at once. It was a dramatic moment! Some woman cried, "Why, that's the *harâmî* that kidnapped my little Mustafâ!" And a man exclaimed, "And stole my cattle!" He was in fact recognised as a brigand chief, a hated terror, and this was to be the end of his evil acts. The furious villagers closed in upon him, and he was lost to my sight, and I have grave hopes that he was torn to pieces.

News reached the authorities with more quickness than accuracy, and in a very few minutes mounted "'askarîs" with sticks charged and recharged the assembly with more zeal than discrimination; tents came down; *artistes* dressed or otherwise fled into the fields; the moulid was utterly wiped out. I was sorry for the honest crowd, who in lynching the villain had done good service, if a bit irregular, but that could hardly have been known to the police till after, and their job was obviously to stop bloodshed and disorder, however caused.

Appended is the account of the lynching affair as given by *La Bourse Égyptienne*:

Criminal Lynched by Mob

On the occasion of the Moulid of Sheikh el-Mazloum, at Sherabia, two policemen were given the responsibility for maintaining order at the site. The policemen noticed that one Mohamed Kassem, a criminal released from prison barely two months earlier, was visiting the stalls and demanding money from the stall-keepers by threatening them with a large metal file. They had to intervene to stop the criminal from making these threats, and they took away the file. Furious at this, Mohamed Kassem took an iron bar from under his robe and wounded Mohamed el-Sayed, one of the policemen. Having had enough of Mohamed Kassem, the crowd rushed forward and attacked him with clubs, bottles and chairs.

The dead body of the criminal was conveyed to the police station at

Mahmasha and the Public Prosecutor's Office was assigned the case. Several people were questioned, and they confirmed the sworn statements of the policemen.

The wounded policeman, in serious condition, has been sent to hospital. An autopsy has been carried out on the criminal's body.

The following year, Sunday, 25 Muharram 1354 (28 April 1935), an English lady who had wandered through Arabia and the Yemen, attracted rather than the reverse by my stories of this moulid, accompanied me in my cab, but when approaching this temporary city of a hundred tents, a wheel subsided in the soft earth at the edge of the embankment, and the cab overturned. Bumping across a well-filled ditch into some rich vegetation, we escaped without broken bones and without broken bottles, for we had brought picnic rations and after getting together a willing fatigue party to get *Humpty Dumpty* up again, and obtaining the '*arbagî*'s blessing and solemn oath that he would send a cab for us, as he was seemingly very grateful for what he considered liberal treatment, and after a preliminary round of the tents, &c, we sat down by running water in a field close by. There was a bucolic atmosphere of fresh soil and spring onions, for we were in a salad field, and the one lacuna in our menu was supplied on the spot. One item was a succulent plant which I have not seen elsewhere. The local swain called it *kurrât* (leek)[100].

The moulid went smoothly this time, and my companion was specially attracted by the conjuring of el-Hâgg Mahmûd, by the shadow shows, and the dancing horses. She indulged in mild gambling of various sorts with enormous luck for the benefit of some appreciative youngsters. But at the latter end, history repeated itself – *breach of promise* by the '*arbagî,* and nothing that my *murâsla* could find to ride but the sumpter mule with the brazen pyramid on its back. To sit fore and aft of this appealed to neither of us, but a donkey cart load of women and children consented to our squeezing in with them – and so to Cairo.

---

100 Could McPherson's companion on that 28th of April have been Freya Stark? Unwell after a failed attempt to reach Shabwa in the Hadhramaut, evacuated to Aden by the RAF, Stark had sailed from Aden Port on the Orient cruise liner S.S. *Orontes*, 10 April 1935, on her way home to Asolo, Italy. That route would have taken her to Port Said and Naples. Although the ship may have stopped for several days at Port Said, easily allowing for a side trip to Cairo, the timing makes such an eventuality unlikely unless she disembarked at Port Said and took a second ship to Italy. In her collected letters, her first from Italy after this voyage is dated 25 May. Doreen Ingrams might also be a candidate for the mishap with McPherson. She was apparently also in the Middle East, but her whereabouts on 28 April 1935 are unknown to the Editor.

Whilst seated, *pro fanum*[101], I have had considerable conversation with pilgrims to the shrine of "Mazlûm", but their information has been neither consistent nor reliable. Some say that his name was not Mazlûm, but that the term is applied to him, almost in the sense of "martyr", on account of his having been falsely accused and put to death.[102] My informants have agreed that he was a friend of the *fallâh* and patron of agriculture. He might also be patron of wanglers, for he usually obtains abnormally long runs and gracious concessions for his moulids: twenty days or more against the Prophet's seven. Even the death of King Fu'ad in 1355 (1936), which checked all such celebrations, only held up this for a time, and really prolonged it; and in 1357 (1938) it must have run for more than a month. When nearing the date of its *apodosis*, it was stopped (for reasons unknown to me), but I am told that the sheikh of the tomb made strong representations to the *ma'mûr*, not without a *soupçon* of menace, which that high functionary had in his mind, when at night Mazlûm himself appeared in a vision and told him roundly that lives could be cut short as well as moulids. The good man (so the local people say) assured his ghostly visitor that he, the ghost, had been misinformed about the curtailment of the moulid, and that it should be consummated with all honour and five nights added to its duration. And it was so – and the writer was present on the final night, Sunday, 27 Rabî' II 1357 (26 June 1938), and enjoyed *quietam noctem et perfectum finem*[103], with the usual picnic meal in the salad field, and rough ride home.

Floreat Mazlûm – and the *ma'mûr*, and may the latter have five years and more added to his valuable life.

M 10 (cf. Sectional Map VI)
MUWAFFAQ

(سيدي موفق)

This moulid seems to have a precarious existence and the votaries of the Saint to be glad of any day of the week or month when they can celebrate his memory and invoke his intercession. In 1353 (1934) it was Sunday 26 Rajab; in 1354 (1935) Tuesday 10 Sha'bân; in 1355 (1936) Thursday 27 Sha'bân; in 1356 (1937) Tuesday 28 Sha'bân; and in 1357 (1938) I fear it was relegated to the Greek Kalands[104].

---

101 In front of the "temple".
102 mazlûm = wronged, ill-treated.
103 A quiet night and a perfect end.
104 Or Greek calends, a time which is expected never to arrive.

It is just behind the great mosque of Abû -l-'Elâ, and therefore passed by trams 13, 14 and 15, and buses 6 and 15.

The squalid little street which contains the tomb of Sîdî Muwaffaq has nothing else to redeem it except just opposite, another tomb, that of Sîdî Mustafâ.

When I found this moulid in 1353 (1934) it was a big affair, with good attendance at the shrines and the usual shows, with a large tent theatre under the Mosque of Abû -l-'Elâ. This disappeared in 1354 (1935) and *Qara Goz* did not survive till the last night, but there were some "ringas", with highly primitive Sudanese music and dancing; a subject of interest and research to the late Professor of Anthropology of the University and other savants who accompanied me. In 1355 (1936) another sort of dancing place was violently raided, but went on again in a few minutes. In 1356 (1937) there were a few gaming tables and an odd pilgrim or so at the shrines, and an attempt at a tiny *zeffa* at 4.30. In 1357 (1938) nil! And I fear since!

M 11 (cf. Sectional Map V)
MUHAMMADÎ (SÎDÎ EL-SHEIKH DEMARDÂSH EL-MUHAMMADÎ)
(سيدي الشيخ دمردش المحمدي)

This is one of the moulids recognised officially (like that of Imâm el-Shâfe'î), by ceremonies of considerable *envergure*,[105] attended by many of the *'ulamâ*, Ministers, High Functionaries, and Notables, descendants of this great local Cairene Saint, and bearing his name, being included.

On the site of the little *zâwia*, where Sîdî Demardâsh meditated, there is now his *tâbût*, and on the patch of land which he cultivated for the poor and for the state four hundred years ago, there is now a splendid mosque and buildings, supplemented at his moulid by pavilions for a great *tashrîfa*. I have had the honour of attending this on several occasions on the final night which is always a Thursday of the second half of Sha'bân, varying from the 17th in 1352 (5 December 1933), to the 26th in 1357 (20 October 1938). It is quite splendid and rendered more impressive by the white-robed candle-bearing devotees. I have not witnessed a *zeffa*, but that may be because I have not come sufficiently early. Before the *tashrîfa* many of the poor are entertained to dinner.

It is best reached by bus 10, but if the train be preferred it is but a short walk from Demardâsh Station, and in any case the lofty illuminated minaret is a beacon guiding one to the *zâwia*, which will be found surrounded by a dense concourse of pilgrims.

---

105 Scale, breadth

This moulid until 1353 (1934) was not only the goal of a pilgrimage but a highly popular event, and the road from the 'Abbâsîya boulevard to the mosque was a gay scene of booths, stalls, *zikr* groups on both sides, and an immense crowd, but on going in 1355 (1936), this track was quite deserted except for automobiles going to, or returning from, the *tashrîfa*. Doubtless the blending of the two was deemed incongruous and inadvisable, but the result was depressing and disappointing to many, so that in 1356 (1937) I rejoiced with many to find that the amusement department still carried on, but in the village at a respectable distance from the track referred to. The same was the case in 1357 (1938), and all passed tranquilly and everyone was edified and happy. Old friends of the people reappeared – the strong man and his dwarf and company, Mahmûd el-Hindî the conjurer, some performing dogs, and the great favourite, *Qara Goz*.

In most cases it is very difficult to obtain consistent information about the life and origin of the saint one is honouring, but from readings at the *tashrîfa,* and the chronicles of Sha'rânî, Muhammadî stands out a very real and attractive character tilling his plot of almost desert soil, till many attracted by his holy life, or benefited by his prayers or the produce of his labour, settled about his *zâwia* and formed the nucleus of the village which bears his name. It comes down to us that his wife, an earnest disciple, shared his cell, and was awe-stricken at the frequency with which he rose throughout the night to perform ablutions, pray, or study the Qurân el-Sherîf. His motto like that of most of *Western* monasticism was evidently, "Ora et labora"[106].

M 12

MUHAMMADÎ (SHEIKH SÂLEH EL-ÂBID SHÂHÎN EL-MUHAMMADÎ)
(الشيخ الصالح العابد شاهين المحمدي)

I hesitate to include this saint in a book of moulids because I have no definite proof that his cult, almost limited as far as I know to the Muqattam Hills and their vicinity, actually extends to a moulid. My main reason for doing so is to dissipate the confusion between him and his contemporary recluse of the same name, Demardâsh el-Muhammadî, a confusion transmitted to me by my informants, and only now cleared by the help of the *Tabaqât el-Kubrâ* of Sheikh Sha'rânî.

Sheikh Sâleh el-Muhammadî was a soldier in the army of the Mameluke Sultân Qâitbâi, and a great favourite of the latter. He accompanied the Sultân in his expedition to Persia but returned to Cairo and settled down to an anchorite's life, living 30 years in a cave or a grave of the Muqattam Hills, dying in great

---

106 "Pray and work".

sanctity about the beginning of the 10th century A.H. (the end of the 15th century A.D.).

He went as naked as St. Onephrius, without the advantage of that saint's beard which reached his feet. He seems to have made a vow of silence, for his visitors and disciples could not persuade him to talk, but gained edification from the pious austerity of this ascetic.

I have been unable to trace his cell in the Muqattam Hills.

One of our sheikh's names being Châhîn or Shâhîn,[107] I was inclined to identify him with Abû Shâhîn, whose lovely ruined mosque merges into the rock, south of the Geyûshî, from which it can be approached by a narrow track skirting in one place a precipice. From this you crawl like a rabbit up through a hole cut in the live rock, avoid falling into a great dark cave on the left, or mistaking a sort of natural *oubliette* on the right for the track, and so hurtling into space, squeeze through a long rock gallery, and emerge on one of the beauty spots of Egypt, perhaps of the world, commanding a view of the Nile, green Ma'âdî, distant Hawâmdîya, the Saqqâra pyramid, and much else (an ideal spot for picnic and a siesta). Thence you climb down to the old mosque with its fine minaret vertically beneath you, and find a gaping hole which once contained the mortal remains of the sheikh, dug up and violated unhappily about 1918, at which time also the wonderful green tiles and all things portable were stolen.

That the clearing up of these points must be left to others was brought home to me at the end of Sha'bân 1358 (1939), when I was assured by a sheikh (without any guarantee of accuracy) that the tomb and Moulid of Muhammadî were behind the *manshîya* of Muhammad 'Alî, and the new *caracôl*, and the moulid, then on. The spot I found in darkness and crowds of children showed me what might have been the tomb, many of them declaring that this was the first year that the moulid had been suppressed.

N. 1 (cf. Sectional Map XVII)
NAFÎSA
(سيدة نفيسة)

Strictly speaking as far as I am aware, Sitna Nafîsa has *now*[108] no moulid of her own, but she shares in a way that of Sitna Sakîna (who was, I think, her great-aunt)

---

107 [McPher.] Either spelling may be used, according to whether we transliterate from the original Turkish chin, or from the Arabic shin. By a paradox, therefore, it is more correct to write this and similar words of Turkish origin with the initial "Ch", but better Arabic to employ "Sh".

108 [McPher.] I have seen in an old book the Moulid of Saida Nafisa referred to as an

near the middle of Gamâd I. On that occasion her tomb seems as much in favour as that of Sakîna, and the amusement park is in a bit of waste land facing the *gabel* close to Sitna Nafîsa's great mosque, and some distance from that of Sakîna.

Bus 18 from Darâsa via the 'Ataba runs to the *gabel* in question, passing Sitna Sakîna. This is one of the most fascinating bits of Cairo and should not be missed. I recommend a visit on Sunday, when there is always a little pilgrimage to the tomb of the great saint (great-grand-daughter of Sidna Hasan, and therefore directly descended from the Prophet) and collateral celebrations suggestive of a small moulid.

Nearly always on the Sunday at the door of the mosque one finds women sitting, selling for three *millièmes* a little orb-shaped *sistrum* of wickerwork on a stalk, which one of them informed me was in remembrance of Nafîsa as a girl, these *sistra* having been her favourite toys. This touching remembrance reminds me much of toys shown in the house of St. Catherine, with which she played as a little girl, and of which replicas can be purchased in the *contrada* at the time of the Palio race at Siena.

There is a more scientific interest in this *sistrum*, in that it supports Prof. Newberry's theory that the royal sceptre was in origin a *sistrum*.

Sitna Nafîsa is held in such esteem and affection by the Cairenes, especially their womenfolk, that she perhaps rivals in that respect her great-great-aunt Sayyida Zeinab. That is largely due to her having spent the last seven years of her life in Cairo, and bringing up a son and daughter here. She married late in life, her early days having been taken up in devotion and good works. Born in Mecca in 145 A.H. (762 A.D.), she passed away in Cairo in 208 A.H. (823 A.D.) at the age therefore of 68 years (Eastern reckoning).

The great Imâm el-Shâfe'î was an ardent votary of hers, praying constantly at her mosque, which is only separated from his tomb, and the beautiful mosque built over it, by the necropolis, *qarâfa*, which contains the tombs of the Fatimite Khalîfas, and always praying the special prayers of Ramadân with her.

N 2 (cf. Sectional Map VI)
NASR
(سيدي نصر)

On the one occasion on which I was present, Thursday 14 Rabî' II 1353 (26 July 1934), this moulid was fairly big and lively. It is held in the Darb el-Nasr, Bûlâq, and is reached in a few minutes from Shâri' Fu'ad el-Awwal, by leaving tram 13,

---

important occasion.

14, 15 or 33 or bus 6 or 7 at Abû -l-'Elâ and going North along the new big street, Shâri' 'Abd el-Gawâd, till that is crossed by the Shâri' Darb el-Nasr. In the open space near the crossing there was a very big *zikr*, and in the *darb*, an amusing little theatre and Punch and Judy.

The Darb el-Nasr is a long picturesque street, full of people at all times, and crowded when this moulid is on, or the moulids of Khasûsî, and of Awlâd Badr, which are both held here in Sha'bân.

N 3 (cf. Sectional Map IX)
NEBÎ (EL-NEBÎ)

(النبي محمد صلى الله عليه وسلم)

I was introduced on 11 Rabî' I 1320 (18 June 1902) to this most august of Moslem festivals by the late Muftî and was amazed, as all must be who visit it, at its magnitude and magnificence. I went the following year a night too late, owing to the misleading notices which I think still persist in the European papers, announcing the day corresponding to 12 Rabî' I as the Prophet's birthday, and a public holiday, but omitting to point out that the great celebration is on the eve of the feast. Again and again, I have met disappointed people who have missed the great occasion in the same way.

Lane in his *Modern Egyptians,* writing over a hundred years ago, gives a splendid account of the moulid in detail, even the words and music employed in the "zikrs" and other religious ceremonies. Those were the days of the *dôsah*, when the sheikh of the Sa'dîya rode over the prostrate bodies of a multitude of dervishes. This was suppressed before the present century owing, it is said, to the Khedive listening to earnest representations made by a European visitor. Butler's name is mentioned, but I cannot believe that the author of the *Coptic Churches of Egypt* could have been capable of such a display of arrogant interference and ignorant narrow-mindedness, and I hope it was not an Englishman. There is no record of anyone having been injured at the *dôsah* during all the years it was observed, whereas in 1353 (23 June 1934) Europeans and Egyptians alike were shocked by the number of people injured by the zeal and impatience of the police, who expected the great square clear the minute the fireworks ceased.

In Lane's days, the Sheikh el-Bakrî had an important role in this moulid as he had in that of Dashtûtî, and all occasions of the *dôsah,* but a custom which concluded the ceremonies in his house, that of eating snakes by Sa'dîya dervishes, had been forbidden already, one reason given being that serpents are unclean and unfit for food. That, I think most people will agree, was "a custom more honoured in the breach than the observance".

The Sheikh el-Bakrî then dwelt on the shores of the little lake which occupied during a big part of the year the site where now we have the Ezbekîya Gardens, and it was there that the moulid was celebrated – by the lake or in its dry bed according to the season in which Rabî' I fell. The religious ceremonies took place largely at the mosque and tomb of 'Ashmâwî in what was then the Sûq el-Bakrî, now Shâri' el-'Ashmâwî. The moulid of that great saint is still held in conjunction with that of the Prophet, the final night being always the eve of Rabî' II.

The site has long since been transferred. For a time, it was at Fumm el-Khalîg. All the early part of this century, it was a desert tract close to the 'Abbâsîya tram, now built over. Then for some years on the 'Abbâsîya parade ground just beyond the *rasadkhâna* (the old Observatory), where the ceremony of the *Mahmal* is now held, and quite recently in the desert between 'Abbâsîya and the tombs of the "Khalîfas", near the water towers. From the terminus of tram 7 it is a walk of about a quarter of an hour. Cab or taxi it is difficult to obtain there. Tram 3 passes the same spot. There is parking accommodation for those who come in cars, and buses run on the evening of the great night between the moulid and the city, passing Sidna Husein. Therefore, though there is regal sitting accommodation in the great pavilions whilst there, going and coming may be tiring. Some years ago, the Carmelite monks of St. Teresa (Shubrâ), including the present Vicar of Mt. Carmel, were invited, and were interested and impressed, but lost their way on the return, and at last, after midnight and half dead with fatigue from the long tramp in the sand got into Cairo somewhere near the top of the Mûskî. When at last they arrived at the little monastery at Shubrâ at an unheard-of hour, the other monks, who had probably completed matins, looked down their noses. The Very Rev. Vicar remarked to me that "Moslem pilgrimages were more austere and arduous than many Christian ones."

Amongst the moulids of Cairo, this for sumptuous magnificence is *facile princeps.* I have seen no celebration of its sort, Islamic or Christian, to touch it. Three sides of an immense square covering many acres are enclosed by vast and handsome tents; in the centre of the south side, the royal pavilion, and royally indeed is it appointed. On each side are the almost equally superb tents of all the Ministries, carpeted, and adorned with palms, parterres of flowers, and decorations indicative of the function of each Ministry, that of War being a great favourite with its display of arms and cannons. The Parliament has its pavilion, and so has the Sheikh el-Bakrî. The east and west sides consist also of rows of tents of the various *tŭrŭq* (orders of dervishes) and of eminent sheikhs. Refreshments and lordly sitting accommodation are provided in all of these, and after the opening ceremonies in the royal pavilion before the king or his representative, the reading of parts of the Qurân, and the Life of the Prophet, the Ministers and others of the high company go to their tents and visit the others, where sheikhs on a dais are already intoning. A *beau geste* of very recent years is the admission of those of the multitude who wish into practically all of the tents about sunset, when in many of them "zikrs" begin. They appreciate this enormously and do not take advantage, or crowd inordinately. The mighty space holds the overflow, which crowd becomes denser and denser, till all are rewarded and entranced by such a brilliant display of fireworks as could hardly be seen at the Crystal Palace.

The marvellous opening procession which Lane describes passed long since into the *Ewigkeit,* with the *dôsah* and much else, to be replaced by this city of tent-work palaces and the fireworks. Early in the century, there was rather a sordid little amusement park without the main precincts; carts and booths of *ta'mîya* and other edibles prevailing, but this developed until a vast assemblage of theatres, "ringas", circuses, *Qara Goz* (Punch and Judy), and the like, occupied a big piece of desert sufficiently removed from the official part. That died in 1355 (1936) with King Fu'ad, for in that year even the fireworks were suppressed as a sign of mourning, and though these were restored in 1356 (1937), little remained of the fair but a few stalls and inferior shows, and happily as a redeeming feature, that most popular attraction, the *Piste à la Mort* of the intrepid Billy Williams. Though this deprivation is a disappointment to the poor people who come from near and far, it does not hit them as at other moulids, owing to the *éclat* of the tents, and the brilliance of the myriad of coloured lamps which illumine them, and of the fireworks.

This major feast of the Prophet is, curiously enough, one of the shortest, officially only a week, and in reality, hardly frequented at all till the great night. Not so in the villages and the provinces, where "zeffas" and "zikrs" are held most nights of the week, and almost all night, and alms and food are given to the poor. In the *'ezba* where I live, swings and goose-nests are put up for the children; all the week prominent villagers supplement the accommodation of their houses by tents for ceremonies of consequence; and sleeping on the roof as I do, I hear special commemorations of the Prophet from the minarets, and the sounds of music and "zikring" almost till the dawn, culminating in a *zeffa* of the Shâzlîya, Sa'dîya, Rifâ'îya and other dervish orders with their *dabâbîs*, "tablas" and "tars", "zummâras" and *kâs*, their banners and insignia, much, I should imagine, on the old original lines.

I think few Egyptians can be aware how far their devotion to the Prophet exceeds that shown in other lands, even in Stambul before its 'yankification'. Recently, I came down from the top of Mount Lebanon on 11 Rabî' I to Beyrouth, the Syrian capital[109] and largely a Moslem city, and in the evening found some boys collecting sticks and paper and lighting tiny bonfires in open places, and a few windows showing a candle flame behind a bit of transparent red paper, and a few pocket fireworks were let off. It is true that the following morning a unique little ceremony was enacted: some sheikhs mounted to the top of a leading mosque and sang, and after the noon prayer went in procession to an outlying mosque, but *voilà tout.*

I gather from accounts Prof. Evans-Pritchard[110] has given me of Bedawin tribes in the far south of Upper Egypt, in Nubia, the Sudan and Abyssinia, with whose ways he is intimately acquainted (with, I think, special reference to the Bisharin[111] and 'Abâbda tribes), that though the cult of their saints is by no means neglected, this does not involve a celebration of their moulids, except in the case of the Prophet himself. In that, however, their *walîs* and the minor *sheikhs* all participate in a way, and are duly commemorated, with naturally special emphasis on any local saint of each district. They too – the tribesmen – at the time of the Prophet's birthday aspire to humble communion with this great company, and to participation in the divine benefits in the gift of these *"favourites, friends and companions* of Allâh".

The last verse of the "Lauda, Sion, Salvatorem" does not ill express their vague yearnings, and generally indeed those of Pilgrims and moulid-goers of the right type:

Tu, qui cuncta scis et vales,
Qui nos pascis hic mortales:
Tuos ibi commensales,
Cohæredes, et sodales,
Fac sanctorum civium.[112]

---

109 Beirut had been the capital of a Syrian governorate, part of the Ottoman Empire, since 1888. After WWI and the collapse of that Empire, Lebanon was placed under a French Mandate. Syria after WWI was briefly independent as the Kingdom of Syria, but that failed and the country was also placed under the French Mandate. In 1943, two years after *The Moulids of Egypt* was first published, Lebanon became independent with Beirut as its capital.
110 [McPher.] Dr. Evans-Pritchard, Research Lecturer in African Sociology at Oxford (but at the moment on active Service on the Abyssinian frontier) is well known to very many of my readers, having been Professor of Sociology at the Egyptian University. Amongst his major works is *"Witchcraft, Oracles and Magic among the Azande"*, and very recently a book on the Nilotic People entitled *"The Nuer."*
111 In Arabic, Bishâriyyîn.
112 "You who know and can do all things,

The only exception to the above generalisation that I am at all sure of is in the case of Sîdî Abû Hasan el-'Abâbdî, who has his own moulid near Qoseir, in addition to his commemoration at that of el-Nebî (cf. Moulid of 'Abâbdî, A 20).

The Aswân "Pantheon", if I may venture to so term it, is a mysterious evidence of the solidarity of the community of Islamic "walîs" and "sheikhs", and holy men generally. Mysterious to me anyway, who has not visited it, and whose sole information thereon is derived from one Sharîf and two or three sheikhs who have been more fortunate, and whose testimony may be summed up as follows:

About a kilometre from Aswan, in the *gabel* sacred to the Prophet, where his blood still is to be seen on the rocks, all the Walis and Sheikhs who have moulids are represented. The *Awlia* (Walis) and those with special repute for holiness have their "dareh", with dome and *tabut,* whilst the rest have at least their names inscribed on a tabut or something to testify to their being of the select company.

They have as guardian, or *naqiba,* as she is there termed, a sheikha named Sofia Abd el-Hakim, who lived a very austere life amongst the tombs until one of the *Awlia* appeared to the mudir and called attention to her privations. His Excellence at once had a house built there for her with water-supply and all requirements.

It is the writer's hope to see and know much more about this mystic epitome of all Egyptian moulids.

The following extract from a Cairo paper indicates a traditional custom of distributing sweets on the occasion of the Moulid el-Nebî. Husein Pâsha Heikal's move was naturally a very popular one. This custom is not confined to Cairo, though it has its variants, such as the substitute of money. I was informed in Tunis years ago that the "Bey" rides amongst the crowd on this occasion scattering purses. I fancy that nothing of that sort will survive in the present *vitiated* atmosphere.

Who feed us mortals here:
Make us there your table companions,
Co-heirs and fellows of the holy citizens."
These are the final lines of the Lauda, Sion, Salvatorem, a prayer written by St Thomas Aquinas for the Roman Catholic Mass of The Solemnity of the Most Holy Body and Blood of Christ.

Moulid el-Nebî

King Farouk at the Moulid el-Nebî. The photo is inscribed: "To my
dear friend, Mr McPherson – a souvenir of honour and friendship.
Farouk, son of [King] Ahmad Fu'ad the Great. 10 May 1941."

The Sugared Almonds of Moulid el-Nebî

There is a tradition that sugared almonds be distributed to Government
officials on the feast of Moulid el-Nebî, that is, the birthday of the Prophet.
The various ministries and administrative bodies have already prepared a list
of officials, employees and temporary workers eligible to benefit from this
distribution of sweets. The funds for purchasing the sugared almonds are taken
from money budgeted annually towards the Moulid's celebration. Ordinarily,
high officials are allotted considerably more of the sugared almonds than the
lower functionaries and "farrashes".

But that's not what is going to happen this year at the Ministry of Public
Instruction, where His Exellency Dr Hussein Heikal Pâsha has it in mind to
use the occasion to bring a bit of joy to the families of those at the lower end
of the scale. He has decided to offer most of the sweets to them and to reduce
the portion going to the higher officials.

King Farouk's presidency for the first time in 1357 (1938) lent a special *éclat* to
the celebrations, as will be seen from the attached extracts from *La Bourse Égyptienne* of that date. (It is regrettable that he was not left in peace on the Prophet's
birthday, but his petitioner seemed very harmless.)

I have included the tract distribution incident, as it is unique – the only example
I know of politics being dragged into a moulid (except on one trifling occasion, when a few students aired some slogan and were promptly and effectively
checked).

To the Court

Office of the Grand Chamberlain
Wednesday, 11 May 1938

At 4:38 p.m., His Majesty the King, accompanied by His Excellency
Mohamed Mahmoud Pâsha, President of the Council of Ministers, left
Abdin Palace by automobile in order to attend the Feast of Moulid el-Nebî
in Abbassia. On his arrival at the royal marquee, His Majesty was received
by Their Excellencies the President of the Senate and Ministries, the Rector
of Al-Azhar, the President of the High Court, the Grand Mufti, the Naqib
el-Ashraf, the head of the religious confraternities, under-secretaries of State,
the vice-president of the Senate, the Chargé d'Affaires of the Iraqi Legation

in Egypt, the Governor of Cairo, and high officials of the Royal Court. Army units taking part in the festivities greeted His Majesty with military honours, and their band played the royal anthem as a salvo was fired to salute the monarch as soon as he was seated. His Excellency the Grand Chamberlain came forward to ask His Majesty to do the honour of attending the military parade; then the heads of the religious confraternities expressed their best wishes and testimony of their devotion to their august sovereign.

His Majesty then deigned to visit the tent of el-Sayyid Abd el-Hamid el-Bakri to hear a recitation of the Hadith of the Cloak (Hadith el-Kisa'). Another salvo was fired in honour of this solemn occasion, whereupon His Majesty, with due ceremony, returned to the Palace.

His Majesty the King has delegated His Excellency the Governor of Alexandria to lead the festivities organised by the Municipality of that city on the occasion of Moulid el-Nebî.

Police Arrest Engineer Distributing Anti-Jewish
Leaflets at Moulid el-Nebî Festival

Yesterday, at the Moulid el-Nebî festival the police arrested an engineer, employed at the Arsenal, caught distributing seditious tracts against the Jews. The leaflets have been seized and the engineer incarcerated pending an enquiry.

The gist of the message in the leaflets is: the Jews in Palestine, who are in continuous conflict with the Arabs there, are aided morally and financially by their co-religionists in Egypt. It is, therefore, important to boycott those Egyptian Jews who have close relations with the Jews of Palestine.

It is to be hoped that the authorities will take the measures necessary to put an end to this state of affairs, which in no way accords with the spirit of tolerance and friendly cooperation between all races and religions living on the hospitable soil of the Nile Valley.

Young Man Tries to Present a Petition to His
Majesty at Moulid el-Nebî Ceremony

Yesterday, as His Majesty's cortège made its way to the Moulid el-Nebî and was approaching the site where the religious ceremonies were taking place, a young man hurried past the cordon of police and proceeded towards the carriage bearing the Sovereign and his Prime Minister.

In his hand he had a roll of paper or, to be exact, a petition which he wanted to present to His Majesty. The young man was arrested by soldiers of the Royal Guard. Nevertheless, the youth succeeded in throwing the petition which came to rest at the feet of His Majesty.

In the petition the young man informs His Majesty of his poverty and asks to be appointed a "maazoun".[113]

An enquiry into the affair has been opened.

I am supplementing the above account by two more cuttings from Cairo papers. The short one indicates the lavish way in which the Prophet's Birthday is honoured in the Egyptian capital, L.E. 8,500 being spent to begin with, in levelling the site and putting on water from the reservoirs close by. The longer one gives some interesting particulars and statistics. It will be noted that its date is 1358 (1939).

May nothing ever happen in Egypt to dim the lustre of the Birthday of the Prophet.

The location of the next Moulid el-Nebî

We have already announced that the authorities had decided that the next Moulid el-Nebi should be held in Abbassia, near the reservoirs and filters of La Compagnie des Eaux du Cairo.

We have since learned that the funds needed to level the ground at the site and to furnish drinking water are estimated at L.E.8,500. For its part, la Compagnie Lebon has undertaken to install, at its own cost, the necessary electricity.

That installation would equally serve other ceremonies, such as the departure and arrival of the Holy Carpet.

Moulid el-Nebî

Moslem World Celebrates Prophet's Birth

Moulid el-Nebî, "The Prophet's Birthday" was celebrated last night by 400,000,000 Moslems all over the world. 1,358 years ago, yesterday, Amina, a "noble lady of Koreish" who had been a widow for some months gave birth to an infant who was destined to proclaim a faith which revolutionized the life of

---

113 ma'zûn = Official authorised to perform Muslim marriages.

Moulid el-Nebî
Some "pilgrims" to the Moulid el-Nebî (McPherson with two
Christian fathers at the Moulid of the Prophet Muhammad).

the Arabs and had far-reaching effect on the peoples of the East.

Yesterday, the Imams of mosques recited the Prophet's life story, the miracles which took place on the day of his birth, the adversity he had to suffer, the fact that although born and brought up among idolators, he had always worshipped one God, and the first inspirations he had as a Prophet and Apostle of God.

Like Christmas for Christians, the Moulid el-Nebî is an occasion for bringing joy to children. Dolls and toys made of sugar are presented to young folks, and although there is no Santa Claus, parents do all they can to make their children happy.

Owing to King Farouk's indisposition, Aly Maher Pasha, Chief of the Royal Cabinet, attended the official ceremony as the King's representative. He was received on arrival at the official marquée at Abbassia by the Ministers, the Ulema and the high officials.

After a military display, Maher Pasha went to the marquee of Sheikh El-Bakry where he listened to the recital of the Prophet's life story.

The marquees of the various government departments, particularly that of the Ministry of Waqfs, were gaily illuminated and the fireworks were admired by the huge crowds which took part in the celebrations.

All Government offices will be closed today to celebrate the occasion.

Celebrations in Alexandria

Over twenty marquees were erected to celebrate the moulid in Alexandria, in the different quarters of the city and refreshments, and alms were distributed on the occasion.

An official marquee was erected by the Alexandria Municipality on the eastern Quay, near the National Court building. Mohamed Hussein Pasha represented King Farouk. Ulema, notables and officials were present to hear Sheikh Rifaat read the history of the Prophet's life. The celebrations continued until well after midnight.

O 1

'OMAR ('OMAR IBN EL-FÂRID)

(سيدي عمر ابن الفارض)

I have been assured by Miss G... , a person deeply interested in moulids that "one is held in honour of Sîdî 'Omar somewhere behind the citadel, in the Imâm el-Shâfe'î direction". I have never been able to confirm it in place, and no date was indicated, but evidently this must centre about the little mosque and *tekîya* of Sîdî 'Omar el-Fârid, behind the rather gruesome little village of Abâgîya, at the foot of the Muqattam precipices, immediately under that most picturesque ruined mosque, Abû Shâhîn.

The fortress-like wall of the Muqattam Hills confronting the citadel teems with weird beauty and interest, and lovely vistas, much obvious enough; but much also hewn in the living rock by monk, Christian and Moslem, for seclusion, security, and worship preserves a good deal of its secrecy to this day and requires a lot of learning. Some particulars of one part of this are given in the account of the moulid of Shâhîn el-Muhammadî (cf. M 12).

I take this opportunity (though late) of thanking the good dervishes of Sîdî 'Omar Ibn el-Fârid for coming to my rescue in a desperate situation. I had introduced a large party – the Cairo Catholic Association – to some of the mysteries of the places; they had scaled the cliff front, squeezed up vertical shafts and through holes and galleries, and arriving at the spot shown in the picture were more than ready for a picnic tea, already spread by my boys except for the tea itself, and for that a kettle was boiling in a deep and windless cave. Then my batman whispered to me that he could not find the packet of tea and must have left it behind. I felt that my guests were entitled to hurl me and the batman from this Tarpeian Rock,[114] but the garden boy Sayed made himself the scapegoat. He slithered down this seeming precipice, flew to Sîdî 'Omar, and up again, bearing a canister of excellent tea and the pious and friendly greetings of the monks.

God bless'em!

O 2 (cf. Map of Upper Egypt)
'OQBÎ = 'UQBÎ or 'UQBA[115]
(سيدي عقبة)

I had never heard of this moulid but lighted upon it accidentally in 1938 (1357), when riding across the fields from my home at Bein el-Sarâyât to a football match at Zamâlek and passing through the big picturesque village of Mît 'Uqba. The precincts of the tomb of Sîdî 'Uqbî were decorated, but it was three days to the big celebration, and not being free then, I sent a *murâsla* on Sunday, 18 Gamâd II 1357 (14 August 1938), who reported that it was quite a considerable event,

---

114 A cliff on the southern side of the Capitoline Hill in Rome. During the Roman Republic it was used as a site of execution, convicts being thrown from the summit to their deaths.
115 McPherson gives both spellings. 'Uqba would more likely refer to the place, 'Uqbî to the person from that place. Valerie J. Hoffman identifies Sîdî 'Uqba as 'Uqba bin 'Âmir el-Juhaynî, a Companion of the Prophet.

with a great concourse at the shrine, and even a theatre of sorts in the amusement department. It was of the simple country moulid type, similar to that of Abû Qureish two nights previously at Zenîn (cf. A 22); but my messenger was assured that usually it is much larger, being reduced this year by the competition, so to speak, of a plethora of moulids – Sîdî Ibrâhîm Desûqî the same evening at the cenotaph of that great founder of the sect of the Desûqîya by the Nile at Gezîrat el-Dahab; 'Abd el-Rahîm el-Tartûrî in the neighbouring village of el-Hatîya, and Abû Qureish of Zenîn, and another, whose name and place I am not sure of, only just over, and the great Moulid of Zefeitî, through which I passed on my way from Bein el-Sarâyât to Mît 'Uqba working up for a grand finale on 22 Gamâd II.

It may be reached by Gîza tram 15, getting out at the first stop after Zamâlek Bridge, and taking the road at right angles to the Bahr el-A'mâ. As it is nearly a two-mile walk, a car is preferable and the road is not bad.

I have not succeeded in obtaining any reliable information about Sîdî 'Uqbî.

In 1358 (1939) the same *murâsla* reported Sîdî 'Uqbî's moulid to have been kept up on Thursday, 24 Gamâd II (10 August 1939) in conjunction with two minor moulids in the same village. These were el-Sheikh el-Lâshîn and Sîdî Gharîb.

There is a mosque and small cemetery of a Sîdî 'Uqba a little south of Imâm el-Leithî, but I am ignorant of any connection between these and the shrine at Mît 'Uqba.

Q 1 (cf. Sectional Map XII)
QÂZÂZÎ
(الشيخ قازازي)

This small moulid I came across accidentally on 28 Sha'bân 1354 (25 November 1935), a little after 10 at night, for whilst interested in the tomb of Sîdî Mustafâ el-Gamel in the Darâsa district, a small zeffa appeared from the direction of Sidna Husein, and following this, we halted at the little modern mosque Qâzâzî in the Shâri' Tamain el-Guwânî. It was a *private* moulid but well attended, though this I was told was only the penultimate night. I was not free to go on 29 Sha'bân.

WÂSTA

Q 2 (cf. Map of Upper Egypt.)
QĂRĂNÎ (UWEIS EL-QĂRĂNÎ)[116]

(سيدي أويس القرني)

I have found this the most elusive of moulids and have been misled about it, to the extent of going to Mazghûna and witnessing that of Sayyid el-Shuhadâ' on the assurance that I was present at the Qărănî moulid.

The frequent mention of it as an important event induces me to include it, and I believe it is in the direction of Wâsta but have no idea of the date.

Also, there is no question as regards the importance of Uweis el-Qărănî in Islam. 'Abd el-Wahhâb el-Sha'rânî gives a long (but to me obscure) account of his sayings and doings, and groups him amongst the earliest dervishes almost at the beginning of the spread of Muhammadanism.

He seems to have had great authority with the *djinn*, so that he was not seen to enter or leave his house sometimes for a year or two at a time, and at his death his body miraculously disappeared.

FAYÛM

R 1 (cf. Map of Upper Egypt.)
RÛBÎ

(الشيخ روبي)

A big and important moulid, I am told, in beautiful surroundings, which I am anxious to see. At present I know nothing about it from personal experience, but believing it to be held at mid-Sha'bân, I sent this year of the Prophet 1359 (1940) my garden boy, and he has come back full of enthusiasm, as he found it compared very favourably with the Cairo moulids of today. Medînet el-Fayûm was crowded with pilgrims and visitors, and the place was full of life by night and by day. There was a great confluence at the shrine and at that of a local sheikh of great holiness and repute, with whom Sîdî Rûbî consorted constantly after he came to Egypt – for according to Sayyid (the garden boy), Rûbî was "Rûmî"[117] by origin and birth, and came somewhat late in life to the Fayûm.

---

116 Said to have been killed at the Battle of Siffîn (37 A.H. / 657 A.D.), fighting on the side of 'Alî. Cf. Article "Uways al-Karami" by Julian Baldick in *The Encyclopaedia of Islam*, 2nd ed.
117 A somewhat ambiguous word in Egyptian Arabic. It could mean either "Greek" or "European"; cognate of "Rome".

Unfortunately, there were no horse races nor performing horses, and other beauties had disappeared in recent years. *Qara Goz* and a shadow show survived, and also a little theatre.

According to all the calendars, the eve of mid-Sha'bân, 14 Sha'bân, coincided with Monday, 16 September 1940, but someone seems to have played about with the moon, as the West (and unhappily the East is following suit) has taken to monkeying with the sun, and the shaking of the Lote Tree of Paradise was put off to the Tuesday. This gave two last nights to Sheikh Rûbî, as the news only filtered through slowly to the Fayûm.

(In Cairo, and doubtless elsewhere, the minarets were lighted up on the Tuesday, not the Monday, and the Citadel celebration was held then.)

S 1 (cf. Sectional Map XVII)
SAKÎNA

(ستنا سكينة)

Though I have witnessed this curious moulid several times, I only once noted the date. That was Wednesday, 12 Gamâd I 1353 (22 August 1934).

Bus 18, which runs via 'Ataba from Darâsa on the edge of the desert on the East to Sitna Nafîsa at the beginning of the desert to the South, passes the mosque of Sitna Sakîna near the latter terminus. Sitna Sakîna in a way shares her moulid with her great-great niece Nafîsa, especially on the secular side, the theatre and all the shows being on the edge of the "gabel" close to Nafîsa's mosque, which excels in beauty the celebrated place which contains the remains of Sakîna, daughter of Sidna Husein. This district, which lies south of Ibn Tûlûn and north of the great necropolis ending at Imâm el-Shâfe'î, remains unspoilt, and abounds in splendid monuments, including these two great mosques, some majestic tombs, and a remarkable tower which was probably used as a beacon; no visitor or resident should omit exploring it. Apart from moulid time, the best day is Sunday, as Sitna Nafîsa is always then *en fête*.

The moulid is big, bright and popular, but on two occasions I have seen it broken up by ragamuffins who swarm on the "rubbish heaps". These are expert stone throwers, often dividing into camps and indulging in pitched battles amongst themselves.

The numerous lights and the large white tent which houses a theatrical troop prove irresistible attractions to the stone throwers, and it is pathetic to see enraged persons, sometimes aided by the police, charging the heights in pursuit of the attackers, and perhaps throwing stones up at them at a hopeless disadvantage. A few plain clothes men, police, or just from the private individuals affected, unostentatiously taking up positions on the higher slopes, concealing good stout whips, would turn the tables on the aggressors and discount the chances of a repetition. Instead of this, on the two occasions to which I have referred, the unsuccessful stormers of the heights – to relieve their feelings, and I suppose with the idea that if the tent had not been there the incident could not have happened – have made an onslaught upon that, stopping the performance, ejecting the spectators; then, extending their attentions to Punch and Judy and other attractions, have finally brought the moulid to a regrettable end.

I have heard doubts cast on the actual existence of the remains of the daughter of the Imâm Husein in the mosque of her name, but 'Abd el-Wahhâb el-Sha'rânî states unequivocally that Sitna Sakîna is buried near Sitna Nafîsa.

I am reminded (whilst this is in the press) by an interesting broadcast by Mrs. Devonshire on "Mausoleums of Cairo" (see "Cairo Calling", 14 December 1940) that in referring above to "Majestic Tombs", I omitted all reference to the Mausoleum of Sitna "Ruggeya" (as I think Mrs. Devonshire rendered her name). Mrs. Devonshire's broadcast is illustrated in "Cairo Calling" by a picture of this tomb.

It is a shrine much frequented, especially on Sundays, is passed by bus 18, and is almost opposite the mosque of Sitna Sakîna, a shade to the south.

I have been told that a small moulid is held in this Saint's honour but have not been able to confirm this.

In the broadcast mentioned above, it was pointed out that she was a relative of Sidna Husein.

I have referred to her in this connection in Chapter I under the name of Rugaiya, taken down phonetically from the words of a local sheikh, but he may have been Upper Egyptian in origin, where they pronounce the "q" as "g"; but if I read her epitaph aright, her name in Arabic may perhaps be transliterated simply as "Ruqayya", though without the diacritical signs to indicate the weak vowels, the doubling of a letter by the "shadda", &c., there is scope for several other pronunciations my various informants have given me.

Alas, this is only one instance of the baffling problem of transliteration!

S 2 (cf. Sectional Map XI)
SALÂMA

(الشيخ سلامة)

This moulid I saw in full swing on Thursday, 13 Gamâd I 1353 (23 August 1934), and on one or two previous dates not noted, but have not been able to find it at that date since.

It is most easy of access, just behind the 'Ataba, and its two opposite parts overlooking Shâri' el-Azhar, the tomb of the saint being on the north side, and a number of dancing cafés, "ringas", etc., on the south.

Like Ma'rûf, this is essentially a moulid for Sudanese and *Barâbira*[118]. It is lively but rather squalid, and though in an old district there is little about it attractive.

S 3 (cf. Sectional Map XII)
SÂLEH (SULTÂN SÂLEH)
(الصلطان صالح الأيوبي)

Many years ago, at the moulids of Sidna Husein, there was always a crowd about singing sheikhs in the Shâri' Nahhâsîn at the far end of the Khân el-Khalîlî, but I did not understand the significance of this until recently reading Lane's "*Modern Egyptians*", written over a hundred years ago, I came across an account of a great *walî*, a "Sultân" (King of Sheikhs), buried at this spot, and whose moulid was held on the same night as that of Sidna Husein. Lane describes the mosque and tomb as dirty, neglected and in the last stages of decay, so my surprise and delight were great when, a few days ago, Mîrâlâi G-A, an authority on these matters took me there, to find the vast chamber in which a *tâbût* is still over the body, clean and perfectly kept. The mosque indeed is mostly gone, but a part is still used for the customary prayers, and what remains is well looked after and very impressive. The *tâbût* is surrounded as in Lane's time by a wooden fence, which he calls a "maksoora"[119], and bears inscriptions, one of which refers to the family of el-Bakrî, *Naqîb el-Ashrâf*.

A worthy sheikh showed and explained much of interest and stated that Sâleh's moulid is *now* always on the night *before* the final night of Sidna Husein, and that it will be certainly held this year.

The spot is well-known: near that marvellous group of mosques, Qalâwûn, Barqûq, etc., but on the other side opposite the gold bazaars.

We enquired about the "Roman Candles", which in Lane's day towered at either end of the *tâbût* but are no longer there; and were told that they are now in the Arab Museum. They were presented, it is said, to the shrine by some mighty but evil person, but the *walî* Sâleh appeared in a vision to the guardian of his tomb, warning him that these candles were full of gunpowder and must be encased in plaster, which was done.

This *malik* el-Sâleh Ayyûb was a great thorn in the side of the Crusaders, taking

---

118 Berbers
119 maqsûra, an enclosure, to which only certain people are admitted.

The Mosques of Sheikh Haddâd (above) and Sultân Hanafî are adjacent to one
another and a short walk to the south of the 'Abdîn Palace. Their overlapping
moulids in the month of Sha'bân were main events in the moulid calendar.

from them the stronghold of Ascalon, the last position held by them. He was con-
queror also at Damascus and the Holy City.

The famous Shagaret el-Durr was Sâleh's wife. The tomb of his mother Fâtima
hatun[120] was shown me in that splendid group of ruins between Sitna Sakîna and
Sitna Nafîsa.

The "muhaddits", as Lane calls them (story-tellers), thirty in Cairo alone, in
his day occupied themselves exclusively in recounting the Romance of el-Zâhir
(el-Sultân Beybars), which turns on El-Malik el-Sâleh, and his son and successor el-Malik 'Îsâ and the rivals and contemporaries of Beybars who ascended the
throne of Egypt in 658 A.H. (1260 A.D.), and vividly describes the pious visit of
'Îsâ and Beybars to the tombs of Sâleh and the Imâm el-Shâfe'î. This recital has
become rare in Cairo. Lane's charming version is well worth reading.

S 4 (cf. Sectional Map XIII)
SÂLEH EL-HADDÂD
(الشيخ صالح الحداد)

On the very numerous occasions on which I have been present, the main night has
invariably been the first Tuesday after mid-Sha'bân, that is the night before the
moulid of Sultân Hanafî.

As the two mosques are contiguous, and the moulids of Sâleh and Hanafî so
nearly coinciding, I refer readers to the account of the latter, which applies to
Sâleh in almost every detail.

S 5 (cf. Sectional Map XVII)
SAMÂN
(الشيخ السمان)

A colourful little moulid, all light and shade, amongst the tombs of the Fatimite
Khalîfas, not far from Sitna Nafîsa, and therefore best reached by bus 18. From
the bus terminus at the mosque of Nafîsa it is about five minutes' walk through
the great necropolis. Or tram 13 may be used, getting off at the street which leads
to Imâm el-Shâfe'î, and taking a rather longer walk, winding in and out amongst
the sepulchres and almost requiring a guide.

On the four occasions on which I have been there on the principal night, that
has been the second Thursday in Sha'bân, eight days after Imâm el-Shâfe'î and
the day before Imâm el-Leithî.

In the account of Imâm el-Leithî (cf. L 1) a longer but more fascinating way

---

120 khâtûn, Turkish for "lady of social prominence".

of visiting this moulid is described, via the Imâm el-Shâfe'î district, the Moulid of Imâm el-Leithî, and through the City of the Dead. Amongst people who have gone with me and fallen under the spell of this weird place were Prof. Hocart of the Egyptian University and his intrepid wife. She consented to put a *nikla* (a two *millième* piece) on the board (or perhaps it was a tomb) for a tiny lad who had lost heavily on the dice and colour game that was being played there. Never have I seen such a run of luck. She was soon in urgent request as a mascot, but nothing broke the spell till we were rescued by some kindly sheikhs, somewhat shocked I fancy, who led us through stalls and tombs to a little *tashrîfa* (a sort of reception), where singing men and *fiqîs* were in full voice and where we were most hospitably treated.

S 6 (cf. Sectional Map XIV)
SA'ÛDÎ (SÎDÎ EL-SA'ÛDÎ EL-RIFÂ'Î)
(سيدي السعودي الرفاعي)

I enjoyed this pleasant little moulid on Friday, 7 Sha'bân 1355 (23 October 1936), and was told that it should have been held in Rajab.

It is strange that the beautiful *Sûq el-Silâh* seems almost an unknown street to Europeans, and yet it is most accessible, emerging as it does into Shâri' Muhammad 'Alî near Sultân Rifâ'î, past which run trams 13 and 23. Its other end near Tabâna is passed by bus 17 from the 'Ataba to Bâb el-Wazîr. The *sûq* has glorious stonework and fine old buildings and is almost unspoilt, and it is approached from either direction through some of the grandest bits of Cairo. The little *maqâm* is on the west side.

I was fortunate in seeing an impressive *zeffa* at about 9.30, with the usual music and banners and an effendi on horseback as *khalîfa*, with a little child, and also a whirling dervish.

It was held this year, 1359 (1940), on the last Friday of Sha'bân, and judging from the night before, Thursday, 23 Sha'bân 1359 (26 September 1940), when I witnessed a *zikr* in a large room adjoining the *maqâm*, it followed the same modest but pleasant lines.

Some local sheikhs think that the tomb is that of the great Sultân Abû Sa'ûd, whose name is invoked almost as often as that of the Companions of the Prophet, particularly in conjunction with that of Sayyida Zeinab and Imâm el-Shâfe'î. There is a mosque, however, in the *gabel*, not far south of Hasan el-Anwar and the Aqueduct of Muhammad 'Alî, which has far more just claims to the honour of enshrining the remains of this great *walî*.

This is well worth a visit, especially on a Tuesday when there is a fair, with visits to the tomb making the occasion very like a moulid. I cannot ascertain that there is any definite moulid beyond this. The walled enclosure of the mosque is very extensive, and near it there is a great confluence of camel tracks named Mîdân Abû Sa'ûd. The full title of the mosque is Sîdî Abû Sa'ûd el-Garhî.

In re-reading Lane, I find ample confirmation to the above views. He states without reserve "The tomb of Aboo-So'ood is among the mounds of rubbish on the south of Cairo." It is interesting that he notes also that on the return of the pilgrims, he was urged in the Mosque of Sidna Husein to offer up a prayer in the names of Sayyida Zeinab, Imâm el-Shâfe'î and "Aboo-So'ood": interesting because these three are neighbours, so to speak, all their shrines being within easy walking distance; also because this prayer was at the shrine of the brother of the first of the three.

The spot is situated at the N-E corner of sectional map XVIII and is best reached by walking south from the terminus of tram 5, or by the new road from Malik el-Sâleh Bridge at right angles to the river, that is due east.

TANTÂ

S 7 (cf. Map of Delta)
SAYYID EL-BEDAWÎ (EL-SAYYID EL-HASÎB EL-NASÎB ABÛ -L-'ABBÂS SAYYIDÎ AHMAD EL-BEDAWÎ -L-SHARÎF)

(السيد حسيب النسيب أبو العباس سيدي أحمد البدوي الشريف)

This provincial moulid, though lacking the brilliance and majesty of the Moulid el-Nebî, as celebrated at 'Abbâsîya, is probably the most popular of all moulids, drawing more pilgrims than any other, and even more in the old days, and perhaps still, than Mecca itself. I am assured that the crowds from all parts of Islam amount to more than a million, at the principal moulid which, independent of the Moslem calendar is always held in the Coptic month, Bâba, our October. On each occasion that I have been present, the great finale has always been the Friday *zeffa*, varying in date from 10th to 26th October.

The beautiful mosque, not far from the station, contains not only the body of Sayyid, but of 'Abd el-'Âl, 'Abd el-Magîd and others of his disciples. The whole district is decorated, and there are numerous public circumcision booths and stalls for vending souvenirs and food, but no secular attractions, unless tattooing be so regarded. But if one follows the multitudes under the railway arch to the out-skirts of the town, one reaches the official and other tents, the place of fireworks, and a perfect city of booths, theatres and improvised dwellings, in which one can wander for hours, or so it seems to me, without reaching its limits. Yet its occupants overflow at night and sleep anywhere and everywhere in the streets and open spaces.

The moulid lasts a week, pilgrims arriving all the time, till on Thursday, the great night, the whole mighty multitude is gathered together in one place to see the fireworks, then scatter to the innumerable *zikrs* and entertainments. But the *clou* of the festival is the *zeffa* beginning on Friday morning and lasting half the day, Egypt's greatest *zeffa*, though Luxor and Qenâ run it close in their great feasts of Abû Haggag and 'Abd el-Rahîm el-Qenâwî, respectively. Of course, all the *tŭrŭq* are represented by their dervishes, banners, insignia &c., the Ahmadîya, the Order of Ahmad el-Bedawî naturally predominating with its red turbans and banners, and the branches of this great order, the Bayûmîya, the Sha'rawîya, the Shinawîya and the Awlâd Nûh. The red turban borne in the procession is partly that of Ahmad, but as he never discarded a turban till it fell off with wear, it is helped out by red material from the *libâs* of 'Abd el-'Âl.

Several years ago, I think 1933 (1352), I witnessed a queer sight at dawn of the last day from my window in the square, a sort of burlesque, but harmless at the time, called locally "zeffet el-Sharâmît"[121]. It was a procession of gaily decorated carts bearing the prostitutes of the town with their admirers, with much music and song. At that date the secular side of moulids had become rather too like ancient Greek and Roman feasts, with Lesbian and mixed dances of a pronounced character, and other unseemly things. These have been properly suppressed, but it would be a disaster if the pendulum were forced to swing too much the other way, and Puritans and Pharisees knocked all life and soul out of these ancient rites. *Stulti qui vitia vitant in contraria currunt.*[122]

This moulid stands unique, as does its great founder. Long before the Fatimites brought saints and relics to Egypt and gave great impetus to the moulid cult and material to support it, pilgrims crowded from all Moslem countries to the tomb of Ahmad Sayyid el-Bedawî three times in the year, particularly just before the winter, and brought so much piety and, incidentally, mirth and money to Tantâ, that Desûq and other cities more or less in the neighbourhood pedestalled their own *walîs* and inaugurated celebrations in their honour, which in due course crystallised into definite and permanent moulids.

Khudeirî Bey who, represents his sainted ancestor Khudeirî at the mosque and moulid of that name, assures me that before this period, moulids such as we now

---

121 "procession of the prostitutes"
122 Horace: Dum vitant stulti vitia, in contraria currunt ("While fools try to avoid one error, they hasten to commit its opposite").

know them did not exist in Egypt, and these early celebrations in honour of some holy man were held without reference to the date of his birth or death.

That even the sanctity, the notoriety, the wide travel and sharif descent, and the miracles he wrought could establish such a vogue is hardly to be admitted, particularly when we remember that Ahmad was a stranger in a country boasting many of the outstanding saints of Islam. Why is his star still in the ascendant when for example that of the Egyptian miracle-worker Dashtûtî is in danger of extinction? Dashtûtî, whose cult in Egypt was enormous and whose moulid was a national event!

The explanation lies in the extraordinary appeal of his character, for I am convinced that Ahmad Sayyid el-Bedawî is one of the world's outstanding personalities. His position in Islam is much like that of St. Francis in Christendom, though their individual traits differed widely. A few notes on his advent in this country may help to suggest his immense virility and spirituality, his human appeal and his mysticism.

Ahmad's family was Meccan and Sharîf in origin and had taken refuge from a slaughter of Moslems in Morocco. He was born in Fez in the year of the *Hegira* 596 (1199 A.D.) so that he was only seven when in 603 A.H. (1206 A.D.), his father, the Sharîf 'Alî, was warned in a dream to migrate to the Holy City and straightway set out on that pilgrimage which occupied four years. 'Alî's elder son, Hasan, who seems to have idolised his young brother, became to a considerable extent his chronicler and recounts how warmly they were received by the Meccans, particularly Ahmad, and how the lad grew in stature and in grace and in favour with God and man – "Et proficiebat sapientia et aetate, et gratia apud Deum et homines."[123] How Ahmad's Meccan companions recognised his horsemanship and heroic qualities and declared that "braver knight never strode a horse", and styled him, "el-Bedawî". How after twenty happy years, the father 'Alî died and was buried there in great odour of sanctity, in 627 A.H. (1230 A.D.).

The brother notes a profound mystical change soon after this date. Ahmad (now Ahmad el-Bedawî) was constantly rapt in meditation, communicated only by signs, and began, like his father, to see visions and dream dreams. His "voices" told him to go first toward the dawn, then toward the sunset, and he interpreted the oracular commands as indicating Iraq and then Egypt, and he lost no time in responding.

At that time Iraq was particularly strong in its spiritual leader, and they at once

---

123 Said of Jesus in Luke 2:52: "And [he] increased in wisdom and stature, and in favour with God and man."

recognised Ahmad as a prophet, and two of their chiefs, Sîdî 'Abd el-Qâdir and Sîdî Ahmad Rifâ'î, representing them all, told him that they had the keys of Iraq, of Yemen and the Indies, of Rûm and of the West and East, and he could take which he chose. He declined with the reply, that "he could take no key except from the Great Opener", and having visited the tombs and holy places, journeyed with his brother Hasan to Egypt; and they were about to enter Tandatâ[124] (Tantâ), when a rough gang opposed them. He used his pugilistic strength and skill flooring the lot, gaining at least their respect, and a further title of Champion Bruiser.

He retired for a time to Umm 'Abîda[125] without giving up the idea of settling in Tandatâ, but Hasan had had enough and returned to Mecca.

Into this time of trial entered the romantic episode of Fâtima bint Bi'rî. Her supreme beauty captured hearts and fortunes, and she doubted not that Ahmad el-Bedawî would prove her crowning conquest, but at his hands she fell penitent, and like the Magdalene became a model of saintly virtue. Ahmad was by no means indifferent to her charms, but he escaped the fate of the lover of Thaïs[126] – helped by a heavenly apparition, as Aeneas was by the vision and words of Mercury.[127] A hâtif[128] stood by his bed and told him his destiny was to enter Tantâ and live there, and named to him 'Abd el-Âl and some of his future disciples. Obeying, he entered hastily the city and the house of Sheikh ibn el-Shâhit[129], and mounting to the roof consummated his Passion. Always standing he gazed up to heaven, and for forty days and nights neither ate nor drank nor slept, till his eyes turned to the fiery red of burning coals.

Then he came down and once more went out of Tantâ, but followed by 'Abd el-'Âl, 'Abd el-Magîd and many others. He asked for an egg from 'Abd el-'Âl, which the lad promised in exchange for Ahmad's green palm stick (a veritable palmer's staff), but his mother, who violently opposed her boy associating with the sheikh, sent back word that there were no eggs. 'Abd el-'Âl was sent back to look again in the sôma'a[130] (egg box) and found it full and fulfilled his word by

---

124 The Coptic name of Tantâ.
125 Also known as Umm 'Ubeida.
126 Presumably, a reference to Massenet's opera of this name, in which the heroine (Thaïs) is a courtesan in Alexandria. Athanaël, a cenobite monk, tries to convert her to Christianity and eventually finds himself lustfully obsessed with her. She, it is revealed, is actually pure in soul.
127 In Aeneid Book 4, Jupiter learns of Aeneas's dalliance with Dido and so dispatches Mercury to Carthage to remind him that his destiny lies elsewhere, i.e., Rome.
128 In Sufism, a hâtif was "a voice from heaven", or as here, an angel speaking to the saint. Curiously, in modern Arabic hâtif is the word for "telephone".
129 Vocalisation uncertain: shâhit is "the begging one", shahhât is "beggar"
130 [McPher.] The soumaa [sôma'a], or safat, a mud structure much used in Egypt for storing

Tantâ

This mosque in the Delta city of Tantâ contains the body of Sayyid Ahmad el-Bedawî.
"The tomb of this saint attracts almost as many visitors, at the periods of the great annual
festivals, from the metropolis, and from various parts of Lower Egypt, as Mekkah does
pilgrims from the whole of the Muslim world."
(E.W. Lane, *Manners and Customs of the Modern Egyptians*)

bringing back a sample. (It is curious that one of the first miracles attributed to St. Joan was her causing the hens to lay inordinately for the supporters of her cause.) Yet the mother did not repent at the hands of the sheikh; but – as she said – she "repented at the horns of the bull", which was about to gore her son to death, and was only prevented by the superhuman courage and strength of Sayyid el-Bedawî, who seizing the bull literally by the horns threw it down.

This exodus of the saint from Tantâ is attributed to jealousies and aversions of some of the leading sheikhs and authorities of the town; and such an overruling of the traditional hospitality of Egyptians seems to have been part of the trial which purified him for his mission.

A delightful *qasîda* on this event by Mr. C. F. O. Scaife of the Egyptian University, was read by the poet himself, in the perfect Arabic surroundings of Major Gayer-Anderson's house at Ibn Tûlûn. The writer and a big company of Egyptians and English were much interested and impressed. The *Scaivian* saga portrays even the trees and the little houses following him to exile till Tandatâ was empty, and the holy man had to be appeased with entreaties to return from those who had in vain attempted to rid their city of him who was to be its pride and its glory.

I venture to give a few quotations from Scaife's "Said el Bedawi", but the whole poem should be read to feel its full beauty and enjoy the atmosphere of old "Tandatâ" so admirably recreated. Incidentally, these citations illustrate the eternal law that the saint wins in the end, and his detractors reap nothing but confusion.

'Who is this man?' the Caliph asked – they told him all the tale:
At last the holy prince arose and looked both stern and pale.
'O arrogant, blind souls,' he said,
'Yours is the most unhappy sin,
You have cast out the man of peace God put your restless town within.'
He ordered them to bring there clay, and straw and joists of wood,
And they rebuilt the beggar's hut in the place where it had stood.
When all was done the Caliph went
On foot towards the north,
And as the twilight died away the stars in heaven came forth.
. . . .
The Caliph knelt upon the ground and kissed his ragged hem;
'The house is ready' then he said, 'be merciful to them,

---

grain, often lends itself when empty to the laying hens.

These children know not what they do.'

The beggar sighed and raised his head –

'God is compassionate, my lord; let us go back' he said.

The remaining forty years or so of Ahmad's life were passed tranquilly in Tandatâ, though most austerely, especially the first twelve spent on the roof. The devoted 'Abd el-Âl was a great comfort and help, cooking for and looking after him, and taking mundane cares off his shoulders. As a *murîd* (disciple) this youth was exemplary, and as an administrator he proved his genius in Ahmad's life and after his death. "The companions of the roof", Ahmad's chief disciples, were the nucleus of many and sent, as it were, apostles in all directions. 'Abd el-'Âl sent Sîdî Ismâ'îl to Imbâba (cf. Moulid of Ismâ'îl Imbâba, I 3), and Abû Tartûr to the desert near it, now the village of el-Hatîya, adjoining Mît 'Uqba. He also has his little moulid (cf. T 2). Sîdî Yûsef, father of Imbâbî has his tomb in Qasr el-'Einî, Cairo, and descendants living nearby of these Ahmadîya apostles.

His old rivals and opponents either went away, or like Sîdî Salîm, whose tomb is in Tantâ, came over to him; and few if any of his followers are reported to have come to the bad, unless the case of 'Abd el-Magîd be so considered. This early *murîd* implored his master to show him his face, which he kept doubly veiled, and was warned that the price of a look was a life. He said he would die rather than forego what he had set his mind on, and die he did before the second veil was removed. (This suggests, rather, "the veiled Prophet of Khorazin"[131], but is the only unsavoury story I have heard about the saint.) Those, however, who condemned his moulid throughout the centuries had a bad time (in this world at least) unless they repented. 'Abd el-Wahhâb el-Sha'rânî in his Tabaqât mentions, amongst other offenders, a man who was eating fish at the time he spoke foolishly, and a bone stuck in his throat, giving him unspeakable torture for nine months till he went repentant to el-Bedawî's tomb at Tantâ and immediately sneezed up the bone. Lane, writing a century ago, mentions a friend of his in Egypt then suffering from the same reason, and within the last year or two I have heard of several instances.

There are people now who seem bent on bringing down this great moulid at Tantâ, and shocking and disappointing a million poor people. Those who persecute moulid-goers at Tantâ and elsewhere should think of the man with the bone in his throat, and consider, too, the feelings of those who come from all over Egypt and most of the world for peace and blessing.

Many records exist of miracles he wrought, before his death and since: how he

---

131 An apparent reference to the poem of Thomas Moore, "The Veiled Prophet of Khorassan".

appeared and even spoke to some, and how he rescued a man in an unfriendly country and flew with him safe to sanctuary in Egypt, and so on. Visitors at his shrine have not been the poor only. Amongst the great ones of the earth who enriched and honoured Ahmad's resting place exceedingly was the great Sultân Beybars, protégé of Sultân Sâleh, now lying in Shâri' el-Nahhâsîn. Indian pilgrims of the highest class have stated that every child in their provinces swears by Sayyid el-Bedawî, and mountains and seas have not kept away his votaries from still more remote regions.

Scaife is not the only poet who has honoured him in song. Lane heard the people singing

Oh, Sheikh of the Arabs! Oh Sayyid!

and I have often heard the same and the like. He is invoked on all sorts of occasions in similar and other words, a favourite expression being O Deliverer! Even in the liturgical prayer from the minarets before dawn, the "aabed"[132], he is called upon with others of the *walîs*, the friends of God – "Yâ Abû Farâg, Yâ sheikh el-'Arab!" "O thou Deliverer, thou sheikh of the Arabs." May he deliver his moulid from all forms of vandalism!

The only news I have in this, the second year of the war, is the following note in this evening's *La Bourse Égyptienne*, 15 November 1940 (15 Shawwâl 1359):

Numerous donations are reaching the Mudîr of Gharbîya Province[133] for distribution to the poor on the occasion of the Moulid of Sîdî Ahmad el-Badawi, which is held in Tantâ.

H.M. the King has deigned to donate 50 Egyptian pounds, which will be distributed among the poor during the closing ceremony.

S 8 (cf. Sectional Map VI)
SAYYID EL-MÂLIK

(الشيخ سيد الملك)

In 1352 (1933), 1353 (1934) & 1354 (1935), this Bûlâq moulid, a very big one at that time, was held on the last Thursday of Safar, but in 1356 (1937) though still on a Thursday it was the last of Rabî' I (3 June 1937).

---

132 This word, given above as McPherson spelled it, is uncertain. 'âbid means the person praying. The Arabic verb 'âbâdâ, ya'bûdû means "to worship". The dawn prayer is called salât el-fagr.
133 Located in the Delta and administered from Tantâ.

The site which is the Saptia end of Shâri' 'Abd el-Gawâd, the same as Abû el-Sabâ', is passed by bus 15 and is near the terminus of buses 2 and 9 and trams 4 and 23.

The moulid has a run of sixteen days, and on the secular side had big theatres, many "ringas", Punch and Judy and shadow shows, with the *Piste à la Mort* of Billy Williams, but there were often rough and unpleasant characters about which reduced its attractiveness for visitors. For that reason, I did not encourage friends to accompany me, but in 1354 (1935), Mrs. Col. R… , a resident, expressed a wish to see what a moulid was like. We went in her car before sunset when, as a rule, things are very quiet but on this occasion we proved an irresistible attraction to the Bûlâq *gamins*, who swarmed on and in the car like flies on sugar. The alarmed chauffeur had difficulty in manipulating a retreat and calculates that we shed at least sixteen kiddies from roof and windows before we regained Shâri' Fu'ad el-Awwal.

The turbulence of the people of this old port of Cairo perhaps brought the decadence which came on their moulid, for in 1356 (1937) it was badly wet-blanketed, in spite of the marvels of Billy Williams and a much-censored theatre. I am not aware if it has been held since.

S 9 (cf. Sectional Map I)
SALÎM
(سيدي سليم)

I enjoyed this pleasant little moulid on Thursday, 27 Rajab 1352 (16 November 1933), but missed it in subsequent years until Thursday, 29 Gamâd II 1357 (25 August 1938), owing mainly to its date being put forward and being variable.

It is situated not far from the Nile in the old port of Bûlâq, near the Caracôl, in Shâri' Suleimân Pâsha el-Qadîm, and easily reached by tram 7 or 13, getting off at the second stop after leaving Bûlâq Bridge, and walking first at right angles to the tram line and then to the left, when it is full in sight. The walk takes about three minutes.

Going in the hope of a *zeffa* at 4 in the afternoon, I was told the *tŭrŭq* were already on the move, but not being very successful in picking up these I settled down and waited in a nice café in the centre of the street, drinking *qirfa,* and reading the Muqattam's account of the ancient ceremony of *'Arûsat el-Nîl* , which had come off the day before with tremendous *éclat.*

A little before 6, the *zeffa* came into sight and sound, to the enthusiasm of the picturesque little crowd which had gathered: first branches of the Qâdirîya with their white, and Rifâ'îya, with their black banners, and vigorously played tambourines and cymbals; then after a discreet interval, for the Shâzlîya are a little exclusive, came over twenty branches of that ancient and most praiseworthy order, with their caps, sashes and banners of white and green, all chanting, book in hand. Each *beiraq* in addition to the designation of the Tarîqa Shâzlîya bore its local name, amongst which I noticed:

Bein el-Sarâyât (my village)
Gezîret Mît 'Uqba
Sîdî Farâg, Bûlâq
Ikhwân Hayy Bâb el-Sha'rîya
Warâq el-'Arab
el-Duqqî
Zâwiet Sîdî 'Atîya
Zâwiet Sîdî Abû -l-Dalâ'il

Last of all came the *khalîfa*, of the same name as his sainted ancestor of over 400 hundred years ago, mounted on a very beautiful black horse. I had the honour of meeting this honourable but most gentle and unassuming sheikh at the tomb of Sîdî Salîm later in the evening, where a pavilion filled the little street, and a goodly company including the Head of the Shâzlîya, Sheikh 'Abd el-Salâm, listened to a *fiqî*.

Making a round also of the little places for acting, dancing, singing, and so on, I was struck by the even more than usual happiness and good temper and behaviour of the people, and the less usual gentleness of the police, who never beat, harried or coerced the people in anyway, but looked smilingly on – but very ready to act if necessary – this, too, in the very roughest bit of Cairo with the tradition of the old port of Bûlâq. I understood why we were enjoying this paradisaic state when I met an old friend of nearly forty years standing, the Qâ'imaqâm A…H… , a high inspector of the Interior, whom the people so like and respect that (as some of them told me after) they would hate to do anything which could annoy him, even if it could be done with impunity. *O, si sic omnes!*[134]

I recommend any old resident who can find little that is beautiful in Bûlâq to go round with the *zeffa* at the next moulid and see the magnificent cupolas and bits of architecture, culminating in the peaceful little square with the Mosque of Salmânîya, just before one regains the street of the moulid.

I gathered little about the history of Sîdî Salîm beyond what his successor and namesake told me – that he was a holy and famous follower of the *tarîqa* of Abû Hasan el-Shâzlî in the tenth century of the *Hegira*.

---

134 "If only everyone were like that!"

S 10
SHA'RÂWÎ
(سيدي شعراوي)

Years ago, I saw a moulid in the Bâb el Sha'rîya district which I suppose was this, but I noted neither name nor date. In 1353 (1934), Dr. 'Enâyet Allâh described it as rather big and important, and it must have been so for him to establish a circumcision booth there.

I do not know if this moulid is in honour of the Sheikh el-Sha'râwî who founded the *tariqa* of the Sha'râwîya as a branch of the Ahmadîya (the great order of Ahmad el-Badawî) but hope to investigate this.

S 11 (cf. Sectional Map XIX)
SHÂFE'Î (IMÂM EL-SHÂFE'Î)
(إمام الشافعي)

This moulid in honour of the great founder of this leading sect of Islam, as far as Cairo is concerned, always terminates on the first Wednesday of Sha'bân, except perhaps that when Sha'bân begins with a Wednesday, the moulid may begin on that day and end on the 8th.

Tram 13 takes one to the spot where normally the celebrations commence, though they retrench more and more every year, and a few minutes' walk brings one to the mosque, and to the place of the *tashrîfa* (reception) where the representative of the *imâm* receives the *'ulamâ*, Ministers and other visitors. This *tashrîfa* used to be on the previous night, the Tuesday, leaving Wednesday to the populace; but since 1351 (1932) it seems to be held on the Wednesday. The solemnity of this overshadows the simple amusements with which both sides of the street from the tram terminus to the mosque were filled, and even the *Qara Goz* and similar shows which favoured the side streets towards the *gabel* have been frozen out. It was still left to the populace to admire the *éclat* of the going and coming of their betters in their cars, and to enjoy the music at the entrance to the *tashrîfa*, but in 1357 (1938) they were driven away from that.

The doyen of the circumcision doctors, 'Enâyet Allâh Effendî, is here at his headquarters and *facile princeps;* his booth with its elaborations and decorations, brilliant illumination and singing men is the most conspicuous object of the moulid. Between his place and the door of the mosque there has always been a *zikr* at the side of the street.

Over the dome of the mosque is a conspicuous object in the form of a boat, intended to hold an *ardab*[135] of corn for the birds – provided for by a charitable

---

135 A dry measure equal to 198 litres.

endowment. Years ago, that was filled, at any rate at the time of the moulid, but if such is still the case, the birds have lost their appreciation for grain, for during the moulid and at other times I have looked in vain for birds, but have never seen one, except sometimes a hawk.

In the good old days, the ceremony of the *dôsah* (cf. Dashtûtî) was annually performed here, as at the moulids of the Prophet and of Sidna Husein and Sîdî Dashtûtî, and the people went home edified and content.

Imâm el-Shâfeʿî, or to give him his full style, Imâmna Abû ʿAbdullah Muhammad bin Idrîs el-Shâfeʿî was Palestinian by birth, but was taken from Ghâza, where he was born, to Mecca when he was only two years old. Like Ahmad Sayyid el-Bedawî, he was a great wanderer, especially in the Yemen and Iraq, and ultimately in Egypt, and early established a reputation as doctor and teacher and was recognised as such by the ʿulamâ of the countries mentioned, and generally. The last four years or somewhat more of his life, from 199 to 204 A.H. (814 to 819 A.D.) were passed in Egypt, mainly in Cairo, where his memory and his tomb are illustrious.

There is a kind of spiritual romance about the affectionate attachment which sprung up between him and the Lady Nafîsa, each recognising the great and saintly character of the other, and withal the attractive and magnetic human qualities. As she lived in Cairo from 201 A.H. till her death in 208 A.H., they were able to associate and to pray together (as they made a point of doing each Ramadân) for about three years, 201 to 204 A.H. The case of these two is, I think, closely parallel to that of St. Francis and St. Clare.

ʿAbd el-Wahhâb el-Shaʿrânî, though he gives the date of the Imâm's death as above, 204 A.H., refers to him as the Prophet's *cousin*. This expression, mysterious to me, is, I daresay, clear enough to my Moslem readers.

S 12
SHÂMÎ
(الشيخ الشامي)

My *murâsla* reports a tiny moulid at Gezîret el-Dahab, close to Gîza, in celebration of this saint. He tells me he was there on the final night and noted the date as Sunday, 5 Rajab 1358 (20 August 1939).

S 13 (cf. Sectional Map XX)
SHATBÎ
(سيدي الشطبي)

On Friday, 9 Muharram 1354 (12 April 1935), I visited this most picturesque little desert moulid, by walking under the guidance of the son of the circumcision doctor, 'Enâyet-Allâh, from his "clinique" by the Mosque of Imâm el-Shâfe'î, half way to the Muqattam Hills. The little shrine is near the line and embankment which run parallel to the hills, not far from the Monastery of 'Omar, as I have heard it called, and the ruined mosque of Abû Shâhîn on the side of the cliff (Imâm el-Shâfe'î is reached by tram 13).

It was not yet sunset, but there were many poor pilgrims there and "zikrs" were proceeding. There was also a little theatre and stalls for simple refreshments.

The beauty of the view and quaintness of the little gathering well repays the walk of a mile or so each way.

EL-SHUHADÂ', MENÛF

S 14 (cf. Map of Delta)
SHIBL (AMÎR EL-GEISH MUHAMMAD SHIBL EL-ASWAD)
(أمير الجيش سيدي محمد شبل الأسود)

Though never present, I have heard the moulid of Sîdî Shibl frequently referred to enthusiastically, and I gather it partakes considerably of the nature of a country fair. The only definite information I possess is the appended short extract from an Arabic paper, which may be rendered as follows—

"MOULID SÎDÎ SHIBL"

The Ministry of Interior has sanctioned the holding of the moulid of the Amîr of the Army Sîdî Muhammad Shibl el-Aswad (who is) lying in his mosque at Shuhadâ', for a period of two weeks, beginning from the 6th July (the present month); and the place of the moulid has become crowded with merchants, and visitors (pilgrims) and the leaders of Sufi Dervish Orders…"

If, as I believe, the cutting is from a 1353 (1934) paper, that fixes the date of the final night as 19 July, that is Thursday, 7 Rabî' II 1353 (19 July 1934). This moulid *at* el-Shuhadâ' must not be confused with the Moulid *of* el-Shuhadâ' (or Sayyid el-Shahîd) held in Upper Egypt, near Mazghûna (cf. Shuhadâ', S 15). El-Shuhadâ' is on the east bank of the Rosetta branch of the Nile, not far from Menûf, on the line between Benhâ and Kafr el-Zayât.

MAZGHÛNA

S 15 (cf. Map of Upper Egypt)
SHUHADÂ' (EL-SHUHADÂ' OR SAYYID EL-SHAHÎD)
(الشهداء أو سيدي سيد الشهيد)

I enjoyed this great desert moulid on Thursday, 22 Muharram 1354 (25 April 1935) under the impression that it was that of Uweis el-Qărănî. On sending my *murâsla*, Mûsa, with some of my neighbours of this village on Thursday, 17 Rabî' I 1359 (25 April 1940), they assure me that el-Qărănî is nearer Wâsta, and that this is in honour of a great number of Moslems who fell fighting in a Holy War *(gihâd)*, and are therefore martyrs *(shuhadâ')*, and that their leader was a famous sheikh, el-Shahîd Sayyid *(shahîd* being the singular of *shuhadâ')*. The word means "one who testifies, bears witness to the faith", and so corresponds to the Church's word "confessor", rather than to "martyr", though its acceptation approaches nearer to the latter.

Mazghûna is on the Upper Egyptian line about half way between Cairo and Wâsta, and less than an hour's walk or half an hour on a donkey (always to be had near the Station at moulid time) from el-Shuhadâ'. Motor buses also run to and from Gîza.

It is curious to note that the two dates of which I am certain, though nearly two months apart by the lunar calendar, to which one would expect them to conform, are the same to a day by the Gregorian reckoning, and by the Coptic (17 Barmûda).

This is one of the few cases of a moulid being in crescendo, for though it was big when I saw it five years ago, my *murâsla* who was also present then reports it as very much bigger now.

The religious observances centre about what might be regarded as a sort of cenotaph of tent work, put up for the occasion by the *tarîqa* of the Shâzlîya, but there are "zikrs" also amongst the numerous stones which still mark the old necropolis of the martyrs.

Like Sîdî Huneidiq, near Ismâ'îlîya, and most desert moulids it is also a fair and exhibits the picturesque element of performing and racing horses and camels. There is found also at least one theatre and Punch and Judy show.

Buffalos *(gâmûs)* are slain for the poor and eaten on the sand, with a curious kind of puff pastry *(fatîr)*, known as Egyptian bread *('eish masrî* or *marahrah)*.

There is much scope here for research. Information I have accumulated is very bulky, but so contradictory or impossible that it cancels down to the few points stated above.

It is pure speculation, but I cannot help fancying that this Moslem moulid was originally in honour of the Christian martyrs who fought under St. George,

Mâr Girgis, against the "infidels". Why otherwise should the Moslem calendar be ignored, and the moulid in 1354 (1935), and 1359 (1940) fall on the same Christian date, and that the time of the Feast of St. George?

One recalls in this connection that the Coptic monastery of St. George at Bibâ[136], some fifty miles further up the river, claimed in a time of riot and outrage to be under the protection of a mythical sheikh Bibâwî who, the monks alleged, dwelt as a *walî* within the walls of their *deir,* causing many a pious Moslem to recite a *fâtiha*[137] and leave an offering before a picture of St. George and the Dragon.

S 16 (cf. Sectional Map VIII)
SUTUHÎYA (SAYYIDA 'AYSHA SUTUHÎYA)
(سيدة عائشة السطحية)

On three occasions on which I have seen this little moulid, the date has been 29 Sha'bân, the last being 1355 (1936).

The little shrine of this sister of Sayyida Râbi'a nestles under the great mass of the Bâb el-Futûh, and is therefore passed by bus 12, which plies between Beit el-Qâdî and 'Abbâsîya.

There is so much doing on this eve of Ramadân, including the Moulid of Sîdî Bahlûl near the Bâb el-Wazîr, that one is apt to miss this small celebration, but at least a short visit should be paid to this majestic part of the old and still unspoilt city, the region of the Gates of el-Nasr and el-Futûh. The lighting up of the tiny tomb in the shadow of the mighty gate, and of the little mosque just beyond the gate to the north, is an impressive sight, and the same may be said of the groups of pilgrims and the "zikrs", and a little way to the south, on the main street, the concourse of simple souls about a café where comic turns are interspersed with more serious performances and singing.

On the same night there are a number of microscopic moulids between and in the neighbourhood of the "Bâbs", which should be seen: of these are 'Abd el-Bâsit in Shâri' Dabâbîya; 'Abd el-Qâsid; Muhammad el-Gamel (Hâret Guwânîya, Bâb el-Nasr); and 'Abd el-Karîm.

(Since writing the above, this tomb unique in style and in beauty, has disappeared, and the Saint has been dug up. The *bâb,* however, is still standing – or was when I passed through it a week or so ago.)

Sic transit decor Aegypti![138]

---

136 Near Beni Suef.
137 The short opening prayer of the Qurân.
138 "Thus passes the beauty of Egypt."

ON THE SUEZ ROAD

T 1 (cf. Map of Delta)
TAKRÛRÎ or DAKRÛRÎ
(الشيخ طكروري)

I have no knowledge of the date nor of the conditions of this little desert moulid, but there are points of interest about the tomb which induce me to introduce it.

Crossing the desert from Cairo to Suez in December 1911, on a push bike, I visited this picturesque shrine and was struck particularly by the number and quaint variety of votive offerings on the *tâbût,* considering that the door was open and, I am told, is always so, and the tomb is quite near and in view of the desert track. The offerings were not valuable certainly, including teeth, hair, rags, pipes, beads, little flags, a sardine tin and small coins. Amongst and attached to some of these I noticed the visiting card of the late W. G. Kemp, and quite recently in reading the book called "*Egyptian Illustration*", which was written and illustrated and I think printed by him, I came across a short account of this tomb, with a woodcut of the interior. He mentions that "large numbers of desert Arabs collect here to celebrate" Sheikh Takrûrî's moulid. He unfortunately does not give the date, and as I met no one there I left my little offerings without obtaining any information.

The tomb is roughly half way between Cairo and Suez, after Dâr el-Baydâ is left on the left, and a little to the right before reaching Station No. 9. Kemp mentions that it is near the "venerable Pilgrims' Tree at the outlet of the Jandalî Valley".

The sheikh died at this spot – murdered, some say – on his return from pilgrimage to Mecca.

T 2 (cf. Map of Delta)
TARTÛRÎ
(سيدي أحمد أبو طرطوري)

This small but attractive moulid is at the little village of el-Hatîya, adjoining Mît 'Uqba in the Imbâba district, not far south of the tram track by the Bahr el-A'mâ, between Zamâlek and the English bridges. I found it a pleasant ride from my home at Bein el-Sarâyât on Thursday, 15 Gamâd II 1357 (11 August 1938). The tomb of the saint and the surroundings were bravely decorated but I was too early in the day to see the ceremonies, and I expect they were somewhat overshadowed by those of the very considerable Moulid of Sîdî Qureishî at Zenîn the same evening.

I have little doubt that the sheikh who is buried and honoured here is the "Sîdî Ahmad Abû Tartûrî", who was placed in the wilderness near Imbâba by

'Abd el-'Âl, the celebrated disciple and friend of Sayyid el-Bedawî. (Some local people, however, refer to him as 'Abd el-Rahîm el-Tartûrî.)

T 3
TARTÛRÎ (HASAN EL-TARTÛRÎ)
(شيخ حسن الطرطوري)

I have heard from a fairly reliable source that there is a moulid in honour of one Hasan el-Tartûrî in the Rôd el-Farag district, and that its date in 1353 was Thursday, 28 Rabî' II (9 August 1934).

T 4
TÛNSÎ
(التونسي)

I regret never having seen this moulid, which has been reliably reported to me several times, but too late, notably on Friday, 2 Muharram 1354 (5 April 1935).

It is the opening moulid, or nearly so, of the Moslem year, and the more popular from that fact, and from its situation in a wild and lovely district beyond Imâm el-Shâfe'î. Friends of mine who went and enjoyed it took tram 13 to its terminus, then walked the rest with an amateur guide picked up near the mosque.

ALEXANDRIA

W 1 (cf. Map of Delta)
WAFÂ'Î (EL-WAFÂ'Î)
(سيدي الوفائي)

My ignorance about Alexandria moulids is complete, and in this compilation I have already attempted much more ground than I had intended, so I must not try to fill this great lacuna and a number of minor gaps.

This ignorance is the more discreditable, as I have spent much time in "Alex", living once in Ibrâhîmîya over two years, when I attended commemorations of Muhammad 'Alî, celebrations of Leilet el-Mi'râg, Leilet el-Qadr, &c, and in honour of the Prophet, but never saw a moulid, and only heard of this one, el-Wafâ'î, which I am told is in the month of Muharram.

Though I have certainly missed much I feel sure that, compared with Cairo, "Alex" has kept little of the old and beautiful in buildings and in ceremonies. As an example of the awful iconoclasm from which this great port has suffered, there is hardly a really ancient and unspoilt Coptic church left, though they form one of the priceless riches of the metropolis.

The appended newspaper account of a Moulid of the Nebî el-Wafâ'î, shows it to be of considerable note in Alexandria and a happy occasion for the poor of the district.

COMMEMORATING THE PROPHET EL WAFAY

To celebrate the anniversary of the prophet "El Wafay" Maher Hassan Farag Effendi, concessionary for the sale of newspapers in Alexandria and Lower Egypt, has organised for this evening a ceremony over which the Governor of Alexandria, Husein Sabri Pasha, will preside. A large gathering of notables is expected to be present.

A marquee has been erected near the Sidi 'Abd el-Razzak El-Wafay Mosque, where verses of the Koran will be chanted by eminent Sheikhs.

As usual, food will be distributed in the afternoon to the poor and needy of the quarter.

W 2 (cf. Sectional Map VI)
WÂSTÎ (EL-WÂSTÎ)

(سيدي الواسطي)

My murâsla, Mûsâ, discovered this cheery little moulid and conducted me to it on Thursday, 30 Rajab 1353 (8 November 1934), but though I have looked for it several times since at about that date, I have never found it in progress.

It is in the Sûq el-'Asr, Bûlâq, and perhaps best reached by leaving bus 15 in Shâri' 'Abd el-Gawâd at Shâri' el-Ansârî (which is near the Saptia end on the left going from Shâri' Fu'ad el-Awwal), then following that little street which nearly cuts it till its lights and music are apparent.

The little mosque is good, and there is a certain picturesque gemütlichkeit about its surroundings, albeit the district is one of the poorest and without striking monuments.

LUXOR

Y 1 (cf. Map of Upper Egypt)
YÛSEF ABÛ EL-HAGGÂG[139]

(سيدي يوسف أبو الحجاج)

This moulid falling on 14 Sha'bân rather unfortunately clashes with that of Sîdî 'Abd el-Rahmân el-Qenâwî held at Qenâ, which is also in the Theban region, as well as with Sîdî Matrâwî at Matarîya, and often with other minor moulids; and in 1357 (1938) it coincided with the great Tantâ moulid of Sayyid el-Bedawî, but this was purely accidental, because Sayyid el-Bedawî does not follow the Moslem calendar but is always in October, and in 1357 (1938) mid-Sha'bân happened to fall in that month. This year, 1359 (1940), it synchronised with Sîdî Rûbî of the Fayûm (cf. moulid R 1).

As explained elsewhere, Sha'bân is crowded with moulids because the next month, Ramadân, excludes these celebrations, and in the following months of pilgrimage they are extremely rare. Moreover, of the nights of Sha'bân none is so solemn as the eve of mid-Sha'bân, when each mortal's term of life is determined and written on the leaves of the Lote Tree of Paradise, the *morituri*[140] losing their leaves this night on the shaking of the tree, and their lives in the ensuing year.

In addition to the characteristics of moulids generally, and the additional attractions of Arab races and trick riding, and the extra freedom and colour of a provincial moulid, there is a peculiarity – shared as far as I know only with the sister moulid of 'Abd el-Rahîm el-Qenâwî – and that is the carrying of *boats* in the *zeffa*, two in the case of Luxor.

This is explained locally by the tradition that the holiness and fervent effectual prayers of Sheikh Yûsef Abû -l-Haggâg saved the ship in which he was returning from Mecca, when the rest of the pilgrim-fleet foundered, but anthropologists recognise in it one of the cases, and an unusually clear one, of the adaptation into an Islamic ceremony of something far more ancient than Christianity or Islam. Hornell has an interesting article in *Man* of September 1938, illustrating the boats[141] carried in the Luxor *zeffa* and pointing out their resemblance to "the sculptured record on the exterior of the western wall of the temple of Ramses III, within the great enclosure of Amun at Karnac", which represents the towing of the royal barge, and that of Mut and Khons. He states that Egyptologists, in the

---

139 A film by Elizabeth Wickett, "For Those Who Sail to Heaven" (First Run/Icarus Films, 1990), is about this moulid and the surviving ancient Egyptian practices in it (information kindly provided by Valerie J. Hoffman).
140 "Those who are about to die."
141 [McPher.] See also *Nature*, about October 1938.

main, regard the Luxor procession as "a shadowy survival of the great water fes-tival of Opet, when the Theban Triad, Amun and his divine companions, Mut and Khons, journeyed up-river from the vast temple of Karnac to visit their shrines in the Luxor temple".

These boats gaily decorated, like the "'Aqaba" in the Cairo ceremony of the "Bride of the Nile", do not take the water as in the case of the "'Aqaba", but mounted on carts are dragged by youths connected with the various *turŭq*, filled with children whose parents are supposed to possess a *sanad* showing their descent from Sîdî Yûsef.

Z 1 (cf. Map of Duqqi District)
ZEFEITÎ (SÎDÎ MUHAMMAD EL-ZEFEITÎ)
(سيدي محمد الزفيتي)

This is an extraordinary instance of a moulid coming into existence, or if it lived years ago, rising Phoenix-like from its ashes, and after a rapid *crescendo* becom-ing absolutely *fortissimo*, the more so as its meteoric rise has been during a period in which *Zeitgeist* and the authorities have been anything but propitious. I have been living since the beginning of 1922 within a mile of the little *qarâfa* of Sîdî Zefeitî, where the simple tombs of my neighbours are grouped about the almost equally unpretentious last resting place of this obscure saint, and still nearer the Bûlâq - Dakrûr road, whence a merry din and even voices can easily reach me, and for over ten years I neither heard the moulid, nor rumours of its existence. I cannot think that it was held at all, or if it were, that it was anything more than a *zikr* or two at the tomb, or at the mosque of Duqqî.

It crystallised into a definite moulid, but a very minute one, in 1351 (1932), when the main night was Sunday, 10 Gamâd I (11 September 1932). Though away when it was held in 1352 (1933), I saw it – still small but grown a little – in 1353 (1934); and in 1354 (1935) it was reported on return from absence to have become a big affair, and to have had a long run. In 1355 (1936), I left Egypt for a couple of months early in Rabî' II, and left it developing – swings, *Qara Goz*, and such like, already very popular, and I was much surprised on my return to find it still going strong, much stronger, in fact. A record run I should think, but I am told it was somewhat intermittent. It culminated that year on Thursday, 24 Gamâd II (10 September 1936), simply immense, a string of booths and tents of all sorts, with spaces for "zikrs", swings, Arab singers, and the rest; extending from the Waqf buildings, at the crossroads (Bûlâq - Dakrûr and the road from the Orman Gardens to the Agricultural Museum), past Duqqî nearly to the line at Bûlâq - Dakrûr. I have only seen this size of a moulid exceeded in Cairo at that of Sidna Husein in 1353 (1934), when the booths fringed the foot of the *gabel* from the end of Shâri' el-Gedîda (the continuation of the Mûskî) to the necropolis outside the Bâb el-Nasr.

In the year of the Prophet 1357 (1938), it was even greater, especially in the magnitude of the theatres and their castes, and of the dancing cafés and "ringas", and though the last night and the culmination was 22 Gamâd II (18 August 1938) and the next day the *khâtima* only, I could then still hear the sound of "tars" and "naqqâras", the cracking of the percussion cap when a strong man pushed the little engine up to the limit of the rail, and the varied sounds and voices of a moulid.

But the *clou* was the marvellous *zeffa* in the afternoon. Sections of it made preliminary tours of the fields before 4 o'clock, and by about 5 all had met in the village of Duqqî. Duqqî is a stronghold of the Qâdirîya, that great primitive and original sect founded by 'Abd el-Qâdir el-Gîlânî, who was buried in Baghdad in 561 A.H. (1165 A.D.), and of the Rifâ'îya, an immensely powerful branch of the Qâdirîya, founded, as its name implies, by the Sultân Rifâ'î, buried in Basra in 578 A.H. (1182 A.D.).[142] Their black banners were very prominent, and their dervishes very fervent, as they rotated, *dabbûs* in hand, in a circular dance to the sound of *târ*, *kâs* and *naqqâra*.

The *dabbûs* is not, as its name would suggest, an ordinary pin, but an anomalous instrument of devotion, torture and music. It is a straight and pointed rod of steel about two feet in length, with a spherical head, either of wood, in which case it resembles the "Jack" played at in bowls, or of hollow metal, and in each case fringed at the top with a number of little chains, bearing at the free end a triangle of metal. These play the part of bells. One young dervish, with a wild *chevelure* which would have been startling even on a Bishârî, in kindly showing me his *dabbûs,* called it a *shakhshâkha sistrum,* as it contained objects which converted it into a rattle. This would interest Prof. Newberry[143], late of the Egyptian University, for in his book on Ancient Egypt, he voices his theory that the royal sceptre was in origin a *sistrum*, with which the king could call to order or reduce

---

142 [McPher.] My authority for the Statement that "Sultan" el-Rifai was buried in Basra is Bliss (see *Religions of Syria and Palestine*), but I understand from Mrs. Devonshire, whose conferences and books on the mosques and other monuments of Cairo are so well known and so much appreciated, that the great mosque of Sultan Rifai opposite that of Sultan Hasan was built comparatively recently about the shrine of El Rifai. Others, including Miralai Gayer-Anderson Bey, who is full of accurate information on such matters, are confident that the shrine in question is no cenotaph, but actually holds the body of that great founder. Is Egypt (and Cairo in particular) indebted to the Fatimites for this precious possession? I wonder!

143 Percy Edward Newberry (23 April 1869 – 7 August 1949), a British Egyptologist.

to silence. What an ideal sceptre for a despotic monarch the *dabbûs* would make! If it did not produce the desired effect when used as a rattle, a blow with the head or a prod with the point, would effectively assert royalty.

But I am delaying the procession! It is preceded by the traditional Alexandrians, in their picturesque boleros and baggy *libâs,* some holding up long poles bearing a kind of highly decorated and tasselled *sistrum*, some dancing or spinning, and in this case one, a bicycle expert, holding his inverted machine in his teeth. Then the dervishes of the *tŭrŭq*, followed by the *khalîfa* on horseback with a couple of baby Bedouins, most picturesque in *lâsa*[144] and *'uqâl*. As the word implies, the *khalîfa* represents the sheikh in whose honour the moulid is held and is chosen from his family. In this case, the Sheikh Abû Zeid filled the rôle with dignity. Then more of the *tŭrŭq* with their banners and their sashes, bearing the insignia, *nishân*, of the sect, and others playing all kinds of music, or gyrating alone or rotating with their fellows in the dance of the *dabâbîs;* some also carrying cressets, *mashâ'il*, to keep the skins on the tambourines taut, though this was not necessary as the thoughtful villagers had kindled tiny fires by the wayside for this purpose. To vary the dancing, certain of the dervishes thrust their *dabbûs* through the lips or cheek; then suddenly going down and impaling themselves with their dabâbîs, in the face, throat, chest or abdomen, they formed a human causeway, *gisr*[145] with their bodies, and a local sheikh of note, Sheikh 'Âyed, representative and descendant of el-Rifâ'î, walked upon them, making a short prayer and exhortation at intervals. An effendi of the tribe of el-Rifâ'î did the same, and this was repeated several times before the *zeffa* had passed out of the village. Lagging behind to see the rest of the *zeffa* pass, I noticed that the theatre company of "Sayyida Fâtima -l-Kisâra", in two well-filled carts, brought up the rear with songs, music and belly-dances. They were a pied and multicoloured and lively party. They gave out papers with some of their photographs, and which notified that Fâtima and her caste were there to honour the Sheikh Muhammad el-Zefeitî.

At length the *zeffa* emerged into the Bûlâq-Dakrûr road, following it west-ward till the canal bridge was reached, shedding all secular elements on the way, the Alexandrines and Fâtima Kisâra's party. Finally, it reached the beautiful spot where Zefeitî's body rests in the lush grass, under mighty trees, an English-looking country spot, such as Gray's elegy might have been composed in. Then "zikrs" were commenced and visits paid to the tomb – visits which must have taken hours, for never in modern times can Zefeitî have seen such a concourse. It was

---

144 White wrapping of fine linen around a skullcap.
145 A bridge.

as significant as it is typical, that when the merry side of a moulid is not checked, the piety of the people is enormously enhanced.

The above description locates the moulid pretty well. To get there from town, bus 4 serves till nearly 9 o'clock, passing right through it. Bus 6 or tram 15 takes one to the English Bridge, whence a walk of a few minutes due west leads to Duqqî and the moulid. Taxis and cabs are always to be found at the English Bridge, and that is the starting point for the Kerdâsa bus, which passes through the moulid, but is very infrequent and ceases to run at or before 9.

A rather striking incident was omitted from the description of the *zeffa*. A remarkably handsome and patrician little lad took from a dervish, doubtless a relative, his *dabbûs* and thrust it in and, I believe, through his own cheek. Was this, I wonder, a variant on or an addition to, the initiation ceremonies of *zikr* and *ward* (rosary)? It reminded one of the "blooding" of a young rider who is well in at the death in a hard hunt.

As for Sîdî Zefeitî, I regret that I have no reliable or consistent information in the way of history or tradition.

Alas, Sheikh Zefeitî's fall was even more meteoric than his rise! I was in Europe when the moulid was held on Sunday, 27 Gamâd II 1358 (13 August 1939), but was told on my return that it had been dreadfully reduced. The reason generally assigned was that the *cafetiers*, owners of booths, tents, etc., who had paid well the previous year for the use of the waste land by the side of the road, had been unable to come to terms with the Waqf officials and others concerned.

This year of the Prophet 1359 (1940), the specious war pretext seems to have given almost the *coup de grâce,* for even swings and such like put up by local enterprise (possibly irregularly in some technical way) were pulled down before the final night on 18 Rajab (22 August 1940), and the people of Duqqî and visitors were bitterly disappointed. I am told, however, that there was a *zeffa* in the afternoon, but by no means like that of 1357 (1938) described above; and that there was no crush of pilgrims at the tomb.

Z 2 (cf. Sectional Map XV)
ZEIN EL-'ABDÎN
(سيدي زين العابدين)

The Moulid of 'Alî -l-Asghar, Zein el-'Abdîn, was formerly one of the great celebrations of Islam, and certainly should be still, seeing that Cairo is privileged to guard the shrine of one of the leading characters in the history and religion of the Prophet, who was Zein el-'Abdîn's great-grandfather.

It was still big and impressive when I saw it on Saturday, 5 Sha'bân 1351 (3

December 1932), in its weirdly wonderful setting of tombs and mighty mosques, but it was not held at all in 1352 (1933), because, I am told, there was a murder somewhere in the *qarâfa*, necropolis, in which the shrine is situated, though I cannot trace any connection between the crime and the moulid.

On Saturday, 6 Safar 1353 (19 May 1934), I witnessed a miserable simulacrum of the moulid, and even this poor ghost was laid until 1357 (1938), when gallant attempts were made by the friends of the saint to bring him into his own again. The *zeffa* and the great night were fixed for Saturday, 17 Gamâd II (13 August 1938), and a week before that the *qarâfa* and the approaches to the shrine were thronged by pilgrims. The treatment it then suffered from the police of Sayyida Zeinab was heart-rending, the more so as of all Cairo moulids perhaps it has the most purely religious character; and being in a cemetery where there is no traffic whatever, the aggression seemed almost wanton. Though the *zeffa* was not allowed, the last night was peaceful and happy[146] and attended by an enthusiastic and goodly crowd, many from remote parts, for invitations had been sent out, and the fame of this great *walî* is as wide as Islam.

The approach, by the way, is very easy, by Khalîg tram 5 or 22; the Qarâfa being near the *salkhâna*[147] and Muhammad 'Alî's Aqueduct.

There was no secular side, no amusement park, and the general character of this celebration did not seem to call for these, though I regretted that the "fiqîs" who sang in the cafés and shops of the district, and who were so much appreciated in the good old days, are no longer heard, or at least I neither saw nor heard them; but I did not wander much from the shrine and its immediate surroundings. I was privileged to enter the holy of holies, where a beautiful grille in metal with a floral design, encloses the tomb, and garlands and bouquets of fresh roses add beauty to it. With some of these I was presented. But WHAT does the tomb contain? That I should be still in uncertainty illustrates the extraordinary difficulty there is to obtain definite or reliable information about these matters. 'Abd el-Wahhâb el-Sha'râni, a recognised authority, in his *Tabaqât*, clearly states: "His head was brought to Cairo and buried near the aqueduct which brings water to the Citadel in Old Cairo." Yet the Sheikh el-Sayyid 'Alî 'Abdîn, whose hospitality I enjoyed,[148] who is, I understand, the spiritual if not the blood successor (but I am told both) of Zein el-'Abdin in unbroken *silsila*, attested by diploma (*sanad*) and who would,

---

146 [McPher.] The result of representations made to the Governorate, which checked the destructive zeal of the local authorities.
147 Abattoir.
148 [McPher.] This sheikh's sudden death was recently announced under strange tragic circumstances.

I suppose, have ridden as *khalîfa,* had the *zeffa* been allowed, assured me that the *entire body* of the *walî* lies there, and was supported by relatives and sheikhs who naturally have inner knowledge. If a casting vote can be taken to decide the question, the sheikh directly in charge of the tomb, on being asked by me if the tomb contained the body, replied: "No, only the Noble Head."

In the *qarâfa,* not many yards from the great door of the *dareih,*[149] through which there was a perpetual passing of a crowd of pilgrims to and from the inner *maqâm,* a gaunt and terrible creature fascinated literally an immense ring of people. He was a *magzûb* from Upper Egypt – in the army once, I was told, now a religious maniac – and never have I met in real life a being with such a powerful and terrible personality. He hurled Jeremiads at the people and kept them entranced and terror-stricken by his voice, his fearsome gestures, and his marvellous whirling and contortions. He was a born witch doctor, and now and again smelt out a heretic or a pious fraud and hypnotised him on the spot. Sometimes the ring was like a spot on the island of Circe, bodies with the head bent back nearly to earth, or circulating upside-down on all fours and looking like scorpions, or bleating cries for mercy in ovine voices, or in the attitude of an ass carrying the *magzûb* on their backs or shoulders, whilst he himself emitted sounds which were anything but human, roars, grunts, and animal notes indescribable. When he took a new victim in hand, he generally fixed him with fierce wild eyes, and with fingers vibrating like claws asked him – "Are you laughing at me?" – for he was as sensitive to ridicule as Cyrano de Bergerac and, I am sure, would just as willingly have run the offender through the body. Without waiting for a reply, and indeed the subject was usually rendered speechless and helpless, he seized him by the hair, nose, or any member, swung him into the ring, made a few more rapid passes with his hand and, if necessary, again used his eyes and voice on him and then at once proceeded to the Circe transformations.

Early on he had not come into his power, and used some restraint, and even passed police scrutiny, though only just. When I was near, he was obviously *gêné* and very conscious of me, and in fact challenged me with his sphinx question, with baleful eyes, and claws working like snakes, but had not quite his usual confidence. I assured him with truth that I was not laughing at him, and to relieve the tension bluffed him by asking if he did not remember me at the Moulid of 'Abd el-Rahîm el-Qenâwî (to which in point of fact I had never then been, but guessed he as a *sa'îdî*[150] would have) and he replied – "Yes, by God, I remember you

---

149 The grave of a sheikh, with dome.
150 i.e., from Upper Egypt.

well". This, I think, was purely the Egyptian instinct of politeness, which conquers all other feelings. It was towards midnight that the Spirit came upon him with unusual power, and he came into "his hour". Then the police kindly and wisely left us alone, except one "saff zâbit"[151] who thought, but was not quite sure, that it was his duty to interfere. In time, he shuddered away like a falling withered leaf. I confess I should have liked to see the *ma'mûr* of the *qism*[152] in the magic ring: he might have been cured like Saul of the persecuting tendencies with which he is locally credited. The last occult triumph I witnessed was the subjugation of a highly respectable-looking sheikh, wearing a green turban, proclaiming him to be of the seed of the Prophet. He was walking past our ring at some distance, but the witch-doctor dashed through the people and had him into the charmed circle in a flash, tearing off his green *'imma*[153], and accusing him of being a false *sharîf*, and daring to approach Zein el-'Abdîn whilst *năgĭs* (in a state of ceremonial impurity).

With flashing eyes, the *sharîf* indignantly expostulated, but he met other eyes, and his went dull, and his face expressionless, and his voice lapsed into *aposiopesis*[154]; and after many antics worthy of *Qara Goz*, at word of command he was down and grunting on all fours, like the companions of Ulysses. Then after dancing a *pas seul,* he performed a lonely *zikr* – Allâh! Allâh! Allâh! – which changed into a mere cry, so full of pain and pathos, and so high-pitched, that it resembled no sound I have ever heard except the dying cry of an animal poisoned by prussic acid. We all appealed to the *magzûb* to desist, to which he responded making a few counter passes, and thrusting the *sharîf* out of the ring with words that sounded like an absolution. He also dealt with two or three other of his subjects still lying about, absolving some, but heaping unheard-of and horrible curses on one and hurling him among the tombs.

Out of curiosity, I followed the *sharîf*, and got into conversation with him, asking him the name of the *magzûb*. He said he did not know, though he had seen him once before, and he was "a very good man". "But", I said, "what he has just put you through must have been dreadful for you." "Anything but dreadful", he replied, "I love a *zikr*". And he looked at me with an expression of great surprise, as though entirely unconscious of his recent canine, ovine, porcine and Punch-like variants.

Seated on a tombstone to meditate on the strange beauty of the surroundings,

---

151 Non-commissioned officer.
152 The head of the police station.
153 Turban
154 ἀποσιώπησις, ("becoming silent"), in Classical Greek denotes a sentence being deliberately broken off and left unfinished.

the whispering of veiled women – vaguely seen – came to me, with the sound of "zikrs", and the singing or droning of holy men, and the animal cries of the untiring *magzûb*. Tombstones all about and a few trees, and in the distance veritable mansions of the dead, some of them fresh with flowers and greenery, and festooned minarets, and their ancient domes glowing softly in some hidden light, partly the effect of the now risen moon. I tried to place him whom we were honouring in the scheme of things. Grandson of the Imâm 'Alî and Fâtima, daughter of the Prophet, he escaped death on the field of Karbalâ' with his father Sidna Husein, "the martyr," and elder brother, 'Alî -l-Akbar, through his being too sick and too young to fight, and died in the year 99 A.H. (717 A.D.) at the age of 58, having founded a line illustrious to this day in the person of the Âghâ Khân and others. For Zein el-'Abdîn, 'Alî -l-Asghar was father of Ga'far Sâdiq, the sixth Imâm, whose son Ismâ'îl was the first of the sect of Ismâ'îlîya, which embraced the Assassins under Râshid el-Dîn, the Old Man of the Mountains, who proved such a thorn, or rather dagger in the sides of the Crusaders, and who levied a tribute (or some call it blackmail) which tens of thousands of Ismâ'îlîyans still pay to his successor, the great Derby winner at Bombay. We owe many Cairo moulids to his immediate family, apart from that of Sidna Husein: Sitna Sakîna, Sayyida 'Aysha, and Fâtima el-Nebawîya among them, the last named, his granddaughter Fâtima, having her *Maqâm* and her moulid, behind the governorate, beneath the windows of the Isti'nâf Prison – a yearly source of delight to the prisoners.

Z 3 (cf. Sectional Map XIII)
ZEINAB (SAYYIDA ZEINAB)
(سيدة زينب)

After the birthday of the Prophet that of Sayyida Zeinab is one of the two leading moulids of Cairo, the other of course being that of her brother Sidna Husein; the two being children of the Imâm 'Alî and Fâtima daughter of the Prophet, and therefore grandchildren of Muhammad himself. Though doubts have been thrown on the authenticity of the tomb in the Cairo mosque, ancient tradition and belief are strong enough to draw the best part of a million pilgrims to this reputed shrine each year. The mosque itself, though attractive, is not old nor famous architecturally; it was built on the site of an older mosque 140 (lunar) years ago by Muhammad 'Alî. The recent modernisation of the square of Sayyida Zeinab and destruction of a fine old tree and tomb and other such objects in the immediate neighbourhood have deprived it of much of the charm it possessed a few years ago.

After a run of three weeks, the moulid terminates on the nearest Tuesday to the middle of Rajab, at least as far as my experience goes: in 1348, 16 Rajab; 1351, also 16 Rajab; 1353, 14 Rajab; 1354, 17 Rajab; 1355, 13 Rajab; 1357, 18 Rajab; 1358, 14 Rajab; 1359, 16 Ragab (20 August 1940).

The writer made an early and strange acquaintance of mosque, tomb and moulid in 1319 (1901), being smuggled into the very exclusive penetralia on one of the early nights by two of the sons of 'Arabî Pâsha and the son of my host, Hâmed Mahmûd, later friend and doctor to Zaghlûl, and now Minister of Hygiene. I was introduced to sheikhs and notables who knew the lads, as a Turkish visitor of great piety, and Harold Base, whom many of my readers must have met, and who also was smuggled in, as a dumb dervish; and we were received with a kindly hospitality which smote our consciences. Seated and drinking *qirfa* (cinnamon tea), I made the most of my very limited Turkish and Arabic, and we were all happy, till someone had the *mauvaise idée* of bringing over to our little group a Bey from Stâmbûl who, he thought, would love a chat with *a fellow countryman.* Hâmed and the 'Arabî boys were in the greatest consternation, and before Base and I realised what course they proposed taking, the 'Arabîs bolted across the mosque, and Hâmed, not then perfected in the ways of diplomacy, did the same. The dumb dervish and I, not knowing what fate might await us, followed them out of the mosque and down Baghâla at high speed.

Any of the Sayyida Zeinab trams 4, 7, 12 and buses 2, 9 take one to the door of the mosque. So well-known is Sayyida Zeinab that this information may seem superlative, but some residents have so concentrated on certain parts of Cairo to the neglect of others, that I dare not omit it – having in mind an incident of some years ago. Dining a few evenings before the big night, with Mr. Humphreys of Bûlâq Dakrûr, who had been resident here since about the end of last century, I asked him if he would like to come with me to the moulid, and he replied, "I should love to, but what is a moulid and where is Sayyida Zeinab?"

A feature of this moulid has always been the numerous "zikrs" in and about the mosque, and in the side streets and courts, and until recent years the singing sheikhs in Sîdî -l-Barânî, who seem unhappily to have, to a large extent, come under the Al-Azhar ban on anything "against religion or morals". Also, the five-legged cow, *Qara Goz* and other characters have been chased from the precincts. But, *en revanche,* quite a big amusement park sprang up away to the east, by the Darb el-Gamâmîz and the Khalîg, with several theatres and many shows, stalls and entertainments. I have not seen a proper *zeffa* with mounted *khalîfa* since 1351 (1932). In 1353 (1934), Billy Williams amazed thousands of people by his daring riding in his *Piste à la Mort*. Recent building on the *terrain vague* which was utilised will make things difficult.[155]

Some ten years or more ago there was a serious *bagarre*[156] at which a number of people were killed, mostly "Sa'îdîs". A most rare occurrence, as a moulid crowd is full of piety and fun, and good temper. And ladies whom I have taken into the thick of the Sayyida Zeinab crowd would add "good manners", for a way is always made for them, politely and pleasantly, and every consideration shown. On one occasion my lady companions were invited into the mosque to visit the tomb, a favour which delighted them and left them most appreciative and grateful. "Sayyida Zeinab was a lady," one of them remarked, "and her votaries here are gentlemen."

---

155 [McPher.] A fresh spot was selected in the direction of Ibn el-Touloun, by the new gardens. The up-to-date aspect of this moulid is touched on in a letter to *The Egyptian Gazette* of 4 September 1940 (2 Sha'bân 1359) and quoted *in extenso* at the end of my Introduction.
156 Brawl (Fr.).

Envoi

It is the hour of sunset, but at the moment of writing I am not sure of the date – whether it be this month, last month or the next. The official date has recently been already changed, as mentioned under the moulids of Matrâwî and Rûbî, and now the *ru'ya*[1] is looking for the crescent of Ramadân to decide whether the month of fasting is to begin, or whether Sha'bân is to claim another day.

Anyway, this is 2 October 1940 A.D., and 22 Tût in the Coptic year of the martyrs 1657, and the eve of the Jewish New Year, 5001 A.M., as well as being the year 1359 A.H., and the cannons will fire and the minarets be all ablaze, if we are to welcome Ramadân.

My list of Egyptian Saints ends appropriately enough with two of the greatest of Islam, the great grandson and the granddaughter of the Prophet, but it is strange and regrettable that the Nebawîya group of the near relatives of Muhammad, of supreme value in religious history, should seemingly have suffered even more than some of the less exalted. The account of Zein el-'Abdîn's moulid, as in the cases of the two Fâtimas, is just a "tale of woe", and one who has witnessed recently their agony is tempted for a moment to repeat the despairing words of Keats in his "*Hyperion*":

"Leave them, O Muse! for thou anon wilt find
Many a fallen old divinity,
Wandering in vain about bewildered shores."

or to paraphrase the words of the same poet:

"Ay, the count

---

1 More properly the *ru'ya* is the sighting of the new moon and not the authority in charge of the sighting.

Of mighty Poets is made up; the scroll
Is folded by the Muses"

substituting "Poets" by Moulids: but what are we to put in the place of "Muses"?

I had proposed holding up the MSS of this compilation till the end of Sha'bân, the completion of the moulid season, but passed all in to the printers on the 18th of this month, rather on the "de mortuis nil nisi bonum" principle, for I found some old friends dead, and others reduced to such lifeless condition that I felt NIL to be the word.

But to adapt the old hymn:

"Sometimes a light surprises
The pilgrim on his road"

The very next day I was summoned to the shrine of Sîdî Hârûn el-Huseinî, and found his recently resuscitated moulid very much alive, an inspiring little scene of spiritual enthusiasm and joyous piety.

Then came the welcome surprise that, although nearly six months late, Sîdî Marzûq was to come into his own, when the hopes of his votaries had faded; and in spite of his moulid being denuded of some of its few popular items, its *zeffa* was so majestic and so true to traditional lines, that these were hardly missed, and *Qara Goz* supplied the pabulum so indispensable with the youngsters. Some account of these two at least I must induce the printers to find a place for.

I cannot ask them to do so in the case of a small discovery the *khalîfa* of Sîdî el-Ansârî helped me to make on 27 Sha'bân – the tiny moulid of the Sheikh el-Gûdârî in a little street of the same name, not far from the Bâb el-Metwallî[2].

Of the others I saw in the latter part of Sha'bân, Sâleh Haddâd, Sultân Hanafî, Hasan el-Anwar, Mansî, Ansârî and Marsafa were black-outs or nearly so, Bahlûl a little better, and Sa'ûdî and 'Abdullah Hagr very small but good as far as they went. But when I sought the beautiful little tomb of that eminent saint, Sitna Sutuhîya, in its ancient place under the Bâb el-Futûh it had simply disappeared, and local people explained that she had been dug up. Of course, her moulid must be struck off the scroll.

I cannot speak for the important moulids of the two great hermits, Barsûm el-'Aryân and Muhammadî of Demardâsh, as they both fell on the eve of the last Friday of Sha'bân, clashing with that of Sîdî Marzûq, and some minor

---

2 Also known as Bâb Zuweila.

celebrations. They were both held, and I am told that the monastery grounds at Ma'sara were thronged much as usual, and that the usual *tashrîfa* was held at the *zâwiya* of Sheikh Muhammadî.

Their date coincided with 16 Tût 1657 (26 September 1940).

The Feast of St. Teresa on 3 October was mentioned at the end of Chapter I as perhaps the nearest Catholic approximation to an Egyptian moulid that we have. This is the last night of the Novena of the "Little Flower", and at more than one minor celebration at which I have assisted during the past week, the vast Basilica (sprung in a few years from a tiny room used as a chapel) has been crowded and the precincts full of life with people of all denominations of Catholic and Ortho-dox Christendom, and many Moslems and Jews, invoking the miracle-working saint or bringing votive offerings to her shrine. (The phenomenal rise of this cult has, I fear, thrown into the shade the ancient miracle shrine of the Amîr Tadros, St. Theodore, in the Hâret el-Rûm, which though in Coptic hands is equally in vogue with Moslems.) The sight at Shubrâ tomorrow afternoon at the time of the Blessing of the Roses will indeed be a striking one, especially for the comparative few who succeed in finding a place within the church.

But there is no longer any doubt about the date. The Cairenes are all agog and, leaving this Envoi for a few minutes, I witnessed the beautiful sight of the glowing minarets. About the *manshîya* of Muhammad 'Alî alone, on the two mosques of Sultân Rifâ'î and that of the citadel, there must be the best part of a thousand lamps ablaze, and the domes of these and of Sultân Hasan are either flood-lit or show up as if they were in their light.

I am being greeted by "RAMADÂN KERÎM" to which I say in reply, as I do to all my kind and patient readers, "ALLÂHU AKRAM".

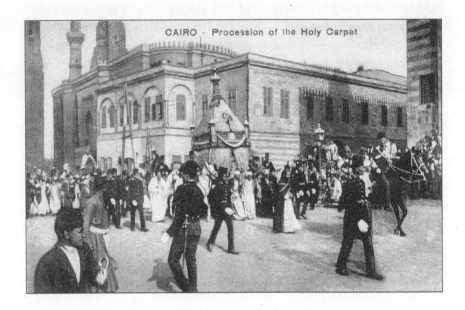

The Mahmal Procession.

Post Scriptum

It is with the greatest hesitation that I take up my pen again after completing the Envoi, but from one cause and another, an unexpectedly long time has elapsed since that date, 1 Ramadân 1359 (3 October 1940), when the MSS were passed to the printers, and the appearance of the book. So that now, at the eleventh hour, seeing in an English paper, a leading article entitled "A PLEA FOR MOULIDS", completely endorsing my point, the temptation to display to my readers such a *rara avis* is too strong for me.

As the writer (to me unknown) of this *leader* refers to a letter *The Egyptian Mail* had published a few days earlier, I have obtained the issue which contained this, and also their issue containing an account of the return of the *Mahmal* referred to therein. Here follow therefore:

From *The Egyptian Mail* of Sunday, 16 February 1941 (20 Muharram 1360) the shorter of two articles on the "Return of the Mahmal";
From *The Egyptian Mail* of Friday, 21 February 1941 (25 Muharram 1360) a letter on "The Mahmal Camel", signed "Abu Masaud";
From *The Egyptian Mail* of Sunday, 23 February 1941 (27 Muharram 1360) the *leader* entitled, "A PLEA POR MOULIDS".

Return of the Mahmal

Yesterday morning Hussein Sirry Pasha, the Prime Minister, as the representative of H.M. King Farouk, drove in State from the Presidency of the Council of Ministers to the Mouled el-Nebi Midan[1] at Abbassia, where the ceremony of the return of the Mahmal to Cairo took place.

The usual review of Egyptian Army units was held, the Prime Minister

---

1 City square, open space.

taking the salute in place of the King, and then the processions of Sufi dervishes went past the great marquee with their banners and drums.

The most interesting part of the programme was that of the camel carrying the Mahmal making the seven rounds in the Square, at the end of which the Emir El-Haj handed its halter to the Prime Minister.

The Prime Minister drove back to his office with the same ceremonial, while a salvo of guns was fired.

The Mahmal Camel

To The Editor of The Egyptian Mail

Sir,

The articles on pages 2 and 3 of the Sunday *Egyptian Mail* concerning the Mahmal ceremony were pleasant and interesting reading, and still more so the view of this fine old function in the eyes of the tens and tens of thousands of people who came from near and far to witness it.

You mention that "the most interesting part of the programme was that of the camel carrying the Mahmal", and so say all of us, though the military and other elements were brave sights.

As on the occasion of the departure of the Kiswah, everyone wanted the camels, and there was some anxiety until they appeared and great relief and joy then, for it was well-known that some pressure had been put on the Prime Minister last spring by – it was believed – a high personage, to mutilate the ceremony by cutting the camel out.

It is a mystery why such people cannot find evils to combat, or good objects to promote, without letting what looks like sheer ignorance and arrogance lure them to such limits as to urge the destruction of a picturesque and majestic national and Islamic custom, which had met with the approval and support of Egypt's leaders and saints for many centuries.

It seems indeed heartless also to wish to deprive the populace, particularly the poor, of one of their remaining innocent and legitimate joys.

I feel confident, Sir, that I have the whole of Saturday's great multitude with me, in thanking the Government and the Prime Minister for preserving the Mahmal ceremony intact, and we utter a heartfelt chorus of *El Hamdu Lillah!*

I am, Sir, Yours, etc.
Abu Masaud
Cairo, 18 February 1941

A Plea For Moulids

A few days ago, we published a letter from one of our readers, protesting against the gradual but relentless process of suppression which is being applied by those in authority to the old traditional ceremonies and merrymaking which have formed the core of Egyptian popular life for centuries.

Traditions die out. That is only natural under changing conditions. Other traditions arise, and some traditions may well be socially harmful, relics of superstition and ignorance, which no one would regret to see disappear. But that is not the same as casting a cold and disapproving eye and enforcing it with all the power officialdom has at its command on the ordinary pleasures of the fellahin and the poorer classes of Egypt.

The repression of all the secular fun and gaiety which used to accompany saints' birthdays in Egypt is one of the most striking instances of this sort of intolerance. For generations, the celebration of the local saint's birthday, commonly called a 'moulid', has been about the only break in the drab and colourless monotony of the peasant's existence. Swings, roundabouts, tumblers, dancers, plays, booths of sweetmeats and cheap finery, flaring lights and sizzling *felâfel*, all the fun of the fair, went hand in hand with the reverent visit to the saint's tomb, the delirious sway of the *zikr*, the solemn procession through the streets and fields to the holy mosque. It is a process which is duplicated all over the world – the very word holiday, so full of gay relief and light-hearted merriment, began its life as Holy Day, and popular rejoicing has always gone hand in hand with religious festivity.

If the dead hand of officialdom has its way, these rejoicings will soon be a thing of the past. Every day new restrictions are placed on the secular celebration of moulids, regardless of the fact that the peasant has little else to brighten his life. He does not read. He knows no games. He cannot afford cinemas, or radios, or modern methods of distraction, even if they were, as they often are not, more desirable. As long as nothing better is provided for his recreation – and where are there signs of it? – he should at least be left the old traditional pleasures that have stood the test of centuries.

My readers will remember a letter in the Introduction, signed Abu Masaud and dated 25 April 1940, voicing the indignation of the people that suggestions had been made to the Prime Minister by a sheikh of Al-Azhar, to abandon the camel part of the *Mahmal* ceremony (as published in *The Egyptian Gazette* of 9 March 1940). That makes the press cuttings in this Post Scriptum clear.

I understand that the further letter of Abu Masaud of 21 February 1941 appeared in *The Egyptian Mail* verbatim, except for the deletion of its heading – "Cacoethes delendi"[2] – and the prudent omission by the editor or censor in the last clause of *"the Prophet's camels",* who were included with the writer and the multitude in returning thanks. I think Abu Masaud had in mind the Quranic text in the *Chapter of the Pilgrimage*:

"And the beasts of sacrifice (she-camels) —
We have appointed them for you as among the symbols of God;
For you therein is good."[3]

One wonders whether the learned sheikh had forgotten this, when he tried to force the hand of the Minister, and to deprive people and camels of a rightful and beautiful fragment of their heritage, and indeed whether the injunction in the *Chapter of the Sanctuary* is not sometimes overlooked:

لا ترفعوا أصواتكم فوق صوت النبي

"Raise not your voices above the voice of the Prophet."

Oh, if the multitude of Egypt's faithful poor were not almost as voiceless as their camels, my feeble plea and the few *voces clamantium in deserto*[4] in defence of their priceless heirlooms would not be needed, for the roar of their chorus would drown the voiceful few who would deprive them of their rightful joys and traditions, and barter Egypt's real gold for dross; and a happy people would continue to enjoy its lovely old customs, which make the charm and fascination of Egypt, and not least of these the MOULIDS OF ITS SAINTS.

---

2 "Bad habits should be eliminated".
3 (Sûrat al-Hajj, verse 36). The English translation is slightly adapted from A.J. Arberry's *The Koran Interpreted*.
4 "Voices crying in the wilderness".

أ تستبدلون الذي هو أدنى بالذي هو خيرٌ

"Would you exchange that which is better for that which is worse?"
(Sûrat al-Baqarah, verse 61)

Glossary (edited and expanded)

'abd = Slave; often used in conjunction with one of the 99 "names" of God for personal names, e.g., 'Abdulhamîd (slave of the praiseworthy).

'afrît = Demon, imp.

'ahd = Covenant.

Alf Leila wa-Leila = The Thousand and One Nights; "The Arabian Nights".

'âlim, *pl.* 'ulamâ' = A learned person; in the plural, the body of professional theologians.

'âlima (*fem.*) = A learned woman; generally, a professional woman expert, e.g., the leader (*kôdya*) of a *zâr*.

aluba = Cane (according to McPherson, otherwise unknown).

a'mâ, *pl.* 'umyân = Blind.

'amm = Paternal uncle; often used as term of respect for older men not in one's family.

'Aqaba = The name of the ship which bears the "Bride of the Nile".

'arbagî = Driver of an animal-drawn cart, horse-drawn cab, &c.

ardab = Dry measure equal to 198 litres.

arghûl = Wind instrument roughly a metre long, consisting of two pipes.

'arûsa = Bride; also, a sugar figurine.

'Arûset el-Nil = "Bride of the Nile" ceremony when a wooden doll, dressed as a bride, is thrown into the Nile to celebrate the annual flood.

'arîs = Bridegroom.

'ashâ' = Dinner.

'âshûrâ = The 10th of Muharram, a day of fasting and mourning; the anniversary of Husain's martyrdom at Kerbala in 60 A.H.

'askarî, *pl.* 'asâkir = Soldier or policeman.

'asr = Afternoon; afternoon prayer.

'ataba = Threshold; the "tram centre".

'ataba -l-khadrâ > el-'ataba -l-khadrâ = The "threshold" of the vegetable market;
    also, in McPherson's words, "the tram centre (recently afflicted with some
    new name)".

'atfa = Blind alley, cul-de-sac.

'athrâ' = Virgin.

'atshân, *pl.* 'atshânîn = Thirsty.

bâb = Door; city gate, e.g., Bâb el-Nasr, Bâb el-Akhdar at Sidna Husein, and
    other important gateways.

bâbâ = Pope, generally in reference to the Coptic pope.

babûr = Fair-ground contraption whereby, with a large hammer, one attempts to
    propel a weight up a pole to ring a bell.

bahlawân, *pl.* bahlawânât = Acrobat; from the Persian *pahlavân*, meaning
    "hero" or "strongman", generally known in the West through its cognate
    Pahlavi, the name of the former royal family of Iran.

badîr = A large tambourine.

badîr 'arûsî = A deep form of large tambourine.

badîr qadrî = A shallow form of large tambourine.

bărăkă = A blessing; also, *bărăkă/yŭbrŭk* (verb past/present), "for a cámel to
    kneel", e.g., in the text where McPherson refers to a camel "summarily
    baraking".

barbarî, *pl.* barâbira = Berber.

barîza = Coin worth 10 piastres.

bâz, *vide* tabl bâz.

beiraq, *pl.* bawâriq or (more correctly) bayâriq = The banner of a Sufi Order.

Benî Isrâ'îl = "The sons of Israel", the Jews.

bimbâshî = Major (in Turkish).

birka = Pool, lake.

birket el-timsâh = Lake Timsah at Ismâ'îlîya ("Lake of Crocodiles").

bûza = A Sudanese fermented barley-drink, also called *marîsa*; *vide* Berthold
    Laufer, On the Possible Oriental Origin of our Word Booze, *Journal of the
    American Oriental Society*, Vol. 49 (1929), pp. 56–58.

caracôl = Police station (in Turkish).

Cutting of the Khalîg = The Khalîg was an ancient canal in Cairo, abandoned at
    the end of the 19th century. The ceremony of "cutting" it was celebrated the
    day the Nile flood reached a level whereat water could be let into irrigation
    canals.

dabbûs, *pl.* dabâbîs = Pin; the dervish dagger used mysteriously to perforate
    one's own body without ill effect, particularly by the sect of the Rifâ'îya.

dâ'im, yâ dâ'im = The Everlasting, O Eternal One!

dalâ'il > el-Dalâ'il el-Sughrâ = A book in praise of the Prophet.

dandurma = Ice cream (in Turkish).

darb el-raml = Fortune-telling while tracing figures, &c. on sand.

darabûkka = A large musical instrument of earthenware, open at one end, but covered at the other (and larger) end by skin.

dareih = The grave of a sheikh, with dome, &c.

dawâ' = Medicine.

dawâh, pl. dawâya = Ink stand, writing having a supposed medical force.

deir = Monastery.

dervish < darwîsh = An initiate into one of the Islamic orders (tŭrŭq).

dilq, *pl.* dulûq = A patchwork coat of many colours, worn by some dervishes, and many *soi-disant* "Holy Men".

Djinn < jinn = Spirits recognised by religion, usually evil or mischievous but may be good.

dôraq, pl. dawâriq = Pitcher, jug; the vessel used by sellers of tamar hindî, 'erq sûs, lîmânâta, &c.

dôsah = The riding by the mounted sheikh of the Sa'dīya Order over the prone bodies of many dervishes, at the Moulids of el-Nebi, Imâm el-Shâfe'î & Tashtûshî, (Leilet el-Mi 'râg).

dûd rûmî ["Greek worms"] = Leeches; in Egypt, these are normally called '*alaq* [pl.], '*alaqa* [s.].

dŭrra = Corn, maize.

effendî = Turkish title of respect; the word's plural means "educated class".

'erq sûs = Licorice root; McPherson calls the drink thereof, "a cold sarsaparilla decoction".

'ezba = Country estate, farm; rural settlement.

fa'r, *pl.* fîrân = Rat.

fã's or fâs, *pl.* fu'ûs = Type of heavy hoe used in Egypt.

fagr = Dawn, time of the first prayer.

fallâh, *pl.* fallâhîn = Native peasants, agricultural labourers.

fânûs, *pl.* fawânîs = Lamp.

fărăh = Rejoicing; wedding festivities.

farrâsh = House servant; office boy.

farqilla = Small whip of cords.

fath (pronounced fatʰh) = A favourite dish of rice, bread, meat and rich sauces.

fâtiha = The short opening chapter of the Qurân.

fatîr = Unleavened (bread).

fatûr = Breakfast; the sunset meal of Ramadân after the day's fast.

feddân = 1.04 acres.

felâfel, = In Egypt, the common word for *ta'mîya*, a sort of vegetable burger.

fetwâ = In Islamic law, a formal legal opinion.

fiqî = Professional singer of the Qurân.

fûl = Broad beans.

fûl medammis = Cooked broad beans with oil.

fûl nâbit = Sprouting broad beans (a decoction of these is a mild medicine).

fulân = Unspecified person, "so-and-so".

Fumm el-Khalîg = "Mouth of the Canal", referring to the old Red Sea Canal, which reached the Nile by Rôda Island in Cairo; the name of that area of the city.

găbĕl = Hill; mountain.

gada', also gaza' = Young man; gallant lad, "young buck".

gallâbîya = Long and loose shirt-like garment worn by Egyptian males.

Galli Galli man = A conjurer in the streets and ports of Egypt who says *galâ galâ* (hey presto!).

Gamâd el-Awwal (or Gamâd I) = Fifth month of the Muslim year.

Gamâd el-Tânî (or Gamâd II) = Sixth month of the Muslim year.

gâmûs = Water buffalo (collective noun).

gâria = Female slave.

gazb = State of religious ecstasy.

gehâd = Jihad, holy war.

Gezîra = In the Nile, the main island in Cairo; otherwise, Arabic for "island".

ghadâ' = Mid-day meal.

ghafîr = Guard, watchman.

ghâziya, *pl.* ghawâzi = Dancing girl.

gink = Turkish word referring to cross-dressing male dancers.

gisr = Bridge.

gô'a = Theatrical troop or caste.

gôz el-hind or gôz hindî = Coconut.

gôza = Narghile.

Hadîth = Collected sayings of the Prophet.

hâgg = Pilgrim; more especially, one who has been on pilgrimage to Mecca or Jerusalem.

hakîmdâr = Officer in charge of a police station.

hâra, *pl.* hârât = Quarter or section (of a city); lane or small street.

harâmî = Thief.

harîm = Harem, women's quarters in a Muslim house; a sacred, inviolable place.

hâtif = In Sufism, a *hâtif* was "a voice from heaven", or an angel speaking to the saint. In modern Arabic, it is the word for "telephone".

hatun, *vide* khâtûn.

hâwî = Snake charmer; conjurer.

hegâb, pl. hegâbât = Amulet, charm; talisman (often containing Qurânic texts or mystic figures); woman's veil.

hegira or higra = The transfer of the Prophet from Mecca to Medina. A.H. is *anno Hegirae*, "in the year of the Higra" (622 A.D.), the Islamic calendar dating from that event.

helba = Fenugreek.

hôsh = Courtyard.

hummusîya = Hard white candy with dry chickpeas.

Iblîs = Satan.

ifrângî = Literally, a Frank or Frankish, meaning West European.

imâm = Imam, prayer leader.

'imma = Turban.

irba, *vide* (q)irba.

ishâra = Sign, indication; used by [E. W.] Lane for *zeffa*, a religious procession.

Ka'ba = The "Sanctum sanctorum" of Islam; the central object of the pilgrimage to Mecca, round which the pilgrim must go seven times to become *Hâgg*. Covered by the *Kiswa*, the holy carpet from Egypt.

kalima = Word; specially applied to the confession of the faith, "There is no God but one, and Muhammad is his Prophet".

kamanga = Fiddle.

kâs = Cymbals.

kashshâf = Search-light.

khalîfa, pl. khulafâ' = Caliph, "Commander of the Faithful"; the rider in a *zeffa* representing the sheikh who is being honoured.

khalîg = Canal; gulf.

khătma = Recital of the entire Qurân.

khâtûn = Turkish for "lady of social prominence".

khayâl el-zill = Shadow show.

khâtima = End, conclusion; final rites at a moulid.

kishâfa = The Boy Scouts.

kiswa = A brocaded covering for the Ka'ba, the *Kiswa* was made annually in Egypt and sent to Mecca with the Pilgrimage caravan.

kôdya = The leading woman at a *zâr*.

kubrî = Bridge.

kurrât = Leek.

lâsa = Large scarf; white wrapping of fine linen around a skullcap.

Leilet el-'Eid = Eve of the feast.

Leilet el-Ghitâs = Eve of 11 Tûba in the Coptic calendar (Epiphany).

Leilet el-Isrâ' = Eve of the Prophet's Ascension.

Leilet el-Mi'râg = Eve of 27 Rajab in which the Prophet made his journey
    through the seven heavens.

Leilet el-Nuqta = Night of 17 June (11 Ba'ûna in the Coptic calendar) when a
    miraculous drop is said to fall from heaven, causing the yearly rise of the
    Nile.

Leilet el-Qadr = Eve of 27 Ramadân, when the Holy Spirit came down – that
    night said to be "more blessèd than a thousand months."

libâs = Drawers, underpants.

ma shâ' allâh = An expression of wonder and admiration. Literally, "O, what
    God has willed!".

magnûn, pl. magânîn = Insane, mad; possessed.

maghreb = Sunset, the time of the fourth Islamic prayer.

magzûb, *pl.* magâzîb = Possessed, entranced (*vide* gazb); idiot.

mahdar = Procès Verbal.

mahmal = Camel-borne litter sent by Egyptian rulers to Mecca at pilgrimage
    time.

malik, *pl.* mulûk = King.

mamlûk = White slave; feudal nobles and a line of kings.

ma'mûr = Official in charge.

Ma'mûr Zapt = Director of the political Criminal Investigation Department
    (CID) for investigating political activists and secret societies.

mandel (or darb el-mandel) = Form of magic where a fortune-teller or medium
    prophesies while contemplating a mirror-like surface.

"Manouli" = Derived from the Greek proper name Manolis; commonly applied
    to a performing monkey.

manshîya, *pl.* manâshî = A city square or open space; more properly, a recently
    built village or suburb.

maqâm = Tomb of a sheikh, about which a moulid centres.

maqbara = Cemetery.

marahrah = Flaky bread, specially used at the Mazghûna moulid.

margûha = Children's swing.

marîsa = A Sudanese fermented barley drink, generally known in Egypt as *bûza*.

masgid = Mosque.

mashrabîya = Projecting window enclosed by wooden latticework.

Maulâwî = Dervish of the Sufi order of Galâl el-Dîn el-Rûmî.

ma'zûn = In Islam, an official authorised to perform a marriage.

meded = An interpolated ejaculation in singing, more or less equivalent to "dynamis" in the Byzantine liturgy and "selah" in the Psalms.

meitam *pl.*, mayātim = Wake, vigil over the dead.

melbûs = Possessed, in a state of religious frenzy.

millième = 1000 millièmes equals 1 Egyptian pound.

minbar, *pl.* manâbir = Pulpit.

mi'râg = The ride of the Prophet to Jerusalem and Paradise on the horse Burâq, celebrated on eve of 27 Rajab.

mîrâlâi = Colonel (in Turkish).

mish'al = Torch; a brazier used in *zeffas*, for solemn effect, light and for tightening the skins of the tambourines.

moulid = A popular religious feast in honour of a saint.

mudîr = Head, director, administrator.

mudîrîya = Approximate equivalent of town hall; town or city administration building.

muftî = Chief Doctor of the Law, with very considerable ecclesiastical and civil jurisdiction (e.g., no capital sentence can be executed without the *fetwâ* of the *muftî*).

muhaddit(h) = Storyteller, especially a recounter of the exploits of "El-Zâhir" Beybars. El-Ẓâhir Rukn el-Dîn Beybars el-Bunduqdârî (died 1277 A.D.) was the fourth sultan of Egypt in the Mamluk Bahri dynasty. A warrior of great renown, he helped defeat Crusader King Louis IX of France at the Battle of Mansûrah in 1250. He also played a leading role in the defeat of the Mongol army at 'Ain Jâlût (in Galilee) ten years later. NB. In Egyptian dialect, pronounced "mihaddis" and "mihaddit".

Muharram = First month of the Muslim year.

mulâzim awwal = First Lieutenant.

mŭnshĭd = Singer, reciter.

murâsla, *pl.* murâslât = A military term meaning "orderly" or "batman".

murîd = Postulant for initiation in one of the *tŭrŭq* (dervish orders), but a step higher in the process than *tâlib.*

mŭrshĭd = Spiritual guide.

mutahhar, *pl.* mutahharîn = Purified; circumcised.

nadr, pronounced nad'r = Vow.

nâ'ib = Representative, agent; deputy.

nagîl = Couch grass (*Elymus repens*).

năgĭs = Impure.

nâqa = She-camel.

naqîb, *pl.* naqâ'ib = Ecclesiastical rank like *qutb* and *walî*, but generally inferior
   to these; descendants and representatives of the first caliphs.

Naqîb el-Ashrâf = The highest naqîb, representing Abu Bakr, the Sheikh
   el-Bakrî of Cairo.

naqqâra, pl. naqâqîr = Small percussion instrument of earthenware, closed at the
   larger end by taut skin.

naqrazân = Small musical instrument of hemispherical shape of the *tabl* (drum)
   class; like a kettledrum, but smaller.

nasrânî = Christian.

nay = Flute.

nebî, *pl.* anbiyâ' = Prophet.

nikla = A 2 millième-piece, worth a ha'penny.

nishân = Sign, mark; medal.

onbâshî = Corporal (in Turkish).

pîr = "Old man" in Persian; in context, refers to a superior in a Sufi order of
   dervishes.

qâ'imaqâm = Lieutenant Colonel.

qal'a = Citadel.

qânûn = A musical instrument of 72 chords, much on the principle of the harp,
   played by two plectra.

qarâfa = Necropolis.

Qara Goz = Variant of Punch (and Judy).

qasîda = Ode; ancient Arabic poem.

(q)irba = Waterskin (of goat or sheep) carried by a *saqqâ'*, water carrier; smaller
   skins are used for churning cream into butter; bagpipe.

qirfa = Cinnamon; an infusion of *qirfa*, cinnamon tea.

qism, *pl.* aqsâm = Police station.

qubba = The dome of a mosque or tomb.

quradâtî = Showman of performing monkey.

Qurân = The sacred book of Islam, of 114 chapters.

qutb, pronounced qut'b = Axis; pole; pole-star; The most holy *walî* only
   occasionally seen by mortals, still sometimes looked for behind the Bâb
   el-Mitwallî (Bâb Zuweila).

rabâb or rabâba = The one-stringed viol with which the *muhaddit* (raconteur) accompanies the recitation of his romance.

Rabî' el-Awwal (Rabî' I) = Third month of the Muslim year.

Rabî' el-Tânî (Rabî' II) = Fourth month of the Muslim year.

raghûl, *vide* arghûl.

Rajab = Seventh month of the Muslim year.

Ramadân = Ninth month of the Muslim year; the month of fasting.

ramûs = Raft of earthen pots bound together by osiers.

raqs = Dancing.

rasadkhâna = Observatory (astron.).

ringa = Sudanese entertainment of music, dancing and "bûza" drinking; the chief musical instrument used, a sort of piano.

riqq = Small tambourine.

ru'ya = Seeing, viewing; the sighting of the new moon.

rukhsa, *pl.* rŭkhăs = Licence.

rŭz or arŭz = Rice.

sabâris = Cigarette butts gathered from the street for re-use.

sâda, *vide* sayyid.

Safar = Second month of the Muslim year.

saff zâbit = Non-commissioned officer.

sâgh = A rank in the army and police forces intermediate between Captain and Major.

sâgha > el-sâgha = In Gamâlîya district, the gold market and assay offices.

sahhâr = Magician, conjurer.

sa'îdî = From Upper Egypt.

sâ'iqa, *pl.* sawâ'iq = Thunderbolt.

salâmlek = Primarily, a reception room or parlour (in Turkish).

salkhâna = Abattoir.

samâ' = The whirling dance of the Sufis, including that introduced by Galâl el-Dîn el-Rûmî at Konya in Anatolia; literally "listening".

sanad = Diploma of initiation to a dervish order.

saqqâ' = Water carrier.

sayyid, *pl.* sâda = Honorific title before the names of male Muslim saints; otherwise, simply Mr. or Sir in common parlance.

sayyida, *pl.* sayyidât = Honorific title before the names of female Muslim saints; otherwise, simply Mrs. or Madame in common parlance.

sebîl = Fountain.

sebîl ullâh = "Fountain of God": free drinks for the populace.

shabâba = Reed pipe.

Sha'bân = Eighth month of the Muslim year.

Shagaret el-Durr = Queen of Egypt at the time of Beybars.

shahâda = Testimonial, credentials, certificate.

shâhid, *pl.* shuhadâ' = Martyr (witness to the faith).

shakhshâkha = Rattle; sistrum, particularly the cylindrical metal rattle of the
 ringa.

Shamm el-Nesîm = A pan-Egyptian feast held on the Coptic Easter Monday (the
 Arabic words meaning "the smell of the breeze"); also, the date of the Giza
 Moulid of Abû Hareira.

sharbât = Drink made of sweet syrup; specifically, a sweet fruity concoction to
 be got in bottles or from a *dorâq*.

sharbâtlî = Seller of the above; the picturesque character who hawks divers
 sweet and iced drinks in the streets.

shâri' = Street.

sharîf, *pl.* ashrâf = Descended from the Prophet; noble.

sharmûta, *pl.* sharâmît = Prostitute.

shatrang = Chess.

Shawwâl = Tenth month of the Muslim year.

shîsha = Narghile, hookah.

sïbs = Small flute.

sidr = A variety of Christ's thorn (*Zizyphus spina Christi*).

sigâda = Carpet, (especially) for praying.

sigât = Castanets of brass.

sikka = A street, smaller than a shâri'.

silsila = Literally: chain. Otherwise, pedigree; family "tree"; the dervish's line of
 descent from the spiritual founder of his "order".

simsimîya = Sesame seed candy.

sîr = The watching spirit of a sheikh, long since dead.

sirâg, *pl.* sŭrŭg = Lamp

skêté, ΣΚΗΤΕ (in Greek) = Monastic enclosure.

sôma'a = Monk's cell; silo for storing grain.

subû' = Ceremony marking the seventh day after the birth of a child.

sûfî = Persian dervish, particularly one associated with Galâl el-Dîn Rûmî at
 Konya; tenets sometimes deemed hedonistic and loose from Quranic
 standpoint.

sufrâgî = Waiter, steward.

sŭlŭs = Egyptian pronunciation of "thŭlŭth": an ornate style of Arabic calligraphy.

sûq, *pl.* aswâq = Market, bazaar.

Sûq el-'Asr = Literally, "afternoon market"; a district in Bûlâq.

Sûq el-Bakrî = Renamed Shâri' 'Ashmâwî.

Sûq el-Harâmîa = Market for stolen goods.

Sûq el-Silâh = Literally, "market for weapons"; a street joining Shâri' Muhammad 'Alî by the Mosque of Sultân Rifâ'î.

Sûq el-Talât = "Tuesday Market" or fair, at Giza and elsewhere.

syce [sâ'is] = Stable groom.

ta'mîya = A vegetable fritter of beans, onion, garlic and parsley.

tabl baladî = Bass drum.

tabl bâz = A variety of small metal kettledrum beaten with a strap.

tabl shâmî = Shallow metal kettledrum with a laced head.

tâbût = Casket or coffin.

takhtarawân, *pl.* takhtarawânât = Animal-borne litter, palanquin.

tâlib = A postulant, candidate for initiation; a student.

tamar hindî = Tamarind (in Arabic, literally "Indian dates").

tanwîn = In Arabic grammar, the addition of a final "n" in the declension of nouns.

târ, *pl.* tîrân = Tambourine.

tarîqa, *pl.* tŭrŭq = "Way"; sect; order of dervishes.

tartûr = High, conical hat of dervishes.

tashrîfa, *pl.* tashrîfât = Social reception; ceremony marking the opening and closing of a moulid.

tayyâra *pl.* tayyârât = Aeroplane.

tekîya = Cell (in Persian and Turkish); monastic retreat; Sufi hospice or "monastery" that developed with the rise of an organised Ottoman network of brotherhoods but is not exclusively Bektashi.

tîl = Hemp.

tûb or tôb = The central object of veneration in the *zeffa* of Sîdî 'Abd el-Rahîm el-Qenâwî, somewhat of the nature of a miniature *mahmal*.

tuhûr = Circumcision; literally, purification.

tunbûr > tambûr (Egyptian pronunciation) = Archimedean screw for raising water to irrigate land.

turmus = The Egyptian Lupin, the seeds and beans of which are eaten.

'ûd = Lute.

'ulamâ' = The body of professional theologians in Islam.

'uqâl = Cord ring used to hold Arab *kaffiyeh* (headdress) in place.

wakîl = Deputy, representative.

walad, *pl.* awlâd = Boy.

walî, *pl.* awliyâ' = Holy man, saint.

waqf = In Arabic grammar, a rule suppressing the terminal sound of a word at
    the end of a sentence.

waqf, *pl.* awqâf = A pious gift or bequest; religious endowment.

waqfa = Eve; eve of a religious festival (*i.e.,* waqfat el-'eid).

ward = Rose; "rosary" in initiation to dervish tarîqa.

wasl = In Arabic grammar, a rule concerning the elision of the final letter of a
    word with the first of that following.

wazîr = Minister (of government).

Wizâret el-Awqâf = The ministry in charge of the government "waqfs",
    corresponding in a way to the English Court of Chancery.

wudû' = Ablution before prayer.

zaghrôta, *pl.* zaghârît = A loud, joyful trilling of the tongue, which women
    produce at weddings, at the passing of a *zeffa* or the *mahmal*, and other great
    occasions.

zâr = Ritual for appeasing or casting out evil spirits.

zarb = A musical term meaning rhythm.

zâwiya, *pl.* zawâya = Cell; small monastery; (literally, corner). Often the
    equivalent to *maqâm* and *darêh* as the tomb of a saint.

zeffa = Dervish procession, the great feature of a complete moulid, brought up
    by the *khalîfa*, the representative of the sheikh whose moulid is being
    observed.

zikkîr = One who takes part in a *zikr*.

zikr = A religious observance whose essential is the repeated utterance of *Allâh*
    or one of the 99 names of God.

zikr el-hadra = A congregational *zikr*.

Zû -l-Higga = Twelfth month of the Muslim year.

Zû -l-Qa'da = Eleventh month of the Muslim year.

zummâra = A reed instrument, consisting of two pipes.

zuhra > el-zuhra = The planet Venus.

zuqâq, pl. aziqqa = Alley.

Life of J. W. McPherson (1866–1946) in Historical and Literary Context

Russell McGuirk

In 1901, the first year of the Edwardian era and the nineteenth of the British Occupation of Egypt, 35-year-old Joseph McPherson travelled to Cairo for the first time. He was a schoolteacher by profession, intelligent and well-educated, who had spent the last ten years in England drifting from job to job. Ready now to try his luck in Egypt, Joseph wanted more than steady employment: he craved excitement and this he would find in abundance, living contentedly as an Anglo-Egyptian for the rest of his life. From the time of his arrival until the outbreak of the First World War, he worked as a teacher. He then became a Red Cross volunteer under fire at Gallipoli; a soldier with the Egyptian Camel Transport Corps in Sinai (aged 50!); an Intelligence Officer in Cairo; and towards the end of the war and during the Egyptian riots of 1919, he was the *Ma'mûr Zapt*, the head of political security. In retirement from 1924, he researched the religious festivals called "moulids" and wrote this book.

*

Joseph Williams McPherson was born 29 August 1866 in a large 17th century house, "The Rookery" at Brislington, near Bristol. He was the sixth son and last child of Dougal McPherson and Eliza Williams, from the Scottish Highlands. The building was at that time an asylum for the mentally ill, and Dougal worked there supervising the care of those inhabitants. Joseph (in his own words) "ran wild"[1]

1 From information provided by Joseph McPherson to the Old Merchant Venturers' Club for

until the late 1870s, when as an adolescent he was sent to the Trade and Mines School in Bristol. He won a scholarship to the Mines faculty (1881 to 1883); then moved to the Royal College of Science in Dublin, where he showed exceptional aptitude in chemistry. During academic year 1886–87, he returned to Bristol as assistant master at the Merchant Venturers' Technical College into which the Trade School had since been merged. In 1887 at age 21, he went to Christ Church, Oxford, again on a scholarship, graduating in 1890 with first class honours in natural science.[2] Henry George Liddell, the Dean of Christ Church, wrote that McPherson "fully justified our choice by his industry and good conduct."[3] (This is the same Liddell who co-authored the Liddell & Scott *Greek-English Lexicon*, and whose daughter Alice achieved greater fame as the inspiration for Lewis Carroll's *Alice's Adventures in Wonderland*.)

To the above bare sketch of Joseph's education, his great-nephew provides some colourful detail.[4] "At Oxford he was successful athletically and socially; he was much involved in strenuous undergraduate pranks, and, through high living with aristocratic friends, ran up large debts which his brothers paid. At the same time, he was devoutly religious…".[5] This early interest in religion, in contrast to his penchant for student horseplay and running up debts, is striking. McPherson had become interested in Catholicism when studying in Dublin and upon his return to Bristol (at age 20) had converted. His parents, though, were strict "covenanters," and the very foundation of this austere 17th century Scottish movement was pro-Presbyterian and anti-Catholic. Did McPherson's conversion affect his relations with his family? Perhaps not. Dougal, certainly, would have disapproved, but he had died in 1883. Joseph wrote of him that he was "of inflexible righteousness and missed his vocation as monk or missionary or martyr …[and] should never have had boys, certainly not me to scowl at habitually".[6] Joseph's relationship with his mother, on the other hand, was ever marked by mutual affection to the end of her life.

His formal education behind him, Joseph faced the prospect of working for a

---

publication: two pages, undated, found in the McPherson archive temporarily at the Bristol Record Office.

2 McPherson wrote in the opening of this book that he had a "BSc (Bris)" and a "MA (Oxon)". Bristol University was not founded until 1909, but in the 1880s the evolving Merchant Venturers Trade School and then the Technical College provided the best scientific education in the city. The Technical College was eventually supplanted by Bristol University.

3 Carman, B. and McPherson, J., editors (1983), *Bimbashi McPherson: A Life in Egypt*, p. 20.

4 John McPherson, co-author of the above.

5 Carman and McPherson (1983), p. 20.

6 Ibid, p. 17.

living without any clear idea of what he wanted to do. Unable to hold a job for long, he did secretarial work in London for the 4th Baron Camoys; then taught science short-term at Clifton College, Bristol;[7] at a school in Wakefield; and another in Shropshire.

In 1900, Eliza Williams died. The loss of Joseph's mother was for him a major turning point. He was thirty-four years old and his employment record undistinguished. He would later write about having sought a solution to his mid-life crisis in the memory of childhood reveries:

> Since boyhood it had been my dream to live in Cairo, and, from that centre, to see and know as much as possible of the places, peoples and languages all round the Mediterranean... Mother's death left a deeper shadow and more terrible void than even my worst forebodings, and nothing in England seemed to rouse much enthusiasm. The old longing for the 'storied shores of the Mediterranean,' which had been repressed while Mother was still alive and anchored me at home, returned now unrestrained.[8]

In short, Joseph decided to seek his fortune in Egypt.

He obtained an interview with an Egyptian government representative, an Englishman, whose job it was to find qualified teachers for Egypt's "Department of Public Instruction". This odd name for a ministry of education was a mark of earlier French influence in the country (the corresponding ministry in France at the time being *le ministère de l'instruction publique*). Ronald Storrs, who was Oriental Secretary at the British Agency in Cairo under Consul-Generals Gorst and Kitchener, made an interesting comment about this entity in Egypt, that "the P.I. was... considered to be the lowest of the low, classed perhaps with... the Scavenging Department. The result, and perhaps the reason, of this absurdity was that none ever remained in the P.I. who could manage to get transferred anywhere else."[9] Joseph, who was offered and accepted a position teaching science and

---

7 Three sources state that McPherson was educated at Clifton College: (i) John McPherson's Prologue to his great uncle's published letters, (ii) the Christ Church Gaudy Oration 1996, and (iii) the article on J W McPherson in the Oxford Dictionary of National Biography (2004). Nevertheless, I am assured by Dr C S Knighton, Principal Assistant Keeper of Archives at Clifton College, that McPherson was never a student at the school. Indeed, McPherson's own summary of his education for the Old Merchant Venturers' Club magazine article only mentions the College in relation to his employment there in the early 1890s as "Research Assistant to Prof. Shenstone".

8 Ibid, p. 20–21.

9 Humphrey Bowman (1942), *Middle East Window*, p. xiii (Introduction by Sir Ronald Storrs).

mathematics at the Khedivial Secondary School in central Cairo, would prove to be an exception to Storrs's rule.

On 1 October 1901, Joseph disembarked at Alexandria from *Le Congo*, an 1870's French steamer, and headed for Cairo, several hours away by train.

The titular head of Egypt at that time was 'Abbâs Hilmî II, who bore the title Khedive. To call the Khedive the country's "ruler", however, would be to overstate the case for two reasons: the first because Egypt was still officially part of the Ottoman Empire; the second because the British had occupied Egypt in 1882, and the man doing most of the ruling in 1901 was British Agent and Consul-General, Lord Cromer.

Cairo, like Alexandria, was remarkably cosmopolitan. The Khedive's relations and most of the rest of the upper class spoke Turkish, French and colloquial Egyptian, a form of Arabic that is quite distinct from that spoken elsewhere in the Arab world. There were also communities of Greeks, Italians, Armenians, Jews, all similarly multi-lingual. In contrast to this Europeanised population there were, of course, millions of native Egyptians, from the educated *effendi* middle-class to the soil-tilling peasants, or *fallâhîn,* whose lives had scarcely changed over a thousand years.

The exotic atmosphere of Cairo at the turn of the last century was intoxicating to Joseph. His letters home overflow with excitement, as if he cannot believe his good fortune.

The Khedivial Secondary School, "a sort of Eton of Egypt" Joseph calls it, was the more exclusive of only two secondary schools for Egyptian boys in Cairo.[10] It was centrally located, just a few minutes' walk from the Khedive's 'Abdîn Palace. The school was held in high esteem by Cairo society, and distinguished graduates included prime minister Mustafa el-Nahhâs, poet Ahmed Shawqî, and journalist Lutfî el-Sayyid. Joseph's earliest letters home describe sailing on the Nile with, and invitations to meals at the homes of, two of his student friends, Ibrâhîm Zakî and Hâmid Mahmûd, the first of whom would become an eminent doctor and the second Minister of Hygiene.

All students and instructors at the school were required to wear a *tarbûsh* (fez), jacket and tie. The atmosphere was militaristic, but apt to be noisy and chaotic. Joseph, who taught chemistry and higher-level maths, had finally found work he enjoyed.

Those same early letters are noteworthy in another respect. During Joseph's first weeks in Cairo, he was already paying attention to Sufi ceremonies and

---

10 Carman and McPherson (1983), p. 27.

moulids. "I left... to follow... a party of the Zikr – religious fanatics who carry mysterious lanterns and invoke [the name of] Allah perpetually."[11] Some months later, he wrote a long description of a *zikr* to his brother Dougal, one which had taken place at night in Cairo's Bûlâq quarter, by the Nile. The crowd was large, and Joseph the only European there. With the drums, flutes and tambourines providing a frenetic ever-quickening rhythm,

> the party were gasping in earnest, most of them... swaying their bodies and several spun like tops and others contorted themselves horribly... For a moment or two, the noise stopped and subsided from sheer exhaustion, but a few rushed forward and danced wildly and with wonderful skill. Then one made an... inspired address, which he punctuated by stabbing himself with a sharp Sudanese spear, and as soon as one spear was thoroughly embedded he seemed to forget its existence and another was given him until he was bristling with steel.[12]

McPherson was entranced as he beheld one wondrous feat after another. Whatever the nature of these phenomena, they had also been witnessed and described, in the 1830s, by E. W. Lane in *The Manners and Customs of the Modern Egyptians*. Joseph would spend much of the rest of his life exploring the mysteries of the moulids, and Lane's book was for him a key source of information. Dougal passed this strange, impassioned letter to a friend at the Birmingham Cosmopolitan Club, where it was published in full as "The Zikr" by J. McPherson.

In 1904, Joseph transferred to the Ra's el-Tîn School in Alexandria. Little is known of what he did there during his two and a half year stay other than continue to teach; and that he speculated on the city's stock market and usually lost. The school was on the small peninsula between the eastern and western harbours, not far from Fort Qait Bey (site of the ancient Pharos). Alexandria was at the time one of the most beautiful cities on the Mediterranean and still deeply Hellenic in character. Lawrence Durrell was not yet born, but Cavafy was just getting into his stride as the city's poet.

On 31 August 1905, the topic of the day in *The Egyptian Gazette* was the previous day's total solar eclipse. Scientists, under the aegis of the Survey of Egypt, had come from Oxford, the US and Russia to view the phenomenon from Cairo,

---

11 Ibid, p. 30. The word *zikr* refers to the ceremony and not the people performing it, as he thinks at first.
12 Ibid, pp. 38–39.

Alexandria, Port Said and Suez; but their main focus of attention was at three positions further up the Nile: Edfu, Aswan and a small riverside village called Demhîd, 30 kilometres south of Aswan. The *Gazette* in its coverage mentions one "Mr MacPherson [sic] and Youssef Effendi [who were collecting the data] at Demhîd, south of the first cataract."[13]

In a long letter home, Joseph wrote that he and several assistants, having camped by the Nile the previous night, spent nearly the whole day of the 30th, "from 10.30 to 6.30", with a combination magnometer/telescope, taking hundreds of readings in very difficult conditions.

> Just as I had taken an absolute set of declination readings, with torsion, azimuth, etc., and was taking each minute a reading of the scale, the temperature which had been [in] previous days steady at about 41° (106°F) – a very pleasant temperature – ran up tremendously and shoals of burning sand were dashed over me and the instrument by violent gusts of wind...[14]

The whole endeavour, meanwhile, was watched suspiciously by a crowd of local Egyptians. As the sun began to disappear,

> ... suddenly a frenzied mob surged up the front more in terror than in anger. Nearly naked women and men and quite naked children! Our native guard of police had disappeared and the Omda (the Mayor of the district) had left command and was not to be seen. Only the Sheikh el-Balad (chief local magistrate) retained any idea of protecting us and when I appealed to him, he rained, in deadly terror himself, frantic blows on the heads and bodies of the villagers with a stout club.[15]

Amidst this chaos, Joseph carried on jotting down precise readings every fifteen seconds, yet managing at full eclipse to steal "two 8-second intervals to admire the marvellous light of the Corona flaming round the jet black moon." The next morning, their mission accomplished, Joseph and his team broke camp and sailed their felucca back to Helwân and home.[16] Neither the letter nor the

---

13 *The Egyptian Gazette*, 31 August 1905, article "At Assouan (From Our Special Correspondent)".
14 Carman and McPherson (1983), p. 56.
15 Ibid, p. 56–57.
16 Helwân, just south of Cairo, is the site of Egypt's main observatory.

newspaper reveals how the school science and maths teacher landed this prestigious few days' work, but that he did so is impressive.

Joseph continued working at the Ra's el-Tîn School until late 1906. There were
far fewer moulids in Alexandria than in Cairo, and in his book he admits, "My
ignorance about Alexandria moulids is complete... the more discreditable as I
have spent much time in 'Alex', living once in Ibrahimia [for] over two years."[17]

On 13 June 1906, an incident occurred at Denishwai, in the Nile Delta, which
brought enormous discredit to British control of Egypt. Officers of the Army of
Occupation caused a riot by shooting privately owned pigeons near the village.
After one officer died, draconian punishment was meted out to the local villagers
involved. Four were hanged, while others were jailed or flogged. "Denishwai"
sparked the rise of nationalist resentment and became a potent symbol of colonial
injustice. Cavafy expressed his revulsion thus:

And when they took him up the scaffold's steps
and passed the rope around him and strangled him,
the innocent boy, seventeen years old,
... piteously... hung inside the void,
with the spasms of black agony...
His mother, martyr, wallowed on the ground...[18]

Joseph apparently was abroad at the time, but the echoes of this ghastly event
would reverberate to 1919 (when, as *Ma'mûr Zapt*, it would be his job to help
control great crowds of rioters in Cairo) and far beyond. In the meantime, it also
brought about the fall of Cromer, even though he, too, had been away. He was
replaced as British Agent and Consul-General by the more liberal Eldon Gorst,
who tried to pacify the local population. In this, he was unsuccessful, and the
situation only worsened.

Joseph's third and final teaching job was at Cairo's Agricultural College, next
to the Zoological Gardens in Giza, where he began work in January 1907. Almost
immediately after returning to Cairo, he found himself in a dangerous situation:
"... a very unpleasant... incident occurred, a scoundrel attacking me with an
ancient pistol when I was shooting in a lonely spot, and I had to defend myself

---

17 Ibrâhîmîya is a city quarter to the east of the Library of Alexandria and west of Sîdî Gâber;
inhabited at the time by Greeks, Jews and other non-indigenous Alexandrians.
18 "27 June 1906, 2pm"; translation by Daniel Mendelsohn.

with my gun."[19] His servant managed to trip up the assailant, but going into a secluded area with a gun seven months after the Denishwai debacle was reckless, to say the least.

By 1909, the spirit of Egyptian nationalism had infiltrated the school system. Certain subjects which had been taught in English and French, such as mathematics, were now taught in Arabic. Egyptian teachers proved to be not as exacting as their European colleagues, and the pass mark was halved from 60 to 30. When the Europeans protested, the local Press got involved, taking the side of native teachers and students. Joseph wrote about furious students storming the test centre and the chief inspector having to be smuggled out the back "like St Paul".[20]

On 20 February 1910, there was another significant rise in the political temperature of Egypt, when Prime Minister Butros Ghâlî was assassinated by a 23 year-old university graduate named Ibrâhîm el-Wardânî. Butros Ghâlî was targeted for having presided over the court that issued the brutal sentences on the Denishwai villagers. But el-Wardânî was not the usual sort of nationalist. He had been educated in Paris and London; his father was the governor of a province and his uncle a *pâsha*. The issue was further complicated by the fact that Butros Ghâlî was a Coptic Christian. The assassin was seen by Egyptians as a national hero, and crowds of students thronged the streets of Cairo shouting

Wardânî! Wardânî!
illi 'atal el-Nasrânî

[Wardani, Wardani,
who killed the Christian][21]

Joseph was horrified at the jubilation among Muslims over the killing. He called on Butros Ghâlî's family to give his condolences and attended the funeral. El-Wardânî was hanged four months after the assassination, and his name, like "Denishwai", became a nationalist slogan for years to come.

Between 1907 and the advent of the First World War, Joseph travelled extensively. His published letters for this period shed little light on his teaching activities, but they are full of his impressions of the Mediterranean world outside of

---

19 Carman and McPherson (1983), p. 76–77.
20 Ibid, p. 79. Reference to St Paul, after his conversion, having to be smuggled out of a window in a basket to escape from an angry crowd (Acts 9:23–25).
21 Ronald Storrs (1937), *Orientations*, p.84.

Egypt. How he paid for this "vagabondage" (as he called it) is not clear, but certainly expatriate schoolteachers, in Joseph's time and for long after, often earned as much, if not more, from private lessons than they did in the classroom. In any case, Joseph's known travels over the seven years included Greater Syria (i.e., Syria plus Palestine and Lebanon), Monte Carlo, Capri, Turkey (twice), Sicily, Russia and England. On the whole, this touring is of little interest, but there is one exception.

In September 1909, shortly after the school examination fiasco, Joseph arrived at the port of Mersin (in south-eastern Turkey) with a view to riding on horseback across the Taurus mountains via the pass known as the Cilician Gates. Turkey at the time was in turmoil: the previous year, the Young Turks had seized power from the Sultan; a counter-revolution had failed; the Sultan was forced to abdicate; and through it all, the large Armenian Christian community in the southeast was increasingly subject to attack, with thousands being massacred. When Joseph arrived at Mersin, there were terrified refugees everywhere trying to get away to Cyprus. After many adventures (some embroidered in the telling),[22] he succeeded in reaching his destination, the town of Ereğli ... and this he did as planned, on horseback.

He proceeded by train to Konya, where he introduced himself to the British vice-consul of both that town and Mersin, Major Charles Doughty-Wylie. When the Armenian massacres had started, this distinguished soldier (who had served with Kitchener in the Sudan, the Second Boer War, and the Boxer Rebellion), had somehow managed to restore order in Mersin and nearby Adana, all with little help from the Ottoman authorities. Joseph spent a few hours with Doughty-Wylie and his wife, though both had been physically affected by the massacres. He had been shot in the arm at Adana; she was convalescing from a fever contracted in the hospital of that city, where she had been nursing sick and wounded Armenians. Six years later, both men would be at Gallipoli. Joseph would be wounded, and Doughty-Wylie would be killed in action and posthumously receive the Victoria Cross.

Before leaving Konya, Joseph visited the mausoleum of Galâl el-Dîn Rûmî and the *tekîya* (monastery) of the Mevlevi Order of Sufis known as the "whirling dervishes". The order exists in Egypt, also, and is mentioned by McPherson in the main text of this book.[23]

---

22 Writing to his brother Dougal, Joseph pretends he could understand the brigands' *sotto voce* conversation in Turkish, a very difficult language of which he had scant knowledge. While mounted on his horse in the Taurus mountains he studied a basic primer of the language entitled *Turkish Self-Taught*, by Thrimm & Hagopian, and practised words and phrases with his guide.

23 The Order is called Mevlevi in Turkey and Maulâwî in Egypt.

*

When the world war erupted in August 1914, Egypt was for several months only indirectly involved. Kitchener, who had succeeded Gorst as Consul-General upon the latter's death in 1911, was away in England, where Prime Minister Asquith appointed him Secretary of State for War. In Kitchener's absence, the most important British official in Egypt was now the senior military officer, General John Maxwell, rather than the top Foreign Office representative as before.

Khedive 'Abbâs Hilmî, like Kitchener, was out of the country when the war began. He had gone to Constantinople on holiday, and there he had nearly been assassinated by another Egyptian nationalist, again a student. Severely wounded, he was still convalescing. He had never hidden his resentment over the British occupation of Egypt, and before he was well enough to travel, he received notice by telegram that henceforth he would be *persona non grata* in his own land. His anglophile uncle, Husein Kâmel, was declared "Sultan" of Egypt, and the title "Khedive" was now discarded.

In September, the German and Austrian diplomatic staffs were expelled, and citizens of those countries resident in Egypt were told to register or be arrested. Some 500 men of military age were sent to Malta for internment.

As the weeks passed, it became apparent to the British that the large Turkish-Egyptian population of over 30,000 was potentially a bigger problem than European enemy aliens. They had always tended to be more accepting of the occupation than the indigenous Egyptians, but the fact was that according to international law, Egypt was part of the Ottoman Empire, notwithstanding its nominal semi-independence; and there were some very distinguished Turks in Egypt who were also senior officers in the Turkish army. No matter how anglophile they were, the situation was clearly delicate. General Maxwell gambled – correctly, as it turned out – that his main problem would not be Egypt's Turks, but the native Egyptian army officers.

Although the Young Turks in Constantinople had initially wavered about which side to join in the conflict, by early November Britain and Turkey were at war, and General Maxwell declared martial law in Egypt. Before the end of 1914, British Intelligence would be warning of an Ottoman army forming in Syria with the intention of crossing Sinai to attack Egypt.

However, the Turks also had an effective intelligence service. They knew, for example, that the entire Army of Occupation, the 6000-man force behind the British presence in Egypt, had been sent to the Western Front early in the war and replaced by inexperienced territorials. In other words, General Maxwell was facing an invasion from the east without fully-trained soldiers. In his favour was the Suez Canal. The Turks would have to cross it; the British only had to defend it, and in those circumstances the Canal would be tantamount to the longest and widest moat in the world. Meantime, an obvious partial solution to the lack of British officers was found locally. Numerous retired British officers were working for the Egyptian government, and many volunteered to return to arms with their own country's forces in Egypt.

In the charged atmosphere of impending invasion, other able-bodied men offered to help fill the ranks of the depleted British force. For example, male members of the Gezira Sporting Club formed a volunteer reserve unit called the Pharaoh's Foot. Joseph McPherson was one of the volunteers in this unit, a sort of Anglo-Egyptian "Dad's Army", a Home Guard, which set about square-bashing and acquiring the basics of soldiering on the Club's grounds.

The Turkish invasion force reached the Suez Canal in early February 1915 and was easily defeated (without the help of the Pharaoh's Foot).

The next crisis to involve Anglo-Egypt came in April 1915 with the first Allied landings at Gallipoli. British and Commonwealth troops poured into Egypt, settled into large tent-cities, and waited to be shipped to the battle zone. Before long, wounded and sick were streaming back to Alexandria and Cairo, where hospitals in both cities filled far beyond normal capacity.

Joseph McPherson, having decided that parading at the Gezira Club was point-less and tedious, joined the Red Cross as "an officer". On 6 August 1915, the first day of the disastrous Suvla Bay landings, he was aboard the hospital ship *Neuralia* headed for the battle zone.[24] When the vessel anchored near the headland of Gaba Tepe on 10 August 1915,

the battle was in full swing, and I should think it is seldom a non-combatant...
has had such a magnificent view at close quarters. The Turkish guns in the
'Olive Grove' were enfilading the beaches on which we had to descend to
bring out the wounded. There was a continuous roar of musketry and machine
guns, and a constant booming of cannon, partly on shore but mainly from the
battleship behind us.[25]

That first day was one of furious activity for the Red Cross workers. Joseph

---

24 Suvla Bay is on the west coast the Gallipoli peninsula; Gaba Tepe is a headland a few miles to the south of the bay.
25 Carman and McPherson (1983), p. 137.

Map of the Gallipoli Area

spent it rushing round the wards of the ship, helping in the operating room, and collecting more casualties from shore.

> ... a small first batch of wounded came alongside, and a few of us went ashore with the boat to help in bringing more. We were soon in the thick of it. The beach and the gully behind it were full of wounded, dying and the dead, and as furious fighting was going on in the gully, an incessant hail of bullets came down, wounding or killing the already wounded, and their stretcher bearers and helpers... So busy was I for one, that I was only vaguely conscious of the ceaseless rattle of rifles and machine guns, of the whistle of bullets...[26]

The next day saw all-out attacks and counter-attacks in the sector, with stray bullets hitting several men on the decks of *Neuralia*. Joseph went to the beach on the ship's launch, but that night, still ashore, a shell burst in the sand behind him.

> I put my arm up to shield my head, and received a shower, apparently of sand and pebbles, which bruised and lacerated my arm and side. One bit, harder and sharper than the rest, a piece of the shrapnel itself, got me just above the elbow.[27]

Wounded and exhausted, Joseph was unable to get back to his ship that day. By the time he did return, a day later, septic poisoning and fever had set in. His four-day participation in the disastrous events at Gallipoli ended with him being hospitalised at the nearby island of Lemnos. That week, two notices appeared in *The Egyptian Mail* reporting on his condition. Meantime, with his wounded arm he penned a mostly illegible note to his family that he had received "...a mild dose of shrapnel... Had a great time. Would not have missed it for anything. Love, Joe."[28]

In a period of just over one week, 6 to 15 August 1915, the tally of Allied dead and wounded at Suvla Bay and adjacent Anzac Cove exceeded 18,000.

The Allies' ill-starred Gallipoli campaign ended in January 1916. In Egypt, the focus turned again towards Sinai, a large part of which the Ottomans still occupied.

Joseph spent four months recuperating, with his arm in a sling. At the age of nearly fifty, he might have taken a safe job with the Red Cross in Egypt, or

---

26 Ibid, p. 138.
27 Ibid, p. 144.
28 Ibid, p. 152.

returned to teaching. But when the sling came off, in December 1915, Joseph straightaway joined the Royal Army Service Corps and was assigned as a second lieutenant to a local formation called the Camel Transport Corps (CTC).

Over the next two years, the CTC supported the British Army in Sinai and Palestine. The majority of its 170,000 men were camel drivers, and their task was to keep water, food and supplies moving.[29] The first drivers were paid volunteers. However, when their numbers began to fall short, the British resorted to their authority over Egyptian officials under martial law, and those officials in turn press-ganged the needed camel drivers and other labour. This, naturally, caused resentment, as General Maxwell had promised at the start of the war that Egyptians would not be involved in it.

The CTC training camp was at 'Ain Shams, in the northeast part of Cairo. The location was convenient for Joseph, whose residence at the time was in nearby Heliopolis. But the work was strenuous and sometimes hazardous, as camels are notoriously bad natured. Joseph's military records for this period mention his multiple hospital visits due to bites and other injuries to legs, head and back.[30]

> ...one day, when superintending watering, I noticed a brute giving sidelong glances... and warned the Adjutant not to come too near him. I had hardly spoken when [the camel] left the water and came for me open-mouthed. As I turned the horse, his jaws met so near my bare knee that he covered it with foam. I was splendidly mounted, but the horse could not get sufficient pace on at once, and the camel missed me again, fixed his teeth in the pony's flank and hung on... My poor beast reared, tried to bolt and finally foundered in a pool of blood, quite done for... I came off scot-free, but a few days later was not so lucky. I was knocked down by a brute and got a nasty wound in the legs, which necessitated a small operation and made me a cripple for some time.[31]

Still limping in February 1916, Joseph was sent to Upper Egypt to find additional drivers and camels for the CTC. He was chosen because he spoke Arabic; he was successful because he was sensitive to the position of the people he was recruiting. He paid them fairly and avoided relying on his authority as a British officer.

---

29 Badcock, Lt-Col G. E., *A History of the Transport Services of the Egyptian Expeditionary Force, 1916–1917–1918* (1925) "Between the date of the formation of the Egyptian Camel Transport Corps in December 1915 to that of demobilisation in 1919, approximately 170,000 camel drivers and 72,500 camels saw service in the Corps." p. 23.
30 National Archives, WO 374/45322.
31 Carman and McPherson (1983), p. 160–1.

Map of Egypt and Sinai

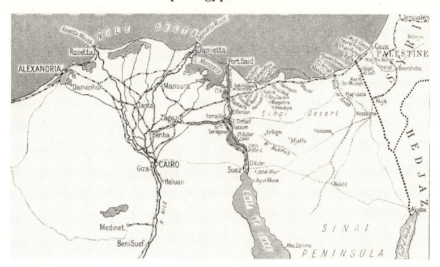

In March 1916, the Egyptian Expeditionary Force (EEF) was formed for the purpose of driving the Turks out of Sinai and Palestine. In June, the EEF seized the town of Romani, thirty kilometres east of Qantara (on the Suez Canal). The ejected Turks, however, remained in the vicinity, awaiting reinforcements from their main force further east. A few weeks later, the CTC's K Company, of which Joseph was a "section officer", was ordered to the front. Departing from 'Ain Shams on

... 21 July, we marched out with 2000 camels, 20 riding dromedaries, 12,000 natives, OC, Adjutant, 5 Sectional OCs including myself, a number of NCOs and the usual attendant... saddlers, ambulance, vets, batmen, orderlies, etc... Half and more of our company moved on to Romani, but my section and half of another were kept at [Q]antara from 26 July to 3 August.[32]

On this last day, the section moved into Sinai with orders to take water to the Worcestershire Yeomanry. The landscape between the Canal and Romani was a combination of high dunes, small oases, sandy plain, and several long, barren hills. The Worcesters were supposed to be at a small oasis about half-way to Romani, and the Turks, for all that Joseph knew, could be anywhere. The section arrived at the oasis to find that the Worcesters had moved on; indeed, were in the thick of battle behind a hill just to the north. Joseph, his section, camels and all, climbed the hill, where they had a clear view of the fighting. The EEF appeared to have the upper hand. Some Turks were surrendering; others fighting on; and their artillery was in action from a palm grove just below where Joseph was standing. Overhead, a German bi-plane was circling.

...I was so fascinated by the sight, and it was so theatrical and dramatic, that I felt rather like the occupant of a stage box at the fifth Act of a tragedy.[33]

Joseph was still wondering how to reach the Worcesters, presumably some-where among the cavalry below, when a second enemy bi-plane swooped down, firing on his position. This caused a stampede of camels but no casualties. Col-lecting men and animals, he descended the hill and hurried towards an oasis on the west side of what had recently been the battlefield, but was now held by the EEF. It was late in the afternoon, and the Red Cross was already there, tending

---

32 Ibid, p. 163–4.
33 Ibid, p. 169.

the wounded. There was no sign of the Worcester Yeomanry, but parched soldiers from other regiments thronged round the CTC's water cans. At 9pm, Joseph
moved the unit to a safer position westward. The Turks, meanwhile, were relocat-
ing to the east to get closer to their main force.

> …at midnight, after a twenty-one-hour day and fifteen and a half hours in the
> saddle without food except a few biscuits nibbled on the march, I settled down
> to bully beef and tea, and made an attempt at sleeping.[34]

Joseph spent the rest of 1916 in Sinai, providing water and supplies to the EEF
as it pushed the Turks back to their main camp at el-'Arîsh. By Christmas week,
the Turks had evacuated that town. Their next strong garrison was at Gaza, on the
south-western coast of Palestine.

The EEF began their assault there in late March 1917:

> …our troops made a disastrous attempt to rush Gaza, and our dead and
> wounded reached many hundreds; I should think, probably, thousands… One
> of our CTC officers with a convoy of 180 camels and 95 men taking water to
> the trenches came under heavy shell fire and only seven camels and two men
> escaped.[35]

In fact, EEF casualties in this first battle at Gaza were over 4000, more than
twice the number for the Ottoman defenders.

On 30 March 1917, Joseph was in casual conversation with Colonel Whit-
tington, the CTC commander, when the latter asked Joseph "if [he] would like
to go up to the firing line". He jumped at the suggestion and was soon working
near the front as a volunteer with a company of Royal Engineers. During this
brief interlude away from CTC duties, Joseph again found himself at the scene
of battle.[36] His letter describing this period tells of aeroplanes fighting overhead;
artillery shells exploding; having to crawl on his belly on a reconnaissance trip to
identify where the latest Turkish trenches were. He was also exhilarated to be able
to attend Easter Mass (8 April 1917) to the sound of whizzing bullets and "…the
crump of trench mortar shells and the rattle of machine guns…"[37]

---

34 Ibid, p. 170.
35 Ibid, p. 185–6.
36 Ibid, p. 190. The date of Joseph's return to CTC duties is uncertain. At the start of the 2nd
Battle of Gaza, 17 April 1917, he appears to be still with the Royal Engineers.
37 Ibid, p. 189.

A second EEF attempt to take Gaza began on 17 April 1917. It, too, failed and its casualties were even higher than at the first battle. A week later, Joseph was again wounded, this time "sniped in the leg".[38] He was not seriously hurt, but his days on desert battlefields were over. He was told (9 May 1917) "to proceed for duty under the Director of Public Security, Ministry of the Interior".[39] Back in Cairo, he was promoted to the rank of major (in Egypt, *bimbâshî*) and temporarily assigned to take charge of political prisoners being held at Giza.

*

Butros Ghâlî's assassination in 1910 had demonstrated the inadequacy of the existing political intelligence service (i.e., the secret police), which had been created by the Ottomans to protect the Khedive and government officials. The person most involved with implementing this change was Harvey Pasha, Commandant of the Cairo City Police.[40] The head, officially called the *Ma'mûr Zapt*,[41] of the revised secret police, was appointed by Harvey;[42] and his appointee was Philippides Bey, a Levantine Christian. In an official memo, Harvey would later write: "Its organisation and supervision I placed entirely in the hands of Philippides Bey."[43] Unfortunately, Harvey's appointee was corrupt. For the next seven years, Philippides used his position to engage in bribery and extortion on a massive scale. Disquieting rumours eventually began to circulate, but Philippides was Harvey's protégé and close to a number of high-ranking Egyptians. The case against him was finally confirmed by Thomas Russell, later famous as Russell Pasha, but then the Assistant Commandant of the Cairo police, whose immediate superior was, of course, Harvey. Russell took irrefutable evidence of Philippides' crimes direct to the senior British official in the Ministry of the Interior;[44] Harvey resigned;

---

38 Ibid, p. 203.

39 British National Archives (Kew), WO 374/45322.

40 Sir George Samuel Abercrombie Harvey (Pasha), KBE, CMG, (1854–1930).

41 "ma'mûr" is a noun meaning "a civil officer or an official"; "zapt" (more properly "dabt") is a noun meaning "control" and related to cognates referring to the police, e.g., dâbit, an officer. So, a literal translation of "ma'mûr zapt" would be "an official [having] control". The words are Arabic, but the title and grammatical construct is Turkish. Military ranks in Egypt were in Turkish rather than Arabic until well into the 20th century. Hence, "bimbâshî" for major.

42 The official name of this force was the Central Special Office (CSO).

43 British National Archives (Kew), FO 141/474, "Note on the Special Political Office of the Cairo City Police".

44 Sir Ronald Graham, Adviser to the Minister of the Interior, who in such matters certainly had more power than the Minister.

Russell replaced him as Commandant; and Philippides was tried, convicted and sent to jail.

The newspaper coverage was extensive, and Joseph must have known about these events. He appears, however, to have been indifferent to them even though the detention camp he was running at Giza was under the supervision of the *Ma'mûr Zapt*.

Joseph got on well with the prisoners. We know that he was proud of having formed and trained a soccer team from among the internees; and that he suspected that some of them had been locked up for failing to pay the stipulated bribe to Philippides. Joseph had been at the camp for seven months when the authorities finally chose a new *Ma'mûr Zapt*, and to his absolute surprise, they chose him.

Looking back on this period three years later, Joseph wrote:

> I do not think that I was at all interested in this *cause célèbre* [the court case], except so far as it threw light on the guilt or comparative innocence of my political internees; but suddenly as I was looking to be sent back to the campaign in Palestine, where I had been supremely happy, I found myself shovelled, willy-nilly, into this invidious post of honour and power.
>
> Those who put me in may have looked to an Englishman to break the traditions of corruption and extortion; or they may have intended me as a harmless figurehead who would not in any way interfere with their own plans.[45]

In appointing Joseph to this position, the authorities doubtless intended to achieve both these aims. Did he realise that he was being handed a poisoned chalice? Probably not, since he says he had not been interested in newspaper accounts of the scandal. And what qualifications did he have for the job? For a non-native speaker of Arabic, his command of the language was far better than that of most Anglo-Egyptians (though claims that he could pass as a native Egyptian are not credible); and he showed courage under fire in battle. On the other hand, he was 52 years old with no experience as a policeman. Nor is it obvious that he possessed the cunning required for the successful pursuit of criminals or political agitators.

Nevertheless, on 22 January 1918, Bimbâshî Joseph McPherson was put in charge of the Egyptian secret police. His official title was acting-*Ma'mûr Zapt*, which clearly meant that the appointment was contingent upon satisfactory

---

45 Carman and McPherson (1983), p. 204–5.

performance of the work. In theory, Joseph reported to the Cairo police commandant, that is, to Thomas Russell, although the two were seldom in touch. His
main support came from a small team of professionals, including a legal adviser;
an adjutant, "...a remarkably straight and nice man, with 37 years' experience in
the Egyptian police"; and an assistant-*Ma'mûr Zapt*, named Abraham Dykes.[46]
Joseph thought all three were first-rate men.[47]

Joseph appears to have assumed his new position with virtually no training.

[Russell] handed me a couple of keys, explaining that they were the sole
keys that opened a box fastened to the wall outside the Governorate [48], in a
rather obscure place, in which from time immemorial had been deposited
petitions, denunciations, and all sorts of secret matter[s], which it was one
of the functions of the Mamur Zapt to deal with. At the same time, he gave
the secret register for these matters, and presented me to the Special Secret
Clerk, a highly educated youth, whose two duties were to help me with these
documents, and to keep his mouth shut.[49]

In 1918, the principal threat to the British in Egypt was not crime as such, but
rising nationalism. Great Britain had many friends in the country, but the fact was
that *most* Egyptians yearned for an end to the Occupation. Three years earlier, T.
E. Lawrence, working for the Arab Bureau, had written: "The Egyptian towns-
men do hate us so. I thought it was only a coldness... but it is a most burning
dislike."[50] His equally brilliant colleague in military intelligence, Aubrey Herbert,
recollected a few years later: "Many of the English thought that we were living on
a sleeping volcano" and "...one used sometimes to get black looks in the bazaar
and scowls from the class of Effendis".[51]

Joseph's letters from 1918 do not give the impression that he understood the
dangerous level of this discontent. He writes to amuse family and friends in
England. His letters begin to bear titles as in detective stories: the case of "The
Golden Needle" or "The Beautiful She-Devil and her Mate". He now seemed to
be performing two roles simultaneously: Holmes *and* Conan Doyle. His great

---

46 His actual surname was Mordekovitch. Before working with the secret police, he was Chief
Ticket Controller of the Egyptian State Railways. Cf. FO 841/182/52.
47 Carman and McPherson (1983), p. 205–6.
48 A building located in Bâb el-Khalq, just east of 'Abdîn Palace.
49 Carman and McPherson (1983), p. 207–8.
50 D. Garnett (1938), *The Letters of T. E. Lawrence*, letter to Hogarth, 2 February 1915.
51 Aubrey Herbert (n.d.), *Mons, Anzac & Kut*, pp. 88 and 90.

nephew described Joseph as "… something of an actor… who would play with some swagger any part life assigned him".[52] Sometimes accounts of his successful cases appeared in the local press: "The Cairo mamur zabt [sic] has raided a house…where gambling was carried on and confiscated L.E. [Egyptian Pounds] 95"; and "Bimbashi McPherson… while bicycling… smelt the odour of hashish, and seeing a boy run at great speed, followed him to a room where he found men smoking the drug. One man was taken to the *caracol*".[53] These are hardly cases for which Egypt needed the secret police, although to be fair there are also two articles about Joseph's men raiding and closing down printing presses for seditious leaflets.

"John" Gayer-Anderson, who knew Joseph well for many years, wrote an amusing description of his friend's police activities, which tends to corroborate that he was "in over his head" as *Ma'mûr Zapt*.

> I once accompanied Mac when he was raiding a political suspect's house in the Mousky. He was strangely quixotic and at the same time in many ways worldly; and always quite unpractical. This raid which he had carefully organised in some parts, but had left completely unorganised in others, turned into a ridiculous fiasco. We reached the dwelling quite unsuspected. We forced the door, but as Mac and his men poured up one well-guarded stair, the suspects poured down another that was not guarded at all, and escaped. This was typical of all his efforts.
>
> No matter what happened, however, he always had a marvellous and quite incredible tale to tell of each of his adventures, a tale which he succeeded in bringing himself sincerely to believe after he had tried it over once or twice. His fertile imagination and facile credence made each adventure, when related, follow the form of those dark and intricate transactions usually met with only in a thriller or on the screen, wherein the atmosphere is redolent of spies, counter-espionage, marked cards, poisoned coffee, daggers, automatics, blackmail, bloodstains, murders and abductions – in all of which the highest in the land as well as the most desperate villain and lowest scum are involved.[54]

The touch of "keystone cops" comedy in the first paragraph of this passage is meant in good humour, but there can be little doubt that Joseph's innate

52 Carman and McPherson (1983), p. 22.
53 Ibid, p. 208. The Turkish word "caracôl" [*polis karakolu*] means "police station".
54 Major Robert ["John"] Gayer-Anderson, unpublished memoir.

Robert "John" Grenville Gayer-Anderson (1881–1945).

eccentricity became more pronounced under the pressure of trying to do work for which he was unsuited.

In November 1918, the world war ended, and Anglo-Egypt's descent into revolutionary nightmare began. Two days after the signing of the Armistice, Sa'd Zaghlûl, the leader of Egypt's nationalist Wafd Party, announced that he wished to attend the Peace Conference to make the case for Egypt's independence. The senior British administrator in Cairo, High Commissioner Reginald Wingate, referred Zaghlûl's request to London, advising that it be granted.[55] The Peace Conference began mid-January 1919 with the request still unanswered. By then, Zaghlûl's popular support was soaring; nationalist agitation was on the increase; and on 8 March 1919, Zaghlûl was arrested and deported to Malta. Inevitably, this sparked violent outbursts across the country. Joseph was involved in the attempted clampdown without fully realising the seriousness of the situation:

> [10 March 1919] …a rowdy mob looted the shops in the Muski, and played the fool generally. They passed the Governorate and commenced to smash the windows there also, and I had a lot of fun with Russell Bey… and my assistant Dykes, chasing them at the head of bodies of police troops and men [from the Sultan's Guards].[56]

The first fatalities occurred the next day in the city of Tantâ (in the Nile Delta), when a mob rushed the railway station and 14 were killed. From then on, the tally rose quickly.

> [13 March] "… the big tram depot at Shubra was attacked, and the crowd [was] only beaten off when two or three had been shot.[57]

> [14 March, the crowd were] "… excited to such a point that [they] attacked a patrol in the Muski, firing revolvers into an armoured car … and smashing and looting houses and shops. They only desisted when … twelve of them were dead."[58]

> [15 March] Denunciations, mostly anonymous, reached me in shoals, and

---

55 The title "British Agent and Consul-General" had been replaced by that of High Commissioner in 1915.
56 Carman and McPherson (1983), p. 222–3.
57 Ibid, p. 223.
58 Ibid, p. 224.

appeals for help came in constantly by telephone, or by letter, or by word of mouth.[59]

On 18 March 1919, the most gruesome incident took place when a mob boarded a train at Dairût (midway between Cairo and Luxor) and killed seven unarmed British soldiers and a prison inspector, mutilating their bodies in the process.

Wingate was in Paris at the time, attending the Peace Conference, so General Allenby was sent to Egypt with a brief to placate the situation if he could, but in one way or another to end the spreading violence.

For Joseph, the worst day of the 1919 uprising must have been 3 April 1919, when his assistant, Abraham Dykes ("a splendid fellow"[60]), was murdered in front of 'Abdîn Palace. Dykes had arrived there in a military car to find a patrol of Australian Light Horsemen attempting to break up a large mob. When he descended from the car to try to help, he was shot in the back. The crowd then turned on the Australians, pulling two of them to the ground. The soldiers managed to escape by firing their revolvers at their attackers, but the enraged rioters then turned to Dykes' body and defiled it.[61] Joseph claimed to know that Dykes' killer was one of the Sultan's Guards – that is, someone who was supposed to be helping the authorities to restore order.[62]

The murder clearly had a profound effect on Joseph, the more so as rumour spread that he had been the intended target. He had never been particularly interested in politics apart from a rather vague belief in the benefits to all and sundry of the British occupation of Egypt. After Dykes' murder, his attitude towards the Nationalists hardened, and his now oft expressed opinion of British policy was that it was too soft *vis-à-vis* criminals, rioters, Zaghlûl and the Egyptian Government. Indeed, Joseph especially disapproved of Allenby, who, in his opinion, went too far in seeking to mollify the local population. Just three days after the deadly riot in 'Abdîn Square, Allenby announced that Zaghlûl would be released from internment[63] and that the five-year-old martial law would be lifted.

Joseph was appalled at this turn of events:

---

59 Ibid, p. 224.
60 Ibid, p. 226.
61 McGuirk, R., *Light Car Patrols, 1916–19: War and Exploration in Egypt and Libya with the Model T Ford* (2013), p. 113.
62 Carman and McPherson (1983), p. 226.
63 Zaghlûl would be re-arrested in late 1921 and deported to the Seychelles. He was allowed to return to Egypt in 1923.

[3 May] Secret agents reported to me a monster procession coming from
Al-Azhar, down the Nahasin [quarter] towards Mohammed Ali Square.
The riotous units had been organised and to some extent armed within the
[Al-Azhar University] Mosque, at leisure and with impunity, for that master
jackass Allenby still upholds the fiction of its inviolability and sanctity, in
spite not merely of my protests, and common sense, but against the urgent
prayers of the better-minded sheikhs of the University.[64]

Joseph carried on as *Ma'mûr Zapt* for another year, until spring 1920. Rioting
in the streets was largely under control by mid-May, but there was still civic
unrest, and the occasional murder of English officials continued. Where Joseph
had been impressively unshakeable under fire in Gallipoli and at Gaza, he was
now increasingly nervous in the belief that he, as an Englishman and head of the
secret police, was an obvious target for the extremists. He was never particularly
competent as *Ma'mûr Zapt*, and now the effectiveness of the whole secret police
division was being questioned. In January 1920, Thomas Russell, wrote that the
force was "not satisfactory"; and a second document from this period reveals that
Intelligence Specialist General Wyndham Deedes suggested "doing away with the
Mamur Zapt and giving the work to the commandant of police" (i.e., to Russell).[65]
Joseph was now seriously stressed and anxious to leave his job. In the week 24
February to 3 March 1920, he sent no fewer than six memos to Russell describing
ostensible plots to assassinate the *Ma'mûr Zapt*. Shortly thereafter, Joseph did
resign, and one may assume that Russell did not object.[66]
     Throughout his two years as head of the secret police, Joseph was still officially
in the British Army. "Demobbed" at last in August 1920, he went back to England
for his first home-leave in six years.[67] This was a much-needed opportunity to
recover from the accumulated stress of four years of war and two of revolution.
The holiday seems to have served him well, as far as one can tell from his letters.
When it was over, and he was returning to Egypt, he was recognisably his old self.
He broke the journey in Paris for a short stay, and went out of his way to pay his

---

64 Carman and McPherson (1983), p. 231.
65 National Archives (Kew), FO 848/6. Both reports in the same file.
66 Of all the officials known by the Editor to have worked with Commandant Thomas Russell,
McPherson is the only one not to have received some mention of commendation in *The
London Gazette*. Nor is he mentioned at all in Russell's autobiography *Egyptian Service 1902–
1946* (1949), despite the book's exhaustive coverage of the Philippides scandal.
67 On 18 August 1920, cf. WO 374/45322. Confirmed in *Supplement to The London Gazette*,
18 October 1920.

Sir Thomas Wentworth Russell (1879–1954), known in Egypt as Russell Pasha. He was the commandant of the Cairo City Police when McPherson was the Ma'mûr Zapt.

respects to Saʻd Zaghlûl, who was staying at the luxurious Grand-Hôtel. Zaghlûl may have been the embodiment of Egyptian Nationalism, but he had also been Minister of Education for two years when Joseph was a school teacher. This gracious social call in Paris contrasts sharply with Joseph's reaction in Cairo, shortly before going on holiday, when he had received an invitation from "His Excellency the High Commissioner and the Viscountess Allenby" to attend the celebration at the Residency of George V's birthday. Asked to RSVP, Joseph wrote on the card "No damn fears," "Anarchy & Shame!", "Invitation rejected. J.W.McP."[68]

Back in Egypt at the end of 1920, Joseph was still in the Civil Service, and retirement was four years away. He secured a post as Intelligence and Passport Control officer at Qantara, on the Suez Canal. Other civil servants might have found this a lonely outpost, but Joseph was delighted with the new job.

I have excellent quarters, I should think the best in all [Q]antara. I feel *chez moi*, but have full membership of the H.Q. mess, the club, &c. Everyone from Earl Stadbrooke, the Base Commander to the Mascot Murasla, who brings me G.R.O.s and other important documents... at odd hours of day and night, are most complaisant and friendly. I have wangled ... all I can want in this world; and there is a pack of hounds, tennis, swimming, cricket, &c.

By order of G.S. "I", G.H.Q., I was appointed G.S. Intelligence Officer pro temps, and A/O.E.T.A. Officer... and at once used my military status...for drawing liquors from the Canteen. My eyes are cheered, as I execute this my virgin typing, by a row of bottles including, Green Chartreuse, Benedictine, Whisky, Vermouth and Beer.[69]

Joseph was responsible for examining the identity and travel documents of all travellers through this border post, located 50 km south of Port Said. The names of suspicious-looking individuals were checked against a "black list" containing thousands of names.

I was happily allowed a very free hand, and had full authority to stop anyone on suspicion, even if his papers were perfect; or to pass anyone who was

68 Carman and McPherson (1983), p. 233.
69 G.R.O.s: General Routine Orders; G.S. "I": General Staff, Intelligence; G.H.Q: General Headquarters; and A/O.E.T.A. Officer: Assistant/Occupied Enemy Territory Administration Officer. "Earl Stadbrooke" is probably a reference to George E. J. M. Rous, 3rd Earl of Stradbroke, who was with the Territorial Army in Egypt. This 1920 letter was in the McPherson Archive temporarily at the Bristol Record Office.

technically without valid authority if I believed him to be harmless and his error unintentional so that I came to run my control almost entirely on impression.[70]

Late in 1921, Joseph was transferred back to the Department of Public Security in Cairo. Once again, he was in the business of suppressing crime in the city streets, but working in a different department and at a much lower level than when he was *Ma'mûr Zapt*. He was now desk-bound in what he called "the dossier garden".

All attempts to enforce order were hampered as usual by Allenby's asininity… gutter urchins … commandeer[ing] the trams and, with the help of bigger roughs, … overturning and burning them [once they were] tired of riding on the tops.[71]

The Egyptian political scene was changing rapidly. In February 1922, at Allenby's urging, the British Government announced formally, but unilaterally, that the British Protectorate was ending; that Egypt was on track to becoming an independent and sovereign state, though Britain would reserve to itself powers and rights to ensure the security of foreigners and to protect the Suez Canal; and that Sultan Fu'ad, who had succeeded his elder brother as ruler in 1917, would become King Fu'ad. This development pleased neither Egyptian nationalists, nor British imperialists, the former objecting to Britain's reserved powers and rights; the latter insisting on continued British control of Egypt. As a consequence of this impasse, violence flared up again, especially in Cairo.

In May 1922, an inspector of the Cairo City Police was assassinated.[72] The killing followed seven unsuccessful attempts on the lives of British subjects over the preceding three months for which no arrests had been made. The man ultimately responsible for finding assassins was, of course, Thomas Russell. He summoned men with experience in countering nationalist extremists to help in this latest emergency, and one of these was Joseph McPherson.

Near the end of 1922, I was dug up, to my joy, and put on to my old Secret Police Work; for assassinations of Englishmen, bombings and all sorts of

---

70 Carman and McPherson (1983), p. 255.
71 Ibid, p. 259.
72 Bimbâshî Wilfred Cunliffe Cave, Assistant Commandant, B Division, Cairo Police.

outrages were becoming of common occurrence, in spite of Allenby's 'bruta fulmina' [stupid thunder claps], posted up everywhere, that any unauthorised person in possession of arms or trading in them would suffer the pain of death.

I was not reinstated as Head of Secret Police... Bimbashi B[aker] occupied that chair...[73]

Joseph was now working "free-lance" for his old department from several basement rooms in Heliopolis, twelve kilometres northeast of Cairo.[74] This office space belonged to an Italian wine-importer, and *secret-agent* Joseph became Signor Martino "...of Italian father and American mother (oh, horrible thought) ...". Joseph's account of what he accomplished in this guise is vague. Apparently, he threatened two scoundrels ("against whom I had hanging evidence") into helping him, and "these two in their turn brought other flies into our parlour".[75]

One is left wondering to what degree these efforts helped curtail assassinations and bombings. In any case, it was not long before Russell reassigned Joseph to the police campaign against narcotics trafficking, and his letter to Joseph about the new and important position shows no sign of scepticism about the latter's qualifications to undertake it.

[Drug trafficking] is literally ruining the race, physically and morally, and as I am always rubbing it into the Government, we Police are practically powerless, as long as its use and traffic [are] barely an offence legally. Thank God, they are at last formulating stringent laws against drugs, and my idea is for you and your dope squad to raid enough to keep the public satisfied, and to take advantage of the present relative openness with which the drug-mongers ply their traffic, to register and card them, and that when the law makes it a crime and gives us the power to deal with them severely and effectively, we can mobilise all our forces and round them up *en masse*.[76]

Joseph was given a former soldier as second-in-command, "an ex-NCO, Berry,

73 Carman and McPherson (1983), pp. 259–60. Major Douglas Baker (1884–1958) was, like McPherson, at Gallipoli in 1915, where he was awarded the Military Cross and twice mentioned in despatches. A close associate of Russell's, he had worked in Intelligence at Army headquarters in Cairo before transferring to the City Police.
74 McPherson had been living in Heliopolis for several years before the war and may have gone back to that area after it. He moved to Giza in 1925.
75 Carman and McPherson (1983), p. 261.
76 Ibid, pp. 262–3.

who was keen, shrewd and intelligent and had a natural flair for this kind of game", as well as several police agents experienced in fighting drugs.

> To these we added sundry 'confidants' drawn from the ranks of dope fiends, and dope dealers. I gave up Café Maraschino [the "office" in Heliopolis] and was authorised to take a five-roomed flat in Abdin...[77]

Joseph describes only one raid from this, his last position with the Egyptian Civil Service. It was carried out in Shâri' Wagh el-Birka (north of the Ezbekîya Gardens), which Joseph describes as "the Boulevard Clichy of Cairo", which presumably implies a street of louche artists and avant-garde cabarets, but there were also – Joseph writes – shops where hashish and other drugs were sold.

> "...Berry and I simply strolled down the street with a large party of agents, confidants, and ordinary police in plain clothes, and dropped a couple of each at each shop to immobilise the occupants. Then, when our force was exhausted, we walked back and searched shops and owners one by one, and found cocaine, hashish or other drugs in every one..., with one exception."[78]

Out of that exception, Joseph weaves a long and bizarre story of how he and his men out-smarted (i) the shop attendant, a young Libyan with Italian nationality who could not legally be searched because he, like other foreigners, was under the jurisdiction of his Consul;[79] (ii) the Italian Consul, who himself was a rogue and suspected of smuggling arms to the nationalists; and (iii) the Consul's *kavass* (consulate policeman) whose presence was required at the arrest. At the story's end, the Libyan is jailed for selling drugs; and the Consul finds himself in trouble with Mussolini because Joseph's friend, the Italian wine-importer in Heliopolis, denounces the man to the Italian authorities as a traitor.[80]

In November 1924, a band of Egyptian students murdered Major-General Sir Lee Stack in the streets of Cairo. Stack was Sirdar (commander-in-chief) of the Egyptian Army and Governor General of the Sudan. The Egyptian Prime Minister at the time was Sa'd Zaghlûl, who had finally returned to Egypt to become the country's first democratically-elected head of government. Because of the killing,

---

77 Ibid, p. 263.
78 Ibid, p. 263.
79 Called the Capitulations, this system dated back to when Egypt was an Ottoman province. It was still in force in the 1920s.
80 Carman and McPherson (1983), p. 264.

Zaghlûl was forced to step down; and Allenby was blamed more than ever for having been responsible for letting matters get out of control. Joseph was characteristically forthright when a member of the Turf Club suggested congratulating Allenby for forcing Zaghlûl's resignation after the murder.

> If anyone is such an ass as to go and flatter the master jackass… after fouling our pitch and [that of the Egyptians] for years, trampling on our prestige and every sane basis of government… let him go. I, for one, would rather shake hands with old Zaghlul. He has been treated like a mouse by a very cruel and silly cat: allowed again and again to run as he liked and then clawed back. He, at least, has remembered his friends… Allenby has let down his supporters, [both] Egyptian and English… Go to him, by all means, and tell him if he wants to benefit England and Egypt, for God's sake, to clear out![81]

*

Late in 1924, Joseph finally retired from the Egyptian Civil Service. He was 58 years old and had only just passed the mid-point of his 45-year stay in Egypt. He would now be, as he put it, "free as the sea".[82]

As in 1901, when he went to Egypt seeking a complete change, he now left urban Cairo and moved to the farming village of Bein el-Saryât, just west of Giza. There, he bought an old villa that had been the property of the Franciscan Order; the building was run-down, but it came with a small orchard of fruit trees: orange, fig, guava and mango. He called the property "Porziuncula", which is the name of the tiny church inside the Basilica of Santa Maria degli Angeli near Assisi and the place where the Franciscan movement originated.

Joseph set about re-inventing himself as a part-time gentleman farmer. He grew vegetables, planted corn; and he had an assortment of farm animals. By the summer of 1925, he was proudly reporting to his family that he owned 87 chickens, 50 rabbits, 100 pigeons, four goats, a lamb and a donkey.[83] To help Joseph run the farm, he enlisted the family of his personal servant since 1916, Gad el-Moula: Gad was "majordomo", his wife was dairymaid in charge of milking

---

81 Ibid, p. 266.
82 Ibid, p. 269.
83 Ibid, p. 270.

and cheese-making, while other relatives comprised the rest of the servant staff –
cook, gardener, etc.

Porzicuncula remained Joseph's main residence for the rest of his life. Gad
and his family were utterly devoted and, before long, could run the property when
Joseph was absent. He took advantage of this and began to travel again – to the
Greek islands, Italian-occupied Libya, French-occupied Tunisia.

For occasions when he wished to be in Cairo, to visit moulids for example, he
still had a small flat in the city centre, and that, too, he retained for all his remaining years.

In 1932, a young anthropologist came to Cairo to lecture at Fuad I University (now Cairo University), his speciality being tribal religion in the upper Nile
region. Edward Evans-Pritchard was renowned for his brilliant fieldwork while
living among the Azande and Nuer peoples of the Sudan. When he and Joseph met,
they had a common interest: Joseph had come to realise that there was a marked
Sudanese influence on certain aspects of Egyptian moulids. The two became close
friends and began to visit the moulids together. Evans-Pritchard left Egypt in
1934, but not before suggesting to Joseph that he undertake a serious study of the
moulids for publication. Joseph, then 68 years-old, was enthusiastic about the idea,
and most of the dated moulid visits described in his book are from 1934 onwards.

In a letter written by Joseph soon after his friend's departure, he addresses
Evans-Pritchard as "Bakurĕmi", this being the word in the Zande language for
"blood-brother". Indicative of Joseph's excitement over the project, and the
warmth of their relationship, while touching on key aspects of the moulids, it is
worth quoting in full.[84]

Porziuncula, Bein el Saryat, 18 July 1934

Dear Bakurĕmi,

Moulids: There has been an almost continuous succession of excellent
moulids, of which Sheikh Farag and Sheikh Nasr are quite new to me, and if
your gentle urging ever overcomes my lazy inertia, and I write my book, there
will be a good deal of new matter (though the behaviour of Qara Goz in the
Punch and Judy shows, and the phallic and lesbian dancings and much else
will have to be left in Arabic, as English versions of Boccaccio and Petronius
leave passages in Italian and Latin). At the moulid of Fatima el-Nebawiya,

---

84 Ibid, pp. 282–3.

there were several booths of a type new to me, but probably you met with
them in more southern Africa. Jet-black boys and girls danced to strange
instruments – the *Ringa*, in a sort of shrine, which was like a small piano
with the jumps, the *mugrizan*, a sort of zither, the *shackshackas*, like cocktail
slings, and a barrel-shaped *tabla* which at times made a noise like guns firing;
the whole a kind of jazz in its primitive *désinvolture*. Booza was passed round
in bowls, and some got very merry.

  Music: After a couple of little dinners here recently in the garden, the boys
and little Zenab Warda, and Antar, have given alfresco displays of quarter-
staff, dancing, mummery, and music, and elicited considerable applause
from the guests, but when Sencourt's boy has danced in with *Sigat* or *Tarr*,
or led with the *Darabuka*, he has brought down the house, and I have handed
castanets to the English ladies and they have danced in too.

  Vale: All here deeply lament your departure. All the villagers, including
my own boys, particularly love you because of the hearty way you return
their salaams, and the human way you laugh and wrestle with them. If you
disappear again into the heart of Africa, as seems imminent, this must be a
most valuable asset and help in research, and a powerful weapon to ward off
dangers from savage primitives.

  Vale, si possis cito veni![85]

Yours,
Mac

*

In April 1936, King Fu'ad died and was succeeded by 16-year-old King Farouk.
The year was an important milestone on Egypt's path to independence. An Anglo-
Egyptian Treaty was signed in August, superseding the 1922 declaration; signa-
tories were the current premier, Nahhâs Pasha, and British Foreign Secretary,
Anthony Eden. The new document stipulated that Egypt was "independent", but
with qualifications, e.g.: the UK would withdraw all troops from the country,
except those needed to protect the Suez Canal; its troops would not be transferred
until new barracks were ready; troops in Alexandria could remain for 8 years; the
UK would defend Egypt against attack; in case of war, Egypt would provide all
facilities and assistance to British forces.

---

85 "Farewell. Come back soon if you can."

Once again, the nationalists protested, but the international situation in 1936 was already menacing. The Italians were at war in Ethiopia, and as they also occupied Libya, Farouk feared they would invade Egypt. By the terms of the Treaty, and because of the young king's fears, British troops were still in Egypt when the Second World War began.

Throughout this whole period Joseph worked on his book, and roughly when the war started, it was ready for publication. He found a publisher in The Nile Mission Press, located on Shâri' el-Manâkh near Opera Square and the Ezbekîya Gardens. *The Moulids of Egypt* was published in 1941.

Joseph was now in his mid-70s and suffering from heart disease. For any business he had in Cairo, he took to riding his donkey into the city. Many years after the war, Egyptian writer Dr Mursi Saad el-Din recalled seeing him astride the animal, wending his way through the city traffic:

"I personally remember Bimbashi McPherson and so does my generation.
During the second world war he was often to be seen riding a white donkey
with his *sayis* [stable groom] striding alongside. He took no notice of the
traffic and wherever his donkey led him he was greeted by many Egyptians."[86]

After the book's publication, British and Allied forces in the Western Desert came perilously close to being defeated by Rommel's Afrika Korps. The distance from Alexandria to the Libyan border is 500 kilometres; by the end of June 1942, the Wehrmacht, pushing east, was a mere 100 kilometres from the city. There was even more cause for concern, when the Nationalists (including recent Prime Minister 'Alî Mâher) began to reveal pro-Axis sympathies. When the British fleet hurriedly sailed away from Alexandria, discomfort among the expatriate population was palpable.

In Cairo on 1 July 1942, or "Ash Wednesday" as some wag famously dubbed it, the air was acrid with smoke as the British Embassy and Army Headquarters burned vast quantities of files, while the streets filled with loaded vehicles exiting the city.

On Friday, 3 July 1942, enemy occupation… seemed inevitable. Our fleet
had gone East, "fled", it was said; GHQ was doing the same. Their bonfire of
papers and that of the Embassy were imitated by civilians, self included. Up
to then, the chief fear for people like myself was compulsory evacuation, but

---

86 Mursi Saad el-Din in "Plain Talk", *Al Ahram Weekly*; reprinted 20 November 2013.

on 2 July, a man in GHQ assured me in confidence that there was no time to apply the scheme drawn up two years before, that civilians could stew in their own juice, for the army would evacuate entirely, and that I might know when the Boche had actually broken through at el-Alamein, by the British Guards in the village decamping. This they did about 2 o'clock that night.[87]

It would be fascinating to know what papers Joseph still had in his keeping, which needed to be kept from enemy eyes. At any rate, he called the night of 2–3 July 1942 the darkest of his life.

Unexpectedly, the British line held; the First Battle of el-Alamein, led by Auchinleck, was won later that month of July 1942; and the Montgomery-led Allied forces won the Second Battle of el-Alamein decisively in the autumn. Churchill famously viewed this victory as the turning point in the war. "It may almost be said, before Alamein we never had a victory. After Alamein we never had a defeat."[88]

Joseph was aged 76 when he burned his papers at Porziuncula, and nearly 80 at the war's end. His friend Evans-Pritchard, roughly half his age, served throughout the conflict: with the Sudan Defence Force against the Italians in Ethiopia; with the Alawites in Syria; and with the British Military Administration in Libya. Released from duty in 1945, Evans-Pritchard briefly returned to Cairo, much to Joseph's delight.

The war has given me many more guests than usual, including I am glad to say, some of our young heroes. At present, Evans-Pritchard is up from Cyrene and making this place and the Abdin flat his HQ, whilst in Cairo for ten days or so. It's delightful having him.[89]

Otherwise, Joseph continued to write – letters, of course, but also articles for the two main English-language newspapers, *The Egyptian Gazette* and *The Egyptian Mail*. His subject for the Press was almost always the moulids and the Egyptian government's attempts to suppress them. In addition, he worked on a long essay, which he called his "Swansong". It contains thoughts on comparative religion and philosophy, a justification for his turning to Catholicism. It is not an easy read, perhaps because he did not live long enough to revise it.

---

87 Carman and McPherson (1983), p. 285. See also, Artemis Cooper, *Cairo in the War: 1939–1945* (1989), pp. 190–4.
88 Churchill, W, (1950), *The Second World War*, Vol. 4, *The Hinge of Fate*.
89 Carman and McPherson (1983), p. 292.

Joseph died on 22 January 1946 at Porziuncula. He was buried in Cairo's New British Protestant Cemetery (next to the Commonwealth War Graves). A tombstone once marked the site, but it has long since disappeared. Nevertheless, Joseph's name is in the cemetery register, and the caretaker is happy to show visitors where he was laid to rest. On the missing tombstone was engraved one word of Classical Greek: XAIPE —

"Hail and Farewell"

On 23 January 1946, *The Egyptian Gazette* printed an appreciative obituary of the man whose articles it had been printing for years.

Bimbashi J. W. McPherson, who died suddenly at Giza yesterday, was a remarkable Anglo-Egyptian character... A great lover of Egypt and a keen scholar, he devoted much of his interest to the study of the Egyptian moulids, saint's day festivals, and produced a valuable and comprehensive work on the [subject] entitled "The Moulids of Egypt". He had attended almost every moulid in Egypt and knew [all] the picturesque characters associated with them.

Despite his four-score years, Bimbashi McPherson was still to be seen a few months ago enjoying the moulids and side-shows in and around Cairo. His one cause for indignation was that so many of them were dying out.

Bimbashi McPherson had little time for modern developments and until his death still rode around Cairo on a white donkey with his devoted servant running behind.

Bimbashi McPherson liked to tell his friends how 20 years ago his doctors diagnosed heart trouble and gave him six months to live. He will be missed by many Egyptian and British friends.

Forty-five years earlier, Joseph McPherson went to Egypt searching for excitement. In that alone, his was an extraordinary success story.

*

There is a surprising epilogue to the story of Joseph McPherson. The teacher-soldier-secret policeman-scholar, who in his lifetime earned a modicum of local fame in Cairo, in death became famous in Great Britain both for his real-life adventures laid out in this essay and as the origin of two separate characters of best-seller fiction.

This metamorphosis began in 1957 with the publication of Lawrence Durrell's *Justine*, the first volume of his Alexandria Quartet. Fifteen years earlier, Durrell and his then wife had met Joseph at the latter's flat off 'Abdîn Square. Durrell's biographer, Ian MacNiven, describes the encounter.

> Knowing his penchant for seeking out unusual personalities, someone introduced Larry to Joseph McPherson... [He] was much loved by his Egyptian neighbours, who considered him a seer and a holy man. When Larry and Nancy visited him, McPherson was about 76, 'white haired and frail' '... of medium height and slightly built with a small and beautiful head which housed eyes of extraordinary luminosity and smiling kindness.' McPherson received them in a room moving in its evocation of his personality: the small crucifix over the bed, a print of the Madonna, a photograph of his mother, a few cherished personal objects.[90]

Several decades after their meeting and long after the publication of *Justine*, Durrell wrote: "I was honoured to be the recipient of what must have been the last complimentary copy of his 'Moulids of Egypt'..., an invaluable work..., which gave one a superb first-hand glimpse of [Egyptian street-life]. My own copy, which I laid under heavy tribute when I needed colour for my Alexandria Quartet, now reposes piously in the... archive at [Southern Illinois University]. It is starred and underlined and cross-hatched in a way which makes clear the extent of my debt." And of its author, Durrell added: "He gave off the most extraordinary scent of human grace."[91]

These touching (almost reverential) words written in the 1970s contrast considerably with the rather squalid character of Joshua Scobie which Durrell created in the Alexandria Quartet and whose personality, physical appearance and living quarters bear a striking resemblance to those of Joseph McPherson.

There are, certainly, considerable differences between the fictional Joshua and the real Joseph. For example, Scobie is a Londoner; one-eyed; prone to malapropisms; parents killed in a motor accident in the London to Brighton Race; fought in the Boer War; is an "old sea dog" with a green parrot.

But the similarities between the pair are too obvious to miss, and not simply because both are "bimbashis", Roman Catholics, of similar age and appearance.[92]

---

90 MacNiven, I., *Lawrence Durrell, a Biography* (1998), pp. 254–5.
91 Carman and McPherson (1983), p. 7.
92 And both were life-long bachelors, of course. Joseph was once asked what he considered

There are moments when Scobie and Joseph are indistinguishable, as when the former says: "Swear you won't say a word... They've made me head of the Secret Service";[93] and "The furnishings of his little room suggest a highly eclectic spirit; the few objects which adorn the anchorite's life have a severely personal flavour... The shabby little crucifix on the wall behind the bed... Nearby hangs a small print of the Mona Lisa whose enigmatic smile has always reminded Scobie of his mother."[94]

As the character of Scobie is developed, it moves ever further away from its model. Still, Durrell's creation of Scobie seems a curious, backhanded way for him to show his admiration for McPherson.

To understand how "Scobie" originated, one must shift the spotlight onto Durrell. When it came to social conventions, he was resolutely Bohemian. Even before he moved to Corfu (1935), he was an aspiring *enfant terrible*. By his mid-20s, he already had a remarkable facility with language and a scintillating, seemingly limitless vocabulary. He was praised and mentored by T. S. Eliot, who tried to restrain his exuberance ("At times it was necessary to cut me down to size; he would do it with such breath-taking elegance and style that it left me gasping.")[95] But his nearest literary soul-mate was not Eliot, but American writer Henry Miller. The two became the closest of friends; and both were at war with the censors: Miller over his *Tropic of Cancer*, Durrell over *The Black Book*. Both books were banned for obscenity. Durrell's book also reveals his taste for the surreal or, to use his term, the "Durreal".

In the opening pages of *Justine*, Durrell's describes Alexandria as a place where "[t]he sexual provender which lies to hand is staggering in its variety and profusion". Thus, Scobie's caricature emerges from this fevered sexual context as a pederast and a transvestite. Ultimately, he is found on the streets dressed up as "Dolly Varden" to be beaten to death by the ratings of HMS *Milton*.[96] Then, in a true "Durreal" moment, the dead Scobie is transfigured into a local saint, whose shrine is visited by both Muslims and Copts during Moulid el-Scob!

None of this, of course, has anything to do with Joseph McPherson. Ian Mac-Niven's view is that "McPherson's was a saintly and monastic nature by contrast

---

his narrowest escape. His answer: "Missing getting married!" (McPherson to the Old Merchant Venturers' Club magazine, issue undated).
93 *Justine*, p. 137.
94 Ibid, p. 111.
95 'The Other T. S. Eliot', *The Atlantic Monthly* 215: 5 (May 1965), 61. Source of quote kindly provided by Prof. John Haffenden.
96 Dolly Varden being a character in Dickens' *Barnaby Rudge*.

with the roguish character Larry was to create". Joseph's friends and relations (indeed, Joseph himself) would likely have found the term "saintly" hilariously misplaced, but MacNiven's point is basically sound.

I discussed the McPherson/Scobie contrast in correspondence with the late Michael Haag, who was an expert on Durrell, no less than on Alexandria and its pre-Egyptian Revolution society.

> As far as I am aware Durrell nowhere says that McPherson was his model
> for Scobie. But clearly, he lifted aspects of McPherson in creating Scobie,
> his eccentric saintliness, the decorations in his room, etc. Ian MacNiven sets
> this out in his biography … while at the same time stating that McPherson
> possessed none of Scobie's 'Tendencies'. I myself have not heard anything
> otherwise.
>
> The link between McPherson and Scobie would not be obvious to the
> average reader; the connection is probably owed to the industry of academics
> who are big on the numbers of angels dancing on pins but poor on whether the
> angels are actually there…
>
> A characteristic technique of Durrell's was to take an aspect of a person
> and attach to that the aspects of another person, a cut and paste job. I clearly
> see Gaston Zananiri and Carlo Suares in Durrell's character of Balthazar.
> The pederasty and transvestism of Scobie does not even have to come from
> another person; … that side of Scobie comes straight off the burlesque stage.
> At any rate Durrell did not get it from McPherson.[97]

*

By the 1970s, Durrell had become famous and a pillar of the literary establishment. Joseph's great-nephew, John McPherson, and broadcaster/writer Barry Carman, set about publishing an edited and annotated collection of Joseph's home letters and photographs. John McPherson contacted Lawrence Durrell, asking him to write a Preface. To give Durrell due credit, he accepted and wrote a short but very gracious introductory piece for the new book. He described his meeting with Joseph, about whom he wrote nothing but praise, and his use of *The Moulids of Egypt* as an important source for his Alexandria Quartet. Joseph's letters were published by the BBC in 1983 in the book entitled *Bimbashi McPherson: A Life in Egypt*. Not only did it sell many copies; there was a 3-programme series about it on BBC Radio 4.

---

97 Michael Haag in correspondence with the Editor, 18 November 2017.

*

Joseph's third literary reincarnation came in 1988, when British novelist Michael Pearce published a volume of crime fiction entitled *The Mamur Zapt and the Return of the Carpet*. In the book, the main protagonist is the Mamur Zapt, but he is a Welshman, named Gareth Cadwallader Owen, and nothing like Joseph McPherson. However, his close colleague in the story is the Assistant Commandant of the Cairo Police, one Bimbashi McPhee who "had spent twelve years teaching in the Egyptian equivalent of a minor public school". Just as Durrell drew from *The Moulids of Egypt* for atmosphere and colour, Pearce has drawn on both that book and *Bimbashi McPherson: A Life in Egypt* for the same purpose.

There have now been nineteen Mamur Zapt books. One volume in the series has won the Crime Writers' Association's Last Laugh Award for funniest crime novel; another was shortlisted for the Ellis Peters Award for best historical crime novel. Joseph McPherson would be delighted to have, in any degree, inspired them.

Sources

Carman, B. and McPherson, J., *Bimbashi McPherson: A Life in Egypt* (BBC, 1983).

Durrell, Lawrence, *Justine* (Faber and Faber, 1957).

—*Balthazar* (Faber and Faber, 1958).

Innes, Mary, "In Egyptian Service: The Role of British Officials in Egypt, 1911–1936", (Thesis for D.Phil., St Antony's College, Oxford).

McPherson, J. W., Papers, Bristol Record Office.

Pearce, Michael, *The Mamur Zapt and the Return of the Carpet* (Collins, 1988).

—*The Mamur Zapt and the Night of the Dog* (Collins, 1989).

Robinson, Samuel, "Joseph Williams McPherson", Christ Church Gaudy Oration, Oxford (1996).

Russell, Sir Thomas Wentworth, *Egyptian Service, 1902–1946* (John Murray, 1949).

—Papers, Middle East Centre Archive, St Antony's College, Oxford.

Seth, Ronald, *Russell Pasha* (William Kimber, 1966).

Sirrs, Owen L., *A History of the Egyptian Intelligence Service, 1910–2009* (Routledge, 2010).

Vatikiotis, P.J., *The History of Modern Egypt* (Weidenfeld & Nicolson, 4th ed., 1991).

Editor's Acknowledgements

I am most grateful: to Terry Walz, who first suggested that I undertake to produce a new edition of *The Moulids of Egypt* and has been unfailingly supportive from the beginning; to Barnaby Rogerson, who immediately recognised the book's importance and referred me to the publisher; to Professor Valerie J. Hoffman, who not only wrote the new Foreword, but having read a quasi-final draft, provided a list of needed corrections and valuable commentary; to Barbara Schwepcke, Stephen Landrigan, Harry Hall and Nigel Grey-Turner of Gingko Library for publishing the book.

I am also grateful to the following for their kind assistance while I was writing the account of the life of Joseph McPherson: Elspeth McPherson; Theo Gayer-Anderson; Ambrose Evans-Pritchard; Bruce Ross-Smith; the late Michael Haag; Greg Olson; C. S. Knighton, Principal Assistant Keeper of Archives, Clifton College, Bristol; Gabriel Sewell, College Librarian, Christ Church, Oxford; Judith Curthoys, Archivist, Christ Church, Oxford; Heather J. Sharkey, Head of Department, Near Eastern Languages & Civilizations, University of Pennsylvania; Marianne Eaton-Kraus; Alon Tam; Philip Grover, Assistant Curator, Photograph and Manuscript Collections, Pitt Rivers Museum, Oxford; Chris Morton, Head of Research & Curator of Photograph and Manuscript Collections, Pitt Rivers Museum, Oxford; Francisco Bosch-Puche, The Griffith Institute, Oxford; Debbie Usher, Middle East Centre Archive, St Antony's College, Oxford; Aaron M. Lisec, Research Specialist, Morris Library, Southern Illinois University; the late Michael Pearce and his daughter Caroline Moughton; and the staffs of: the Bristol Record Office; the National Archives, Kew; the British Library Newspaper Archive; SOAS Library; the London Library.

Sources of Illustrations

Front cover: Original postcard – Editor's private collection

Pages ii, vi, xxii, 5, 34, 40, 54, 149, 151, 167, 191, 201, 203, 227, 242, 246, 267, 271, 279: Original book

Page xviii: Ambrose Evans-Pritchard

Pages 18, 26, 48, 75, 286, 314: Original postcards – Editor's private collection

Page 61: Library of Congress, "A Howling Dervish, Cairo, Egypt", reproduction no. LC-DIG-Stereo-1S20938. Rights advisory: no known restrictions on publication

Page 68: *Le Monde Illustré*, undated – Editor's private collection

Pages 90, 216, 354: Gayer-Anderson Estate

Page 174: *Egypt: Descriptive, Historical, Picturesque* (1887), by G. Ebers (London: Cassell & Co. Ltd.)

Pages 185, 358: Internet, Public Domain

Page 344: *Gallipoli Memoirs* (1929), by Compton Mackenzie (London: Cassell & Co. Ltd.)

Page 347: *The Desert Campaigns* (1918), by T. Massey (London: Constable & Co. Ltd.)

Rear cover: Original postcard – Editor's private collection

AN EXTRAORDINARY

NEW ENVIRONMENT

MASTERPIECE
SERIES

HIGHLAND PARK / ALTERSTUDIO

ESSAYS BY ROBERT McCARTER AND MARLON BLACKWELL WITH JONATHAN BOELKINS
REFLECTION BY CARLOS JIMÉNEZ | PRINCIPAL PHOTOGRAPHY BY CASEY DUNN

OSCAR RIERA OJEDA
PUBLISHERS

CONTENTS

ESSAY

BY ROBERT McCARTER

Suspended Refuge and Shadowed Prospect:
A Place Constructed of Complementary Contrasts

Alterstudio has built its reputation as one of the best architects of houses practicing in US through a series of designs carefully constructed to take advantage of the natural characteristics of their sites in order to provide the maximum experiential richness for the inhabitants with the minimum investment of resources. Many of these houses are positioned on the edges of steeply sloping ridges overlooking the expansive natural landscapes of the river, lake, and creek valleys on the western side of Austin, Texas, where the firm is based. These houses provide prospect by opening to the expansive views over heavily forested hillsides on the private side of the house, while providing refuge by being largely closed to views inwards on the public side of the house, facing the street. Prospect, the ability to see outwards from within, and refuge, the ability to not be seen from without, have been identified as being necessary to the comfortable inhabitation of landscape and architecture.[1] Rather than being an oppositional duality, prospect and refuge are best understood as complementary contrasts, which together provide us with repose and allow us to dwell comfortably in the space within. In contradistinction to the dramatic hillside sites of many of their houses, Alterstudio's Highland Park House in Dallas, Texas,

exemplifies the architects' capacity to make a domestic realm of repose on a visually restricted, physically circumscribed, flat suburban site, where providing prospect through expansive views outward would have compromised the refuge and privacy of the inhabitants. The windows of the large neighboring houses look into the site from all four directions—across the public street to the south, across the two narrow alleys to the west and north, and from the neighboring site on the east. Before construction of the new house, the 2/3-acre site was an open grass field devoid of any mature trees to provide shade, privacy, or a sense of place, without even the smallest remnant of the pre-existing landscape of densely clustered live oak trees that is typical of this part of north Dallas.

In response to this exposed, almost treeless site in a wealthy neighborhood of over-scaled, historicist mini-mansions, the partners of Alterstudio—Kevin Alter, Ernesto Cragnolino and Tim Whitehill—have entirely transformed the existing situation by conceiving the house and site as an integrated spatial composition, weaving together architecture and landscape to construct a contemporary interpretation of the courtyard house, the oldest and most widely deployed house-type in the world. The house, set back from the street to the south, forms a U-shape in basic massing, and along with the concrete wall and linear bamboo grove to the

ROBERT McCARTER is a practicing architect, author, and, since 2007, Ruth and Norman Moore Professor of Architecture at Washington University in St. Louis; he has previously taught at the University of Florida (1991-2007), where he was also the founding Director of the School of Architecture; Columbia University (1986-1991) where he was also Assistant Dean; and as visiting professor at University of Arkansas Fay Jones School of Architecture; the University of Venice School of Architecture (IUAV); the Pontifica Universidad Católica del Perú in Lima (PUCP); the Berlage Institute in Rotterdam, the Netherlands; University of Louisville; and North Carolina State University, as well as being Visiting Scholar at the American Academy in Rome on three occasions. Since 1982 he has had his own architectural practice in New York, Florida, and St. Louis, with twenty-five realized buildings. He is the author of twenty-four books, including *Louis I. Kahn* (2nd edition, 2022; 1st edition 2005); *Modern Architecture and the Lifeworld: Essays in Honor of Kenneth Frampton* (2020, edited with Karla Carrara Britton); *Place Matters: The Architecture of WG Clark* (2019); *Grafton Architects* (2018); *The Architecture of MacKay-Lyons Sweetapple: Economy as Ethic* (2017); *Marcel Breuer* (2016); *The Space Within: Interior Experience as the Origin of Architecture* (2016); *Steven Holl* (2015); *Aldo van Eyck* (2015); *Herman Hertzberger* (2015); *Alvar Aalto* (2014); *Carlo Scarpa* (2013); *Understanding Architecture: A Primer on Architecture as Experience* (2012, with Juhani Pallasmaa); *Wiel Arets: Autobiographical References* (2012); *William Morgan* (2003); and *Frank Lloyd Wright* (1997). Among his many awards, McCarter was one of seventy-one International Exhibitors selected for "*Freespace*," the 2018 Venice Biennale of Architecture, and he was named one of the "Ten Best Architecture Teachers in the US" by *Architect* magazine in December 2009.

north, shapes a courtyard and garden at its center, onto which the public, shared spaces of the house open. Due to the angled alley on its west side, the wedge-shaped site is significantly wider at the rear, to the north, than at the front, to the south, and the western wing of the house aligns with this angle, so that the wedge-shaped courtyard opens to the north and northwest.

The house, for a young family with a significant art collection and associated on-site gallery, is organized so as to allow the private and public lives of the family to take place in parallel, intertwining, but non-conflicting precincts and pathways. The thoughtful and appropriate fitting of the complicated program of domestic rooms and art gallery spaces into the house, and of the house to its unpromising and constrained site, exemplifies the principled nature of Alterstudio's practice, and is a typical characteristic of all their designs. Yet, in the case of the Highland Park House, it is the ways in which the materials and methods of construction are deployed to shape and characterize the experience of the inhabitants of the house and the visitors to the art gallery that allows it to attain a remarkable and rarely achieved level of resolution.

Entering the site from the southeast corner, the first of the complementary contrasts structuring the experience of the house is immediately evident in the massing of the front elevation,

where an almost entirely solid, closed, stone-walled, one-story volume is elevated into the air and suspended above an almost entirely voided, open, glass-walled, one-story volume, which is set on the ground. The solid-walled, levitated upper volume, clad in light-colored vertical limestone slabs, houses the private spaces of the bedrooms, while the open, glass- and black steel-walled, grounded lower volume houses the public, shared rooms of the house. The solid, enclosed, suspended volume provides refuge for the private rooms, while the open, expansive, grounded volume beneath provides prospect for the public rooms. The larger volume of the suspended place of refuge overhangs and casts into shadow the grounded place of prospect on all sides, providing both environmental and experiential comfort in the Texas climate. The outward prospect of the ground floor public rooms originates from within the refuge made by the shadows cast by the overhanging private upper floor above.

On the ground floor of the house, the expansive living room and dining room occupy the center of the southern portion of the U-shaped plan. These largely glass-walled rooms open to both the front yard, where views inward are blocked by densely planted berms at the street and alley, and to the rear courtyard garden, where views inward are blocked by a bamboo garden along the north alley. The family room is placed in the left, western wing,

View from the street towards the house, with the stone-clad second floor volume cantilevering over the entry court at center right, and the view through the first floor living and dining rooms to the rear garden court at the left.

View from inside the gallery office, looking through 14-foot-tall windows to the reflecting pool and entry court in the foreground, with the cantilevering, stone-clad volume and its opening to the sky overhead.

with the kitchen and breakfast room acting as the pivot or hinge at the corner. A separate, single-story building, which forms the ivy-covered east wall of the courtyard garden, houses the gallery office, the large art gallery, and the pool cabana / guest suite, and the gallery and cabana can be opened to the west onto the pool terrace at the rear of the courtyard. A half-level below the ground floor, the garage is buried beneath a series of bermed terraces that step down into the courtyard garden, which allows the rear, north portion of the courtyard, where the swimming pool is located, to open to the west without losing privacy. Another half-level down is the exercise room and the media room, which opens onto a stone-walled sunken garden.

The public entry to both the house and the art gallery occurs at the southeastern corner of the U-shaped plan, and here the complementary contrasts structuring the experience of the house construct an appropriately dramatic threshold. In the entry court, the primary volumetric elements of the house and gallery overlap and interweave to form a spatial pivot or hinge that intertwines and integrates all the spaces, while at the same time clearly demarcating the territories of the family and gallery functions. The entry court is formed by the dramatic thirty-five-foot cantilever of the solid, stone-walled upper floor, which creates a shadowed space opening to the street to the south and framed by the glass and steel wall of the house foyer on the left, the glass and steel wall of the gallery directly ahead, and the property-line privacy wall on the right. An off-center, white glass-walled court is opened in the cantilevering overhead volume, bringing daylight into the shadow, and a large tree, rooted in the ground below but opening its foliage into the void above, both fills and anchors this levitated court.

In the entry court, a complementary contrast is constructed between the anchored and embedded art gallery, its lower floor level necessary to keep its height within required limits, and the levitating and cantilevered overhead volume, which somewhat surprisingly is found to contain the spaces of the parents' bedroom and bath suite. The suspended stone-walled volume overhead is separated from both the privacy wall and the gallery wall by narrow voids open to the sky, which are filled with trees along the privacy wall and grounded by a reflecting pool and rock garden along the gallery wall. The light-colored limestone outer walls, white glass inner walls, and white stucco ceiling of the cantilevered volume overhead form a complementary contrast with the darker-colored shadowed glass, black steel walls and glazing mullions, and black reflecting pool and rock garden on the ground floor below. At the northwest corner of the entry court, an opening between the house and the art gallery allows a diagonal view into the courtyard garden for those entering the house or the gallery, and, along with the voids between, emphasizes the spatial independence of the volumes comprising the house. In counterpoint to this use of slices of light to separate spaces, the shadow cast by the cantilevered volume continues uninterrupted into the interior spaces of the house, subtly indicating the primacy of that entrance from the court.

The full-height wooden front door opens into the entry foyer, which is formed by the massive fireplace wall, and the living room beyond may be accessed by walking past the two diagonally-positioned art walls to the left, or by walking past the steel and wood-walled powder room to the right. The living room is anchored and enclosed at the entry end by the two-story, vertical limestone-clad fireplace wall, and at the opposite end by the art wall of the dining room, and both rooms open out to both the front yard and rear courtyard garden through oversized full-height glazing, which can be completely opened on the courtyard garden side. The living room is the only double-height space in the house, and as such it is the only room to occupy portions of both the lower, grounded, shadowed, open prospect volume and the upper, suspended, solid, closed refuge volume. Opening in all directions, the living room centers the house by being the intersection of all three of its axes—the north-south axis from front yard to rear courtyard garden, the east-west axis from entry court to kitchen and family room, and the vertical axis from grounded public living rooms to elevated private bedrooms.

Movement from the more public entry court to the east to the more private family spaces to the west takes place beneath the single-story zones that run along the largely-glazed outer edges of the living and dining rooms, adjacent to the front yard and the rear courtyard garden. In contrast to the white and light limestone walls framing the solid ends of the living and dining room, the kitchen, breakfast room and family rooms at the west end of the ground floor are enclosed in a combination of solid, flush, staggered ribs, or open slat walnut wall paneling and cabinetry, all of which is vertical in orientation. The family room, occupying the angled west wing, opens to the courtyard terrace through full height glazing, and the built-in bench of the breakfast room, occupying the fully-glazed, hinge-like southwest corner joining the south and west wings, opens to the front yard and the garden along the west alley, where it is shielded from neighbors' views by an open vertical walnut slat screen-wall set in front of the glazing. The joint between the south and angled west wings of the house, which occurs at the juncture between the kitchen and the family room, is articulated by the only two full-height, curved glass windows in the house, the larger-radiused one along the edge of the courtyard terrace, which is echoed in the curved limestone cladding of the upper floor above it, and the smaller-radiused one forming the J-shaped end of the breakfast room, which extends downwards into a matching glazed curve at the lower level that brings daylight to the media room. Large rectangular limestone tile flooring ties all the rooms of the ground floor together as well as extending out to form the floor of the courtyard terrace, set beneath and in the shadow of the overhanging upper floor.

On the L-shaped upper floor of the house, the double-height portion of the living room separates the parents' suite on the east end from the three children's bedrooms in the angled western wing, with the playroom acting as the pivot or hinge at the corner, above the kitchen, and with the home office, shielded by a vertical walnut slat screen-wall, placed above the dining room. The stairs to the upper floor are located in the solid walled block separating the dining room from the kitchen, rising from the courtyard garden side of the ground floor to the landing illuminated by daylight from the garden court that runs along the south façade. The outer wall of the rock-floored garden court is formed by the same vertical limestone slabs that clad the entire upper floor, with pieces removed to form an irregular pattern of light and shadow. The garden court provides daylight to the playroom, stair, home office, parents' shower, and the upper portion of the living room, while also shielding those inside from being seen from the street. In counterpoint to the limestone floors at the ground, the upper floor hallways, gallery, and home office have wide plank, white oak wood floors, with light-colored carpet in the bedrooms and large white marble slabs on the bathroom floors.

Among the numerous complementary contrasts on the upper floor are the 40-inch-deep steel I-beams in the outer walls that support the 35-foot cantilever at the entry and the other spans, which rather than being positioned together at the floor or at the ceiling, are set at the roof on one side of the house and at the floor on the other side. While these beams are not literally exposed,[2] their presence is subtly revealed by the positioning of the few window and courtyard openings in the otherwise largely solid limestone-clad façades. On the south, southwest and northwest façades, facing the street and the alley, the four windows of the children's bedrooms are set at the top of the wall, with the glass rising past the ceilings, and the vertical openings of the garden court are also at the top of the limestone wall. On the north façade, facing the courtyard garden, the parent's bedroom window, the only aperture on this side, is set at the bottom of the wall, with the glass sliding down past the floor. That this variation in position of the steel beams is determined by experiential intentions is indicated by the appropriate upward orientation towards the sky allowed by the children's bedroom windows, which encourage views over the roofs of the neighboring houses, and the contrasting but similarly appropriate downward orientation of the parents' bedroom window, encouraging views into the garden rather than of the neighboring houses. Perhaps the most

surprising complementary contrast on the upper floor is the fact that the most visually exposed element of the entire house—the cantilevered volume forming the entry court, with its fully-glazed void court at the center—houses the most private spaces of the house, the parents' baths and dressing rooms. Inside, the glass walls forming the elevated central court rise past the ceiling and slide down past the floor, allowing filtered daylight into the bath and a carefully circumscribed view out into the tree canopy through the full-height glass wall of the dressing room.

Among the many other experience-enhancing complementary contrasts that are constructed into the fabric of the house, mention should be made of the way the public or guest entry sequence into the house, already described, is counterpointed by the "everyday" back entrance sequence used by the family. Rather than entering from beneath the cantilevered stone volume, family members enter from the garage, set a half-level below the main level and at the other end of the house. The horizontal board-formed concrete walls of the garage, which is buried beneath the landscape terraces of the courtyard garden, is contrasted with the vertical limestone-clad upper floor volume that hovers above it, the two separated by the hallway glazing, with the back door opening in the angled joint between. The rear entry foyer, onto which the back door and garage door opens, is also the mid-landing of a remarkable stair, which acts as a spatial hinge or pivot between the main floor of the house above and the lower floor. Hovering cantilevered stone treads with open risers, supported by steel plates, ascend to the main floor from this landing, while, in complementary contrast, solid stone tread and riser blocks descend to the level below, with larger, double-tread-sized blocks of stone, as much excavated as built, forming terraces stepping down beneath the cantilevered treads. Whether ascending or descending this stair, the views along both back entry paths terminate in the (already-mentioned) double-height curved glass corners at the kitchen and media room, effectively uniting the activities of these two levels.

In conclusion, the Highland Park House of Alterstudio is a masterful exercise in the careful articulation of the space within, made possible by the precise deployment of a limited palette of materials and restrained detailing, that together have resulted in the construction of a dwelling that acts as the background or framework for the daily life that takes place within it; that provides its inhabitants both prospect and refuge; and that allows them to have comfortable use of the spaces of the house and garden. Because of these attributes, the house may be said to achieve an atmosphere that allows its residents a sense of repose—the highest goal possible for a work of architecture.[3]

[1] The concepts of prospect and refuge in the experience of the landscape originated in Jay Appleton, The Experience of Landscape (New York: Wiley, 1975, revised edition 1996); the application of prospect and refuge to the experience of architecture is in Grant Hildebrandt, The Wright Space: Pattern and Meaning in Frank Lloyd Wright's Houses (Seattle: University of Washington Press, 1991).

[2] Here Alterstudio is closer in spirit to Frank Lloyd Wright, who did not believe structure had to be exposed, than they are to Louis Kahn, who believed that exposing structure was an ethical imperative. When asked why the steel beams that made the extensive roof cantilevers of the Robie House of 1907 possible were not exposed, Wright famously responded, "Why should you always expose structure? I call it indecent exposure." Wright, An American Architecture (New York: Horizon, 1955), 84.

[3] The terms, "the space within," "background or framework for daily life," "comfort and use," and, above all, "repose" were all employed by Frank Lloyd Wright in describing what for him constituted appropriate design goals and evaluative measures of domestic architecture.

ESSAY

BY MARLON BLACKWELL
WITH JONATHAN BOELKINS

Having known Kevin Alter for over a decade, I have become a great admirer of his work, particularly those projects that I've been fortunate enough to visit in person, primarily in Austin, Texas. I've also come to know him as an educator, appreciating his ability to establish a critical dialogue between theory and practice. By pursuing this balance intensely, Kevin and his partners Ernesto Cragnolino and Tim Whitehill at Alterstudio Architecture have built an exceptional body of work that consistently demonstrates a profound sensitivity and responsiveness to site and a passion for foundational and canonical works of 20th-century architecture, resulting in a clear and distinct architectural language all their own.

When offered the opportunity to visit and review the Highland Park Residence in Dallas, Texas, I accepted immediately, eager to see the latest iteration in Alterstudio's patient process. Located 4 miles due north of downtown Dallas in the Highland Park neighborhood that flanks Turtle Creek, which eventually flows south into the famed Trinity River, and home to the Dallas Country Club, Highland Park is one of the most prestigious neighborhoods in Dallas, if not the most. Though dominated by stately traditional houses, there are important exceptions like the Turtle Creek House by Antoine Predock and The House on Turtle Creek, initially designed by noted Dallas architect Bud Oglesby and subsequently renovated by Larry Speck. These rare exceptions are remarkable for the precedent they set, departing from faux historicism and being willing to embrace the natural landscape.

Coming from the Dallas–Fort Worth airport and forty minutes of massive highways and interchanges, Highland Park is a parallel universe — or perhaps a perpendicular one – that is quiet, calm, and lush. Gradually descending into a wooded ravine along Turtle Creek, the sound of the city's relentless highways falls away, creating a feeling more like a park than a neighborhood. Framed by a primary street to the south and a generous service alley to the west, the house roughly aligns with its neighbors to the east and west, then bends north along the service alley. This strategy takes some exploration to uncover as the house is set back considerably and shrouded by trees along the perimeter. Protected by a rocky, desert garden berm along the street that might have seemed out of place in Dallas were it not for the heat, the floating second story wrapped in stone immediately commands attention, also risking the feeling of being foreign and heavy. On the contrary, it became clear throughout our visit that everything belonged – the landscape, the architecture, the art – all contributing to that rare symbiosis to which we all aspire, where each emboldens and enriches the other.

MARLON BLACKWELL, FAIA, is a practicing architect in Fayetteville, Arkansas, and serves as the E. Fay Jones Distinguished Professor at the Fay Jones School of Architecture and Design at the University of Arkansas. Work produced in his professional office, Marlon Blackwell Architects (MBA), has received national and international recognition with significant publication in books, architectural journals and magazines and more than 160 design awards. Blackwell is the recipient of the 2020 AIA Gold Medal, the Institute's highest honor, which recognizes those whose work has had an enduring impact on the theory and practice of architecture. Other honors Blackwell has received in his career include the Cooper Hewitt National Design Award in 2016, being named the William A. Bernoudy Architect in Residence at the American Academy in Rome in 2019, and admittance into the American Academy of Arts and Sciences in 2023.

JONATHAN BOELKINS, AIA, is a practicing architect, educator, and writer. As the former Studio Director of the internationally renowned Marlon Blackwell Architects, he made significant contributions to numerous award-winning projects. He is a Co-Editor of a new monograph titled *Radical Practice: The Work of Marlon Blackwell Architects* (Princeton Architectural Press, 2022) and has authored numerous essays and papers with international publishers. Essays from his writing partnership with Marlon Blackwell have been featured in several books, including Brian Healy Architects' monograph *Commonplaces: Working on an American Architecture* and Jones Studio's upcoming monograph *Strive*.

Only a winding footpath interrupts the tough berm at the street, its paving interlaced with grass to blur its edges, gradients rather than lines. Passing through the front row of trees, the walk gently rises towards the entry court until the house comes into full view, its austere upper volume now seemingly weightless though clad in Indiana limestone, their grooved patterns providing scale and texture in the stark sunlight. Rather than being dominated and determined by the site, the site is instead being actively shaped by ideas of frontality and figure. That the primary orientation of the main bar of the house is East-West reveals a commonsense approach to environmental responsiveness, but the overall composition is stubbornly resistant to being confined to or shaped by its context. A genuine desire for self-determination as a building and a work of architecture is evident in a studied relationship between inside and outside.

Knowing visitors like us would need shade, the stone upper bar cantilevers 34 feet over the stunning entry court that serves the house itself, the landscape behind it, and a detached art gallery. Entirely in the shade from the street, the entry court isn't clearly visible, and an unexpected delight. One can't help but look upwards on arrival, first to marvel at the effortless power of the stone levitating overhead and then up through the opening in the courtyard and the single tree within, a theme that will unfold throughout the house. Encountering an entry like this, the realization is clear that a journey is being choreographed through a landscape that carefully contrasts the hard and the soft in an episodic and unexpected way, half seen, half unseen.

The heat and heaviness of the stone are gone, replaced by shade and a soft breeze rippling across the koi pond that marks a change in section down slightly to the art gallery and rear landscape. These shifts are subtle but still generous, composed from a curated material palette and interlocked with the landscape. Through a gap between the upper level of the house and the detached art gallery, direct sunlight finds its way through, reflecting off the pond and flickering on the soffit above the massive wooden front door.

Pushing inward with ease, the door revealed the first of many stunning works of art on the backside of a stela that frames the east end of the main living and dining space. The opposite side facing the living area is lined with a smaller-scale version of the limestone panels that clad the exterior. Closer inspection reveals almost imperceptible saw marks left on their surface, just enough to let them feel made. Like the entry court, the living and dining area space opens upwards, overlapped by a desert courtyard upstairs and revealing the backside of the limestone screen. The articulation of the room moves the eye upwards and outwards to reveal a very controlled set of relationships with exterior plantings

and spaces. Tangential experiences are choreographed to push and pull against the sequence of spaces along the intended pathway, working laterally, up and down, and across in a gently dynamic way, engaging the defined, the implied, and the in-between.

Framed by thick walls clad in blackened steel on the outside and wood veneer on the inside at the ground level, structure and services are elegantly hidden so the living and dining area is otherwise seamlessly connected to the front and rear lawns, accessed equally by operable glass walls that can be made to disappear. The broader character of the landscape becomes evident, changing from a straightforward and reserved front lawn to an oasis behind the house with subtle shifts in topography to mask the garage and pool. Though located in an established neighborhood of significant two-story houses, the landscape framed by the house and the art gallery is private and a world apart, a paradise willed into existence out of a nondescript site without any significant trees. Framing the site's east side behind the house, the art gallery is almost entirely camouflaged by ivy but connects directly to the landscape through an enormous sliding door. The magical experience of pushing the door open and allowing fresh air into the gallery calls to mind the Louisiana Museum in Denmark and its nuanced interrelationship between art and nature.

Viewing the house from the rear landscape, the way the house bends to follow the street corner becomes evident, as is the placement of the kitchen at its elbow. Separated from the main living and dining area by a staircase and other services, the kitchen is generous and convenient, with a family banquette in the outside bend of the house, set between expansive windows and a wooden screen for privacy along the street. The conceptual focus on the importance of gathering and dining as a family is evident, as is the intensely thoughtful detailing of custom millwork and upholstery. Outside the mitered glass corner window above the banquette, a stone stair disappears into the lush landscape, revealing another world below.

Discreetly connected to the garage and basement through a bend in plan and shift in section, the volume of the house increases once again, this time downwards via an elegant limestone and painted steel stair framed by art on the inside and continuous windows on the outside. The wood handrail reveals so much about the thought and precision that is obvious but not overwhelming throughout the house. The outside face of the railing is vertical, edges rounded for softness to the hand, and the backside eased inward to be more easily grasped though never seen.

The details are a variation on a theme, a tight theme, offering variety that is both situational and resonant, reinforcing the whole.

And it is whole, the elusive complete work of architecture. This realization wafts over you, hitting you first at the front door, brushed away from a lifetime of skepticism, thinking, "It can't all be this good." But it is, and then time really slows down, the experience sinking in as we shift downstairs. Brought back to the elbow of the house below the kitchen, we rediscover the stone stair outside, now delivering a pool of daylight across an otherwise dark floor. The attention to detail and to experience never wavers — even in the basement — as every light switch and cabinet face is perfectly placed and aligned, materials are coursed out and remain gentle to the touch, all evidence of mastery.

As we move upstairs to the family level, that sense of wonder and delight passes over us again. The stair itself is lit from above by a skylight and by light passing through the limestone screen and desert garden shared by the living and dining area downstairs and the office upstairs. Set between the main living and dining area and the stair, the office stands between the desert garden outside and a generous hall that doubles as an art gallery, connecting the children's playroom and bedrooms to the west and the main suite to the east. The main bedroom enjoys another hefty wooden door that pushes open easily, revealing a comfortable and elegant suite. Occupying the area over the entry court at the east end, the bathroom and closets enjoy ample daylight from the internal opening to the sky. The upper level is otherwise inwardly and upwardly focused, with light only where needed, considerably darker overall than the ground floor.

With time to relax for a moment, we took to the living room, trying to reconcile the monumentality and the intimacy that are present in equal measure while also discerning the architectural references embedded throughout. Aalto, Le Corbusier, and Mies are all here, but more in spirit than specifics, a sotto voce. Instead, it becomes clear that through a commanding knowledge of the history and discipline of architecture, Alterstudio has emerged

into a language that is certainly distinct, a dialect that is somehow international – precise and direct — at the same time as being Southern in the best way — sweet and slow. Having fully absorbed and synthesized this language over time, Kevin, Ernesto, and Tim have clearly established their own voice, which is resounding, confident, and mature.

In this command performance, Alterstudio challenges the immediacy, the selfishness, and the vanity of our time — the instant gratification, the introspection without reflection. This lack of depth is evident in so much of today's architecture, dominated by nearly seamless relationships between interior and exterior and overlit interiors. Instead, the modern paradigm of overtly transparent space is challenged by an architecture that asserts a variable and continuous dialogue between light and dark and more complex spaces. So, while modernity accelerates towards clarity, commonality, and transparency, Alterstudio turns instead, slowly, to the implied, to the bespoke, and to the oblique.

The lessons taught here are plentiful and powerful, ones that every student of architecture should learn – lessons about the history of architecture and the breadth of its vocabulary, the importance of details and the necessity of understanding materials, the varying qualities and levels of light, and the power of the landscape, to name but a few. Any lens for comprehending or experiencing architecture could be used here as the basis for a master class or, better yet, a beginner class. The desire to bring students here is the same one felt at canonical houses that create their own mythical landscapes like Alvar Aalto's Villa Mairea and Rudolf Schindler's King's Road House, and that is indeed the territory and company of this house, the Highland Park Residence. Elevation into the canon takes some time, and clearly there's no formal process, but as this book attests, there is something intensely valuable captured here that time will continue to reveal. And time is on the side of this house as it consciously avoids stylistic tropes and any whiff of fashion. Alterstudio clearly has no interest in the latest 'ism,' as Rick Joy would say. Instead, there is a deliberate timelessness that makes it difficult to date the work precisely, a quality that ensures its longevity. That kind of elan and elegance is the product of a lifetime of earnest dedication to architecture, its history, and its future.

As the time came to leave, there was a deep sense of gratitude for the opportunity to marvel at the work of a true friend who is an architect in full command of the discipline and for the sheer experience of it. Wanting to soak in every last minute, we sat outside in the entry court, watched the light flicker through the top of the lone tree in the center, and recognized that rare feeling that only comes from experiencing a complete work of architecture.

DESIGN

DESCRIPTION

The Highland Park residence offers a counterproposal to the contemporary Tudor mansions and French chateaus of this tony Dallas neighborhood. On a property without any significant natural features and neighbors looming on either side, the design presents an enigmatic presence in the neighborhood, a singular interior environment, and an invitation to live in unexpected ways. An unadulterated limestone bar hovers precariously at the building line, bends to define a private setting, and cantilevers 34' at the entry. A separate gallery building supports this private milieu behind, and provides a carefully calibrated setting for a significant rotating collection of art. A series of expectations are created from the outset, and unanticipated spaces unfold as the visitor meanders through the property. Inside, one is alternatively drawn horizontally into the landscape and further into the house; the living room is carved into the stone bar above providing a space of unexpected height, while an open ground floor encourages the easy transition through the building into the landscape. Constructional aplomb and careful attention to detail are ubiquitous throughout the house, where spatial and material qualities rely on constructional poise. A significant steel structure lays inconspicuously inside the 2nd floor stone volume and allows for the cantilever at the entry. Here, an oculus is carved into the master-suite as an abstract glass volume that opens the entry to the sky. A similar protected courtyard is carved into the middle of the volume to provide another source of light and view, as the limestone wall unravels into a screen. Raw and refined finishes are paired ubiquitously while delicate site-glazed window walls were detailed to work with an enormous operable door system. Glass is employed both for transparency and reflection, and the two curved glass panels add a multifaceted sensibility to the overall ensemble. The underlying steel structure was adjusted from wall-trusses that would have required significant chords at the top and bottom of the structure to a pair of W40 beams, running low on the front and high on the back, to allow the upstairs courtyard to delicately reach the sky and the master window to effortlessly break the bottom of the stone volume. Set out with the understanding that architecture is primarily understood intimately, beauty is defined here as something tactile; the building provides both a tangible material presence and an abstract ground against which the vicissitudes of nature, art and social occasion are highlighted.

PRESENTATION DRAWINGS

Site Aerial View (above) Context Photographs (below)

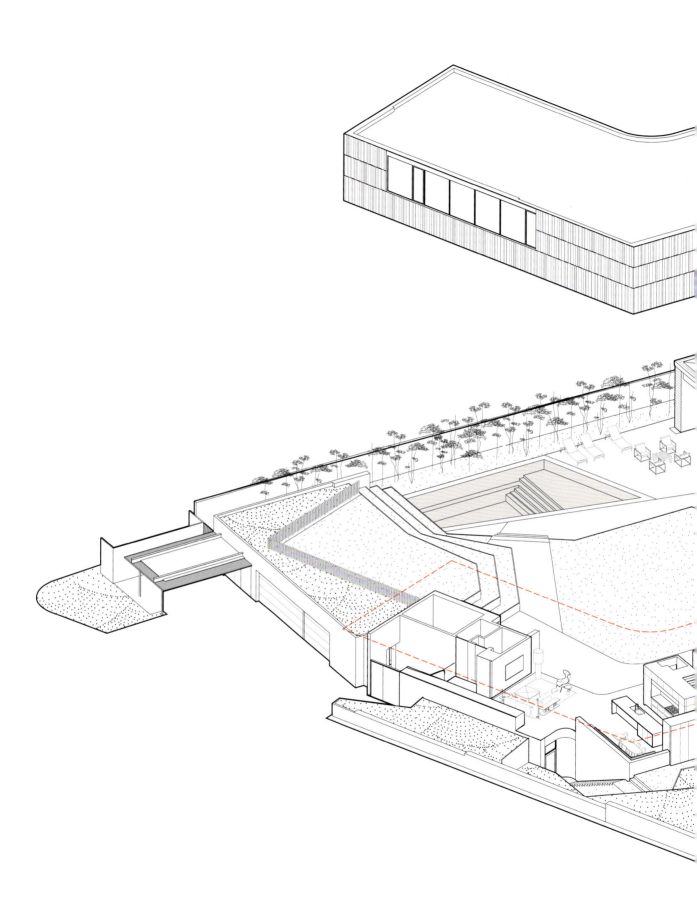

Axonometric

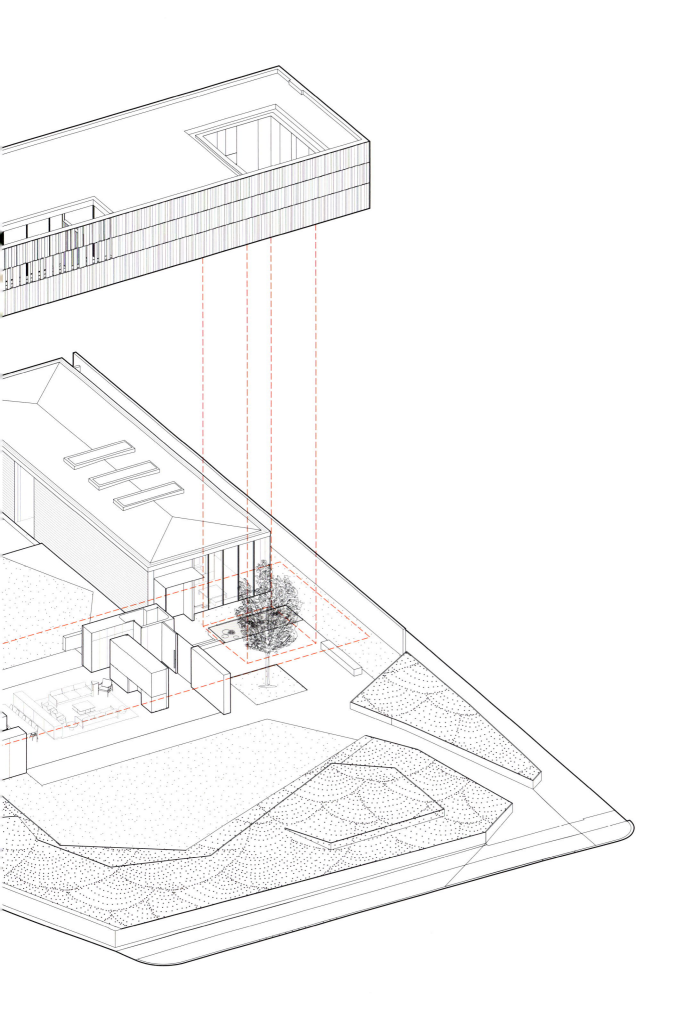

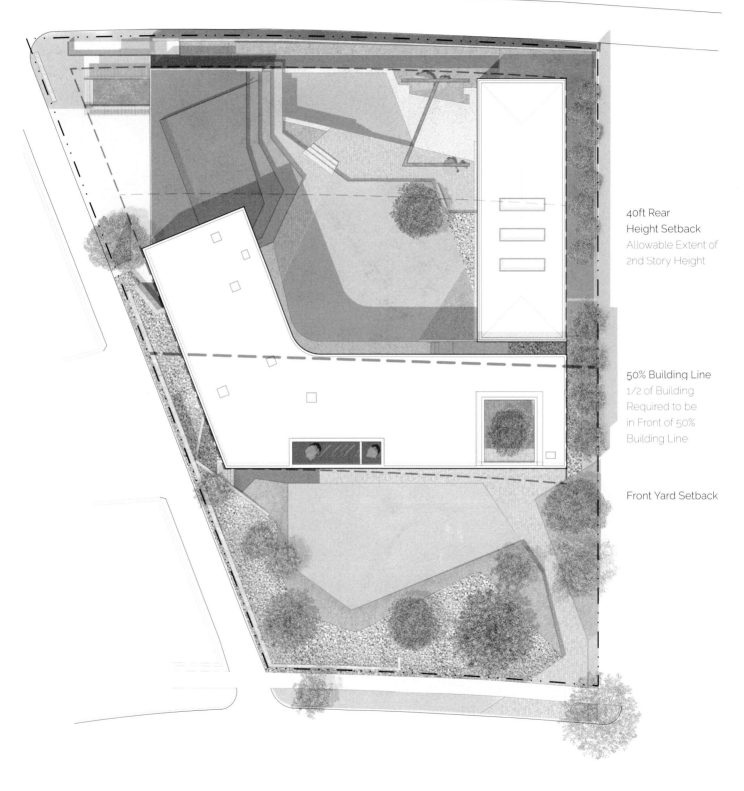

40ft Rear
Height Setback
Allowable Extent of
2nd Story Height

50% Building Line
1/2 of Building
Required to be
in Front of 50%
Building Line

Front Yard Setback

Site Plan

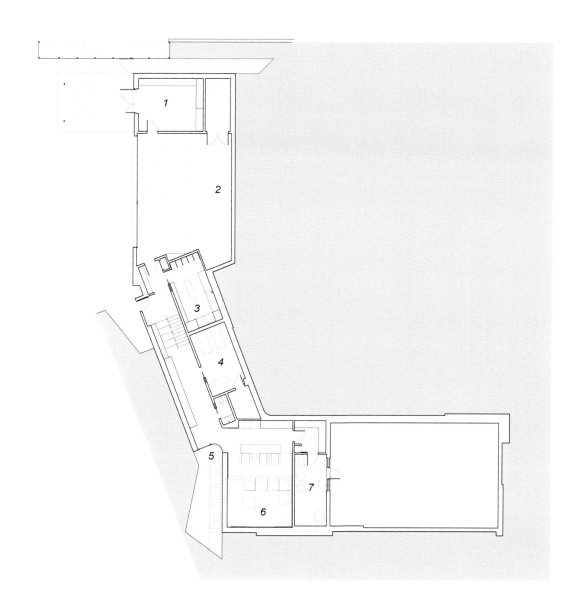

Basement Floor Plan

1 Work Shop
2 Garage
3 Laundry
4 Gym
5 Garden Court
6 Media
7 Mechanical

5'   10'   20'

First Floor Plan

1 Kitchen
2 Pantry
3 Dining
4 Office
5 Den
6 Living
7 Entry
8 Gallery Court
9 Gallery
10 Cabana

5' 10'   20'

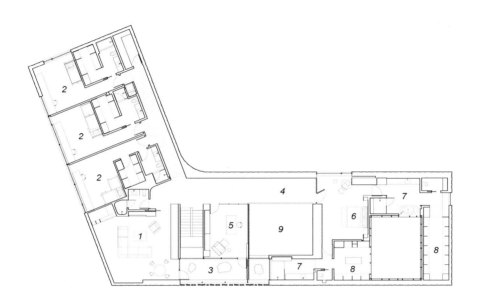

Second Floor Plan

1 Playroom
2 Bedroom
3 Garden Court
4 Gallery
5 Office
6 Primary Bedroom
7 Primary Bath
8 Primary Closet
9 Open to Below

5'   10'   20'

Concept Renderings

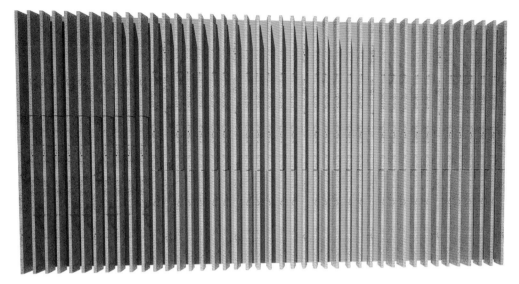

3 3/4" 3"

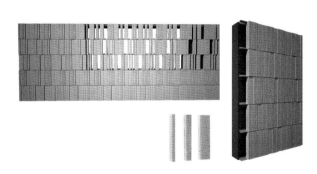
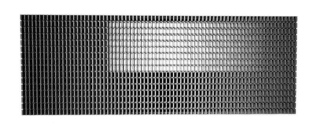
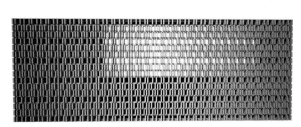
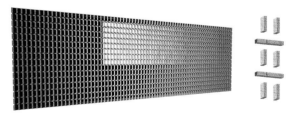
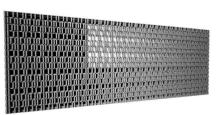

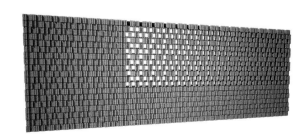

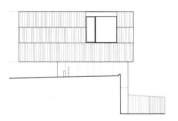

West Wing - North Elevation

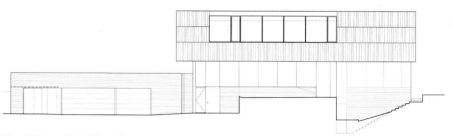

West Wing - West Elevation

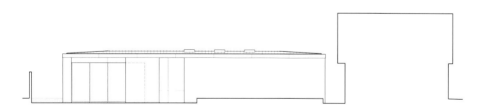

Gallery - West Elevation

Gallery - South Elevation

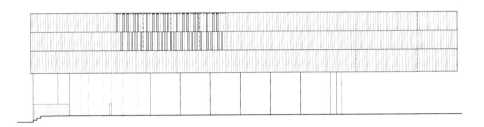

South Wing - South Elevation

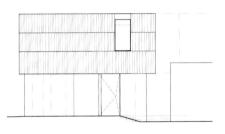

South Wing - East Elevation

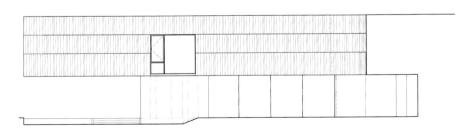

South Wing - North Elevation

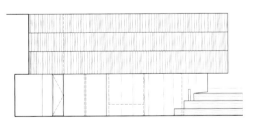

West Wing - East Elevation

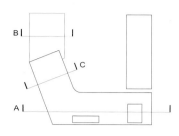

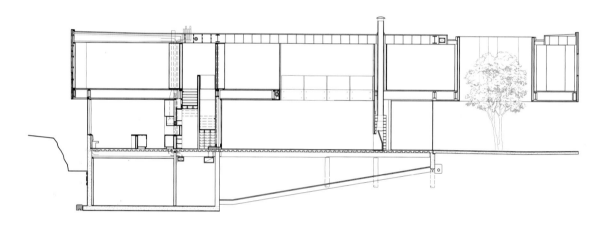

A. Longitudinal Section

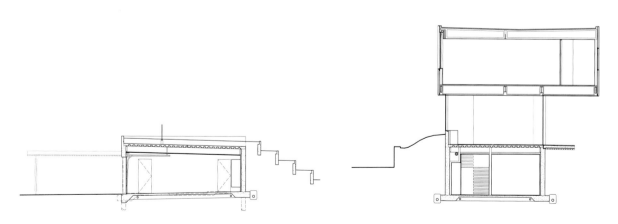

B. Garage

C. West Wing at Patio

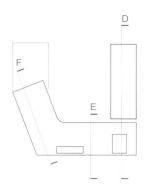

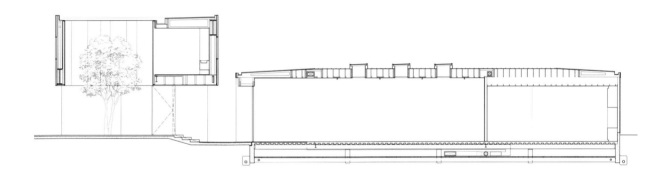

D. Longitudinal Section

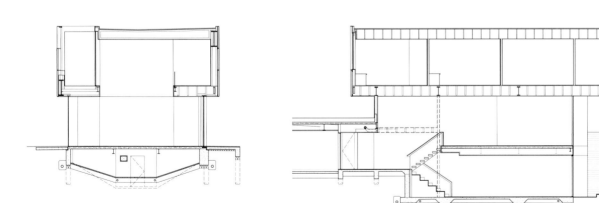

E. Section at Living

F. Section at West Wing

CONSTRUCTION

DETAIL DRAWINGS

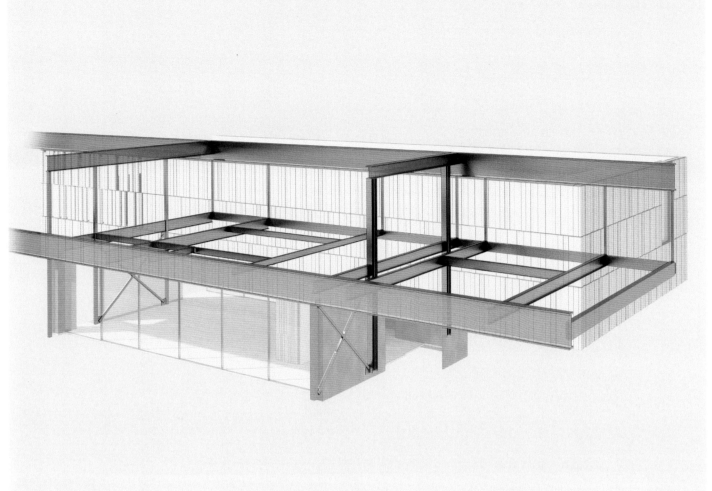

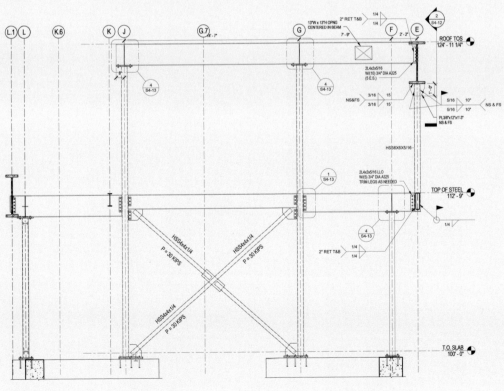

Structural Diagram

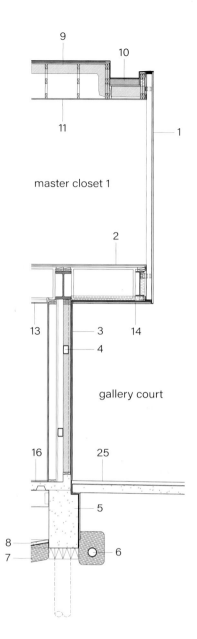

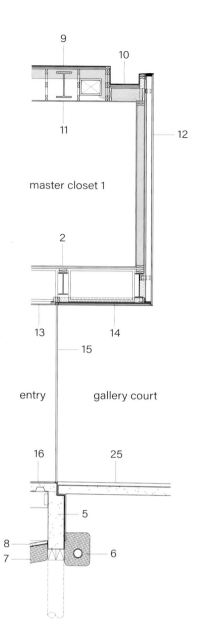

Wall Section
Gallery Court at Steel & Glass Walls

1 Curtain wall: 1" insulated glass unit with privacy film over
aluminum mullion system
2 Floor assembly: carpet over 1 1/8" wood subfloor over wood floor trusses
3 Steel panel wall: steel panel over vertical 7/8" metal hat channels over
WRB over 1/2" plywood sheathing over wood framing with spray foam insulation
4 Structural steel braced frame
5 Crawlspace wall: 1" rigid insulation board over drainage composite
with filter fabric over waterproofing membrane over concrete foundation wall
6 Subsurface drain system
7 Under-slab drain system
8 Crawlspace floor: 2" concrete slab over reinforced crawlspace vapor barrier

Wall Section
Gallery Court at Glass Walls

9 Membrane roof: fully adhered roofing membrane over 1/2" cover board
over 1" rigid insulation over 3/4" plywood sheathing over wood roof trusses
with spray foam insulation
10 Membrane gutter: fully adhered membrane roofing over 1/2" cover board
over tapered rigid insulation (1/4:12 slope) over 3/4" plywood sheathing over
wood framing with spray foam insulation
11 Second floor ceiling: 5/8" gypsum board over wood roof trusses
12 Curtain wall: 1" insulating glass unit over aluminum mullion system with
aluminum plate shadow box panel over air space over 1/2" plywood
sheathing over wood framing with spray foam insulation
13 First floor ceiling: 5/8" gypsum board over 2x4 framing attached
to wood floor trusses
14 EIFS soffit: EIFS with 1 1/2" insulation board over WRB over 1/2"
plywood sheathing over wood framing with batt insulation
15 Site-glazed 1" insulating glass unit
16 Concrete floor assembly: stone flooring over 6" composite concrete floor slab

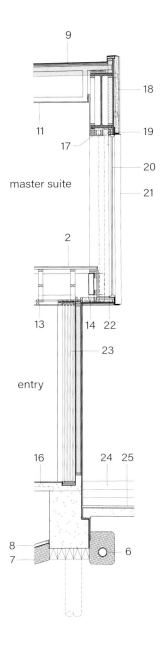

9

18

11

19

17

master suite

20

21

2

13   14   22

23

entry

16   24 25

8

7

6

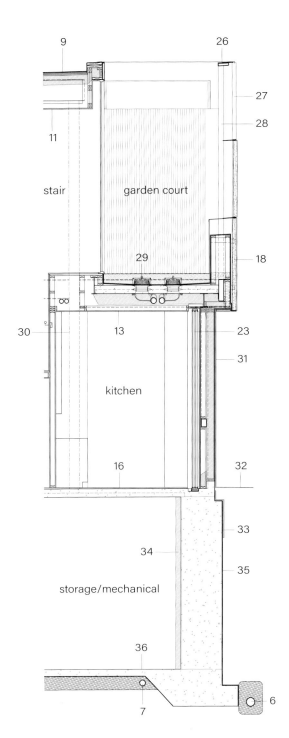

9   26

27

28

11

stair   garden court

29

18

30   13   23

31

kitchen

16   32

33

34

35

storage/mechanical

36

6

7

Wall Section
South Wing at Steel Wall & Window

17 Curtain track
18 Stone panel wall: 3" thick stone panel over air space over WRB over
1/2" plywood sheathing over wood framing with spray foam insulation
19 Motorized blackout shade with metal shade pocket
20 Window system
21 Aluminum window surround
22 Wood flooring over 1 1/8" plywood subfloor over steel outriggers
23 Pocketing sliding glass doors
24 Site stairs
25 Stone pavers over concrete slab on grade

Wall Section
South Wing at Steel Wall & Garden Court

26 Horizontal steel girt
27 Stone panel beyond
28 Steel post beyond
29 Green roof drain with perforated enclosure
30 Steel column in wall beyond
31 Steel panel over vertical 7/8" meta furring channels over WRB over
1/2" plywood sheathing over wood framing with spray foam insulation
32 Finished grade
33 1" rigid insulation board, extend 3'-0" below grade
34 Spray foam insulation
35 Basement wall: drainage composite with filter fabric
over waterproofing membrane over concrete foundation wall
36 Concrete floor slab over vapor barrier

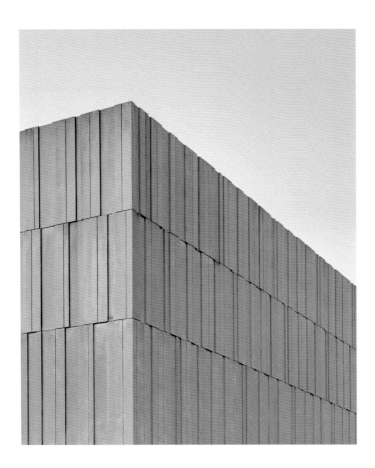

Plan Detail (6" = 1'-0")
Typical Corner at Stone Wall

1 Open cell spray foam insulation in 2x6 wall framing
2 6" or 9" stone at corner, or custom width
3 Embedded stone anchor below, bolted through
1/8" x 1" stainless steel bent strap
4 1/8" x 3" stainless steel stone anchor set in
non-staining sealant; position above
embedded stone anchor
5 Line of 1/4 x 3 steel bar below
6 Sealant joint & backer rod
7 1/8" x 3" stainless steel split-tail stone
anchor set in non-staining sealant
8 Fully adhered WRB over 1/2" plywood sheathing

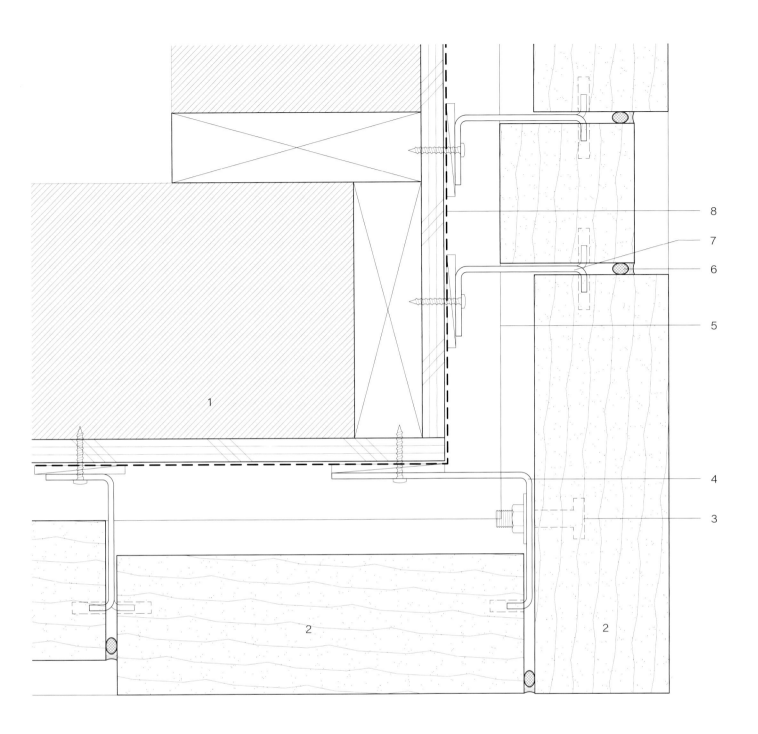

8

7

6

5

4

3

1

2

2

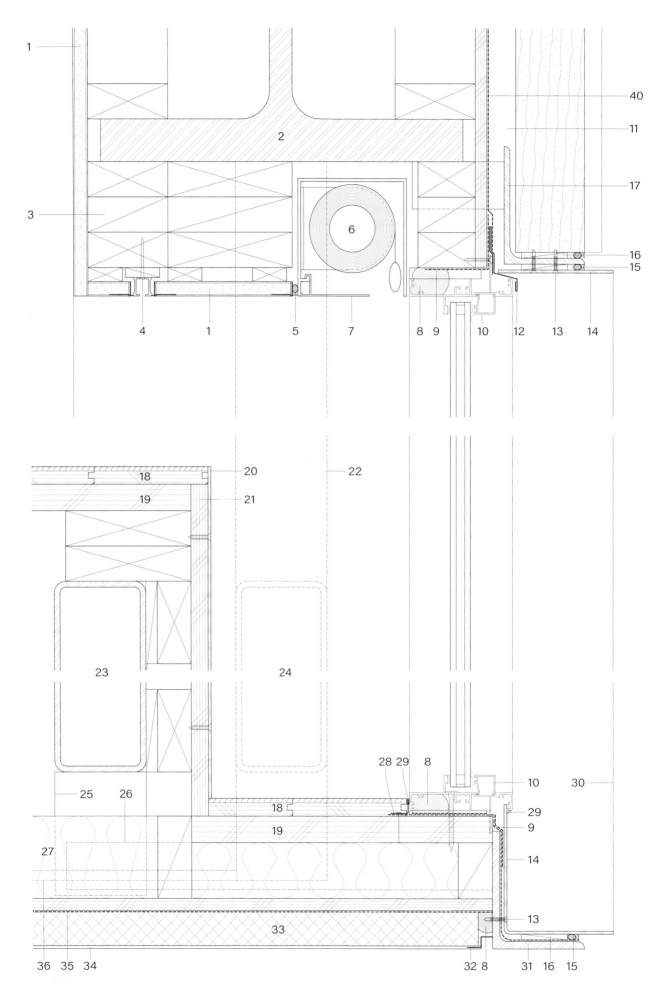

Section Detail (3" = 1'-0")
Stone Screen

1 Painted gypsum board
2 Steel girder
3 Wood blocking
4 Recessed curtain track with
L-mold & sealant on both sides
5 L-mold & sealant
6 Motorized roller window shade
7 Shade flap & housing, painted
8 Low-expansion foam sealant
(air seal)
9 Extend WRB into rough opening
10 Aluminum window
11 3" thick stone, set per pattern
12 Stainless steel head flashing
with leading edge set in sealant
13 Countersunk self-tapping screws
14 Painted 11 GA steel or 0.125
aluminum window trim
15 Sealant joint with backer rod
16 HDPE shim
17 Steel shelf angle, painted
18 Blind nailed engineered
wood flooring

19 1 1/8" subfloor
20 11 GA steel sheet
21 3/4" plywood
22 Line of steel tension
column beyond
23 Steel tube beam
24 Steel tube beam beyond
25 Steel supports between
outriggers and beam
26 Steel outriggers
27 Batt insulation
28 3/4" x 3/4" galvanized steel
angle back dam,
bedded in sealant
29 Sealant joint
30 Line of window trim beyond
31 Steel shelf angle, painted
32 Aluminum reveal trim
33 1 1/2" rigid insulation
34 EIFS soffit
35 WRB over 1/2"
plywood sheathing
36 Bottom of steel beam beyond

Section Detail (3" = 1'-0")
Stone Screen

1 HSS 4" x 2" x 1/4" post, painted
2 Continuous galvanized metal cleat
3 HSS 8" x 2" x 1/4" beam, painted
4 Painted continuous 1/8" x 8"
steel flat bar, welded to HSS
5 1/8" x 2" wide stainless steel stone
anchors set in non-staining sealant
6 PVC-clad metal with metal backing
plate & continuous sealant at laps
7 Continuous saw-cut kerf to receive
coping & stone anchors
8 Line of projecting stone beyond
9 3" thick stone set per pattern
10 Steel peg
11 Plate bevel welded around steel
tube; grind & sand smooth
12 Countersunk stainless steel
self tapping screws
13 Sealant & backer rod
14 HDPE wedge shims

15 Brake-formed 11 GA steel
cap, painted
16 Sealant with bond breaker
tape beyond
17 Tack weld or screw fasten
1/8" Z-cleat
18 11 GA steel sheet, painted
19 26 GA stainless steel flashing cap
20 Self-adhered underlayment
lapped over WRB
21 1/2" plywood
22 Line of HSS post
23 Sealant
24 Two-piece 26GA stainless steel
flashing collar with soldered seams
25 Solder flange of post flashing
to stainless cap
26 26 GA stainless flashing cap
turned down both sides 3" minimum
27 WRB over 1/2" plywood sheathing

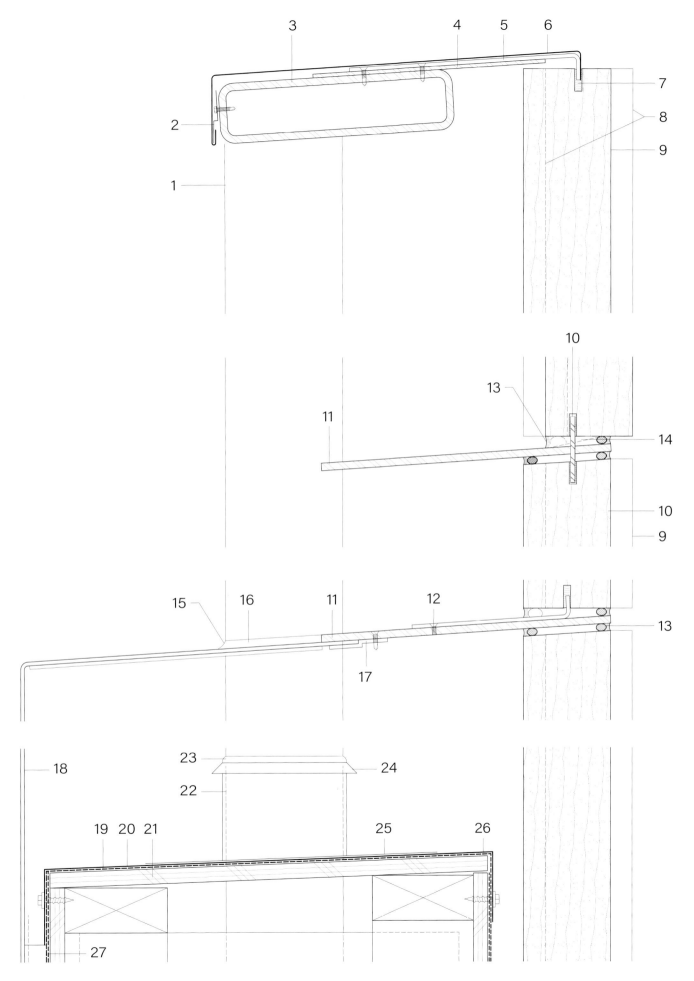

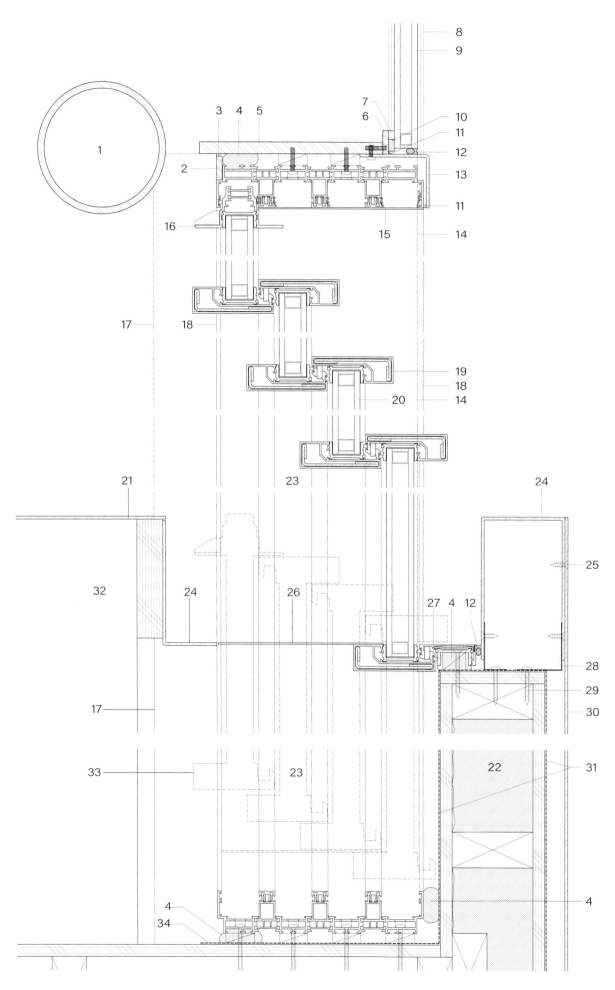

Plan Detail (3" = 1'-0")
Multi-Sliding Door Jamb at Living

1 Steel column
2 Painted 1/4" x 1" aluminum flat bar, adhered to door jamb
3 Sealant joint
4 Low-expansion foam sealant (air seal); join with air seal at head & sill
5 1/2" x 8" cold-rolled steel flat bar mullion, painted, tapped to receive machine screws
6 Painted 1/4" x 1" aluminum flat bar fastened to mullion with countersunk #10 x 1" stainless steel machine screws @ 12" O.C.
7 Tooled silicone structural seal (& air seal)
8 Line of aluminum channel below
9 1" insulating glass unit
10 1/4" glazing tape spacer
11 Continuous sealant joint (weather seal)
12 Sealant & backer rod
13 Continuous 11GA brake-formed painted steel closure, 2 1/4" x 3"
14 Edge of slab below
15 Cover strip
16 Latch stile of multi-sliding glass door
17 Line of slab recess below

18 Line of sliding door sill below
19 4-panel multi-sliding glass door system
20 Insulating glass unit by sliding door manufacturer
21 Cabinetry end panel
22 Open cell spray foam insulation in 2x4 wall framing
23 Multi-sliding door bottom tracks below
24 Brake-formed 11GA steel sheet closure
25 Countersunk black oxide screws
26 Pocket closure panel by sliding door manufacturer
27 Pocket jamb trim by sliding door manufacturer over plastic shims
28 Vertical galvanized steel furring
29 Galvanized steel screws
30 11 GA steel panel
31 Fully adhered WRB over 1/2" plywood sheathing
32 Cabinetry
33 Sliding glass doors in open position
34 Extend WRB into rough opening

Section Detail
Stone Shelf Angle at Girder

1 Line of roof beyond
2 1/2" plywood sheathing
3 Painted brake-formed 11 GA
sheet steel
4 Roofing underlayment
5 Wrap roofing membrane base
flashing over parapet and hot air weld
to membrane-clad metal coping
6 Membrane-clad metal coping with
metal backing plate & continuous
sealant at laps; set into stone with
non-staining sealant
7 Continuous saw-cut kerf to
receive coping
8 Lap roofing underlayment onto WRB
9 7/8" galvanized steel furring channels @ 48" O.C. with two fasteners per
channel only; fill pre-drilled holes with
sealant prior to driving screws and
treat screw heads with sealant
10 Fully adhered roofing membrane
base flashing with factory-formed
inside corners where membrane
meets wall
at roof beyond
11 Membrane-clad metal with
metal backing plate & continuous
sealant at laps
12 Sealant & backer rod
13 Sealant & bond breaker tape
14 Painted aluminum tube, 4" x 1" x 0.125"
15 Horizontal wood beam spanning
between built-up studs at each
side of opening

16 Tapered wood blocking
17 Aluminum channel 1 1/2" x 1 1/2" x
0.125" inside vertical tube; fasten with
countersunk stainless steel screws
from top & sides
18 1" insulating glass unit
19 Batt insulation
20 1/8" x 3" stainless steel
split-tail stone anchor set in
non-staining sealant
21 Metal angle brackets at each stud
22 WRB over 1/2" plywood sheathing
23 3" thick stone, set per pattern
24 Line of projecting stone beyond
25 Lap WRB over through-
wall flashing
26 Steel clip angles welded
to steel beam
27 Weep holes at 24" O.C. max.
with masonry vent screens
28 Through-wall flashing
29 HDPE shim
30 Steel shelf angle, painted
31 Low-expansion foam sealant
32 Aluminum reveal trim
33 EIFS soffit
34 1 1/2" rigid insulation
35 Silicone setting block
36 1/4" glazing tape spacer
37 Structural glazing tape
38 Painted brake-formed 0.125"
aluminum Z sill
39 Steel angle sill support, welded
to clip angles
40 0.125" painted aluminum
shadow box panel
41 Steel girder

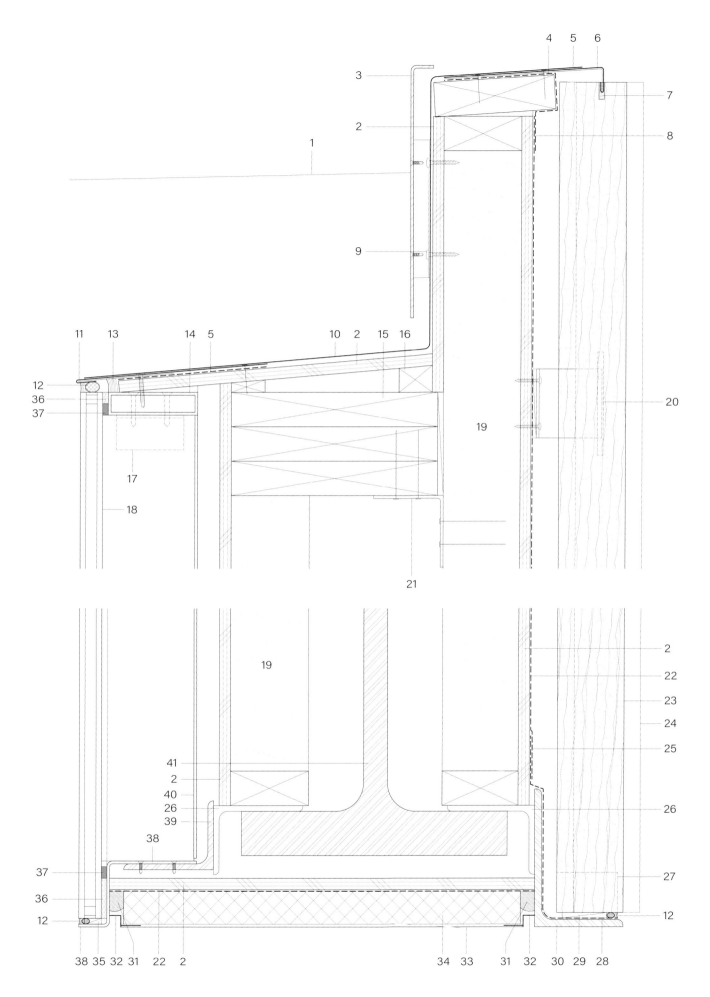

057

Plan Detail (3" = 1'-0")
Entry Pivot Door Jamb

1 Line of aluminum channel below
2 1" insulating glass unit
3 Painted 1/4" x 1" aluminum flat bar,
fastened to mullion with countersunk
#10 x 1" stainless steel machine
screws @ 12" O.C.
4 Painted countersunk screws
5 Low-expansion foam sealant (air
seal); extend down to waterproofing
membrane at slab below;
join with air seal at door head above
6 4" x 3" x 3/16" steel plate at top &
bottom of mullion; anchor into
wood header & floor slab with
countersunk screws
7 Tooled silicone structural seal
(& air seal)
8 1/4" glazing tape spacer
9 Sealant & backer rod (weather seal)
10 Painted wood door stop, attached
from back with 4" countersunk screws
11 Weatherstrip
12 Brush gasket with concealed
fasteners
13 Line of stone threshold below
14 Painted 1" x 4" cold-rolled steel
flat bar mullion, tapped to receive
machine screws
15 Painted wood trim
16 Painted wood door jamb over
plastic shims
17 Brush gasket
18 Wood perimeter blocking fastened
to steel frame & mortised to
accommodate brush gaskets
19 Keyed deadbolt
20 Fully adhered WRB over 3/8" plywood sheathing
21 Cover pan of pivot hardware below
22 Door cavities filled with 2" rigid
insulation board
23 3/8" plywood sheathing
24 Vertical 3/8" x 3-1/4" wood tongue
& groove siding with 1/8" x 1/8"
reveals at joints
25 Welded 2" x 2" x 14GA tube steel
frame, typ.
26 Center-hung self-closing pivot
hardware below
27 Edge of slab below
28 Fully adhered WRB over 1/2"
plywood sheathing
29 11GA steel panel, typ.30 Galvanized
steel screws, typ.
31 Countersunk black oxide
screws, typ.
32 Continuous 11GA brake-formed
steel door stop over plastic shims
33 Open cell spray foam insulation in
2x6 wall framing
34 Extend WRB into rough opening
35 1/2" plywood blocking
36 Vertical 7/8" galvanized steel furring

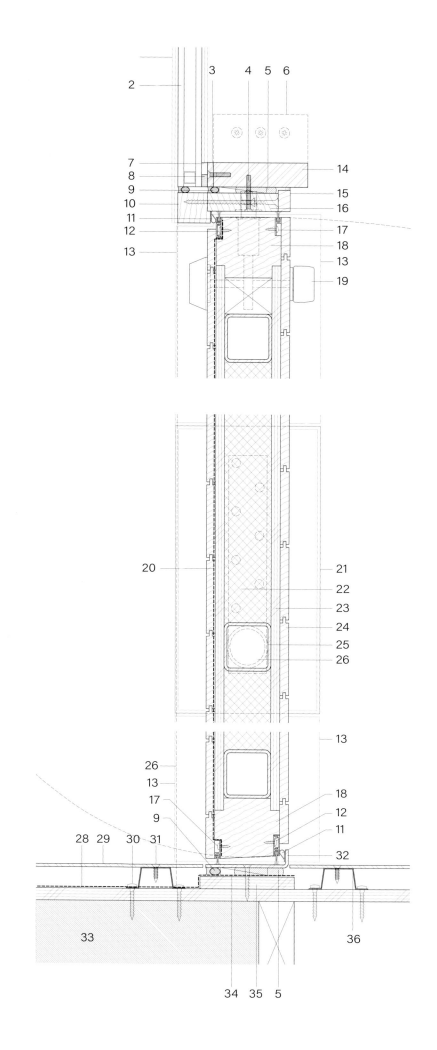

Plan Detail
Breakfast Room Screen

1 Wood blocking
2 Wood dowels
3 Steel window mullion
4 Leading edge of steel column
5 Vertical wood slat
6 Aluminum reveal trim
7 Wood trim
8 Veneer plywood
9 Cushion
10 Plugged pocket screw
11 Concealed light fixture
12 Gypsum board ceiling

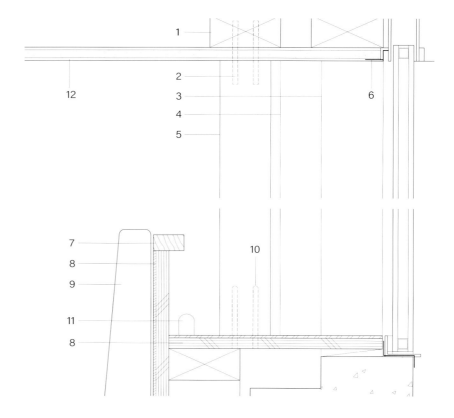

Plan Detail
Breakfast Room Screen

1 Cushion, below
2 Wood trim, below
3 Steel window mullion
4 3/8" wood dowel stained black and glued into hole at wood slats
5 Vertical wood slats, 1 1/4" x 2 1/2" at 3" O.C.
6 Steel column

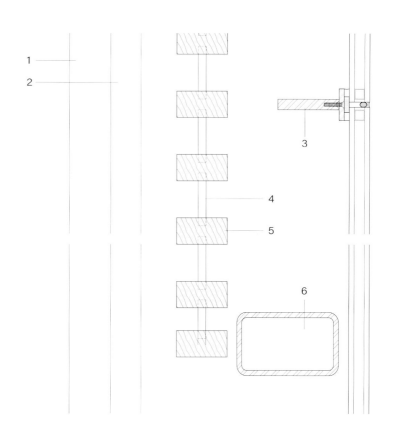

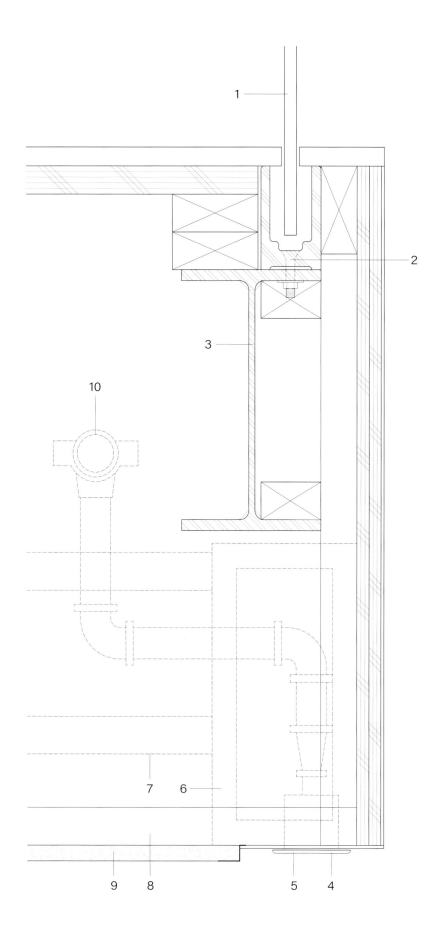

1

2

3

10

7   6

9   8   5   4

Section Detail (3" = 1'-0")
Guardrail

1 1/2" tempered glass guardrail
2 Guardrail glazing shoe
3 Steel beam
4 Sprinkler head
5 Speaker beyond
6 Supply plenum
7 Supply duct
8 Ceiling framing
9 Gypsum board ceiling
10 Fire sprinkler main

Section Detail
Overflow Outlet & Fresh Air Intake

1 Makeup air duct
2 Duct insulation
3 Fully adhered WRB over 1/2"
plywood sheathing
4 11 GA steel panel fastened to furring
channel behind
5 Self-adhered flexible flashing lapped
over steel flange
6 Insect screen closure
7 2x6 cut to accommodate duct
8 Continuous 1 1/2" x 11 GA steel flange
around all 4 sides
9 Open cell spray foam insulation
10 Vent cap with insect screen
11 Sealant around duct penetration
12 Low expansion foam sealant (air seal)
13 Extend WRB into rough opening
14 Line of steel panel at jamb beyond
15 11 GA brake-formed painted steel sheet
with continuous weather welds
16 Overflow drain pipe
17 Sealant around pipe penetration
18 Plastic shims
19 Line of side panel beyond
20 Painted 11 GA steel fascia, fastened
with painted countersunk screws
21 Full-height foundation waterproofing
membrane; extend onto top of curb
22 Concrete curb
23 Finished grade
24 1" rigid insulation board with drainage
channels (on side facing waterproofing)

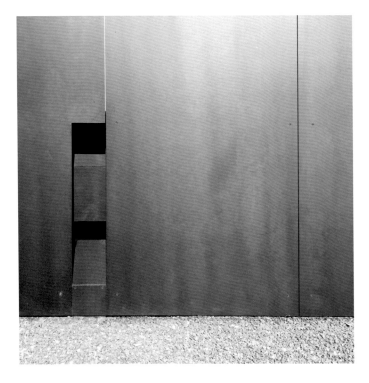

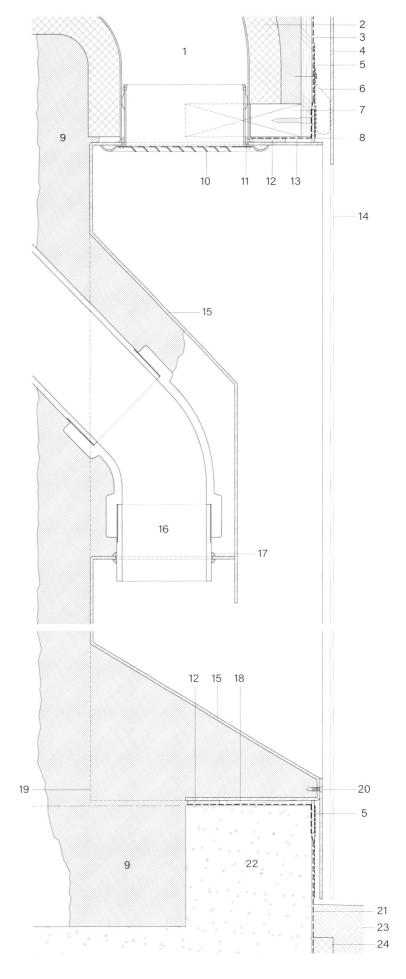

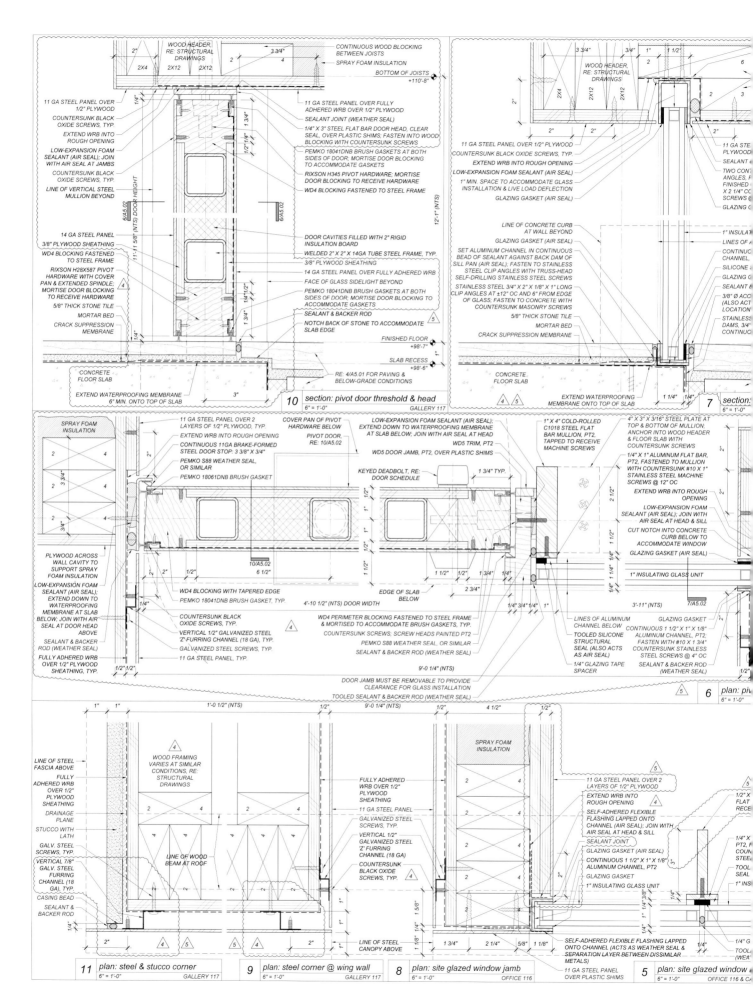

section: pivot door threshold & head — 10
6" = 1'-0"   GALLERY 117

section: — 7
6" = 1'-0"

plan: piv — 6
6" = 1'-0"

plan: steel & stucco corner — 11
6" = 1'-0"   GALLERY 117

plan: steel corner @ wing wall — 9
6" = 1'-0"   GALLERY 117

plan: site glazed window jamb — 8
6" = 1'-0"   OFFICE 116

plan: site glazed window — 5
6" = 1'-0"   OFFICE 116 & CA

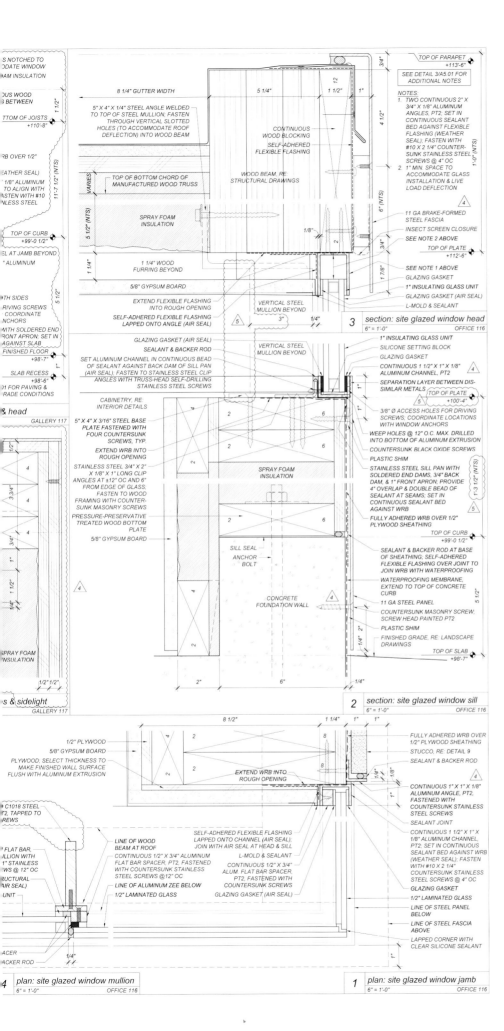

Section 3 — section: site glazed window head — 6" = 1'-0" — OFFICE 116

TOP OF PARAPET +113'-6"

SEE DETAIL 3/A5.01 FOR ADDITIONAL NOTES

NOTES:
1. TWO CONTINUOUS 2" X 3/4" X 1/8" ALUMINUM ANGLES, PT2; SET IN CONTINUOUS SEALANT BED AGAINST FLEXIBLE FLASHING (WEATHER SEAL); FASTEN WITH #10 X 2 1/4" COUNTER-SUNK STAINLESS STEEL SCREWS @ 4" OC
2. 1" MIN. SPACE TO ACCOMMODATE GLASS INSTALLATION & LIVE LOAD DEFLECTION

8 1/4" GUTTER WIDTH
5 1/4"   1 1/2"   1"

5" X 4" X 1/4" STEEL ANGLE WELDED TO TOP OF STEEL MULLION; FASTEN THROUGH VERTICAL SLOTTED HOLES (TO ACCOMMODATE ROOF DEFLECTION) INTO WOOD BEAM

CONTINUOUS WOOD BLOCKING
SELF-ADHERED FLEXIBLE FLASHING

WOOD BEAM, RE: STRUCTURAL DRAWINGS

TOP OF BOTTOM CHORD OF MANUFACTURED WOOD TRUSS

SPRAY FOAM INSULATION

11 GA BRAKE-FORMED STEEL FASCIA
INSECT SCREEN CLOSURE
SEE NOTE 2 ABOVE
TOP OF PLATE +112'-6"
SEE NOTE 1 ABOVE
GLAZING GASKET
1" INSULATING GLASS UNIT
GLAZING GASKET (AIR SEAL)
L-MOLD & SEALANT

1 1/4" WOOD FURRING BEYOND
5/8" GYPSUM BOARD

EXTEND FLEXIBLE FLASHING INTO ROUGH OPENING
SELF-ADHERED FLEXIBLE FLASHING LAPPED ONTO ANGLE (AIR SEAL)

VERTICAL STEEL MULLION BEYOND

2 — section: site glazed window sill — 6" = 1'-0" — OFFICE 116

GLAZING GASKET (AIR SEAL)
SEALANT & BACKER ROD
SET ALUMINUM CHANNEL IN CONTINUOUS BEAD OF SEALANT AGAINST BACK DAM OF SILL PAN (AIR SEAL); FASTEN TO STAINLESS STEEL CLIP ANGLES WITH TRUSS-HEAD SELF-DRILLING STAINLESS STEEL SCREWS

VERTICAL STEEL MULLION BEYOND

1" INSULATING GLASS UNIT
SILICONE SETTING BLOCK
GLAZING GASKET
CONTINUOUS 1 1/2" X 1" X 1/8" ALUMINUM CHANNEL, PT2
SEPARATION LAYER BETWEEN DIS-SIMILAR METALS
TOP OF PLATE +100'-4"

CABINETRY, RE: INTERIOR DETAILS
5" X 4" X 3/16" STEEL BASE PLATE FASTENED WITH FOUR COUNTERSUNK SCREWS, TYP.
EXTEND WRB INTO ROUGH OPENING
STAINLESS STEEL 3/4" X 2" X 1/8" X 1" LONG CLIP ANGLES AT ±12" OC AND 6" FROM EDGE OF GLASS; FASTEN TO WOOD FRAMING WITH COUNTER-SUNK MASONRY SCREWS
PRESSURE-PRESERVATIVE TREATED WOOD BOTTOM PLATE
5/8" GYPSUM BOARD

3/8" Ø ACCESS HOLES FOR DRIVING SCREWS; COORDINATE LOCATIONS WITH WINDOW ANCHORS
WEEP HOLES @ 12" O.C. MAX. DRILLED INTO BOTTOM OF ALUMINUM EXTRUSION
COUNTERSUNK BLACK OXIDE SCREWS
PLASTIC SHIM
STAINLESS STEEL SILL PAN WITH SOLDERED END DAMS, 3/4" BACK DAM, & 1" FRONT APRON; PROVIDE 4" OVERLAP & DOUBLE BEAD OF SEALANT AT SEAMS; SET IN CONTINUOUS SEALANT BED AGAINST WRB
FULLY ADHERED WRB OVER 1/2" PLYWOOD SHEATHING
TOP OF CURB +99'-0 1/2"

SPRAY FOAM INSULATION

SILL SEAL
ANCHOR BOLT

CONCRETE FOUNDATION WALL

SEALANT & BACKER ROD AT BASE OF SHEATHING; SELF-ADHERED FLEXIBLE FLASHING OVER JOINT TO JOIN WRB WITH WATERPROOFING
WATERPROOFING MEMBRANE, EXTEND TO TOP OF CONCRETE CURB
11 GA STEEL PANEL
COUNTERSUNK MASONRY SCREW, SCREW HEAD PAINTED PT2
PLASTIC SHIM
FINISHED GRADE, RE: LANDSCAPE DRAWINGS
TOP OF SLAB +98'-7"

4 — plan: site glazed window mullion — 6" = 1'-0" — OFFICE 116

8 1/2"   1 1/4"   1"   1"

1/2" PLYWOOD
5/8" GYPSUM BOARD
PLYWOOD; SELECT THICKNESS TO MAKE FINISHED WALL SURFACE FLUSH WITH ALUMINUM EXTRUSION

EXTEND WRB INTO ROUGH OPENING

LINE OF WOOD BEAM AT ROOF
CONTINUOUS 1/2" X 3/4" ALUMINUM FLAT BAR SPACER, PT2, FASTENED WITH COUNTERSUNK STAINLESS STEEL SCREWS @12" OC
LINE OF ALUMINUM ZEE BELOW
1/2" LAMINATED GLASS

SELF-ADHERED FLEXIBLE FLASHING LAPPED ONTO CHANNEL (AIR SEAL); JOIN WITH AIR SEAL AT HEAD & SILL
CONTINUOUS 1/2" X 3/4" ALUM. FLAT BAR SPACER, PT2, FASTENED WITH COUNTERSUNK SCREWS
GLAZING GASKET (AIR SEAL)

1 — plan: site glazed window jamb — 6" = 1'-0" — OFFICE 116

FULLY ADHERED WRB OVER 1/2" PLYWOOD SHEATHING
STUCCO, RE: DETAIL 9
SEALANT & BACKER ROD
CONTINUOUS 1" X 1" X 1/8" ALUMINUM ANGLE, PT2, FASTENED WITH COUNTERSUNK STAINLESS STEEL SCREWS
SEALANT JOINT
CONTINUOUS 1 1/2" X 1" X 1/8" ALUMINUM CHANNEL, PT2; SET IN CONTINUOUS SEALANT BED AGAINST WRB (WEATHER SEAL); FASTEN WITH #10 X 2 1/4" COUNTERSUNK STAINLESS STEEL SCREWS @ 4" OC
GLAZING GASKET
1/2" LAMINATED GLASS
GLAZING GASKET (AIR SEAL)
LINE OF STEEL PANEL BELOW
LINE OF STEEL FASCIA ABOVE
LAPPED CORNER WITH CLEAR SILICONE SEALANT

06.17.2016
02.29.2016

alterstudio, LLP

1801 lavaca street
austin, tx 78701
512.499.8007

	EXTERIOR DETAIL REV	04.13.2016
4		
5	REVISION 5	06.24.2016

exterior details gallery

scale   AS NOTED

A5.02

PROCESS

BUILDING

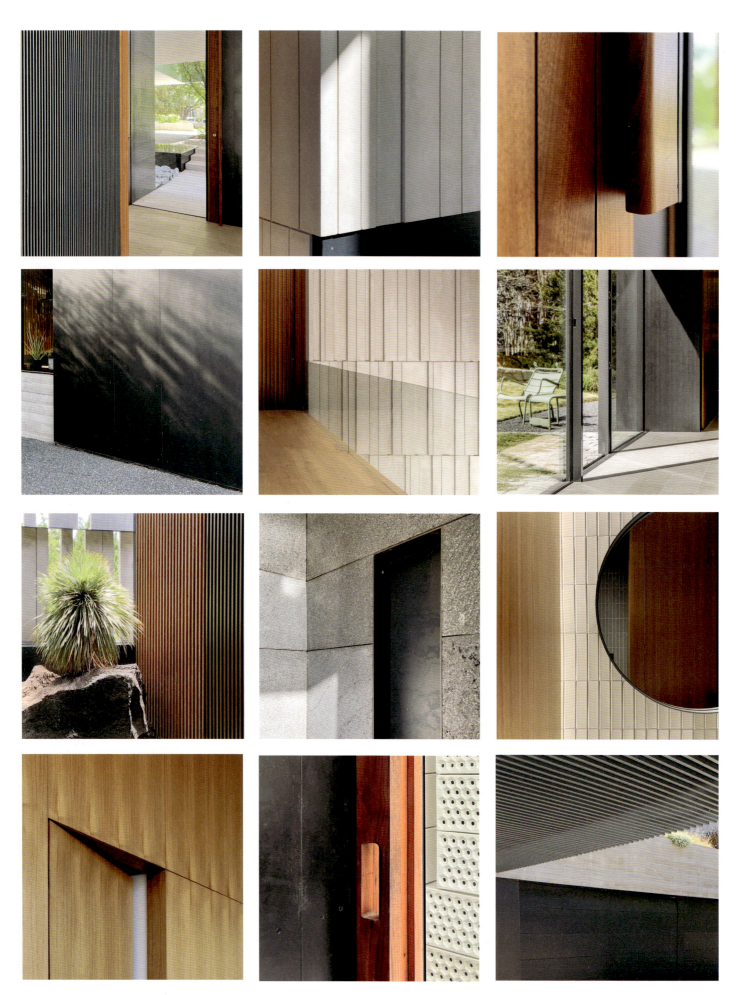

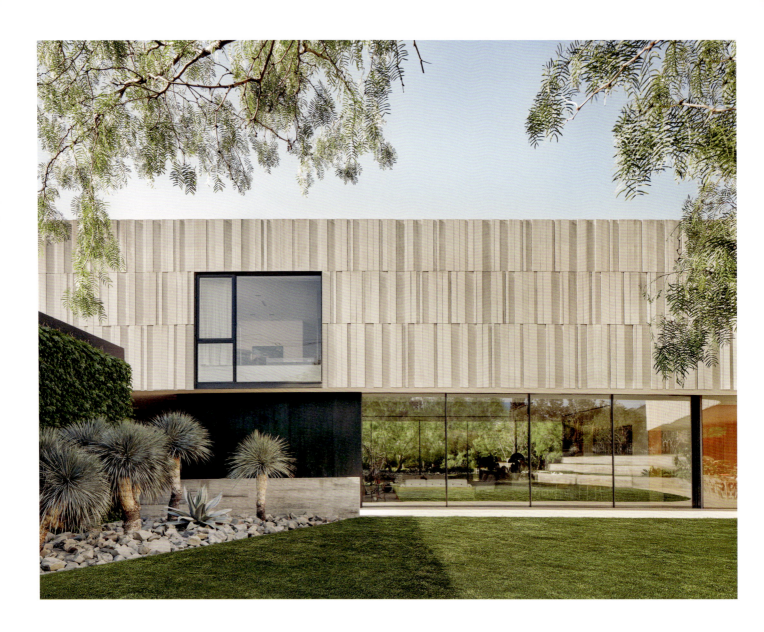

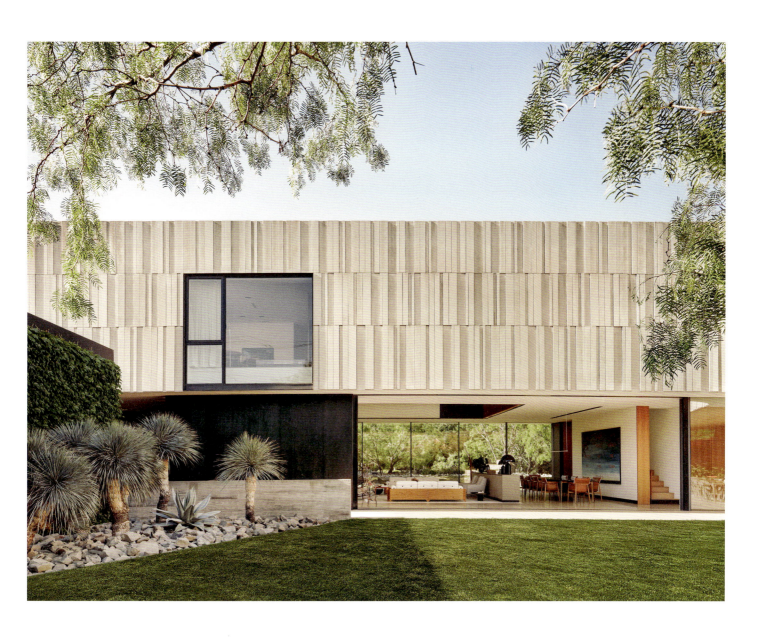

EXCEPT   NO   ONE

IN   THIS   TOWN

TRAVELS

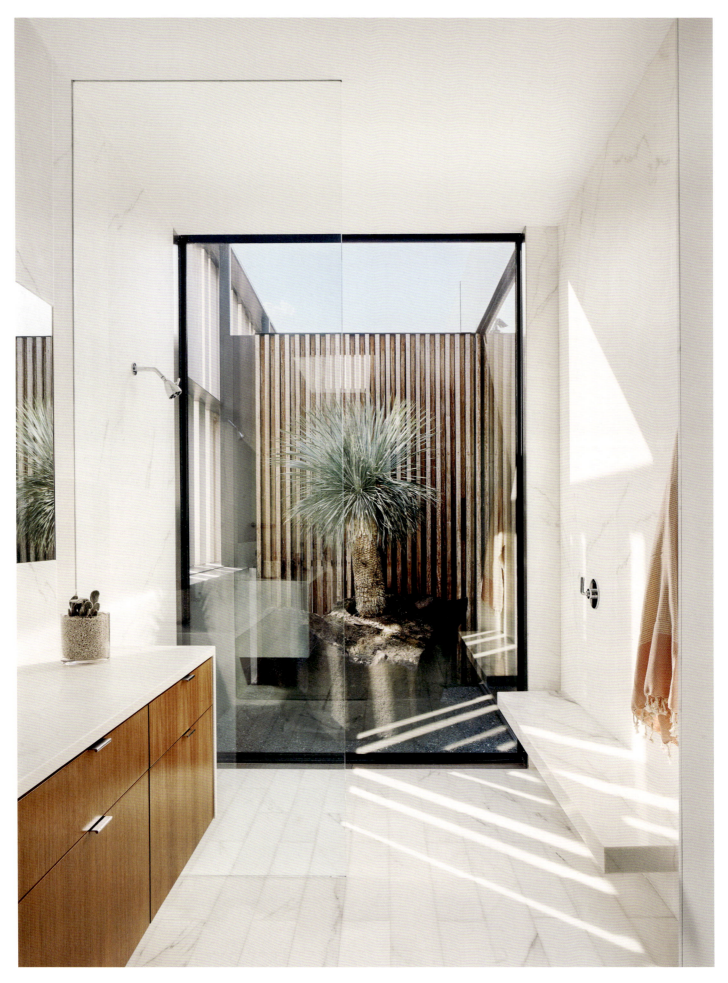

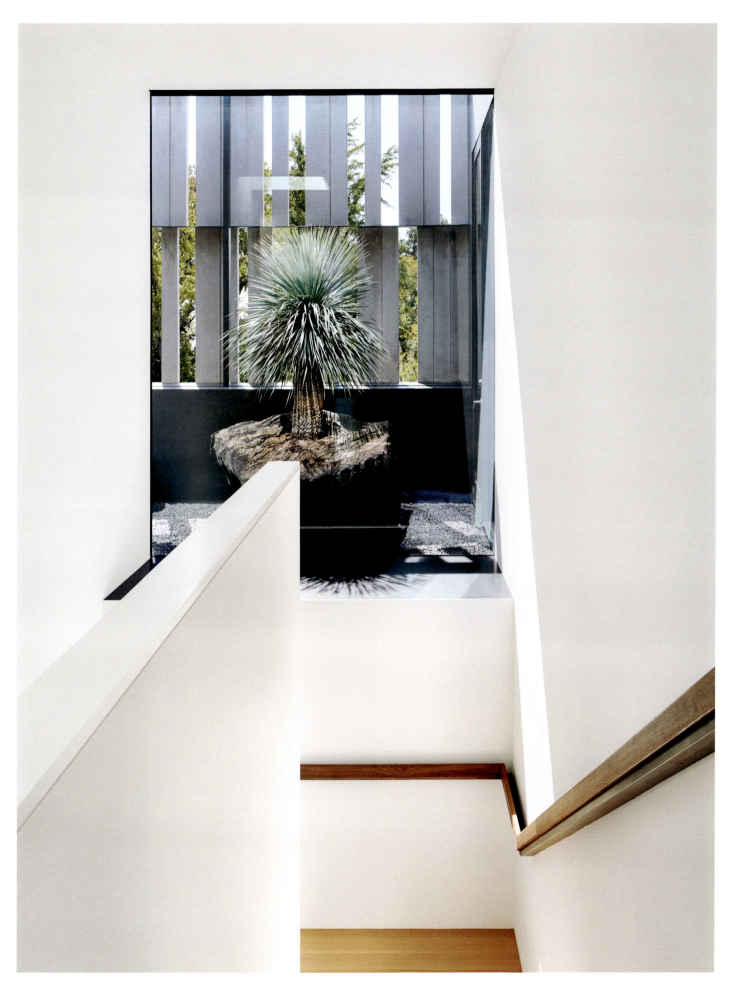

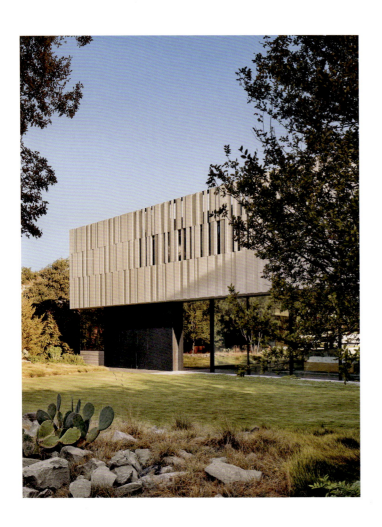

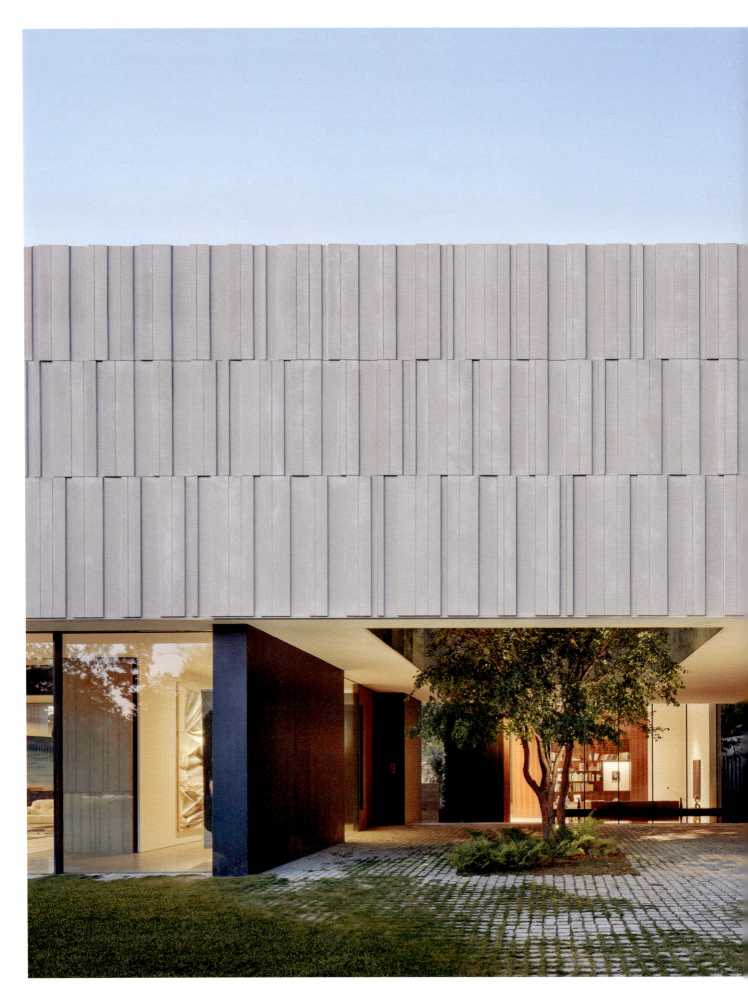

REFLECTION
BY CARLOS JIMÉNEZ

An oasis in Highland Park

Since its founding in 1907, the Dallas, Texas, suburb of Highland Park has nurtured the construction of medium-sized to large houses in its bucolic setting. The idyllic, tree-lined streets that outline this Dallas enclave have accumulated practically every architectural style popular in the twentieth century. Though many of the houses might seem exaggerated or out of place, they wear their Texas-sized grandeur proudly, casting aside any qualms about architectural propriety. Throughout its development, Highland Park has proved fertile ground for works of architecture that transcend historical reproduction and stylistic appropriation. Many celebrated American architects, from Frank Welch to Antoine Predock, have built insightful works whose inventive, careful integration of form, landscape and infrastructure stand in discreet counterpoint to their extravagant neighbors.

Alterstudio's house on Lexington Avenue probes these conditions with imagination and aplomb. We encounter an architecture that asserts singular presence yet dissolves in the larger context of innovative site strategies. Like most properties in Highland Park, the site had no distinct features, no noticeable topography or venerable trees. It did have looming neighbors on either side. Alterstudio and landscape architects Hocker Design Group cleverly edited them out with an unexpected, almost wild landscape that welcomes visitors

CARLOS JIMÉNEZ was born in San José, Costa Rica (1959), and moved to the United States in 1974. He studied at University of Houston College of Architecture (B.Arch.1981) and established Carlos Jiménez Studio in Houston in 1983. He was named Tenured Professor at Rice University School of Architecture in 2000 and is also a Visiting Professor at Southern California Institute of Architecture; Texas A&M University; the University of California in Los Angeles and Berkeley; the University of Navarra, Pamplona, Spain; Williams College; Tulane University; the University of Houston; the Graduate School of Design at Harvard University; the University of Texas at Arlington and Austin; the University of Oregon; and Washington University in Saint Louis. Jiménez is a frequent lecturer, critic and jury member at national and international architecture events. From 2001 to 2011 he served on the jury of the Pritzker Architecture Prize. Jiménez is an Academician of the National Academy of Design and has received multiple awards for excellence in design from Architectural Record, the American Institute of Architects, the Chicago Athenaeum, Architecture, Progressive Architecture and the Architectural League of New York, among others. His work has been published in numerous architectural journals, dedicated monographs and authored books such as *Carlos Jiménez* (Barcelona), *Carlos Jiménez Buildings* (New York), *Carlos Jiménez House and Studio* (Cambridge), *Crowley* (Singapore), *Carlos Jiménez Trim Sessions 07* (Valencia), *Carlos Jiménez 30 Years, 30 Works, AV 196* (Madrid), and *On Won Buddhism and the circularity of things* (South Korea).

approaching the property from Lexington Avenue. The lush vegetation is a prelude, delineating a surprising pathway to the main entrance. Alterstudio delights in choreographing promenades that encourage the simple pleasure of meandering, lingering in places, delaying arrival at the covered entry. We are given multiple choices to either access the house, veer off to a sun-drenched clearing, or proceed to a private gallery sited to the north. The body of the house appears to soar with its rhythmic façade of vertical limestone strips, a pattern that subtly intones a musical texture. The two-level structure mediates two contrasting exterior spaces: one the porous, meandering entry sequence, the other a private terrace and courtyard at the back of the property. These verdant spaces engage their respective topographies, providing all interior spaces with privacy and intimacy.

The openness of the ground floor masterfully interweaves indoor and outdoor spaces, expanding or contracting their respective volumes in complementary exchanges. This produces the effect of being exposed to, yet protected from, the elements. Being in the house is akin to being in an oasis. Seen from the street the house appears like a sanctuary, the farthest from an all-imposing figure on a suburban pedestal. The exquisite precision and craftsmanship that permeate all aspects of the architecture are reiterated in the integration of landscape and infrastructure (especially evident in the camouflaging of the garage). Alterstudio has achieved

a consummate work of architecture on Lexington Avenue, a work where it is not important to account for square footage or spell out its retinue of materials. Generous as these are, what matters most is the pleasure that emanates from the assured deployment of materials, textures and light. One is reminded of the houses of Alvar Aalto, where the interaction between buildings and their surrounding landscape, and the interplay of materials and details, take center stage. On a recent trip to Dallas – three years after my first visit – I returned to visit again. It took some effort to find the house as the mature trees occluded my remembered view. Yet there it stood, quietly taking in the dappled light of a warm summer afternoon, so near to its site yet so far away from its neighbors. An oasis in Highland Park.

Carlos Jiménez, July 2023

APPENDIX

FIRM PROFILE

Alterstudio Architecture

The work of Alterstudio Architecture is rooted in deep-seated virtues of architecture – generous space making, shrewd manipulation of day-lighting, and meticulous attention to detail. The heightening of direct human experience and the framing of the complex circumstances of specific situations are at the core of each project. Underlining all the work is the belief that architecture should deepen everyday experience at the same time that it elevates an awareness of a larger, changing world.

The practice specializes in precise and creative buildings, landscapes and interiors that sensitively respond to their environment and ecologies of place. Their commitment to enhance and protect both the cultural and natural environments of the communities they serve is evident in the technical craftsmanship and long-term sustainability of their projects. Alterstudio promotes ecologically responsive designs that acknowledge the impact of finite resources as a positive contributor in the creation of an ethical architecture. It compels, informs and guides the designs from conception through construction. This approach to sustainable design goes beyond logistical and mechanical concerns to create an architecture that is uplifting to its users and in harmony with its cultural context and natural surroundings.

The attention to all elements of design has been a constant in the firm's philosophy. Alterstudio Architecture has received more than two hundred design awards and been widely published.

Partners:

Kevin Alter
Ernesto Cragnolino
Tim Whitehill

Associates:

Haifa Hammami
William Powell
Daniel Shumaker
Matt Slusarek
Elizabeth Sydnor
Michael Woodland

Samuel Alamo
Jim Chen
Ana Escobar
Mabel Loh
Dylan Treleven
Amy Vaughan

PROJECT CREDITS

Architect
Alterstudio Architecture

Project Team
Kevin Alter, Partner
Ernesto Cragnolino, Partner
Tim Whitehill, Partner
Michael Woodland – associate
Joseph Boyle
Jenna Dezinski
Tyler Noblin

Location
Highland Park, Texas

Project
2014

Completion
2018

Area
12,398 sq. ft. (conditioned)

Principal Photography
Casey Dunn

Portrait Photography
Chad Wadsworth

Additional Photography
Alterstudio

Landscape Architect
Hocker Design Group
David Hocker
Dylan Stewart
Shane Friese
Zewen Allen Yu

Landscape Installation
Texas Land Care

Interior Designer
SZ Projects
Silvia Zofio

Art Consultant
Rob Teeters

Lighting Design
Essential Light Design Studio

Structural Engineer
Ellinwood + Machado
Structural Engineers

Civil Engineer
Monk Engineering Consultants

Mechanical Engineer
Positive Energy

Contractor
Steven Hild Custom Builder

Masonry
Stone Cladding and Flooring –
Indiana Limestone
Stone Pavers and Landscape
Boulders – Oklahoma Silvermist

Stone Fabrication
Holland Marble Company, Inc.

Tile
Ceramica Suro
José Noé Suro Salceda

Fenestration
Steve Hild Custom Builder
MHB (Steel full-lite door)
Western Windows (Upper
floor and Cabana Slider)
Sky-Frame (Multi-sliders at Living)
Glazing Vision (Skylights)

Door Hardware
FSB

Millwork Fabrication
All Woods Cabinetry

Lighting
Amerilux
Bega
BK Lighting
Delta Light
Gotham Lighting
HE Williams
Juno
LF illuminations
Lucifer
Luminart Lighting
Luminii

Furnishings
Custom Furniture - SZProjects
Espasso
ABC Carpet
Paula Silva Ruvalcaba
Future Perfect
Cassina
B.Lux
Suite NY
Artefacto
B&B Italia

Appliances
Sub-Zero Group, Inc.
Miele, Inc.
Best
LG
Fisher Paykel

Plumbing Fixtures
Duravit
Hans Grohe
Blanco
Dornbracht
Julien
Kohler

Awards
2023 The Dallas Architecture
Forum Design Recognition
2022 AIA National Housing
Design Award
2021 Residential Architecture
Design Award
2021 Residential Design
Architecture Award
2020 The American Architecture Award
2020 The Plan Award finalist
2020 Society of American Registered
Architects National Design Award
2020 Architecture Newspaper Best
of Design Award
2020 Builder's Choice Custom
Home Design Award
2019 Interior Design Magazine Best
of Year Honoree
2019 Texas Society of Architects
Design Award
2019 AIA Austin Design Award

PHOTOGRAPHY CAPTIONS

A hovering limestone volume bends to define a courtyard garden, and an articulated landscape of zoysia terraces and board-formed concrete retaining walls rises above the home's garage.

Peering over the berm, the house presents a hovering limestone volume above a transparent ground floor. The pattern of stone pulls apart to reveal an upstairs court, and a rich interior beyond.

The façade's pattern is comprised of stone panels in three widths, set at two depths, and sized for two individuals to install without the aid of a crane.

The visitor enters under a 34' cantilever and through a lush landscape of plantings and hardscape that blurs the boundaries between landscape and building.

Entering from the street, the visitor meanders along a cobblestone pathway, through an unexpected landscape of rich plantings, riprap berms, native trees, wildflowers, cactus, sedum and zoysia.

The abstract stone volume cantilevers out towards a stand of trees that screens the property to the west.

Inside the gallery office, minimally glazed 14' tall windows encourage one's gaze across the black reflecting pool, under the cantilevering stone volume and towards the street.

Indiana limestone is paired with mill-finished steel.

A cobblestone path draws the visitor under the cantilevering volume and to the building's entry.

The intersection of stone, steel and glass is carefully calibrated and presented abstractly.

Boston Ivy clads the gallery as the second-floor limestone volume slips past behind.

Organized along three courses, the façade is made from stones of three widths, set at two depths; creating a volume that is at once singular and variegated.

The stone volume slides out further into the backyard to cover an outdoor dining area, and is reflected in the pool against the dusk sky.

Under the cantilever and around a remarkable Cedar Elm, the visitor turns to enter and is greeted with a floor-to-ceiling pivoting door and 3 Units Aluminum Death Shifter, an enormous 1992 canvas by Steven Parrino, inside.

Peering over the berm, the house presents a hovering limestone volume above a transparent ground floor. The pattern of stone pulls apart to reveal an upstairs court, and a rich interior beyond.

The cantilevered volume frames a view back towards the street while light and reflection stream through the void above.

From the shadow of the elevated volume, the glass walls of the elevated void sparkle with reflection and sunlight.

The home has a restrained palette of materials: stone, steel, glass and timber. Here, the elevated stone volume bends to enclose a private courtyard.

Entirely clad in glass, a hole pierces the stone volume and creates a multifaceted space of reflection, transparency, light, and shadow.

A home office, discreetly positioned behind a vertical timber screen, hovers over the dining room and Travel Agency, 1983 by Ed Ruscha.

Minimal detailing imbues the void with an unfamiliar sense of abstraction and reflection, in contrast to the solidity of the volume it cuts through.

From the gallery, blackened steel defines the threshold, door and return air grill. Photograph by Alterstudio

The brilliant sun and sky of Texas animate the myriad reflections of this voided space.

Staggered stones at the fireplace encourage the visitor's gaze around the volume. Photograph by Alterstudio

A massive, floor-to-ceiling Ipe door, pivots effortlessly while providing an appropriate sense of weight to the entry.

A bespoke pull fits the hand and is a measure of the weight of the front door. Photograph by Alterstudio

The double-height living room is anchored and separated from the entry by the two-story, vertical limestone fireplace wall.

Steel panels act as a primed canvas for a constantly changing array of light and shadow.

The stone cladding appears inside only at the massive fireplace wall. Peering out from behind is Black painting, 2016, by Paul Sietsema.

A glass guardrail exposes the second-floor gallery to the double-height living room. Photograph by Alterstudio

The only opening on the courtyard side of the elevated volume, a window from the primary bedroom slips below the floor and breaks the stone façade.

Sliding glass panels slip behind walnut and steel cabinetry. Photograph by Alterstudio

A yucca plant grows out from a large volcanic stone in the upstairs court, here seen from the living room below.

Circulation on the ground floor occurs along the window walls, where a connection from kitchen to dining room also houses a wet bar.

Steel niches contrast with the rough volcanic stone at the outside kitchen. Photograph by Alterstudio

The limestone volume curves to define a courtyard garden, and frame the ever-changing sky, as well as the flight path to Dallas Love Field.

The subtle gradation in color of custom tile from Guadalajara is highlighted in the powder bathroom. Photograph by Alterstudio

Full-height glazing is barely present under the levitating limestone volume.

Walnut paneling disguises a pantry lurking under the stairs.

The same full-height glazing disappears into the steel-clad volume below, taking with it the reflections but adding a direct connection with the courtyard garden.

A custom steel door & Ipe pull and ceramic blocks from Guadalajara define the entry to the gallery building. Photograph by Alterstudio

A curved glass panel seamlessly continues the glazing as the volume turns to enclose the rear courtyard garden.

The articulated leading edge of the carport aligns with the board-formed concrete of the garage. Photograph by Alterstudio

The kitchen and breakfast room occur at the hinge between front yard, side alley and courtyard garden behind. A tightly-radiused curved glass panel pushes into the building to define the edge of this space and make room for an exterior stair to provide light to and a second means of egress from the rooms below.

Oversized, full-height glazing opens to connect the living room with the courtyard garden behind.

A vertical walnut screen set in front of the glazing and evergreen trees behind shield the breakfast room from the alley and neighbors beyond.

Stairs to the upper floor are nestled in the solid block separating the dining room from the kitchen and family room.

A built-in banquet provides an intimate enclave and allows a view towards the street and alley, through a line of evergreen trees.

The subtle gradation in color of custom tile from Guadalajara wraps the powder bathroom.

A delicately glazed window wall connects the home office to the upstairs court.

Light and shadows from the west cascade into the family room and down the pathway to the back door, laundry, garage and media room below.

Inside the primary bedroom, a large window slips below the floor to the bottom of the stone volume, screened by sheer curtains which, when open, direct one's gaze downward into the courtyard garden.

Stone stair treads span a steel panel and walnut wall.

Floor-to-Ceiling glazing opens one primary shower entirely to the upstairs courtyard: private, but with a view of the same planting that is seen from the living room.

A delicate steel and stone stair ascends from its massive stone counterpart, demonstrating the craftsmanship and precision of the overall enterprise.

A freestanding bath, itself floating in a field of white marble, is softly illuminated by the obscured glass from the void that is evident at the entry.

A home office, discrete behind a walnut screen, is positioned at the center of the home, between public and private realms, and able to observe both simultaneously.

The primary stair is animated by its relationship to the upstairs court, and the plantings ensconced in large, volcanic stones from Guadalajara.

Light pours in from an opening that connects the upper courtyard with the double-height living room along a continuous timber screen.

A second home office associated with the gallery building rests 18" below the entry level, excavated to ensure its interior height remains within the required zoning limits, separated by a slot of light and just beyond a black reflecting pool.

An upstairs gallery connects to the primary bedroom while overlooking the living room. Site specific installation Salubra 2, 2009 by Sherrie Levine.

Stone paving runs uninterrupted into the gallery.

The stone wall enclosing the upstairs court pulls apart, allowing light and views to filter through.

Monolithic corner glazing opens the gallery office resolutely to the out-of-doors.

Flush glass and a zero-edge reflecting pool encourage a landscape of simultaneous reflection and transparency.

The interior of the cabana is clad in custom tile from Guadalajara and walnut cabinetry, behind which lies a murphy bed. An enormous stone slab of slides out to the garden beyond.

A built-in sofa, blackened steel and a vintage upholstered chair are points of stasis against the ever-present pull of the out-of-doors.

The unadulterated stone volume bends to define the garden courtyard and is animated by sun and shadow.

Staggered custom ceramic blocks by Ceramica Suro screen the gallery's entry hall from the office and serve as a backdrop to the vintage furniture.

The variegated pattern of stone cladding is enlivened by the omnipresent Texas sun.

Light is carefully calibrated to display a variety of works from the owner's collection. Corten sculpture by Donald Judd.

The stone volume also cantilevers out over the sod terraces that rise to cover the garage.

The concrete floors, stark white walls and carefully calibrated skylights of the gallery suggest a provisional character, appropriate for a rotating series of exhibitions from the owners' collection and scaled to display the 36' long Helter Skelter II, 2007, by Mark Bradford.

Board-formed concrete and limestone walls alternatively serve as foreground and background, highlighting the varying conditions of circumstance, nature, and light. Photograph by Alterstudio.

A huge wall panel slides discretely away adjacent to Clean Painting, 2017, by Michael Williams, opening the gallery to the courtyard garden and inviting an easy flow between.

An Oklahoma Silvermist limestone stair ascends from the lower level through a narrow court carved into the limestone ground, accompanied by densely planted ferns more accustomed to shade than full sun. Photograph by Alterstudio

Set inside the ivy-covered gallery, a steel panel opens and connects the gallery to the pool deck.

The vertical limestone slabs touch the sky delicately, and open to form an irregular pattern of light and shadow. Photograph by Alterstudio.

At the end of the gallery building a pool cabana/guest room opens directly onto the pool deck to the west and east to an intimate garden behind.

The varied textures of the surrounding plantings weave through the project. Photograph by Alterstudio.

Blackened steel and board-formed concrete serve as a primed canvas for the vicissitudes of nature. Photograph by Alterstudio

Riprap berms topped with Indian Blanket wildflowers frame a view of the hovering stone volume while shielding the ground floor from onlookers. Photograph by Alterstudio

Rich plantings surround and are ensconced in volcanic stones from Guadalajara. Photograph by Alterstudio

Cactus and yucca grow out from the large volcanic stones placed throughout the property and upstairs court. Photograph by Alterstudio

Glazed volcanic stone tiles by Ceramica Suro line the inside of the pool and imbue it with an unexpected ethereal quality. Photograph by Alterstudio

Cobblestones encourage overlapping conditions of landscape and paving. Photograph by Alterstudio

Zoysia, alternatively cut short and grown wild, animates the front lawn and demarcates different areas. Photograph by Alterstudio

Custom tile from Ceramica Suro is juxtaposed against the abstraction of blackened steel, both enlivened by the shadows of Boston Ivy. Photograph by Alterstudio

Dichondra repens grows around the limestone cobbles, further entwining building and landscape. Photograph by Alterstudio

Evergreen Clematis vines envelop the steel trellis at the pool deck. Photograph by Alterstudio

Prickly pear cactus grows through the riprap Silvermist berms alongside wildflowers, grasses, and native trees, creating an edge to the home's precinct. Photograph by Alterstudio

Boston Ivy dances across the datum established by the board-formed concrete walls. Photograph by Alterstudio

Rough and abstract textures are juxtaposed ubiquitously. Photograph by Alterstudio

A rich variety of planting grows through the riprap stone berms that define the southern and western edges of the property, along the street and alley respectively. Photograph by Alterstudio

The mirror-like, black-lined reflecting pool is enlivened by water lilies and koi. Photograph by Alterstudio

Variegated stone shards form a basis from which an array of native plants grow through. Photograph by Alterstudio

Cobblestones allow a seamless transition from dressed stone interiors to landscape. Photograph by Alterstudio

Corner glazing at the breakfast room furthers the impression of a levitating stone volume above.

Shade and sun enliven the reflecting pool, variously exposing it as mirror-like and full of depth and life. Photograph by Alterstudio

In sun, the upper courtyard lies in the shadows behind the reflective stone screen.

Rough-hewn stone contrasts with abstract steel panels. Photograph by Alterstudio

Board formed concrete walls define stepped sod terraces that rise up under the floating stone volume.

The pool's zero edge allows water to drain through a tight slot, next to the cobblestone floor. Photograph by Alterstudio

At the entry, a handsome, multi-stem Cedar Elm tree rises through the hovering stone volume. The house transforms as the sun begins to set, exposing a luminous interior and focus of attention.

Along the alley, the limestone volume hovers over an ivy-clad, board-formed concrete and steel paneled garage. A generous back entry slips underneath, while windows from the secondary bedrooms reach up to the sky and define the edge of the stone volume.

In the evening, light emanates from within, the upper court transforming into a lantern.

The articulated edge of a carport casts shadows on the board-formed concrete garage.

A sculptural cedar elm rises through the void in the cantilevered volume, towards the sun and brings light, shadow, pattern and serendipity to the overall ensemble.

Along the alley, the articulated edge of a carport casts shadows on the board-formed concrete and steel garage.

Seen from the street, the house presents an enigmatic presence to the neighborhood.

A newly planted row of Mexican Buckeyes and Juniper trees along the western alley casts shadows on a board-formed concrete wall and rough-hewn limestone stairs that descend to the lower level.

The solidity of the stone volume contrasts dramatically with the openness of the ground floor.

BOOK CREDITS

Graphic design by Florencia Damilano
Art direction by Oscar Riera Ojeda
Copy editing by Kit Maude

OSCAR RIERA OJEDA
PUBLISHERS

Copyright © 2024 by Oscar Riera Ojeda Publishers Limited
ISBN 978-1-946226-77-8
Published by Oscar Riera Ojeda Publishers Limited
Printed in China

Oscar Riera Ojeda Publishers Limited
Unit 1331, Beverley Commercial Centre,
87-105 Chatham Road South, Tsim Sha Tsui, Kowloon, Hong Kong

Production Offices
Suit 19, Shenyun Road,
Nanshan District, Shenzhen 518055, China

International Customer Service & Editorial Questions: +1-484-502-5400

www.oropublishers.com | www.oscarrieraojeda.com
oscar@oscarrieraojeda.com